XML Schemas

XML Schemas

Chelsea Valentine
Lucinda Dykes
Ed Tittel

SYBEX

San Francisco · London

Associate Publisher: Richard Mills
Acquisitions and Developmental Editor: Tom Cirtin
Editor: Judy Flynn
Production Editor: Jennifer Campbell
Technical Editor: Piroz Mohseni
Graphic Illustrator: Tony Jonick
Electronic Publishing Specialist: Nila Nichols
Proofreaders: Emily Hsuan, Dave Nash, Laurie O'Connell, Yariv Rabinovitch, Nancy Riddiough
Indexer: Nancy Guenther
Cover Designer: Caryl Gorska, Gorska Design
Cover Photographer: Glen Allison, PhotoDisc

To Nana. I love you!
—Chelsea Valentine

*To Wali, with thanks for taking care of things so I can
write; to Dru, with thanks for reminding me to remember
why I'm here; to Mom, Doris Dykes, with thanks
for fostering a deep love of reading and books; and to
Yvonne Adams, with thanks for being the one friend who
might actually read this book.*
—Lucinda Dykes

*To the talented team at LANWrights: thanks for making
this the best 10 years of my life. To Mom and Dad, for
making the whole thing possible: thanks for making me
the person I am today. To Blackie: thanks for walking me
so regularly and helping me keep sane!*
—Ed Tittel

Acknowledgments

As always, thanks to Mary for her endless support and dedication to this project. I would also like to thank my coauthors Ed Tittel and Lucinda Dykes for their hard work on this project. I'd also like to thank the folks at Sybex. A round of applause goes out to Tom Cirtin, Jennifer Campbell, Judy Flynn, Piroz Mohseni, and Nila Nichols. Thanks to all of those who helped to keep me sane.

—Chelsea Valentine

A huge thanks to Mary Burmeister for making it possible for a team to work together to create a book. Mary holds all the threads together and keeps things moving. Thanks, Mary, for all the pep talks and the laughter, as well as the excellent editing and advice. Thanks to Ed Tittel for his continuous support and encouragement and for offering me the opportunity to participate in this project. Thanks to Ed Tittel and Chelsea Valentine for having the vision for an XML Schema book, and thanks to Chelsea for all her help and support in making this book possible.

Thanks to all the people at LANWrights and Sybex who helped to make this project move from a vision to a book.

—Lucinda Dykes

Thanks to Sybex for making this book possible, especially Jordan Gold, Richard Mills, and Tom Cirtin. Thanks to my coauthors Chelsea Valentine and Lucinda Dykes for shouldering such a large share of the work. Special thanks to Mary Burmeister who put this book together so very, very well. You guys are all the greatest.

—Ed Tittel

Contents at a Glance

Contents

Introduction

To many XML believers and purists, there's been a canker at the heart of the beautiful rose that is XML since its very inception. Worse still, some believe that canker was put there by design. That canker is, of course, the Document Type Definition, or DTD, that defines the very essence of XML. DTDs are "foreign imports" based on an older, more complex markup metalanguage called the Standard Generalized Markup Language, otherwise known as SGML.

Why would some characterize this apparently innocuous SGML DTD as a "canker at the heart of the beautiful rose"? you might ask. Perhaps it's because SGML uses its own different (and complex) syntax and structures to define markup and document structures. Perhaps it's because SGML is a bear to learn and a monster to master. Perhaps it's simply because XML should be capable of defining itself, given its nearly universal capabilities to capture and represent data and metadata of all kinds.

To the most ardent XML lovers, XML Schema is the perfect replacement for the SGML canker that would otherwise stay in XML's heart. This is because XML Schema lets you use XML structure, syntax, namespaces, and all the other appurtenances you'll find in the XML environment to define XML documents, not just to express particular document instances.

Of course, not everyone agrees that SGML DTDs are evil, and not everyone thinks that XML Schema should replace SGML DTDs altogether. Each of these document definition technologies has its strengths and weaknesses, and each is particularly suitable for certain applications. Then, too, SGML's been around for nearly 20 years, and XML Schema is less than a year old as a standard, less than 3 years in its current making. Thus, experience and knowledge weigh more heavily on the SGML DTD side than on the XML Schema side—at least for the time being. Within the ins and outs of these technologies, and in the details that make XML Schema such a powerful and capable tool, lie the seeds of XML documents, data structures, applications, and information exchanges as yet unknown. We hope to map out this strange and wonderful territory and compare the major XML metadata alternatives in a way that permits content creators and software developers to make the best of both of these worlds.

XML Schema

When building XML documents, builders must first understand the tools at their disposal and the raw materials with which they must work. An analysis of metadata—information that describes the structure and contents of other information—becomes a central theme in the exploration of both SGML DTDs and XML Schema. Given that the focus of this book is the latter (XML Schema) rather than the former (SGML DTDs), we make fairly short shrift of what could be a much longer story to concentrate on an exploration of XML Schema in this book.

We've been building XML documents and applications for almost four years now, and in those years we've learned much about the limitations of SGML metadata and the frequent need to develop ancillary software to augment what validating an SGML document can do for quality control, constraint and bounds checking, and so on. We've built numerous custom lint utilities to help our XML development work. (In the Unix world, *lint* is a time-honored name for a tool that does syntax and structure checking on various programming languages; we borrow the term because of the similarity of the task involved in testing and debugging XML metadata and XML documents.)

Our biggest hope in tackling XML Schema was that its richer datatypes and more powerful data declaration and constraint mechanisms would make the job of designing XML documents easier and provide more automated assistance for quality control. Although it's not perfect in either of these ways, we did find that for data-intensive XML applications, XML Schema has a lot to recommend compared to SGML DTDs. That said, we also ran into plenty of applications—primarily documents rich in text with relatively simple structure—that could be described with equal facility by XML Schema or SGML DTDs.

For us, the biggest benefit of writing this book was the depth of understanding of XML Schema that it afforded us, not to mention the experience we gained. As you work through the contents of this book, therefore, we urge you to experiment, to implement, and to employ what's covered here, because that's where the best and most useful learning experiences will occur. It definitely worked that way for us; we suspect it will be the same for you.

The Approach

Thus, as you read about XML Schema constructs and datatypes, you should endeavor to put what you're reading about to some use. For example, build a simple address book application to get a sense of how to mix text and numeric datatypes. As you learn about value and existence constraints, you can put the old "Friday night problem" aside forevermore as you prevent a phone number without a name to go with it from having the right to exist (and to torment you unendingly).

Likewise, we urge you to explore the various XML Schema implementations that have already been defined for both "official standard" and unofficial use. Working your way through their designs and implementations will give you a valuable reality check on some tendencies you might otherwise develop to exercise too much control over your data, documents, and applications. Experience will also help you develop a strong sense of the data and content you must capture, organize, and present to your users.

The Tools

Although we mention numerous tools that can aid your design and development work for XML Schema documents throughout the book, we urge you to start with the plain-text editor of your choice and sufficient elbow grease to help you slide your way up the learning curve.

Once you become familiar with the basic constructs, data modeling tools, and datatypes that XML Schema provides, we believe you'll understand why XML Schema is more than just a consistent way to implement XML document designs. It's a powerful, useful, and fairly usable technology. But if you start with a visual or list-driven tool that "liberates" you from mastering the details of XML Schema, you may never develop the depth of understanding necessary to decide when information associated with document elements should be captured as element content and when it should be captured as an attribute value associated with an element (to choose just one example).

It's only when you've explored and fooled with the XML Schema vocabulary and its sometimes arcane structures and content modeling methods au natural that a good design tool will really stand up and bark for you anyway. Before then, you're more likely to be overwhelmed with the options and choices at your disposal than to make the most of what those options and choices enable in your designs.

If only you knew how to use the capabilities of XML Schema to their fullest, what wonders of content and data could you not create? On the other hand, basic understanding of what this technology can do best, and how to realize that understanding, goes a long way toward requiting such unfulfilled longings!

This Book

This book begins with a short, sharp look at the first principles, terms and concepts, and parent technologies that make metadata so important to modern computing. The book also takes you through the pros and cons and strengths and weaknesses of the two primary mechanisms used to describe XML documents—namely SGML DTDs and XML Schema. Most important, this book explores the rules and details that govern the structure, use, and implementation of XML Schema to design XML documents and content of many different kinds.

In a world where XML is rampant, and where it promises to be in places tomorrow where it isn't already today, understanding how to use XML grows increasingly important. When it comes to designing and using XML-based content and data, XML Schema offers the keys to realizing such designs and maximizing such use. We hope you'll find our book both illuminating and illustrative of such designs and uses.

CHAPTER 1

Introducing Metadata

- Introducing metadata concepts and terminology

- Understanding the role of metadata in markup languages

- Understanding SGML and XML metadata

- Understanding two specific types of metadata used with XML: SGML Document Type Definitions (DTDs) and XML Schemas

- Understanding the specific roles that metadata plays in defining and using XML

The word *schema* comes directly from the Greek, where it means *form* or *appearance*. In general terms, *schema* as it applies to XML has an interesting context but generally refers to a structural representation for a set of things, in the sense of a general scheme, layout, or outline.

This general notion of a description, layout, or outline for a set of things—in the case of XML, the description, layout, or outline refers to a set of documents governed by some specific schema or another—strikes at the core significance of formal schemas in general and XML Schema in particular. That is, such schemas define the structure of and describe the types of content that is allowed to appear in whatever documents or data collections they govern.

In computing terms, *metadata* is a special kind of data that exists to describe and contextualize other data. Hopefully, even this brief definition—which we expand on considerably in the body of this chapter—indicates why our discussion of XML Schema begins with an analysis and discussion of metadata. It's because XML Schema represents a particular kind of metadata that needs to be understood in the overall context of metadata itself. It's also useful to understand XML Schema in the context of other ways of defining metadata for markup languages in general and for XML and other specific, related markup languages in particular.

Introducing Metadata Concepts and Terminology

We'll begin our exploration of metadata with a more detailed definition: Metadata is a kind of data that describes other data, particularly complex collections of data. Thus, metadata often includes some or all of the following kinds of information:

- *Data that describes the overall structure or layout of other data elements.* This may be understood as a kind of recipe that describes in what order data elements must or may appear and that also describes how elements may be identified or recognized as such. The recipe involved may be as simple as requiring that data elements in actual records or documents match the sequence in which they appear in a metadata description of such records or documents, or it may be more complex and involve required and optional elements or even conditional elements (this is covered more completely in the item on relationship data that follows later in this list). By convention, we distinguish data or document elements in this book by using special typography (a monospaced font). For example, it's easy to see that the book element is an element named book and not an ordinary, real book because we used the special typography for the word *book*.

- *Data that describes individual data elements, where such elements are normally given names and associated with specific forms of representation known as datatypes, data ranges, or value domains.* Describing how values associated with data elements are to be represented is itself another form of metadata (and one that draws a lot of attention in the XML Schema arena).

- *Data that defines constraints on element values.* For example, a valid zip code or telephone number (both of which are reasonably well-understood types of element data and therefore should make sense to readers) can be distinguished from an invalid zip code or telephone number. In some cases, values may be constrained to belong to a certain set of valid numbers, names, or other restricted sets of data rather than only to a general type. For example, the values "male" and "female" are normally the only values from which an element that represents a person's sex may be drawn. On the other hand, the values for an element of type "name" could be just about any string of alphabetic characters.

- *Data that describes necessary or possible relationships between data elements.* Certain elements may require that specific relationships exist between them and thus may differ from relationships in which there are requirements imposed by metadata that govern overall structure or layout of data records or collections. For instance, a certain document that includes a data element named `person` may require that additional data elements named `name`, `address`, `SSN` (for social security number), and `sex` exist so the `person` element can be completely and properly defined. In other cases, certain special identifier values called *keys* may be required to appear in multiple records as a way of linking a specific `paycheck` element to a specific `person` element to identify whose paycheck that element represents. In fact, this explains why most paychecks include an employee ID number or a Social Security number as well as other information; that unique identifier is the key that links the `paycheck` element to the `employee` element.

This detailed explanation of metadata makes it possible for us to provide a shorter, more cogent definition of the essential role that metadata plays in computing: Metadata essentially explains how to read, interpret, and internalize other data. Making this information explicit can be time-consuming, difficult, and complicated, but it's an essential exercise in making it possible for computers (and humans) to exchange data freely and reliably.

Without metadata to explain what's inside any particular file, record, or document, we'd be unable to exchange data with one another. This fundamental principle is important but easy to overlook because so much metadata is implied in our understanding of how things work. For example, when you look at the files on your hard drive on a Windows machine, you understand that files with an `.exe` extension are executable programs, that files that end in `.txt` are plain-text files, and that files that end in `.doc` are probably word processing documents of some kind. Windows PC applications share this understanding through a formal mechanism called *file association*, which tells the computer that when you double-click the name of a file that ends in .exe, it's supposed to attempt to execute that file, but when you double-click the name of a file that ends in .txt, it's supposed to open that file using some kind of text editor.

Metadata becomes increasingly difficult to ignore or overlook as the complexity of the data itself becomes more obvious. This is why the importance of metadata is undeniable for complex collections of data such as documents or databases. Without some kind of map for record structures and relationships in a database, database engines would be unable to read and interpret the databases they manage. Without access to a style sheet or formatting rules, a word processor wouldn't be able to take the text in a document and give it the appearance it's so often painstakingly designed to display. In both cases, the metadata that describes the database or the document and its contents is the key that opens some specific data collection that follows its rules for perusal, update, or analysis.

In fact, the term *schema* as it's used in this book (and throughout most of the computing field) originally meant a technique to formally describe the structure, contents, and relationships that occur within databases. You'll notice an outright preoccupation with datatyping and data representation, as well as document structure and element relationships, as you learn more about XML Schema in this book. We come by this preoccupation honestly and fairly, because it derives directly from database notions about schemas (or schemata, as the plural is sometimes also expressed using the Greek form). From a database perspective, we see schemas as collections of metadata that describe record or table structures, the data elements of which they're composed, the relationships between elements and other objects, and even the functions or operations that may be performed within one specific database or another.

In modern databases, schemas exist separately and independently from the data collections they describe. Although it's necessary for database software to access and internalize schemas to enable them to access and manipulate the contents of specific databases, the schema is applied to the data collections that individual databases represent. Unlike most of the document metadata discussed in this book, ordinary database files do not typically include labels that identify individual data elements. Rather, schema information is used to create a map of data structures in databases. These structures may be called *records* or *tables*, depending on the type of database in use (or the context of such use).

At this point, we've covered enough ground that a summary list of key concepts and terminology used so far to talk about metadata and schemas will be helpful. For convenience, we present this list in alphabetical order, along with an observation that even those who might ordinarily be disinclined to plow through a mere list of terms will probably benefit from a quick scan through its contents:

conditional element   An element whose existence depends on the existence or inclusion of another, related element within a data collection.

content model   In a document definition or a schema, the content model expresses what forms a document's organization (or the sequences of elements and associated content or values its organization comprises) may take.

data collection   A set of multiple data elements that may represent a database, a document, or some other such set of data elements. When metadata governs a data collection, it may be said to define that collection's organization, contents, and internal relationships.

data domain   The set of all possible values that a data element may assume.

data element   A specific item of data within some data collection. Generally, data elements have names, types, and values; names identify specific element instances within a data collection's structure, and types identify how to interpret the value or values associated with an element. Some data elements may assume only a single value, whereas others may assume a fixed number of values, and still others may contain arbitrary lists or sets of values. Part of what a content model defines is the kind of relationship between elements and the number of values (or subcomponents) they may or must take.

data range   The set of all possible values that performing a function or an operation on some data value may produce (similar to a data domain, but representing the result of some operation or another on a data domain).

database   A data collection that consists of one or more organized sets of element values, where such sets may be called records or tables (see *record* and *table* for more information about these element value sets).

database structure   The metadata that describes how a database is organized or what forms of organization or sequences of data elements it may take; information about element values or representations is part of the schema but not necessarily part of the database structure.

datatype   A specific form that the value or values associated with a data element may assume; alternatively, you may assume that an element value's datatype describes how to represent and interpret any associated value or values.

document   A data collection that consists of content (usually, but not always, textual data) along with metadata that in turn consists of content labels plus processing or rendering instructions. (Sometimes, but not always, this metadata is also in text form and is called *markup*; for XML documents, this is always the case.)

document definition   A type of metadata that defines valid content models and document elements and attributes (including rules governing element content and properties) for some specific document or class of documents.

document structure   The metadata that describes how a document's data elements may or must be organized or what forms of organization or sequences of data elements it may follow; information about element values or content is part of a document definition or schema but not necessarily part of the document structure. See also *content model*.

Document Type Definition (DTD)   A special form of document definition that is expressed with SGML. It defines a content model and document elements (including rules governing element content and properties) for some specific document or class of documents. All HTML documents are governed by SGML DTDs; many XML documents are governed by SGML DTDs, but XML Schemas are designed as a purely XML-based metadata alternative.

element attribute   A named property for an element (which may also have one or more associated values) that qualifies that element beyond the content or value associated with the element itself. In the Extensible Hypertext Markup Language (XHTML), for example, any document element may have an associated id attribute whose value must be unique (and that therefore defines a unique identifier for each particular element that possesses an id attribute so that it may be identified solely on the basis of its associated id value).

element content   For XML documents, element content refers to text associated with some specific, non-empty XML document element. In general, it refers to the data (also called an *element value*, which is more in keeping with database schema terminology) associated with any specific element.

element name   A string identifier associated with an element that identifies an element within the context of a particular data collection, be it a document (part of a content model), a database (an element in a table or a record), or some other kind of data collection (a named component of that other collection, whatever it may be). Because multiple instances of the same element—for example the paragraph, or p, element in XHTML—may occur in a single document, an element name is only seldom a unique identifier (see *element attribute* to learn about a qualifying value that can make any element instance uniquely identifiable).

element value   The actual data associated with a specific data element in a document, database, or some other data collection as distinguished from an element name (which identifies the element) or an element's properties or attributes (which qualify or identify an element and its associated content or value[s]).

file   A container for binary or textual data, or some combination of both types, that normally exists within the context of a file system on a computer. A file is a kind of data collection as well, and XML files are designed to include or refer to explicit metadata about their contents that defines them completely and correctly.

function   A form of data analysis, extraction, abstraction, or transformation that performs various operations on the values in a data collection to produce some kind of desired result, be it a report, trending information, ad hoc query processing, or other kinds of output.

identifier   A unique name or attribute value that permits single element instances in a data collection to be unambiguously identified.

identifier value   The unique value that pinpoints a single element instance in a data collection.

key   A special identifier—usually in a database—that identifies some specific instance of an element with special significance or meaning, such as an employee in a payroll or HR database, where the employee identifier is also a key to obtaining information about payment, training, vacation and sick leave balances, and so on.

metadata   Literally, data about other data, metadata is what defines structure, organization, data elements and interpretation, and even sometimes functions or operations of elements in a data collection. For the purposes of this book, *metadata* effectively means the DTDs or XML Schemas that govern XML documents and related content.

TIP   See Chapter 11, "Using Appropriate Metadata," for more about metadata.

operation   A form of data analysis, extraction, abstraction, or transformation that performs various systematic functions on the values in a data collection to produce some kind of desired result—be it a report, trending information, ad hoc query processing, or some other kind of output.

optional element   Within a content model, optional data elements are those that may or may not appear, depending on the specific content to be represented within a document, a database, or some other form of data collection.

record   Within a specific type of database, a record represents a set of related data elements that together define a single, coherent database entry of some specific kind or another; the kind of database entry is subject to that database's schema and any applicable constraints.

record structure   Within a specific type of database, the record structure defines the map for a single, coherent collection of data elements that together define a single database entry. Inherent in the record structure are the results of applying value, existence, and other constraints to data elements and their associated values within that collection.

required element   Within a content model, required elements are those that must appear with a document, a database, or some other form of data collection to meet the structure and content requirements defined within that model.

table   Within a specific type of database, a table represents a set of related data elements that together define a single, coherent set of database information. By convention, the columns in a database table define the individual elements in database records, and the rows define individual records. Thus, using a table may, to some extent, be considered a way of collecting all records of the same type together within a single data structure.

table structure   The way in which a set of related data elements is organized, wherein, by convention, the columns define individual elements in database records and the rows define individual records of the same type.

value domain   The set of all possible values that a data element or attribute may assume.

Having set the stage for XML-related metadata in general, we proceed to more closely examine the two specific sources of metadata for XML documents in the following sections. We start with a discussion of the Standard Generalized Markup Language (SGML) and its metadata capabilities and then discuss the Extensible Markup Language (XML) and its metadata capabilities.

SGML Metadata Explored and Explained

To begin our overview of SGML metadata, we provide a general background and history of this fascinating technology. SGML has been enshrined as an official International Organization for Standardization (ISO) standard, ISO 8879, since 1986. But the steps leading up to its official standardization and the uses to which this technology has been put will help add context to our discussion of metadata, so it's worth recounting its chronology and development process.

The Development of SGML

The antecedents to SGML lie in what might jokingly be called the "antediluvian mists" of computing, as far back as the 1960s. The SGML Users' Group document "A Brief History of the Development of SGML" identifies the first recognizable implementation of a markup language in the movement away from proprietary, application-specific control codes embedded in documents and toward generic coding, which uses descriptive tags to label document elements that occurred in the latter part of that decade. The Graphic Communications Association (GCA, still active today at www.gca.org) formed a generic coding project in its Composition Committee in 1968. This project evolved into the GCA's GenCode Committee, which was also later instrumental in the creation of the ISO SGML standard.

In 1969, a group of researchers at IBM began work on computerized law office information systems that were designed to permit the then completely separate computer systems used to edit, format, and store legal documents to exchange data readily and easily. Charles Goldfarb was the leader of this group that also included Edward Mosher and Raymond Lorie. Together, their efforts produced the Generalized Markup Language (GML) for IBM. Not coincidentally, the first letters of the last names of the three men behind this technology form the same initialism.

Instead of using simple document tagging, GML implemented the use of a formal Document Type Definition (DTD) that not only explicitly spelled out document tags called *elements*, but also defined rules for their order of appearance and their relationships with other elements. This profound insight produced a clean way to separate document structure and containers for content (metadata) from the content itself. This approach continues to describe how SGML and XML work to this very day.

IBM continued on to implement major portions of GML in the form of powerful, mainframe-based publishing systems, which were soon echoed in similar implementations from other vendors. Because many experts recognize IBM as a publisher on a global scale (the SGML Users' Group document states that the company is "reckoned to be the world's second largest publisher"), its adoption of GML was a significant commitment to its own technology and a significant inducement for other industry players to participate in the phenomenon. As recently as 1990, it was estimated that over 90 percent of IBM's publishing efforts were split between GML- and SGML-based systems.

Once Goldfarb's team was through with GML, he continued his research in the area of document structures and related concepts and technologies. He takes credit for the development of the term *markup language* in 1970 and helped implement IBM's multisite, multinational publishing system, which contained 11 million master pages by the end of that decade. SGML is in fact an industrial-strength technology that has been used successfully for all kinds of extremely large document collections on the order of the IBM collection just described.

In 1979, the American National Standards Institute (ANSI) established a committee for the processing of text, which Goldfarb joined. In that capacity, Goldfarb led a project to create a text description language based on GML, in which the GCA GenCode Committee also took part. This would ultimately result in the publication of the first working draft of SGML in 1980, and the sixth working draft became a GCA industry standard in 1983 (GCA 101-1983). The U.S. government took a strong interest in this technology, which was adopted by the Department of Defense and the Internal Revenue Service shortly thereafter.

In 1984, additional working drafts based on feedback from the GCA standard were completed. The ANSI project was reorganized under its own auspices as well as those of the ISO, so that two parallel and complementary efforts soon got underway. One group began meeting regularly as an ISO working group under the direction of James Mason of the Oak Ridge National Laboratory, while William Davis of SGML Associates chaired the ANSI effort. Goldfarb acted as a technical leader for and liaison between the two groups while also serving as the project editor for each group. (Note that in a working group charged with drafting a standard or some similar document, the editor is the manager responsible for producing that document. Goldfarb is, therefore, justified in thinking of himself as the "inventor" of SGML, although it was very much a team effort.)

In 1985, the publication of an ISO working draft was followed relatively quickly by the publication of a draft proposal for SGML. Groups in the U.S. and Europe worked quickly to react to these drafts and provide feedback, which led to the publication of an ISO draft international standard in October 1985. This draft standard was immediately adopted by the European Community's Office of Official Publications. Following another year of comment and review, the final text was produced and published as ISO standard 8879:1986 in record time; an SGML-based publication system was used to produce that document with great fanfare. A heavily annotated (and updated) version of the document forms the basis for Goldfarb's *SGML Handbook* (Clarendon Press, 1990).

Since SGML's adoption as an international standard, it has become widely used outside the halls of IBM where some might argue that it began its life. Important adoptions are widespread. Some of SGML's better-known applications include the following:

- The Association of American Publishers application for book, journal, and article creation, a source for creating books, white papers, and articles. This application also defines the foundation for the popular Z39.59 ANSI CD-ROM publishing standard.

- The Computer-Aided Acquisition and Logistics Support (CALS) initiative, which originated at the U.S. Department of Defense, that all branches of the military use today for procurement and publishing of systems and related documentation. A similar initiative in the aerospace industry provides a framework for capturing all documentation for modern aircraft, where a single plane's documentation and maintenance records may run into hundreds of thousands of pages in length.

- Strictly speaking, the Web markup languages known as HTML and XHTML are SGML applications (that is, they were originally defined using SGML DTDs).

- Until use of XML Schema became possible, in fact, the only way to define XML markup was to use an SGML DTD. Thus, it's also possible to argue that SGML enabled the definition and use of XML itself.

Until XML-based publication systems became available in the late 1990s, the only heavy-duty, industrial-strength standards-based publication systems were based on SGML. This probably explains why other large companies besides IBM—including Novell, Netscape, Cisco Systems, Adobe Systems, and many others—used SGML publication systems to help them run their businesses (and why many still do so).

Understanding SGML

Of course, there's more to SGML than its chronology and a list of some of its many important applications. Here, we'll review SGML's important characteristics and explain its metadata facilities at a high level. (Chapter 9 is devoted to SGML DTDs and how to convert them into XML Schema.) Then we'll review SGML's pros and cons, partly to explain why so many experts found it necessary to create XML itself and also to explain why XML Schema represents a necessary and logical metadata alternative to (or replacement for) SGML DTDs.

To begin with, SGML is itself a markup language. To explain what this means, we quote from Charles Goldfarb's *SGML Handbook* (pg 5):

> *Text processing and word processing systems typically require additional information to be interspersed among the natural text of the document being processed. This added information, called "markup," serves two purposes:*
> *a) Separating the logical elements of the document; and*
> *b) Specifying the processing functions to be performed on those elements.*

But as a generalized markup language, SGML seeks to separate information that describes the contents and structure of a document from information that describes how that document should appear when displayed, printed, or otherwise rendered for viewing. This is why SGML documents require style sheets to be defined and referenced to govern appearance and why they also require metadata documents to be defined and referenced to govern structure and content.

To better understand the notion of generalized markup consider this quotation from the *SGML Handbook* (pp 7–8):

> *… "generalized markup"…does not restrict documents to a single application, formatting style, or processing system. Generalized markup is based on two novel postulates:*
> *a) Markup should describe a document's structure and other attributes rather than specify processing to be performed on it, as descriptive markup need be done only once and will suffice for all future processing.*
> *b) Markup should be rigorous so that the techniques available for processing rigorously-defined objects like programs and data bases can be used for processing documents as well.*

Describing "a document's structure and other attributes" explains why metadata is necessary. However, the call for "rigorous" markup explains why SGML offers so much power and capability for defining metadata and why the resemblance between SGML metadata (and XML Schema by extension) and database schemas are not at all unplanned or accidental.

That said, SGML is a large and complex specification for describing and handling text. Although SGML itself is based entirely on a simple text-only character set (one of the things that makes it so attractive for computerized document interchange), the environment that SGML defines and supports is both powerful and sophisticated. By way of contrasting SGML to XML, the SGML specification is over 500 pages long, whereas the XML specification barely exceeds 50 pages.

For a long time, SGML-based publishing systems and software were suitable only for large companies and organizations because the cost of implementing the power and complexity that SGML provides perforce limited the size of its audience. Whereas Microsoft (and other application vendors) has embraced XML and is or has integrated it extensively into its software (in Office 2000, Word and PowerPoint use XML to represent file contents and structures internally), the only vendors who've likewise integrated SGML into their products are typically those such as Frame Technologies or ArborText, whose text processing tools typically cost more than $1,000 to $1,500 per user. Full-blown text management or publishing systems that support SGML cost anywhere from $10,000 and up (most cost significantly more than that).

SGML Metadata: DTDs

In its most general sense, metadata is data about other data; it can be either descriptive (to say what it is) or prescriptive (to state rules about what elements and values must occur, in what form, in what order, and so forth). When it comes to SGML-based documents, three ingredients are necessary for an SGML-aware system to be able to properly internalize, interpret, and render such documents for display, analysis, printing, or other uses:

- A DTD that defines the document's elements, content model, and other prescriptive rules for structure and content

- A style sheet that defines rules for how the document is to be rendered for some particular form of output

- Actual document content (usually in a document file) that conforms to the rules set in the two preceding items

Although it's common for each of the preceding items to appear within its own file, there's no requirement that this be the case, and a single valid SGML document can include both inline DTD declarations and inline style sheet information as well as actual document content.

Because the focus of this book is on metadata, we concentrate the rest of this discussion on the SGML DTD declarations, with the understanding that, although the other parts mentioned are necessary, they're not germane to this discussion. The keys to understanding the role that DTDs play for the SGML documents they govern lie in understanding the terminology that describes the components that go into creating DTDs:

attribute definition   A specific type of SGML declaration that defines an individual attribute's name, its associated value or values, a datatype, and an optional default value.

attribute list   A collection of one or more attributes associated with a specific document element.

base document element   Fundamentally, every SGML document consists of a single element called the *base document element* (it's also called the *root element*, particularly when talking about XML documents).

CDATA   Character data that is treated as raw input in an SGML document without further interpretation or examination.

character set   A named collection of character codes with associated renderings used to represent text data in SGML documents. SGML "understands" the International Organization for Standardization/International Electrotechnical Commission (ISO/IEC) 10646 standard character set, also known as Unicode, which may be used to represent characters from most known human languages along with a wide range of symbols, diacritical marks, specialized punctuation, and so forth.

comment   Data inserted into an SGML document or DTD solely for the purpose of explaining or elucidating its content (comments are not parsed and are generally ignored by document processors).

content   Document element data (normally text) that makes up the information contained within a document.

content model   In an SGML DTD, the content model expresses what forms a document's organization (or the sequences of elements and associated content or values that its organization comprises) may take.

document element   Any named document component with an associated content model, optional attribute definitions, and default value(s) is an SGML document element.

element attribute   As in our earlier definition list, an attribute is a name-value pair (where the value may be a single value or a list of values) that modifies or adds information to a specific element instance. In an SGML content model, attributes can be optional or required and may be assigned default values as needed.

element declaration   In an SGML DTD, a special declaration in which an element is named and its associated datatype and/or content model information is defined.

entity   A fascinating shorthand structure in SGML, entities define information (such as strings, pointers to external resources, and so on) that is parsed in at the beginning of document processing and then substituted for entity references encountered later as a document is processed.

external   Some element, attribute value, link, or other data resource that is defined outside the scope of the current DTD or a specific document's inline declarations.

ID   A unique identifier used to distinguish each individual component within an SGML document or DTD.

internal   Some element, attribute value, link, or other data resource that is completely defined within the scope of the current DTD or a specific document's inline declarations.

markup minimization feature   A feature of SGML that permits markup that identifies elements (also called *tags*) to be shortened or omitted. It also permits abbreviation of entity references.

notation   A way of defining content data when the built-in lexicon of SGML datatypes does not suffice to represent particular element or attribute values. Invoking a specific notation often permits the document processor to call another program to handle that specialized data, which then returns control to the processor when its work is done.

PCDATA   Parsed character data that is subject to parsing and analysis (and can therefore include entity references) as an SGML document is handled.

public identifier   A special identifier that provides a location for a DTD or other external data on a system other than the one where a document resides; public identifiers often point to public, standard DTDs and related resources and are generally accessible from anywhere on the Internet.

system identifier   A special identifier that provides a location for a DTD or other external data on the same local system where the document resides.

Why Not Simply Stick to SGML?

With this baseline of SGML terminology and concepts in mind, you'll find that the following observations about SGML will help answer the inevitable questions that any brief exposure to its powerful representational abilities provokes: Why doesn't everybody simply use SGML for document representation and processing? or Why not use SGML as is on the Internet?

The answers to these questions are reasonably straightforward, but they also hide some subtleties that we'll try to expose for your consideration. They are as follows:

Complexity   In some sense, complexity plays a role in nearly every factor included in this list. SGML is a complex technology that is difficult to implement and therefore expensive to acquire and use. Also, from a purely formal perspective, SGML is challenging: Its syntax is complex and difficult and its vocabulary of reserved words and terminology is large (the definitions section of the specification runs to 38 pages). In other words, many people steer clear of SGML because it's more than they want to deal with; certainly, the enormous popularity of the Web stems from the extreme simplicity and ease of use associated with HTML. That phenomenon would not have occurred with direct use of SGML.

Enormous bulk   Because SGML has so much representational power, provides so many alternatives for document processing, and includes minimization features, its internal complexity means that lots of code is needed to create, process, or handle SGML documents. This aspect of complexity translates into expensive tools, which helps explain why general adoption never happened. The sheer size of the code and its impact on Internet access times and delivery helps explain why it was never widely used for document interchange on the Web.

Learning curve   Any complex language takes significant time and effort to learn, and even more time and effort to master. Although there are plenty of competent SGML (and XML) professionals in the workplace, they're outnumbered by HTML- literate (or XHTML-literate) professionals by at least an order of magnitude. The learning curve associated with SGML has always made it a rarefied expertise.

Kitchen sink mentality   Because of SGML's roots in enterprise-level document management systems (from its inception as GML, in fact), it has always had extraordinary capabilities, an enormous set of features and functions, and more bells and whistles than most document designers ever dream of using. This too plays off complexity and imposes learning curve issues. It also helps explain why SGML tools are cumbersome and expensive and why they didn't have the mass appeal that HTML enjoyed.

Inadequate datatypes   Although SGML has a reasonable set of primitive datatypes (the basic datatypes that define element content and attribute values), it falls far short of the kinds of capability you'd find in a database development environment or in a modern programming language such as C++, Java, or Perl. This is somewhat less onerous for text-intensive documents in which structured data isn't terribly important or prevalent, but it's quite taxing for value-intensive or record-structured data collections. We'll revisit this topic in another chapter; for now, suffice it to say that SGML doesn't permit sufficient specificity when defining element content or attribute values to allow document validation to check that such values are within specific ranges or that particular formal relationships exist between such values. Perhaps the best way to understand this limitation is to say that the lack of support for this kind of behavior often requires development of special data-checking tools that must be applied to documents in addition to SGML validation checks. Most content developers prefer that this be handled in a single step, for all kinds of good reasons.

Behind the times   Because SGML was designed in the 1960s and completed in the 1980s, it has not kept up with more recent developments in document definition and processing technologies. For example, it fails to provide support for XML namespaces, a technique used to reference and incorporate external markup definitions in XML documents. Because public, standard namespaces, as well as private namespaces, are becoming more prevalent and widely used, this omission can be frustrating for document designers, even though well-understood workarounds exist.

In the final analysis, SGML's size, complexity, and perceived difficulty of implementation and use all contribute to its relative obscurity. By contrast, HTML's nearly nonexistent learning curve, based on its simple syntax and small vocabulary, has translated into enormous success and popularity. But unlike SGML, which has abstract capabilities to define markup and content models, HTML is a closed system that cannot be extended without altering the very SGML DTD that defines it.

XML (Schema) to the Rescue

Technically, XML is a proper subset of SGML. In plain English, XML supports many of the capabilities and most of the representational power of SGML more or less exactly. But until XML Schema was envisioned, the only valid technique for creating XML metadata was to write SGML DTDs. Thus, it's entirely correct to see XML Schema as a way to use XML to define XML metadata, because any XML Schema—as the name hopefully implies—is itself an XML document. This allows you to define and use XML in its pure form without relying on SGML in any way shape or form.

However, unlike SGML DTDs, which require SGML-capable processors, development tools, validators, and so forth, XML Schema can be processed with the same software that can process any XML document. To understand why this is important, we need to take a brief detour to explore the reasons why XML was invented and what new capabilities it brings to the public at large, and to the Web in particular.

The XML Impetus

If you revisit the list of things that made SGML unsuitable for general public use on the Internet and the Web—specifically, complexity, enormous bulk, learning curve, and kitchen sink mentality—you'll get your first inkling of what created the impetus for XML. That is, XML was deliberately designed to be simple to parse and process so that the overhead of handling XML markup would not impose a severe penalty on Web browser developers or users. The World Wide Web Consortium (W3C), which oversees the specifications for HTML, XML, and lots of other Web stuff, succeeded so well in its aims that some experts argue that XML is easier to process than HTML!

Some mention of HTML is also essential to an understanding of XML, because it was the W3C's frustration with its need to continually redefine HTML that propelled it to produce XML specifications. For one thing, user desires and requirements for markup features and functions changed far more quickly than the specifications that governed the language ever could. For another, stymied by the slow, stately pace of standards development, the major browser vendors—meaning Netscape and Microsoft, mostly—took it upon themselves to add all kinds of proprietary document elements to the definitions that their browsers would process, thereby effectively subverting the whole standards process. Worse, this forced Web designers to build multiple versions of identical Web pages in some cases so both Netscape Navigator and Microsoft Internet Explorer users could interact with their content as effectively as possible.

One subtlety of this phenomenon stems from the requirement that a Web browser must be an HTML document processor. Thus, browser software must internalize some version of an SGML DTD for HTML so that it can process HTML documents. This phenomenon permitted the big browser vendors to add their proprietary tweaks as they built these facilities. Because so many liberties were taken with HTML, and because its original design was not completely clean from a parsing and processing perspective, other profound impetuses toward XML included the following:

- *XML uses completely regular and rigorous document syntax.* Whereas HTML is lax about syntax requirements (it also offers some markup minimization in earlier versions, such as it doesn't always require attribute values to be quoted, and most browsers don't seriously enforce content models), XML is fanatic about a completely regular and rigorous syntax. Although this makes more work for content creators who aren't used to such regularity and rigor, it's easy for tools to deliver—more important, it's easy for tools to check for such rigor. Finally, insistence on regular, rigorous syntax makes it much, much simpler to write document parsers and processors to handle content that adheres to such syntax and to reject documents that fail to follow the rules.

- *XML documents can (and should) be completely described.* Both DTDs and XML Schema share the cardinal virtue of providing a complete description of a valid document's content model, elements, attributes, and so forth. That such metadata can be explicitly imported into a document processor—such as a Web browser—means that the processor uses the metadata that describes the document to process the document itself. In addition to vastly simplifying the jobs of browser developers (because they can rely on an authoritative external source for metadata), this also explains how extensibility can be supported easily and efficiently.

- *Extensibility means existing XML metadata can be altered and custom XML markup created at will.* The *X* in *XML* stands for *extensible*, meaning that XML may be used to define arbitrary document content models, document elements, and so forth or that existing metadata can be altered for custom use. As long as a complete document description is available to an XML processor, that processor should be able to handle any document that adheres to that description. This opens the door to a vast array of possible markup languages—usually called XML applications or XML vocabularies—that users can cheerfully and confidently access, even if they've never seen that particular kind of document before.

Hopefully, these important features and functions of XML also help explain some of the excitement surrounding this technology. We also think it helps explain why so many industries, technical niches, and special-interest groups—genealogy, medical records, e-commerce, and on and on—are building their own XML applications so they can exchange and access data more easily and directly than ever before.

Among other things, XML's self-contained nature—which might be restated as "XML metadata can always be made available for XML content" to make our point more strong—is what makes data exchange and access possible. This is because such XML data incorporates or references all the metadata necessary to internalize, interpret, and render the content it conveys.

The Joy of XML Schema

Without going too far overboard, it's important to understand that document designers' wishes to avoid full-blown SGML DTDs pale by comparison with their desire to be able to use the same tools to process both XML documents and XML document descriptions. Aside from avoiding a bigger, more complex syntax and the need for additional, expensive design and development tools, XML Schema makes it much easier for developers to stick to an entirely consistent metaphor for designing document metadata as well as for creating documents (or document content).

Then, too, XML Schema also addresses some of the other shortcomings we've noted that affect SGML DTDs—namely, their relatively weak datatyping facilities and their lack of support for XML namespaces. As you'll learn in great detail in Chapter 7, XML Schema includes support for as wide a variety of predefined datatypes (sometimes called *data primitives*) as you'll find in most modern programming languages. And like such languages, XML Schema also supports the ability to combine and customize these data primitives into complex, compound definitions. Likewise, XML Schema includes built-in support for XML namespaces so that any public or private namespace you wish to use to define markup in an XML document becomes available using the proper referencing techniques (discussed in Chapter 5).

Does This Mean the End for DTDs?

At this point in the discussion of the relative merits of DTDs versus XML Schema, many people start to infer that DTDs are dinosaurs, doomed to inevitable distinction. However, for some applications, DTDs remain preferable to XML Schema; for other applications, XML Schema clearly provides the right tool set. In most important aspects—except for datatypes and XML namespaces—the two technologies are nearly equivalent. To some extent, this means it's okay to use whichever technology you know best. We assume you wouldn't be reading a book on XML Schema unless you were leaning in that direction—or maybe you're just curious—but we believe that DTDs are by no means dead or dying.

On the other hand, it's clear that there's a meaningful distinction between what might be called *text-intensive* XML documents, in which the content consists almost entirely of text, and *data-intensive* XML documents, in which the content consists almost entirely of record- or table-structured data. For example, think of the difference in designing a book that covers a technical specification or designing a book that contains thousands of movie reviews, alphabetized by title. Whereas the former is to some extent a single, coherent narrative document, the latter is nothing more than a nicely formatted database snapshot.

Conventional wisdom is that DTDs are still eminently suitable for text-intensive XML documents and that XML Schema is better suited for data-intensive XML documents. This is not to say you can't use XML Schema for text-intensive documents or DTDs for data-intensive ones, but the idea is that these metadata technologies work best for building document descriptions when they play to their strengths.

Murray Altheim, one of Sun Microsystem's preeminent SGML and XML gurus, has put together a terrific Web site at www.doctypes.org, in part to stem the momentum of opinion away from DTDs and toward XML Schemas. In this context, we'd like to quote the opening paragraph from his home page before we recap some excellent points he makes regarding the continued value—and right to exist—that DTDs should enjoy going forward.

> *DTDs have been getting a lot of bad press lately. There seems to be an idea that in order for XML Schemas to live, DTDs must die. I hear voices chanting "XML Schemas, XML Schemas, XML Schemas will solve all of our problems…" Many of these voices come from the database community, where the concept of 'structured data' is important but the priorities quite different. There is a battle going on for the heart of XML: is it for documents or for data? We keep hearing that XML Schemas will provide the necessary content validation suitable for databases and object oriented programming. Okay. But you'd almost begin to think that DTDs were no longer suitable for what they were designed to do, and do quite well: validate the markup structure of a document.*

Add to validation another important concept—namely, modularization, as practiced with the XHTML 1.1 specification or the XHTML Modularization specification that preceded it—and you've got a pretty powerful combination of capabilities. As it happens, the much-vaunted combination of namespaces and schemas didn't buy as much for XHTML modularization as some had hoped. Thus, most of the work in defining meaningful subsets of the XHTML specification (which in turn define the modules into which XHTML markup is divided) have focused on DTDs rather than XML Schema—at least up to now. It will be interesting to see how the work now underway to implement XML Schema proceeds toward completion.

The point that `doctypes.org` seeks to make is that it's not really a question of DTDs versus schemas, nor is it a matter of whether schemas can (or could) replace DTDs. Rather, it's a matter of finding appropriate uses for both approaches and applying each where it makes the most sense. Just as `doctypes.org` is worth a visit, so are the points it makes worth pondering. The long list of entirely useful DTDs on the home page makes a pretty strong case that DTDs are indeed far from dead and still have a lot to contribute to the mix, especially for what Altheim so circumspectly calls "human-readable documents."

Summary

When it comes to exchanging data between systems or applications, the metadata that describes the data being exchanged, how it's structured, and how to interpret its values and content is critical in enabling such exchanges. Of course, metadata is equally important to describing content models and elements for data collections of all kinds—as witnessed by the pivotal role that schemas and DTDs play for databases, documents, and all kinds of other data collections.

It's also important to understand that metadata embraces many kinds of information, each of which is subject to numerous nuances. Thus, document or database metadata not only covers the way in which data or content is structured or organized, it's also capable of stating rules or constraints that govern outright existence requirements, relationships between data elements, and attribution information (such as who entered a value, when it was entered, when it was last updated, and so forth).

The term *schema* has a rich and complex heritage, but the meaning that resonates most closely with its intention in the world of XML Schema is as a description, layout, or outline for a set of data elements as they're handled in modern database management systems. When it comes to XML documents however, it's also important to consider that SGML DTDs represent the traditional form in which document metadata is captured and that XML Schema represents a new and emerging alternative to DTDs for creating document metadata.

The representational power and capability of SGML is enormous and well known, but its very strengths lead to significant complexity in learning, using, and implementing that technology. In particular, SGML has proven unsuitable for direct use on the Web because its complexity and cost make it prohibitive to implement on the Internet's global scale. XML, on the other hand, has been designed for Web access from the ground up and benefits greatly from 30-plus years of experience with GML and SGML, as well as 10-plus years of experience with various versions of HTML.

XML Schema has the advantages of working within normal XML document processing models and tools and supporting rich, complex datatypes as well as XML namespaces. This makes XML Schema particularly attractive for applications that may be described as *data intensive*, whereas DTDs appear to be best suited for applications that may be described as *text intensive*. As you make your way through the rest of this book, we urge you to consider how your own content- and information-handling needs fit within the various descriptive models that DTDs and XML Schema provide. Though our focus is on XML Schema, we hasten to point out that we do not see it as either necessary or inevitable that XML Schema completely supplants and replaces all SGML DTDs.

CHAPTER 2

Of DTDs and Schemas

- Understanding basic schema structure

- Examining the basics behind DTDs

- Comparing schemas and DTDs

- Looking toward the future

Recently, there's been a lot to say about schemas and Document Type Definitions (DTDs). As XML has moved from its document-centric roots to a more data-centric environment, the tools necessary for validation have evolved as well. DTDs, a long-standing part of the Standard Generalized Markup Language (SGML), were (and still are) quite good at defining document structure. However, because XML is being used within e-commerce applications and for business-to-business (B2B) transactions, developers quickly learned that DTDs were not equipped to handle data-centric information.

This is not to say that DTDs have outlived their usefulness; however, schemas are giving them a run for their money. As developers, we now have options for validation. Two options come from the W3C: XML Schema and XML DTDs. However, you're not limited to only those two options. In addition to XML Schema and XML DTDs, there are several other schema languages that are circulating throughout the XML community. Two worth noting are REgular LAnguage description for XML Next Generation (RELAX NG) and Schematron, which are both lightweight schema languages that offer functionality similar to the functionality XML Schema offers. Find out more about RELAX NG and Schematron in Chapter 12.

In this chapter, we focus on basic underlying concepts of XML Schema and XML DTDs. It's important to understand the strengths and weaknesses of both approaches before you choose the appropriate validation tool for your application.

Understanding DTD Structures and Functions

DTDs have provided structure to XML documents for a long time. Whereas flexibility is one of XML's primary strengths, there are instances where structure is important—even a requirement. Defining a document model provides a structure to which documents must conform. E-commerce and B2B transactions are two common scenarios that require strict document models.

There are several reasons you might want to use a validation mechanism:

- If multiple developers will be working with the document model, the DTD would provide a framework from which they can work.

- If your document model contains required elements (such as a price for your product), DTDs allow you to define element and attribute behavior.

- If you're developing a document model that will continue to evolve, a DTD could help guide that process.

DTD validation was the first solution for defining document models and is over 20 years old. DTDs have several key functions:

- Provide a structural framework for documents

- Define a content model for elements
- Declare a list of allowable attributes for each element
- Allow for limited datatyping for attribute values
- Provide default values for attributes
- Define a mechanism for creating reusable chunks of data, with some limitations
- Provide a mechanism for passing non-XML data to the appropriate processor
- Allow you to use conditional sections to mark declarations for inclusion or exclusion

In this section, we define notable DTD components.

TIP   As you probably know, DTD validation is no longer the only option for defining document models. XML Schema offers a flexible solution to the preceding scenarios.

Declarations

DTDs consist of declarations that provide rules for your document model. Each declaration defines an element, set of attributes, entity, or notation. These four declaration types make up the bulk of any DTD:

element declarations   Identify the names of elements and the nature of their content. DTDs do not allow for complex content model definitions. Rather, DTDs allow authors to provide information about element hierarchy. The only datatype you can define for element content is parsed character data (PCDATA).

attribute declarations   Identify which elements may have attributes, what attributes they may have, what values the attributes may hold, and what the default value is.

entity declarations   Allow you to associate a name with some other fragment of content. That construct can be a chunk of regular text, a chunk of the document type declaration, or a reference to an external file containing either text or binary data.

notation declarations   Identify specific types of external binary data. This information is passed to the processing application.

When defining DTD declarations, you have to follow a few rules governing the order of their occurrence. If multiple declarations exist for the same element, entity, attribute, or notation, the first one defined takes precedence (the other redundant declarations are then ignored). You also have to be careful when defining entities. Parameter entities (entities defined and used within the DTD) must be declared before they can be referenced.

The syntax used to create declarations allows for white space anywhere within the declarations, but there are a few delimiters that have to be written accurately (such as the exclamation point in !ELEMENT. The follow declarations are all correct:

```
<!ELEMENT book (title, author)>
<!ELEMENT        book        (title, author)>
<!ELEMENT book (  title,
                author)>
```

Declarations can reside inside the XML document or can be defined as a stand-alone document. If defined as a part of an XML document, the collection of declarations is referred to as the *internal subset*. If the declarations are defined externally in a separate file, that file is referred to as an *external subset*. Many times, you'll find that you need to use both internal and external subsets. The collection of all subsets is known as the DTD. Listing 2.1 provides an example of a small collection of DTD declarations defined as a part of the internal DTD subset.

Listing 2.1   An XML Document Containing an Internal DTD Subset

```
<?xml version="1.0"?>
<!DOCTYPE publications [
   <!ELEMENT publications (book+)>
   <!ELEMENT book (title, author)>
   <!ELEMENT title (#PCDATA)>
   <!ELEMENT author (#PCDATA)>
]>
<publications>
   <book>
      <title>Mastering XHTML</title>
      <author>Ed Tittel</author>
   </book>
   <book>
      <title>Java Developer's Guide to E-Commerce with XML
        and JSP</title>
      <author>William Brogden</author>
   </book>
</publications>
```

This example defines only element type declarations. In most cases, your document model would be more complex, also allowing for attributes, notations, and entities. For each element, there's a corresponding content model defined. For example, the book element is allowed to contain only a title element followed by an author element.

Internal Subset

Internal subsets are handy if you plan to import declarations from external DTD subsets. This is because you can override externally defined declarations by defining a new declaration in the internal subset. The declaration found first (the XML parser reads the internal subset before the external) takes precedence.

There are a couple of restrictions placed on internal subsets:

- You cannot use conditional sections to mark the inclusion or exclusion of DTD declarations. Conditional sections make it easier to combine DTD subsets, therefore allowing you to modularize your DTD.

- Your parameter entity usage is limited. According to the XML 1.0 Specification, you cannot define and use a parameter entity within another declaration.

Listing 2.2 provides an example of an internal subset.

Listing 2.2   **An XML Document and Its Internal DTD Subset**

```
<?xml version="1.0"?>
<!DOCTYPE Publications [

    <!ENTITY mxhtml "graphics/mxhtml.gif" NDATA gif>
    <!ENTITY jdgexj "graphics/jdgexj.gif" NDATA gif>
    <!ENTITY jdgsj "graphics/jdgsj.gif" NDATA gif>

    <!NOTATION gif SYSTEM "image/gif">

    <!ELEMENT publications (book+)>
    <!ATTLIST publications xmlns CDATA #FIXED
      "http://www.lanw.com/namespaces/pubs">
    <!ELEMENT book (title, authors, pubDate, publisher, size,
      cover?, topics, errata?, description, website?)>
    <!ATTLIST book isbn    CDATA    #REQUIRED
                   edition CDATA    #REQUIRED
                   cat     NMTOKENS #REQUIRED
                   id      ID       #IMPLIED
    >
    <!ELEMENT authors (author+)>
    <!ELEMENT size EMPTY>
    <!ELEMENT cover EMPTY>
    <!ATTLIST cover img ENTITY #REQUIRED>
    <!ELEMENT topics (topic+)>
    <!ELEMENT errata EMPTY>
    <!ATTLIST errata code CDATA #REQUIRED>
    <!ELEMENT title (#PCDATA)>
    <!ELEMENT pubDate EMPTY>
    <!ATTLIST pubDate year CDATA #REQUIRED>
    <!ELEMENT publisher (#PCDATA)>
    <!ELEMENT description (#PCDATA)>
    <!ELEMENT website (#PCDATA)>
    <!ELEMENT title (#PCDATA)>
    <!ELEMENT author (#PCDATA)>
```

```
      <!ELEMENT topic (#PCDATA)>
]>

<publications xmlns="http://www.lanw.com/namespaces/pubs">
<book isbn="0782128203" edition="1" cat="XML XHTML HTML"
   id="mxhtml01">
<title>Mastering XHTML</title>
<authors>
   <author>Ed Tittel</author>
   <author>Chelsea Valentine</author>
   <author>Lucinda Dykes</author>
   <author>Mary Burmeister</author>
</authors>
<pubDate year="2001"/>
<publisher>Sybex</publisher>
<size pp="1019"/>
<cover img="mxhtml"/>
<topics>
   <topic>XHTML</topic>
   <topic>HTML</topic>
   <topic>XML</topic>
   <topic>Web Design</topic>
</topics>
<errata code="mxhtml01"/>
<description>Newly revised and updated, Mastering XHTML is a
   complete guide to the markup language that is leading the
   world of Web development from HTML to XML. You know the
   dangers of being left behind in this field, and this book
   ensures that you aren't, teaching you step by step how to
   convert existing HTML sites to XHTML and how to build new
   sites using this specification. It's a great way to hone your
   current skills and acquire new ones.
</description>
</book>

<book isbn="0782128270" edition="1" cat="Java ECommerce XML"
   id="jdgexj01">
<title>Java Developer's Guide to E-Commerce with XML
   and JSP</title>
<authors>
   <author>William Brogden</author>
   <author>Chris Minnick</author>
</authors>
<pubDate year="2001"/>
<publisher>Sybex</publisher>
<size pp="464"/>
<cover img="jdgexj"/>
<topics>
   <topic>Java</topic>
   <topic>E-Commerce</topic>
   <topic>XML</topic>
```

```
</topics>
<errata code="jdgexj01"/>
<description>Your Java programming knowledge will go a long way
    toward building an effective e-commerce site. XML is the
    missing piece, and Java Developer's Guide to E-Commerce
    With XML and JSP gives you expert instruction in the
    techniques that unite these closely aligned technologies.
    Covering the latest Servlet and JSP APIs and the current
    XML standard, this book guides you through all the steps
    required to build and implement a cohesive, dynamic,
    and profitable site.
</description>
</book>
</publications>
```

External Subset

An internal subset allows you to override externally defined declarations or to add new elements or attributes to a specific document. Other than that, you'll likely be working with external DTD subsets. More times than not, a common vocabulary will be defined using an external DTD subset. For example, the Extensible Hypertext Markup Language (XHTML), Scalable Vector Graphics (SVG), and the Synchronized Multimedia Integration Language (SMIL) all have externally defined DTDs. Every document that adheres to the defined model just has to include a DOCTYPE declaration that points to the external DTD subset. Separating the grammar rules from the data keeps your file sizes manageable. Listing 2.3 highlights an XML document that references an external DTD subset.

Listing 2.3   An XML Document Referencing an External DTD Subset

```
<xml version="1.0"?>
<!DOCTYPE publications SYSTEM "publications.dtd">
<publications xmlns="http://www.lanw.com/namespaces/pubs">
<book isbn="0782128203" edition="1" cat="XML XHTML HTML"
    id="mxhtml01">
<title>Mastering XHTML</title>
<authors>
    <author>Ed Tittel</author>
    <author>Chelsea Valentine</author>
    <author>Lucinda Dykes</author>
    <author>Mary Burmeister</author>
</authors>
<pubDate year="2001"/>
<publisher>Sybex</publisher>
<size pp="1019"/>
<cover img="mxhtml"/>
<topics>
    <topic>XHTML</topic>
```

```
    <topic>HTML</topic>
    <topic>XML</topic>
    <topic>Web Design</topic>
</topics>
<errata code="mxhtml01"/>
<description>Newly revised and updated, Mastering XHTML is a
    complete guide to the markup language that is leading the
    world of Web development from HTML to XML. You know the
    dangers of being left behind in this field, and this book
    ensures that you aren't, teaching you step by step how to
    convert existing HTML sites to XHTML and how to build new
    sites using this specification. It's a great way to hone your
    current skills and acquire new ones.
</description>
</book>

<book isbn="0782128270" edition="1" cat="Java ECommerce XML"
    id="jdgexj01">
<title>Java Developer's Guide to E-Commerce with XML and
    JSP</title>
<authors>
    <author>William Brogden</author>
    <author>Chris Minnick</author>
</authors>
<pubDate year="2001"/>
<publisher>Sybex</publisher>
<size pp="464"/>
<cover img="jdgexj"/>
<topics>
    <topic>Java</topic>
    <topic>E-Commerce</topic>
    <topic>XML</topic>
</topics>
<errata code="jdgexj01"/>
<description>Your Java programming knowledge will go a long way
    toward building an effective e-commerce site. XML is the
    missing piece, and Java Developer's Guide to E-Commerce
    With XML and JSP gives you expert instruction in the
    techniques that unite these closely aligned technologies.
    Covering the latest Servlet and JSP APIs and the current
    XML standard, this book guides you through all the steps
    required to build and implement a cohesive, dynamic,
    and profitable site.
</description>
</book>
</publications>
```

If you wanted to alter a declaration or add a new element or attribute, all you would have to do is add an internal subset, as follows:

```
<xml version="1.0"?>
<!DOCTYPE publications SYSTEM "publications.dtd"
```

```
[
  <!ATTLIST book updated CDATA #IMPLIED>
]>
<publications xmlns="http://www.lanw.com/namespaces/pubs">
<book isbn="0782128203" edition="1" cat="XML XHTML HTML"
   id="mxhtml01" updated="091801">
…
</book>

…
</publications>
```

In this example, we added an updated attribute to be included with the attribute set declared for the book element. Introducing redundant element type declarations would result in the overriding of the secondary declaration. However, adding additional attribute-list declarations works differently. If the new attribute list declaration contains new attributes, the new attributes declared in the internal subset are simply added to the collection of attributes for the specified element. If you introduce redundant attribute names, the internal subset declarations would override the secondary declaration. Note that the difference here is that it's not the entire attribute list declaration that is overridden, only the part that pertains to each individual attribute.

Elements

Elements are defined in the DTD using element type declarations. Every element must have a corresponding declaration that provides information about its content model. There are several types of content models:

element   May only contain child elements

```
<!ELEMENT book (title, author)>
```

mixed   Can contain character data only or a mix of character data and other child elements

```
<!ELEMENT author (#PCDATA)>
<!ELEMENT para (#PCDATA | em | b | i)*>
```

EMPTY   Does not contain anything

```
<!ELEMENT img EMPTY>
```

ANY   May contain any child elements or character data

```
<!ELEMENT book ANY>
```

In certain cases, you can also define content model behavior. For example, you can define that a book element may contain multiple book elements. The following are examples of element type declarations:

```
<!ELEMENT publications (book+)>
```

```
<!ELEMENT book (title, author)>
<!ELEMENT title (#PCDATA)>
<!ELEMENT author (#PCDATA)>
```

Attributes

Attributes are often used to add metadata to your document model. As modifiers, attributes add information about a defined element. Like elements, all attributes that you expect to use in your document model must be declared. For any given element, a set of attributes is defined with an attribute-list declaration. This is different than element type declarations, which allow only one element to be defined at a time. In this case, all the attributes are defined as a set. White space is commonly used to enhance readability. For each attribute, you must define the element that the attribute modifies (book), the attribute name (isbn), the datatype (CDATA) and the default type (#REQUIRED):

```
<!ATTLIST book isbn      CDATA    #REQUIRED
               edition   CDATA    #REQUIRED
               cat       NMTOKENS #REQUIRED
               id        ID       #IMPLIED
   >
```

Attribute declarations allow for minimal datatyping. In this example, we use three of the possible 10 attribute datatypes: CDATA, NMTOKENS, and ID. The 10 datatypes are as follows:

- CDATA contains character data or text.
- ID contains a unique name.
- IDREF references another element containing the same value identified as an ID.
- IDREFS contains a series of IDREFs delimited by white space.
- ENTITY contains a predefined external entity.
- ENTITIES contains a series of ENTITY names (predefined external entities) delimited by white space.
- NMTOKEN contains an XML NMTOKEN.
- NMTOKENS contains a series of NMTOKENs delimited by white space.
- NOTATION contains a notation (a description of how information should be processed).
- (enumerated value) contains a set of acceptable values.

See Chapter 4 for detailed descriptions of each datatype.

Notations

When you're creating and using XML documents, you might need to include binary data, as well as plain ASCII text. For example, you might want to include a graphic or an audio file. Notations allow you to include non-XML data in your documents by describing the format of the non-XML data and allowing your application to recognize and handle it.

Each notation contains a name that identifies the format used in the document, a SYSTEM or PUBLIC keyword, and an external ID or public ID.

```
<!NOTATION gif SYSTEM "image/gif">
```

Entities

DTDs allow you to reuse information in both the DTD and the XML document. As place-holders for content, entities are defined in the DTD and referenced (used) as many times as you like throughout your document or DTD. Constructive use of entities will streamline your DTD and enhance readability. There are several reasons you might use entities:

- To define reusable chunks of data
- To serve as a stand-in for reserved characters or for characters that do not appear on your keyboard
- To use in conjunction with notations to reference non-XML data

The XML 1.0 Specification defines several different types of entities. Each type uses a specialized syntax; however, all follow one of two basic structures:

```
<!ENTITY entity_name "replacement_text">
<!ENTITY entity_name SYSTEM "URI">
```

For more on entities, see Chapter 4.

Understanding Schema Structures and Functions

XML Schema is the new validation tool for building XML document models. Taking into account the new data-centric role of XML, XML Schema brings datatypes and complex content models to XML. Whereas XML DTDs were the answer for document-centric documents, XML Schema was created with e-commerce systems, Internet applications, and B2B interactions in mind.

In addition to allowing developers to define stricter datatypes and content models for their document models, XML Schema allows developers to take advantage of namespaces.

XML Schema is defined by three separate specification documents:

- The first defines a set of simple datatypes that can be used by elements and attributes. In addition to defining a set of predefined datatypes that you're free to work with, XML Schema allows you to create your own patterns based on any of the predefined datatypes.

- The second specification document defines a method for describing structure. In this document, you'll find an explanation of the XML Schema vocabulary that is used for declarations and definitions.

- The third and final specification document is a primer intended to explain XML Schema in a not-so-frightening way. This primer provides simple explanations, by way of examples, that define what schemas are and how to use them.

XML Schema is a more complex and involved language than XML DTDs and is largely based on many objections voiced about DTDs by the XML community. Listing 2.4 is an example of an XML Schema document.

Listing 2.4   An XML Schema Document

```
<?xml version="1.0" encoding="UTF-8"?>
<xsd:schema xmlns:xsd="http://www.w3.org/2001/XMLSchema"
            xmlns="http://www.lanw.com/namespaces/pub"
            targetNamespace="http://www.lanw.com/namespaces/pub"
            elementFormDefault="qualified">
   <xsd:element name="publications">
     <xsd:complexType>
       <xsd:sequence minOccurs="1" maxOccurs="unbounded">
         <xsd:element ref="book"/>
       </xsd:sequence>
     </xsd:complexType>
   </xsd:element>
   <xsd:element name="book">
     <xsd:complexType>
       <xsd:sequence>
         <xsd:element ref="title"/>
         <xsd:element ref="author"/>
       </xsd:sequence>
     </xsd:complexType>
   </xsd:element>
   <xsd:element name="title" type="xsd:string"/>
   <xsd:element name="author" type="xsd:string"/>
</xsd:schema>
```

Complex Type Definitions

An element is defined as a *complex type* if it allows for child elements and/or may take attributes. There are two ways to define complex types. First, you can create a complex type definition that can then be used in an element type declaration. Each complex type definition can contain element declarations, element references, and attribute declarations. For example, the following is a complex type definition:

```
<xsd:complexType name="bookType">
  <xsd:sequence>
    <xsd:element name="title" type="xsd:string"/>
    <xsd:element name="author" type="xsd:string"/>
  </xsd:sequence>
</xsd:complexType>
```

In this example, we created a complex type definition that can be used in element declarations. For example, you can declare a book element that is defined to follow the bookType definition:

```
<element name="book" type="bookType"/>
```

The sequence element is a compositor. *Compositors* are used within a complexType to define content model behavior. The sequence compositor requires child elements to be used in the order defined by the declaration. In the previous example, the title element would have to be used before the author element.

The second way to declare complex types is to define them as a part of the declaration itself. In this case, you do not define a complex type that you reference later. The complex type definition is used directly within the element declaration itself:

```
<xsd:element name="book">
  <xsd:complexType>
    <xsd:sequence>
      <xsd:element name="title" type="xsd:string"/>
      <xsd:element name="author" type="xsd:string"/>
    </xsd:sequence>
  </xsd:complexType>
</xsd:element>
```

Simple Type Definitions

A *simple type* is defined for elements that cannot contain child elements or for attributes. By default, an attribute is a simple type. Simple types are based on built-in datatypes, which are defined by the XML Schema Part II: Datatypes specification. XML Schema provides a set of facets that may be used to constrain the set of permissible values for simple types. These facets include length, precision, scale, pattern, and enumeration. Facets allow you to create new simple types that apply constraints on data values to keep your data clean and consistent. The following example defines a simple type for a `zipcode` datatype:

```
<xsd:element name="zipcode">
  <xsd:simpleType>
    <xsd:restriction base="xsd:string">
      <xsd:pattern value="[0-9]{5}"/>
    </xsd:restriction>
  </xsd:simpleType>
</xsd:element>
```

Element Declarations

Element declarations provide the mechanism for defining complex content models, including providing default values and behavioral patterns. This is an improvement upon DTD content models and allows developers to design complex models with more accuracy. Elements can be declared locally or globally. A global declaration is declared as a direct child of the schema element rather than as a part of a complex type definition. Once declared, it can be referenced in other definitions. A local declaration is declared as a child of any element other than the schema element:

```
<xsd:element name="book">
  <xsd:complexType>
    <xsd:sequence>
      <xsd:element ref="title"/>
      <xsd:element ref="author"/>
    </xsd:sequence>
  </xsd:complexType>
</xsd:element>
```

In this case, we've created a book element with a content model that allows for one title element and one author element. Listing 2.5 provides an XML document with multiple element declarations.

Listing 2.5   **An XML Schema Document Containing Element Declarations**

```
<?xml version="1.0" encoding="UTF-8"?>
<xsd:schema xmlns:xsd="http://www.w3.org/2001/XMLSchema"
   xmlns="http://www.lanw.com/namespaces/pub"
   targetNamespace="http://www.lanw.com/namespaces/pub"
   elementFormDefault="unqualified">
<xsd:element name="publications">
  <xsd:complexType>
    <xsd:annotation>
      <xsd:documentation xml:lang="en">
       content model modified 10.15.01
      </xsd:documentation>
    </xsd:annotation>
```

```
        <xsd:attribute name="isbn" type="xsd:number"/>
        <xsd:attribute name="cat" type="xsd:string"/>
        <xsd:attribute name="id" type="xsd:ID"/>
        <xsd:sequence minOccurs="1" maxOccurs="unbounded">
          <xsd:element ref="book"/>
        </xsd:sequence>
      </xsd:complexType>
    </xsd:element>
    <xsd:element name="book">
      <xsd:complexType>
        <xsd:sequence>
          <xsd:element ref="title"/>
          <xsd:element ref="author"/>
        </xsd:sequence>
      </xsd:complexType>
    </xsd:element>
    <xsd:element name="title" type="xsd:string"/>
    <xsd:element name="author" type="xsd:string"/>
</xsd:schema>
```

Attribute Declarations

Attribute declarations allow you to define information about your attributes. For each attribute, you can define a default value, behavior patterns (required or optional), fixed values, and a datatype. Attributes are always defined as simple types because they can contain only data. The advantage of XML Schema attribute declarations is that they allow for more complex datatypes. For example, you can define a string datatype (similar to CDATA); however, you can also use other datatypes, such as date, decimal, or boolean. In addition to countless predefined datatypes, you can derive your own datatypes based on preexisting ones. Listing 2.6 shows an XML Schema document that contains attribute declarations (which are in bold).

| Listing 2.6 | An XML Schema Document Containing Attribute Declarations |

```
<?xml version="1.0" encoding="UTF-8"?>
<xsd:schema
    xmlns:xsd="http://www.w3.org/2001/XMLSchema"
    xmlns="http://www.lanw.com/namespaces/pub"
    targetNamespace="http://www.lanw.com/namespaces/pub"
    elementFormDefault="unqualified">
    <xsd:element name="publications">
      <xsd:complexType>
        <xsd:annotation>
          <xsd:documentation xml:lang="en">
```

```
          content model modified 10.15.01
        </xsd:documentation>
      </xsd:annotation>
      <xsd:attribute name="isbn" type="xsd:number"/>
      <xsd:attribute name="cat" type="xsd:string"/>
      <xsd:attribute name="id" type="xsd:ID"/>
      <xsd:sequence minOccurs="1" maxOccurs="unbounded">
        <xsd:element ref="book"/>
      </xsd:sequence>
    </xsd:complexType>
  </xsd:element>
  <xsd:element name="book">
    <xsd:complexType>
      <xsd:sequence>
        <xsd:element ref="title"/>
        <xsd:element ref="author"/>
      </xsd:sequence>
    </xsd:complexType>
  </xsd:element>
  <xsd:element name="title" type="xsd:string"/>
  <xsd:element name="author" type="xsd:string"/>
</xsd:schema>
```

Namespaces

XML Schema supports namespaces and uses them quite often. There are two schema-dedicated namespaces:

- The XML Schema namespace used for W3C XML Schema elements. You can define this namespace as a default namespace or with an xsd prefix. The namespace URI is `http://www.w3.org/2001/XMLSchema`.

- The XML Schema Extensions namespace, for W3C XML Schema extensions used in instance documents. This namespace should be defined with an xsi prefix. This namespace is defined only if you're using XML Schema extensions. The namespace URI is `http://www.w3.org/2000/10/XMLSchema-instance`.

XML Schema not only defines two schema-dedicated namespaces, but it also allows you to declare your own namespace that is to correspond with the declared elements and attributes. The XML Schema vocabulary uses a target namespace (`targetNamespace="http://www.yournamespace.com"`) to define the namespace to which the corresponding XML document should adhere. The following XML document uses a namespace (in bold):

```
<?xml version="1.0"?>
<publications xmlns="http://www.lanw.com/namespaces/pub">
  <book>
    <title>Mastering XHTML</title>
```

```
      <author>Ed Tittel</author>
   </book>
   <book>
     <title>Java Developer's Guide to E-Commerce with
       XML and JSP</title>
     <author>William Brogden</author>
   </book>
</publications>
```

If you were to define a namespace within a DTD, you would be forced to use an attribute list declaration, such as this:

```
<!ATTLIST publications xmlns CDATA FIXED
   "http://www.lanw.com/namespaces/pub">
```

However, this doesn't truly represent a namespace. On the other hand, XML Schema allows you to define a target namespace for any document that is to conform to the schema:

```
<schema targetNamespace="http://www.lanw.com/namespaces/pub">
…
</schema>
```

Listing 2.7 shows an XML Schema document that defines the mandatory schema namespace as well as a target namespace for the document model. The second namespace defined (xmlns="http://www.lanw.com/namespaces/pub") is necessary because once a target namespace is defined, any references made to declared elements must fall within the scope of that namespace. This concept is defined in Chapter 6.

Listing 2.7   An XML Schema Document Illustrating XML Schema Namespace Usage

```
<?xml version="1.0" encoding="UTF-8"?>
<xsd:schema
    xmlns:xsd="http://www.w3.org/2001/XMLSchema"
    xmlns="http://www.lanw.com/namespaces/pub"
    targetNamespace="http://www.lanw.com/namespaces/pub"
    elementFormDefault="unqualified">
  <xsd:element name="publications">
    <xsd:complexType>
      <xsd:annotation>
        <xsd:documentation xml:lang="en">
          content model modified 10.15.01
        </xsd:documentation>
        </xsd:annotation>
      <xsd:sequence minOccurs="1" maxOccurs="unbounded">
        <xsd:element ref="book"/>
      </xsd:sequence>
    </xsd:complexType>
  </xsd:element>
  <xsd:element name="book">
```

```
      <xsd:complexType>
        <xsd:sequence>
          <xsd:element ref="title"/>
          <xsd:element ref="author"/>
        </xsd:sequence>
      </xsd:complexType>
    </xsd:element>
    <xsd:element name="title" type="xsd:string"/>
    <xsd:element name="author" type="xsd:string"/>
  </xsd:schema>
```

Annotations

Rather than using XML comments (<!-- -->) throughout your schema document, XML Schema provides a more formal annotative mechanism.

XML Schema defines three elements to add annotations to your schema documents. These annotations can be defined for the benefit of both human readers and applications. For human-readable information, the documentation element is used. If you're defining information intended for an application (such as tools or style sheets), the appInfo element is used. For both types of annotations, a parent annotation element must be used. Listing 2.8 uses an annotation to add human-readable notes about the content model.

Listing 2.8   An XML Schema Document Containing an Annotation

```
<?xml version="1.0" encoding="UTF-8"?>
<xsd:schema xmlns:xsd="http://www.w3.org/2001/XMLSchema"
    xmlns="http://www.lanw.com/namespaces/pub"
    targetNamespace="http://www.lanw.com/namespaces/pub"
    elementFormDefault="unqualified">
    <xsd:element name="publications">
      <xsd:complexType>
        <xsd:annotation>
          <xsd:documentation xml:lang="en">
            content model modified 10.15.01
          </xsd:documentation>
        </xsd:annotation>
        <xsd:sequence minOccurs="1" maxOccurs="unbounded">
          <xsd:element ref="book"/>
        </xsd:sequence>
      </xsd:complexType>
    </xsd:element>
    <xsd:element name="book">
      <xsd:complexType>
        <xsd:sequence>
          <xsd:element ref="title"/>
          <xsd:element ref="author"/>
        </xsd:sequence>
```

```
        </xsd:complexType>
    </xsd:element>
    <xsd:element name="title" type="xsd:string"/>
    <xsd:element name="author" type="xsd:string"/>
</xsd:schema>
```

Document-Focused versus Data-Focused XML

When designing a document model, one of the first questions you should evaluate is what type of data you are working with. Typically, there are two basic types of data models: data-centric and document-centric. HTML is a document-centric language, whereas XML is becoming more data-centric because it's used for e-commerce and B2B applications.

Are document-centric documents better than data-centric documents? Sometimes there's no obvious answer. But because XML was designed with data exchange in mind, it's likely that many XML documents will typically be data-centric. That is not to say that XML can only be data-centric.

Document-centric design involves a liberal use of free-form text such as paragraphs and other block-level elements. This type of document is designed to store content fragments, such as paragraphs, chapters, and glossary entries, and may include document metadata, such as author names, revision dates, and document numbers. These types of documents are usually managed on the file system. The following is an example of document-centric information:

```
<book>
    <title>Mastering XHTML</title>
    <description>Newly revised and updated, Mastering XHTML is
        a complete guide to the markup language that is leading
        the world of Web development from HTML to XML. You know
        the dangers of being left behind in this field, and this
        book ensures that you aren't, teaching you step by step
        how to convert existing HTML sites to XHTML and how to
        build new sites using this specification. It's a great
        way to hone your current skills and acquire new ones.
    </description>
</book>
<book>
    <title>Java Developer's Guide to E-Commerce with XML
        and JSP</title>
    <description>Your Java programming knowledge will go a long
        way toward building an effective e-commerce site. XML is
        the missing piece, and Java Developer's Guide to
        E-Commerce With XML and JSP gives you expert instruction
        in the techniques that unite these closely aligned
```

```
        technologies. Covering the latest Servlet and JSP APIs
        and the current XML standard, this book guides you
        through all the steps required to build and implement
        a cohesive, dynamic, and profitable site.
    </description>
</book>
<book>
    <title>Java Developer's Guide to Servlets and JSP</title>
    <description>Are you ready to put your Java programming
        knowledge to work building a dynamic, database-driven
        Web site? Java Developer's Guide to Servlets and JSP
        gives you exactly what you need: expert instruction
        in the techniques for constructing a powerful enterprise
        site from custom servlets and Java Server Pages. Covering
        the latest APIs, this book is your introduction to
        technologies that will fundamentally change your approach
        to Web site development.
    </description>
</book>
```

On the other hand, data-centric documents are typically easier to process with computer programs because the data is better organized. Data-centric documents are those in which XML is used as a data format for data transport (e-commerce and B2B). For example, a data-centric document might include purchase orders or scientific data. Data-centric documents typically contain a fairly regular structure with little or no mixed content models. The following is an example of data centric information:

```
<book price="39.99" isbn="0782128203" quantity="37"/>
<book price="49.95" isbn="0782128270" quantity="44"/>
<book price="49.99" isbn="0782128092" quantity="20"/>
```

Schemas or DTDs?

When deciding on a validation mechanism, there's a clear advantage to each type. To begin with, DTDs do not do well with data-centric documents. DTDs don't allow for complex content models or datatyping and therefore don't offer much support for data integrity. In this case, XML Schema would be the best choice.

On the other hand, if you were working with document-centric documents, such as research documents or online book publishing, DTDs might just do the trick. But keep in mind that XML Schema can be used in this scenario as well. If you don't mind paying the training costs for your developers to learn a new validation technology, it might be worth it to go ahead and use XML Schema as your validation tool.

TIP   Most schema editors provide a DTD-to-XML-Schema conversion component that can also be used to reduce conversion costs.

Both DTDs and schemas provide document structure descriptions. In an effort to define structures, the emphasis is on creating readable descriptions that can be understood by automated processors such as parsers, editors, and other XML-based tools. Both validation schemes also provide information for humans, describing content models for elements, how those elements can be used, and what interactions may take place between parts of a document. Although both use a different syntax, they both create documentation.

DTDs and schemas provide basic grammar rules that define a set of expectations that all XML parsers must abide by. Developers can also use DTDs and schemas as a foundation on which to plan transformations from one format to another. If a DTD or schema has been agreed upon, developers have accepted a set of rules about a document vocabulary and structure. With a document model defined, it's easier to define independent development tools that process documents.

One significant difference between XML Schema and XML DTDs is that XML Schema uses XML syntax. This simple fact doesn't translate into an improved document description; however, it does allow for those descriptions to be more extensible. XML Schema allows developers to define complex internal structures for declarations that can take advantage of XML's containment hierarchies (rather than XML DTD linear declarations) to add additional information where appropriate.

Another advantage that XML Schema has over XML DTDs is a vastly improved datatyping system. Whereas XML DTDs focus on document-oriented data, and therefore, document-oriented datatypes (CDATA and PCDATA), XML Schema provides a more data-oriented approach. XML Schema supports built-in datatypes (string, decimal, and date) while simultaneously allowing for *user-derived datatypes*, which allow developers to build upon predefined datatypes (such as, decimal, date, or string) to create their own datatype libraries.

XML Schema also allows authors to define reusable content models, similar to DTD parameter entities, that allow for more complex structure definitions. Instead of including an exact translation of parameter entity functionality, XML Schema allows developers to create complex type and group definitions that can be reused throughout the schema document. These definitions group a set of elements, attributes, or a combination of both for reuse.

And yet another advantage to using XML Schema is that it's namespace aware. It appears that when the W3C made the move to create an alternative to DTDs (one that supported both data- and document-oriented applications), the decision was made to not redesign XML DTDs to support namespaces. This is not to say that you cannot use namespaces within a document that conforms to an XML DTD; however, there is some dancing that has to be done to allow the two to coexist. Bear in mind that even if you create a DTD that will work with your namespaced vocabulary, the DTD does not recognize the namespace.

It's safe to say that XML Schema has several advantages over XML DTDs. XML Schema is new, which is one of the primary disadvantages to using it, but it was designed to work well in a data-centric XML environment. We are not saying that DTDs should never be used: One advantage to using DTDs is that they are tried and true. DTDs have been around for over 20 years. Their syntax is simple, and they are easy to learn.

If you're working with data-centric information, we recommend looking toward a schema language. However, if you're dealing with document-oriented data and don't have the time to learn a new document modeling language, DTDs will do the trick. Many developers are also working with DTDs to support legacy XML 1.0 applications or to support integration with SGML.

TIP   Transitioning from one technology to another can be difficult, but because the function of DTDs and schemas are quite similar, there aren't likely to be many changes that have to be made to your document model. If you're not ready to make the transition, remember that you might want to in the near future; therefore, always develop DTDs with an eye toward future conversions. Lucky for us, there are tools on the market that are ready to convert those documents for us. We like to work with XML Spy (`www.xmlspy.com`). See Chapter 14 for more on XML Schema tools.

Summary

XML Schema has been a long time coming, and the XML community has been anxiously awaiting its arrival. In the meantime, several other languages have been created and have become viable alternatives for validation. There's no way to predict what will happen in the future; however, you can expect to see a strong dependence on schemas, whether they be formally defined by the W3C or by other schema languages. Going forward, there are three options for XML document model design:

DTDs   Ideal for use in legacy XML 1.0 applications and for integration with SGML applications

XML Schema   Will likely be used for most XML applications that require validations

Free-form XML (without a validation)   Used for situations in which describing document structures is unnecessary and counterproductive

When deciding whether to use a schema language or XML DTDs, the first step is to identify the data you're working with. There's also the consideration of skill set for your application. If you're working with document-centric data (for example, online book publishing), it's possible to use a DTD to define your document model. However, if you're creating a document model to define a purchase order vocabulary to contain data-centric information, you most likely want to use a schema language to define your document model.

XML Schema enjoys several advantages over XML that might compel most developers to embrace schemas as their validation tool of choice regardless of their data model. Most of these advantages are a direct result of objections voiced about DTDs noted by developers:

- XML Schema is namespace aware.

- XML Schema is an XML application and is therefore extensible.

- XML Schema allows for complex datatyping, including user-derived datatypes.

- XML Schema supports complex content models, allowing developers tighter control over content model behavior.

- XML Schema provides a mechanism for defining reusable definitions and declarations to be used throughout the schema document.

CHAPTER 3

The Document Design Process

- Understanding document basics: content, structure, and presentation

- Understanding the document design process

- Identifying the document's purpose

- Identifying the document's requirements

- Defining the document information content

- Defining the information relationships

- Defining the document structures

- Identifying reusable structures

- Identifying datatypes

- Identifying custom datatypes

XML Schema lets you define the structure of a class of documents and validate specific instances of that document type to conform to that structure. However, before you can make use of that power, you have to design your document. Because you'll generally be developing schemas for documents that will have long lives and/or be used by many users, it's important to invest the time up front to properly structure your document. If you don't, you'll discover that your document probably won't meet your users' requirements and you'll be investing an unnecessarily large amount of effort in document maintenance in the future.

So in this chapter, you'll learn how to design a document, starting with understanding the various aspects of a document and ending with schema-specific design selections. The process you'll learn is designed to help you ensure that your final document content model is complete and modular and requires minimal effort to implement.

Document Design Basics

When you design an XML document, you specify the information items it will contain and how those information items are related. You can then specify your design using a Document Type Definition (DTD) or a schema. Such a specification of a document's structure is called a *content model*. When a user creates a document that conforms, or at least is supposed to conform, to your document description, it's called an *instance* of your document type. Normally, you won't bother to create a document content model unless you expect that there will be a need to create a reasonably large number of document instances. Otherwise, the investment of your time to create the content model won't normally be cost effective.

Here are some key terms you should remember:

content model   A description of the structure and contents of a type of document

document type   A type of document, such as an invoice

document Instance   A specific document that belongs to a document type and that conforms to the content model for that document type

Content models are powerful because they allow XML parsers to determine whether a given document instance conforms to the designer's description of what should belong in the document. This allows software to help ensure that a document instance is properly constructed and contains all of the specified information. This can dramatically improve productivity. For example, if you and your suppliers interact via documents with content models, then every time you send them a purchase order, you'll know, before you send it, that it contains all of the necessary information.

Documents fulfill a number of purposes. The primary purpose is to convey information. The information can be conveyed to people directly (you read a report) or through software (you examine a report generated by a program that analyzed a document). To achieve their purpose, documents contain information (someone's address) as well as relationships (such as the person's phone number) and they are to be viewed by *people*. These aspects of a document can be described as follows:

Content   What's in an instance of the document

Structure   How the information elements in the document are related

Presentation   The appearance of the document

These are described in detail in the following sections.

Content

The content of a document is the actual information contained by an instance of the document. For example, a typical letter includes the following contents:

- The name of the recipient—"Mom"

- The body of the letter—"Am hungry. Send money."

- The signature—"Love, Tony"

Although the document structure defines how the contents are grouped, the actual content is usually only associated with a document instance.

TIP   You can specify default values for some of the parts of a document in that document type's schema. Those default values are referred to as boilerplate values. If a document instance doesn't override those default values, part of the document instance's content will be contained in the schema.

The people who create document instances are the end users of your document design. If you're not the end user, you need to work with the end user to define what the content of a given document should be. For example, if you're company asks you to create a standard XML document to describe action items, you need to work with as many of the people who will generate, use, and/or monitor action items as you can. If you don't, you may encounter problems when you roll out your document definition. Just as users will tend to avoid using software that doesn't work the way they want it to, they'll also eschew using your document if the document doesn't meet their needs and expectations. You'll learn more about how to engage future users in your document design process in the section "Step 3: Identify the Document's Requirements" later in this chapter.

TIP Remember that all the work you do with document design and schemas is aimed at providing end users with the content in a usable format. Content is king!

Structure

The structure of the document defines the groupings and relationships between its various components. Because the objective of XML is to allow computers to "understand" the meaning of document content, it's important to label the various elements of a document in a computer-comprehensible format.

TIP In the context of document design, an element is a labeled piece of information. It may be defined in your final schema as an XML element or an attribute.

Returning to our letter example, we'd like it to be easy for a software application to identify who the letter is for, who sent it, and what the message is. A key part in the document design process is identifying what the elements of the documents are and how they relate. For example, if you're generating a document for all letters, you probably won't break up the contents of the letter body any further. There are too many possible letter contents to create a detailed schema. On the other hand, if you're creating a document type for a specific type of letter—for example, a billing statement to a client—you may want to specifically define a variety of information pieces in the message. The basic rule is to create information elements for any piece of information that should be accessible by software. Therefore, if you want your software to be able access the area code of a phone number, you should define one element for the area code and another for the local part of the phone number.

TIP The document structure doesn't impose any restrictions on the way the user interacts with the document content. Even if you store the area code and the local phone number in different elements, the software that creates the document instance can input the phone number as a single item and the presentation software that formats the document for display can show the phone number as a single item.

The structure of a document essentially defines what knowledge other software tools will have of the document contents. If our letter document defines the name of the sender as an element, then applications that access a letter document instance will be able to easily find the name of the sender. On the other hand, if our letter document structure has all of the message body in one element, software tools won't be able to easily access items inside the message body. For example, software tools won't be able to apply formatting such as bold or italic to individual words inside the message if the document structure doesn't identify those words as independent elements. But if we add an "emphasis" element as a subelement of our message content, software tools will be able to access the content contained in those elements.

Presentation

The presentation of a document determines how the document will appear when viewed by a human. In the modern multimedia world, the same document may have to be viewed on paper, a TV screen, a computer monitor, a cell phone, and a personal digital assistant (PDA) as well as in color or black and white. A key strength of XML is that it allows document designers to decouple a document's informational structure from its appearance. In fact, when designing a document, you never have to directly address the details of the document presentation. For example, you don't have to worry about displaying important text in red. On the other hand, you do need to be concerned about the presentation of a document when you define the document structure.

Essentially, various formatting languages, such as the Extensible Stylesheet Language Transformations (XSLT) and Extensible Stylesheet Language Formatting Objects (XSL-FO), can access only the elements of a document that are defined by the document structure. In our letter example, formatting tools wouldn't be able to access pieces of the message body (to underline them, for example) unless that type of text has been defined as an element in the document. As a result, although you can be oblivious to the specific formatting that will be used for your document, you have to be very concerned about which information items may require unique formatting.

Whereas the information items that use unique formatting in your document will often be the same as those that software tools that use the content of your document type will need to access, they can be other elements as well. For example, you may want to allow your end users to underline certain words in the letter body. That underlining may only be for human readers of the document and may be ignored by any software analysis tool. You still need to define an underlined element that identifies that the text contained in that element is to be underlined. That element is there just to support the eventual display of the document.

Don't make the mistake of not worrying about the presentation of your documents. If instances of your document type will be viewed by people, it's critical that the document be well formatted or your users will avoid it. Even if your document type is designed to be used only for software-to-software communications, formatting can be important when you're debugging the system. The software developers will have to go over many instances of your documents during the development process. Being able to display your documents in an easily comprehensible way can really help minimize the time spent debugging the system.

The Document Design Process

Developing an XML document content model requires rigor and attention to detail. Generally, a document content model will be in use for a long time by a large number of users. As a result, it's a worthwhile investment of resources to carefully analyze the requirements for the document and ensure that the final structure makes it easy for all the people who work with the document type to achieve their objectives.

The process shown in Figure 3.1 isn't some canonical truth. Rather, it's one workable approach that helps you make sure you've touched all of the key aspects of the design process. Feel free to tailor this process to meet your specific needs and objectives. Of course, the level of effort that you put into this process will depend upon the nature of your document. If you're quickly developing a short document for use in a rapid prototyping exercise for a B2B system, you'll probably breeze through the process in as little as a few minutes. On the other hand, if you're defining a standard action item document for a multinational corporation, you may spend months on this process.

FIGURE 3.1:
The document design process

Step

1. Define the basic purpose of the document type.
2. Define who will use the document.
3. Define document requirements.
4. Define what information the document should contain.
5. Define information relationships.
6. Define information structures.
7. Identify reusable structures.   7A. Identify importable structures.
8. Identify datatypes for information.   8A. Identify importable datatypes.
9. Define custom datatypes.

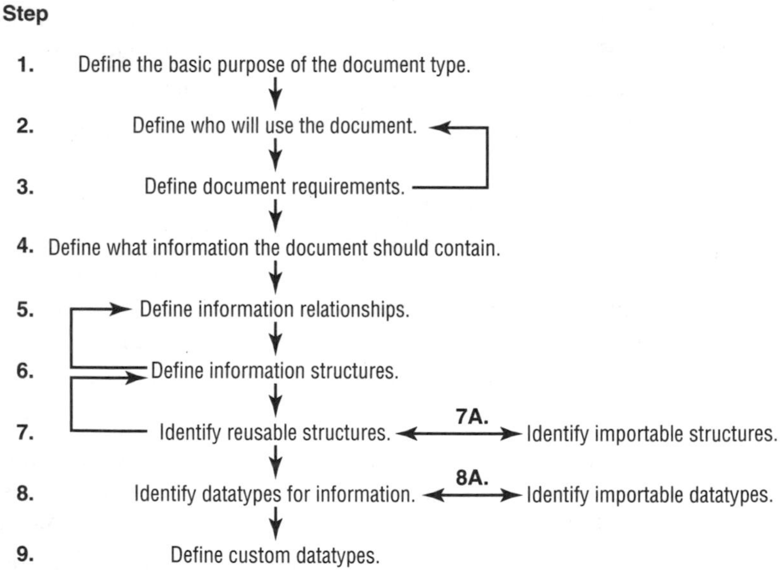

That brings us to the question of budgets. If your boss says, "Get me a new document type by tomorrow COB," you'll have a different rigor than if design and deployment of your document type is a key objective of your company's fiscal year plans. Throughout this process, you'll have to weigh the complexity of meeting any given requirement against the available resources. The input from the software developers who have to write the code to support the document will be very helpful in letting you scope the cost impacts of various requirements. Similarly, the available schedule will help you determine if you have the time to follow a consensus-building, cyclic approach to the document definition or if you'll have to ask for requirements via e-mail and work with whatever you get.

TIP You won't see a lot of schema-specific content in this process because it's generally applicable to any type of document design. In the final steps of the process, where there are schema-specific concepts, we'll cover them in sufficient detail so you can understand their relevance to the process. You'll see much more schema-specific design guidance in Chapter 8.

The following sections will walk you through each of the steps in the document design process. They explain the objective of each step and provide suggestions as to what you should do to reach those objectives. Of course, you should feel free to tailor the steps or leave some of them out, depending on your specific needs and what works best for you.

Step 1: Identify the Document's Purpose

The first step in the process is to figure out what you want to do with the document type. Is it intended to double your company's stock price or is it simply going to make it easy to communicate with your suppliers? Usually, you'll get the objectives of the document as an assignment: for example, "Fred, we need a standard format for action items." There are cases in which you define the objectives of the document yourself, such as when you discover that to implement a task, such as automating of the processing and monitoring of action items, you need a new document type. At this stage, you don't really need to have a detailed understanding of what the document will do. You only need an understanding sufficient enough to let you start the process of collecting requirements. Often, all you'll need to know is who will be using your document type so you know where to go next. If you're developing the document type for your own use, you can skip to Step 3, identifying the document's requirements.

Throughout this process, we'll use a document that describes an action item or a letter in our examples. Action items are tasks that have to be performed by a certain date. A typical action item might be updating a database or defining the requirements for a software program. The examples are all of limited scope and don't contain all of the items that would be contained in the content model of either document type.

WARNING This step often is done by different people than the folks who do the rest of the process. In addition, the process can stop right here if you decide the document doesn't need to use XML.

Step 2: Identify the Document's Users

Regardless of the details of the process you use, the most critical step is to identify who will be using the document you're defining. After you've identified who will be using the document, you need to work with those people to determine what they want to ensure that you have a complete and correct set of requirements.

In the traditional world, the end users of documents are the people who read them. In the new world of XML documents, there are a variety of users as, shown in Table 3.1.

TABLE 3.1:   Who Will Use Your Document Type?

User	How They Use the Document	What They Care About
End user	Read, modify, or use the information in a document instance	Presentation of information, structuring of information, what information is present
Software developer	Write code to create, edit, display, or store instances of the document	Document structure, ease of access to information
Document designer	Integrate your document with theirs	Complete, coherent, and selectable information
Document maintainer	Modify the document over time to ensure that it's current	Coherence, modularity, and flexibility of the document structure

The end users of your documents include the same people who would have used your document type in a traditional paper office as well as in software applications. Even now, the paperless office is not yet a reality and won't be for some time. As a result, many of the documents you design will end up being read off of a physical medium of some sort, such as paper or transparencies. Even the ones that aren't will probably be read from a computer screen or a cell phone. The concerns human end users have are the same ones they've always had: They want an easy-to-read, easy-to-understand, complete presentation of the information they consider important. From a requirements perspective, that means you need to ensure that all of the information the user wants is present.

For example, if you're defining a letter type, you should check with your end users to see if they care if the sender's return address is present. If they do care and you don't include it, they're forced to check some other document or database to reply to the letter, which means you have failed to meet their requirements. But having the information present isn't enough. You have to ensure that it's structured so it can be displayed in a user-friendly fashion. For example, if a letter document's structure didn't have an element for the sender's phone number or e-mail address, presentation software wouldn't be able to access these important pieces of information, resulting in the end user having to wander through the letter body to find them. You can't ensure that a document will be well formatted by giving it good structure, but you can help guarantee that it's poorly formatted if you fail to create elements for the key information items.

Because XML makes it possible for software to understand the informational content of a document, it has spawned a new class of end users: software applications. XML has taken off, in part, because it provides a good way for software-to-software communications. Your company's purchasing software can use XML documents to exchange information, as opposed to just bits, with your supplier's sales software. Many XML document instances are never viewed directly by humans. Instead, they're used by software. These software programs are another set of end users. Of course, you can't interview them to find out what they want, but you can talk to their designers.

Because XML document instances aren't generated with paper and pen but with software applications, it's crucial that you work with the software developers when designing your document. Of course, if you're the developer, that objective is easily accomplished. If you have access to the development team, you need to work with them to determine their requirements. Whereas software can do wonders and can be developed to work with the most poorly structured documents, you'll find that your software development costs will skyrocket as a result. Working with the software team will help you ensure that the information they need is easily available and that your document structure is easy to work with.

What if your organization is such that the software developers don't normally work as part of an integrated design team? This can occur when you use commercial software to create and display your XML documents. For example, you might use XMetal to create documents that are displayed on an XML-enabled browser. In that case, you need to understand the strengths and limitations of the tools that will be used. These will vary from tool to tool, but the speed of processing and the memory required as the document structure grows in complexity are common issues.

TIP Record the idiosyncrasies of the tools you work with in a database or easily accessible document. Lessons learned on one project can help reduce your costs on the next.

You may be wondering how document designers could be the users of your document design. This occurs because one of the growing trends in information management is cross-linking information in multiple documents. We've all seen the utility of hyperlinks on the Web, and more and more information architects are giving end users seamless views into complex information structures that are contained in multiple documents. For example, if you're developing a standard document for action items, an information architect may want to link your documents to an earned value cost accounting system in order to let managers see how value is earned as action items are closed. If your document is poorly structured, it may be difficult to easily construct such connections. In this example, if the accounting area of responsibility for the action item isn't present in your document, it will be difficult to book completed actions against the accounts in the earned value document.

You need to consider document maintainers if your document is going to be around for more than a few weeks. Remember that the document maintainer who has to work late hours to upgrade your document may be you! Generally speaking, the best answer to the question of how to define a given document type will change with time. These changes can occur because a business practice, the business environment, or the software used changes. Of course, you can't predict the future, and you can't usually talk to the people who will maintain your document in the future—they might not be born yet—but you can and should take some time to examine how easy it would be to modify your document.

Stand back and try to look at your document with an objective eye. See if you've made any assumptions that may cause problems later. A simple example of this would be storing phone numbers as a single element. If you do so, anyone who wishes to look at the area codes of those numbers will have to write custom software to extract the area code from the full phone number. Another good way to check your document is to have someone who hasn't been involved in your design process look over your candidate content model to see if it's easy to understand. An easily understandable content model dramatically increases the chance that your document will be easy to use and maintain.

Step 3: Identify the Document's Requirements

Identifying the requirements for an XML document type is very similar to identifying the requirements for a software package. In both cases, you have to see how the item is going to be used and who is going to use it. In addition, to minimize maintenance costs, you have to look to the future to see how the document or software will be used years down the line. Unfortunately, there's no perfect process for deriving requirements for either software or XML document types. On the plus side, that means that you can feel free to recycle processes you currently use in your organization for other tasks.

A good first step in defining requirements is to talk to all of the people who will use or interact with your document type. You identified them in Step 2 of the process, so now you should talk to them. It's often a good idea to construct a preliminary list of requirements to help focus the discussions, but you can also just send them an e-mail describing your objective (developed in Step 1) and asking them for their input.

Unless you're both the document designer and its only user, you'll probably encounter two problems with dealing with users: They will ignore you because they're already overloaded with work and don't see any personal advantage to helping you, or they'll ask for an incredibly gold-plated document definition that far exceeds the scope of your objective. Your job will be to learn enough about the document type's purpose to keep a laser sharp focus on the document's objective. If you don't do so, you may end up with a document that fails when brought into production because you left some required information out or one that doesn't make it to production because you ran out of money or because you tried to put too much information in it.

A good way to extract requirements is to decide what questions people will be asking of a document. Table 3.2 contains a partial sample set for a document type that describes action items.

> **TIP**   All of the analysis shown in this chapter for the action item document type is representative, not complete. The full analysis for a standard action item document for a large corporation would take up more space than this chapter. You might want to try to see what sort of requirements have been left out as an exercise.

TABLE 3.2: Questions Users Ask About an Action Item Document

Question	Who Asks
What is the action?	End users
Who has the action?	End users
When is the action to be closed?	End users
What accounting category covers this work?	Information architect
Will this document instance have to be stored in a database?	Software developer
What is the phone number of the owner of the action?	Document designer
How does the action relate to the master schedule milestones?	End user, information architect

You can turn each of these questions into one or more requirements by determining what the document must contain (and in what datatype) for it to be able to answer the question. For example, the question Who has the action? translates into the requirement that the document contain some sort of information that identifies the person responsible for executing the action.

> **TIP**   Datatypes are discussed in detail in Chapter 7. They describe the type of data in an item. Typical types are `string`, which contains text, and `time`, which contains a time in a standard format.

The last question in Table 3.2 translates into a requirement that the document contain some type of information that will allow a third party with access to the master schedule milestones to determine what milestones are impacted by the action. The following is a partial list of the requirements that could be derived from the questions in Table 3.2:

- The document type must contain a description of the action.

- The document type must specify the individual responsible for the action.

- The document type must contain a date, or a specific milestone, by which the action is to be completed.

- The document type must contain the phone number of the person responsible for the action.

- The document type must contain a list of the program milestones that are dependent upon the action being completed.

Another complementary way to extract requirements is to simply define things the document has to do.

TIP   Keep in mind that a document type can't do anything. When we discuss an action for a document type, it's understood that the document type has to have the right information, organized in the right way, to allow some piece of software or a human to perform the action.

Here are some of the things our action item document type might have to do:

- Keep track of all actions in a project

- Allow insight into the history of the action item

- Enable automatic notification of action item holders when they're late

- Control who can authorize or modify action items

These can be converted into requirements for the document. For example, the first function the document type must perform is to keep track of all actions in a project. This may seem straightforward unless you're working on a project that involves subcontractors; then there are a number of new implications. First, you probably want to identify the company to which the action holder belongs. Second, you may need to support some sort of security requirement.

For example, you may not want the subcontractors to see each other's actions or all of the actions in your company. Because documents can't actually do anything, how can our document type support this function? A good start would be to ensure that the document content model contains a unique identifier. The content model will also probably need to contain the information necessary to define the sharing rules. For example, there may be an item called "share with" with potential values of "everyone," "prime contractor only," "subcontractor 1," "subcontractor 2," and so on. In this vein, a partial list of the requirements that could be derived from the actions the document type has to support might be as follows:

- The document type must contain a unique identifier.
- The document type must be able to contain a change history identifying when a document instance has been changed and how it was changed.
- The document type must contain the e-mail address of the user.
- The document type must identify the company responsible for the action.
- The document type must contain a list of individuals who may modify the document instance.

As you work through the requirements process, you may find the scope of the document expanding beyond what you defined in Step 1. This may lead to an expansion of the users you should contact. That's why Figure 3.1 shows a process flow from Step 3 to Step 2.

The definition of requirements is the heart of this process. If you do a good job defining requirements, you'll probably end up with a good content model. If you miss requirements, you'll undoubtedly end up having to rework your content model—usually after it's been deployed, which will probably cause you to spend more time than you'd like in the office. The bottom line is that if you have limited time to spend on this process, make sure to invest a lot of it on requirements definition.

Step 4: Define the Document Information Content

At this point, you've defined the requirements for the document type. The next step is to determine which information has to be in the document to meet those requirements. A good idea is to create a cross-reference matrix, as shown in Figure 3.2. It will help you ensure that you have completely met all requirements.

In many cases, you'll find that multiple pieces of information may be needed to satisfy a single requirement. For example, to send the holder of the action an e-mail to let him know it's overdue, you'll need his name (to include a salutation in the e-mail content) as well as his e-mail address.

After you've identified the required information content, you should see how many times it can occur in the document. Some items may be present in a document instance or they may not. For example, if your document describes a book and it contains a coauthor item, that item need not appear in document instances for books with a single author. On the other hand, items may also appear more than once. A genealogy document will require that items describing a child appear more than once in a given family.

Required Document Information

	Action Description	Action Holder Name	Dependent Milestones	Action Holder E-Mail Address	Responsible Company
The document type must contain a description of the action.	✓				
The document type must specify the individual responsible for the action.		✓			
The document type must contain a list of the program milestones that are dependent upon the action being completed.			✓		
The document type must contain the e-mail address of the user.				✓	
The document type must identify the company responsible for the action.					✓

During this step, you generally don't have to worry about how the information is structured. For example, it doesn't matter if the action holder's phone number is going to end up as a child element of the action holder item or as a child of the document root. In fact, you don't even have to worry about what information is easily accessible. If your requirements specify that the document must contain both an area code and a local phone number, you can just specify one item: a phone number with area code. In Step 6, you'll decide if the area code should be a separately accessible information item.

If you discover information items that you think belong in the document type but you can't trace them to a requirement, you should carefully reexamine your requirements to see if you've missed something. If you decide you haven't, you should remove the unnecessary information. Conversely, if you find a requirement that doesn't correspond to any of the information items, you should verify the correctness of the requirement and then see what information you should add to the document definition.

Step 5: Define the Information Relationships

To make your document type easy to understand, construct, modify, and maintain, you should carefully examine the relationships between the different pieces of information it contains. This process is akin to how you would define an object hierarchy in an object-oriented programming language or how you'd segment data into pages when designing a Web site. The objective is to group related information to provide a coherent structure. Identifying groupings, relationships, and dependencies lays the foundation for actually defining specific information structures in the next step.

There are a variety of types of relationships you should look for. The most common are as follows:

Belongs to   A phone number belongs to a person.

Requires   If an order has shipped, for example, a FedEx tracking number is required; however, if an order has not been shipped yet, a FedEx tracking number isn't required.

Looks like   The information for the action holder and the information for the person who assigns the action look similar in terms of what they contain.

Depends on   The cost of a part may depend on who the purchaser is.

"Belongs to" is the most common relationship you'll find. It describes the hierarchical relationship of pieces of information. For example, in our action item document, it's clear that the action holder's e-mail address, phone number, company, and name are all related. There seems to be a natural relationship that would define all of these parameters as belonging to a single piece of information that we could call "action holder." These relationships appear to be natural because, in real life, phone numbers and e-mail addresses belong to people. On the other hand, it doesn't seem too reasonable for a phone number to belong to an action item.

The "belongs to" relationships you find will define the hierarchy of information in your document type. If the information items in your document have no "belongs to" relationships, your content model will be flat—everything will be a child of the root element. On the other hand, a rich set of "belongs to" relationships will translate into a modular and hierarchical structure.

"Requires" is a less frequently observed relationship that specifies that one type of information is present only if certain other types, or specific values, of information are present. For example, a piece of information called "personnel record" would only have a subelement called "employee number" if the individual were an employee—contractors don't have employee numbers. Hence, unless the `employee?` element is true, there is no need for an employee number element.

"Looks like" is a different sort of relationship. In a "looks like" relationship, two information structures that occur at different points in a document are identical, or nearly identical. For example, the information about the sender of a letter and the information about the recipient of a letter look a lot alike. Both contain the person's name, phone number, address, e-mail address, and so on. One of the key strengths of XML Schema is that it allows you to reuse information structures. Identifying "looks like" relationships will help you identify where you can simplify your document's description by using a single information structure to fill multiple roles.

"Depends on" defines a potential action relationship between the specific values of information in a document instance. For example, the cost of a part may depend on who the purchaser is because different purchasers may get different discounts. This sort of relationship won't necessarily directly affect your document structure description, because the document itself does nothing. You may find that taking these types of relationships into account can simplify the job of the software developer who will have to implement the function that ensures that the "depends on" relationships are always maintained. It would be bad for business if your best customer didn't get his or her expected discount.

There are other types of relationships you could define as part of your design process, but these four are the most common and the most useful in helping you structure your documents.

As with the basic process of defining requirements, there's no magical way to peruse the information you've defined as necessary and discover all of the useful relationships. The best approach is to carefully examine the informational elements you've defined and see what types of real-world relationships they have. For example, when looking for "belongs to" relationships, you should see what information elements belong to other elements in the real world. In the real world, an e-mail address belongs to a person, as does a phone number. It makes sense then, that when defining the "world" of your document definition, e-mail addresses and phone numbers belong to people.

You should also go through your requirements to see if they imply certain types of relationships. Requirements will often contain indications of "depends on" and "requires" relationships.

To keep track of your analysis of the relationships between the elements of your document, you may want to create a simple spreadsheet similar to the one shown in Table 3.3.

TABLE 3.3: Some of the Relationships in the Action Item Document Type

Item 1	Relation	Item 2	Description
Phone number	Belongs to	Action holder	The action holder's phone number is something associated with him or her and no other item in the document.
Change event	Requires	Change history	You need to establish a container for various change events before you create the first change event.

Continued on next page

TABLE 3.3 CONTINUED: Some of the Relationships in the Action Item Document Type

Item 1	Relation	Item 2	Description
Action holder	Looks like	Authorized to change	Both are descriptions of people with name, contact information, etc. Their structures look similar.
Dependent milestones	Depends on	Master schedule	This is an example of a relationship that extends beyond the document structure. As items are changed in the master schedule, the milestone(s) associated with this action may change.

Notice that these relationships don't have to be confined to your document. It's important for you to consider cases in which changes to other types of documents could require that the contents of your document type be updated. Although your structure won't actually do any updating, you may find that properly organizing the information in your document will make it easier for the developers who implement the linkage to do their job. For example, assigning unique element names to such items may make it easier to locate them as opposed to requiring the software to walk a complex hierarchy structure to find the relevant values.

Using relationships is a concrete way to list the interactions of the various information items that make up your document content model.

Step 6: Define the Document Structures

After you've determined what information goes into a document and the relationships between the components of that information, the next step is to decide how to structure it. You'll find that people who are either very experienced or have no experience tend to jump right to this step when they design a document. In the case of very experienced designers, it's an illusion. They actually perform the first five steps, but they do so quickly and in their head. Of course, for large or complex documents, they'll follow a more formal process. Although you should feel free to skip the formal implementation of any step in this process, it's very important that you at least think about the concepts in those steps before you begin your document structure. Defining your document structure is the most complex, intellectually challenging, and risky part of designing a document. Problems with your structure can lead to significant downstream costs and user problems. Before jumping into the definition of your document's structure, make sure you have a good understanding of your objectives, requirements, and user needs, in your head if nowhere else.

There are two steps to structuring a document:

1. Define what the specifically accessible information items are.

2. Define how those items are grouped.

You should define an information item for each piece of accessible information in your document. An accessible piece of information is one that is unambiguously labeled so that a software program can access it. For example, if your document type has an element for a phone number, something like the following, then the phone number is accessible:

```
<phone_number>555-555-5555</phone_number>
```

On the other hand, if the phone number is embedded in other data, as in the following line, the information isn't accessible, at least by XML parsers:

```
<message> my phone number is 555-555-5555</message>
```

TIP   Information that isn't accessible can be accessed by writing special software to extract it from the data surrounding it. However, this defeats the purpose of XML, which is that all necessary information can be obtained using a standard XML parser.

Make sure you know what information the user wants to access. In the preceding examples, if your user would like to sort items based on the area codes in the document instances, he or she would have to write special software because the area code isn't labeled as an information element in either of those examples.

You'll find that your requirements analysis provides a solid foundation for defining what information items you'll need. For example, if you have a requirement to access the sender's zip code, you know that you need a separate item for zip code. However, if the only requirement for your document is to get the address, you could have the entire address, including zip code, in a single information item.

Here is a general rule to follow: If you're not sure if a piece of information should be accessible, make it accessible. The only cost is more elements in the document. Look at the following phone number example:

```
<phone_number>
   <area_code>555</area_code>
   <local_number>555-5555</local_number>
</phone_number>
```

If you store the area code and the local phone number as two separate information items, it won't prevent presentation or analysis software from grouping the two items. For example, if you use XSLT to transform your XML document into HTML for presentation on the Web, it's easy to convert the preceding XML markup into the following:

```
The phone number is <b><font color="#0099ff">555-5555</font></b>
```

On the other hand, if the area code isn't accessible, you'll have to write custom software to count the number of phone numbers from a given area code. An additional problem with not having information accessible is that once you've built up a large library of document instances with the information inaccessible, converting them to accessible versions can be very complex. Imagine if your document had items like this:

```
<action_holder> John Smith chief architect</action_holder>
<action_holder>Smith,John The Boss</action_holder>
<action_holder>Owner of the Black Smith John Smith</action_holder>
```

In these elements, the first and last names of the individual, and his title, are combined. Imagine having to write a program that would go through several thousand of these documents and separate the first name, last name, and title—the last one would require a pretty sophisticated piece of software.

Once you've defined the information items that your document type will contain, you can begin to organize those items based on the relationships you defined in Step 5.

A powerful tool to use in figuring out how to link the information items in your document is to develop a visual representation of your document's structure. There are a variety of approaches you can use, but one of the simplest is to draw a treelike diagram. Because all well-formed XML documents are trees, you can be sure that a simple tree, with a single root, will always be sufficient to represent your document structure.

TIP   The nodes in the tree will be the accessible pieces of information in your document.

There's no right or wrong way to diagram your document structure, but Figure 3.3 shows a simple approach that contains the key information you'll probably want for each information item. Each piece of accessible information in your document is shown as a node on the tree. The top part of the node is the name of the piece of information and the bottom part contains the datatype for the information.

TIP   You'll learn more about datatypes in Chapter 7, but for now, just think of them as defining which values are allowed. For example, the action holder's name is a string, which means any combination of letters or digits is legal. The due date is a date, which means only legal dates are allowed in any document instance for this piece of information.

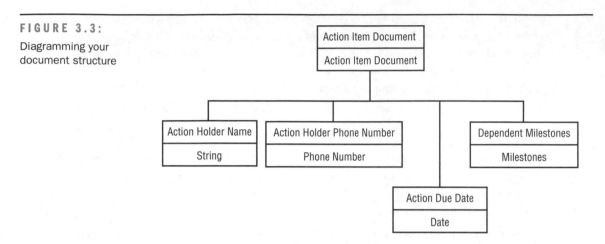

Diagramming your document structure

Dependency goes down in the sort of diagram shown in Figure 3.3, so the Action Holder Name node is a child of the Action Item Document node. That is equivalent to saying that there is a "belongs to" relationship between Action Holder Name and Action Item Document—Action Holder Name belongs to Action Item Document. These sorts of diagrams can help you decide on document structures. One thing you can do is create a diagram in a drawing program and then shuffle nodes around looking for natural structures based on the relationships you've found.

The first decision you should make is about the top level of the document. All XML documents consist of a root node and its descendents. A key decision in your structure definition will be what elements are the children—that is, the first-generation descendents—of the root node. If all of the informational elements are children of the root node, you have a flat structure, as shown in Figure 3.3. But you can start using some of the relationships you defined in the preceding step to improve your structure. Those relationships will help you develop a more modular hierarchical structure, as shown in Figure 3.4.

Of course, for some documents, flat is best. The ongoing argument between flat structures and those that have complex nesting is based on a variety of different objectives and understandings. There's no right answer, but you'll usually find that your documents are somewhere in the middle between the two extremes.

FIGURE 3.4:

A hierarchical
structure

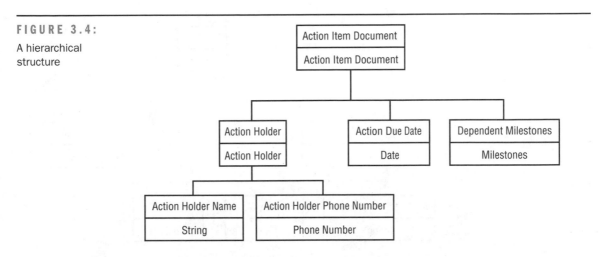

FIGURE 3.4:

A hierarchical
structure

Generally, flat structures are best for information items that are siblings. For example, in our standard letter, the sender's address, the message body, and the recipient are all siblings. None of them naturally belongs to the other. On the other hand, if you decide to create separate elements for the sender's name, street address, state, country, and zip code, a hierarchical structure starts to make sense. The pieces of an address naturally group as parts of an address and are not on par with the major elements of the document structure. Figure 3.5 shows a piece of the document as a flat structure.

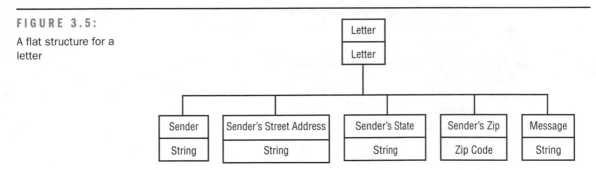

FIGURE 3.5:

A flat structure for a
letter

Figure 3.6 shows a hierarchical structure that seems more intuitive and has the advantage that changes to the sender's address don't impact any other parts of the document.

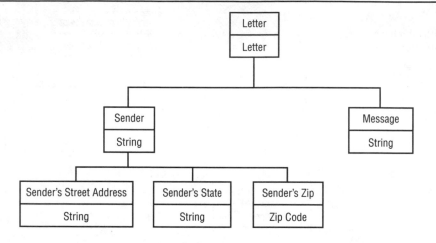

There are different levels of hierarchy that you can use. For example, Figure 3.7 shows a more hierarchical version of Figure 3.6. It has the advantage of being able to recycle the address structure. Let's look at the actual markup structures associated with these two design options. Here is a piece of the document corresponding to Figure 3.6:

```
<letter>
   <sender>
     <senders_street_address>112 S. Stone
         </senders_street_address>
     <senders_state>CA</senders_state>
     <senders_zip>55555</senders_zip>
   </sender>
```

And here is an equivalent listing for the structure in Figure 3.7:

```
<letter>
   <sender>
     <name>
        <first>Louis</first>
        <last>Trinko</last>
     </name>
     <address>
        <street_address>112 S. Stone</street_address>
        <state>CA</state>
        <zip>555555</zip>
     </address>
   </sender>
```

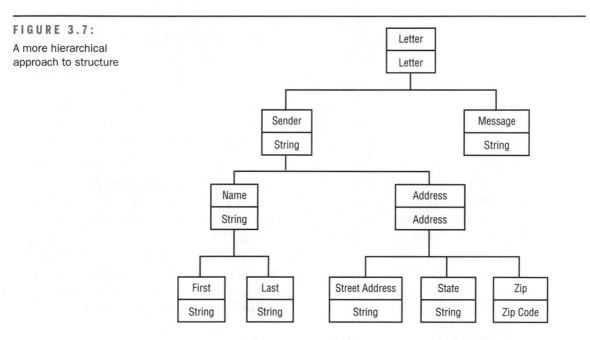

In Figure 3.7, you have two generic structures, Name and Address, that can be reused in a variety of places in a document and in differing documents. For example, you could recycle the Name and Address structures in the recipient structure, as shown in Figure 3.8.

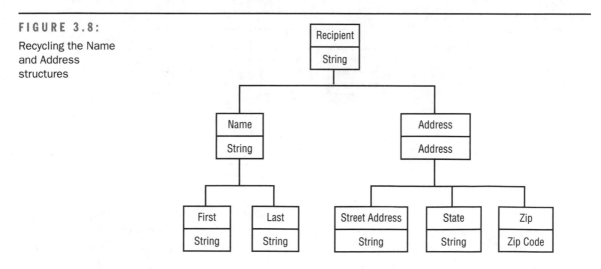

Although deep structures have a number of good features, including reuse, they do have some drawbacks. The software that will be accessing information from the document may have to contain information about the structure in order to access information. For example, if your document uses the structures in Figure 3.7 and 3.8, any software that wants to find the sender's name will have to know to look for an item called Name inside the Sender item. The software can't look for items called Name because there's another item called Name, which is the name of the recipient. That's not too bad unless the structure of the document changes in the future. Then the software that uses the document type will have to be modified.

On the other hand, if your structure had unique items, `sender_name` and `recipient_name`, the software would only need to know the name of the item, not where it was in the document structure. This is one of the cases where real-world practicality may overcome theoretical ideals. Another reason to avoid deeply nested structures is that they may take more memory and/or more time to parse than flatter structures.

If you've memorized Figure 3.1, you remember that there was an arrow going back from Step 6 to Step 5. That's because, as you begin to define your document structure, you may see relationships between information that you didn't see before. Feel free to annotate your diagrams with relationship information, as shown in Figure 3.9, and to update your list of relationships.

FIGURE 3.9:

Annotate your structure diagram to remind yourself of relationships.

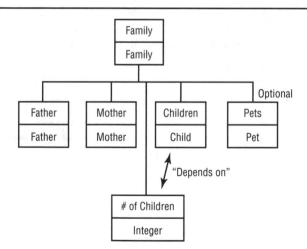

Figure 3.9 also shows an annotation indicating that the Pets information structure is optional. That's a part of the next step in defining your information structure. You have to indicate the number of occurrences allowed for various items. Optional items are those that may appear or not appear in a document instance. For example, a family may or may not have a pet, so a document instance based on a content model with a structure like that shown

in Figure 3.9 may or may not have a Pets item. The Children item may have 0 or more Child items. Other items may have to occur once and only once. In our action item schema, there will be one and only one action item description, for example.

You may want to annotate your diagrams as shown in Figure 3.10 so they contain information about how often an item may appear. Of course, an annotation of the number of times an item can occur refers to occurrences at a specific location in the structure. The Name item can appear only once as a child of the Sender item . There can be 0 or more Sender items as children of the Letter item, which is the only place the Sender item can appear.

FIGURE 3.10:

Note in your diagrams how often items can appear

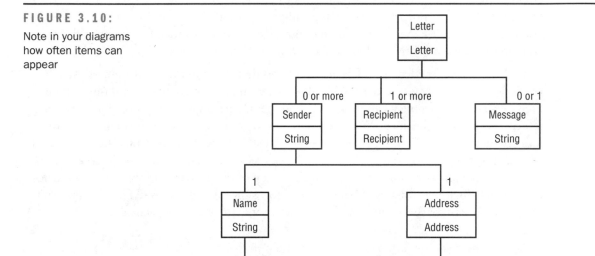

The final step in defining your document structure is optional. It's identifying whether items are to be elements or attributes. It's quite reasonable to postpone this decision until you actually write the content model as a schema. On the other hand, you may find it useful to add annotation to your diagrams to indicate which items should be elements and which should be attributes. Given the vigorous and ongoing arguments about how to decide if an item should be an attribute or an element, you should feel free to use whichever you are most comfortable with.

Step 7: Identify Reusable Structures

The less work you have to do, the better life is. Tried-and-true solutions deserve to be reused. Trite sayings? Not really. After you, or your organization, have defined a number of documents, you'll find that it's not uncommon for a variety of basic structures to keep popping up. A very mundane example of that is someone's address. A typical address may have several elements—street address, apartment number, state, country, zip code—and make a natural information structure. It's good business sense to define this structure once and reuse it. An additional advantage of standardized structures is that they can help you establish a disciplined approach to document development. If you're a programmer, you can think of these structures as being similar to the design paradigms you use to accomplish basic functions. If you're a Web site designer, these reusable components are very much like the style sheets you use to impose a consistent look and feel to your Web site.

XML Schema allows you to reference structures defined in multiple documents. As a result, you can save your standard, reusable schemas in one directory tree and they can be used by all of the documents your organization uses. More important, you can modify these structures and all of the documents that use them will automatically be updated. For example, let's say that you've defined a personnel record that has worked well. All of a sudden, management says you've got to include the employee's nickname. No sweat. You just edit one document, the one containing the schema definition of the personal information data structure, and all documents that use that structure now support nicknames. Of course, this isn't magic, so you still have to figure out how to get people to enter their nicknames.

TIP	XML can help you enter those nicknames. If the personnel record contains the users' e-mail addresses, you can write an XSLT script to query a database to automatically fill in the missing nicknames.

Another way to save yourself work is to look through the large and growing set of standard schemas available on the Web. Sites such as www.schema.net have references to a continually expanding set of document descriptions. You may find structures that you can import into your document content model. Many use DTDs, but the information structures they contain can be easily converted to schemas. It's especially important to examine existing document definitions if you plan to share instances of your document with other companies. Whereas XML allows companies to dynamically transform your structure into one they like to use, it will make life easier if you use an industry standard rather than creating your own.

TIP   A good, and fairly cheap, way to improve your organization's productivity is to create a simple database that contains descriptions of all of the reusable structures you have created or gotten from third-party standards. That way, you and your teammates can quickly find what structures may be usable. If you want, you can even use the database as the repository of the standard schema description for the structure.

If you identify structures that you can reuse, either from your internal set or from some external source, you should feel free to go back to Step 6 and modify your document structure. Reusing structures almost always makes sense and will end up reducing your workload, stress level, and project cost.

Step 8: Identify Datatypes

One of the big advantages of schemas over DTDs is that schemas support a large set of built-in datatypes. In addition, the XML Schema standard also allows you to define custom datatypes. The utility of this is that, whenever you validate a document instance, you can verify whether the types of values assigned to the various information elements are correct. Of course, you can't be sure that an action item description contains intelligible text, but you can make sure that items such as dates are entered properly. These datatypes bring to XML the same sort of functionality that JavaScript brought to early Web forms. Instead of having to send the user's input over the Web to be validated by a server-side application, Web developers could use JavaScript to check a user's input, on the client, and make sure it met minimal standards before forcing the user to wait for the response from the remote server. Similarly, the XML datatypes allow the content of a document to be checked whenever it's validated. Most tools that will generate XML document instances contain validating parsers. As a result, it's possible to continually check the document instance the user is creating to ensure that the contents conform to the document model.

In this step, you shouldn't feel constrained to use the XML Schema standard's built-in types (which are discussed in Chapter 7). Instead, try to define the perfect datatypes. For example, the current XML Schema specification doesn't contain a specific datatype for American-style phone numbers. But clearly it would be nice to be able to ensure that the user entered a valid phone number as opposed to one that lacks digits or contains characters. By recording the ideal datatypes, you can more easily construct the right datatypes in Step 9.

After you've defined your ideal datatypes, you should go through them and see which are covered by the built-in datatypes of the XML Schema specification. During that process, it will pay to make a note of those that are similar to the built-in datatypes. This will help you in the next step where you define custom datatypes.

After you've looked through the built-in datatypes, you should look through your tool kit of recyclable datatypes to see what you may be able to reuse. For example, once you've defined a custom datatype for phone numbers, there's no reason why you shouldn't use it in all of your documents that contain phone numbers.

TIP   With reusable structures, you can improve your productivity by having a simple database in a low-cost tool, such as FileMaker Pro, that contains all of your recyclable datatypes. This will make it easy for you to search for the existing structures you can use in your document.

You should also look around at various public schemas to see if they contain datatypes that meet your needs. Defining and testing a custom datatype can take a while, so if someone else has done the work for you, feel free to avoid unnecessary work and use it.

Step 9: Identify Custom Datatypes

After you've identified all of the datatypes you want to use and you've gone through public definitions and your own organization's list of reusable definitions, you may need to define new custom datatypes for some of your information items.

Before investing time in defining custom datatypes, make sure you know why you need them. You can always have arbitrary content in an information item if you use the datatypes built into schemas. The only reason to define a custom datatype is to allow a validating parser to check the value of an information item in a document instance to see if it's valid. This makes sense for something like a part model in a purchase order. You really don't want your customers to accidentally send you a purchase request that includes a nonexistent part number. On the other hand, you probably don't really care if a visitor to your Web site enters a non-color word, such as *decline*, into an information item that is supposed to describe his or her favorite color.

Even if you find you'd like a certain datatype, you may find that it's really not practical. You'll learn more about how to judge the potential complexity of a custom datatype in Chapter 7, but a good rule is that, if determining whether an entry is acceptable requires thinking, then it's too complex. For example, there are so many different ways to describe colors that, although it's technically possible to create a color custom datatype, it would be prohibitively complex.

Summary

Using a simple design process can be helpful when you're designing the content model for your document. The effort spent in defining the requirements for your documents, including working with those who will be using your document type, will provide significant benefits and will reduce overall cost. Making sure that your document design is correct early in the implementation cycle will reduce costs because the cost of modifying your document structure late in the cycle is much higher than designing it correctly from the beginning.

You've seen a structured and repeatable process that will help you make sure that your document design is complete without being bloated. It's critical that you start the process by clearly defining what the customer wants the document to do. Many software projects have turned into disasters because the development team didn't work closely with the customer—and end users—to ensure that what was being developed was what was really needed. A key aspect of this activity is to identify the end users so you can incorporate their needs and/or interests into the requirements definition step.

The next step is to convert the description of what the document is to do into a set of testable requirements. You've seen a number of ways to extract the requirements and to verify that they are complete. These requirements will help you ensure that the document you design is the one that will meet your customers' needs.

After you've defined your requirements, you begin the detailed design of your document by defining the information items it should contain. The key here is to ensure that all the information items (such as a person's first name) needed by any software that will use the document are easily accessible. When in doubt, it's generally better to define more items than fewer.

With the building blocks of the document and the information items in hand, you can define the relationships between those elements to complete the top-level description of the document. You've seen that there are several types of relationships between elements. Relationships can vary from the simple "belongs to" relationships (a phone number item belongs to a person item) to conditional relationships such as "requires" (a state sales tax item is required only if the purchaser is in the same state as the seller). As you define the structure, you look for common or reusable substructures such as addresses. Recycling structures will reduce your development and test costs.

The last part of the process for XML Schema is to define the datatypes for the information items. As with information structures, it's a good idea to reuse datatype descriptions so as to minimize the amount of testing you'll need to do.

The most important thing to remember is that, although it can seem to be a burden to execute a document design process, especially when the boss has given you a killer deadline, you'll end up spending less time on it by planning your document at the beginning.

CHAPTER 4

The Role of DTDs in XML

- Understanding DTD element type declarations

- Working with attribute-list declarations

- Creating notation and entity declarations

- Using DTDs to design useful document models

One of the advantages XML enjoys over other information architecture designs is that it's flexible. Flexibility is not, however, always an advantage. There are several applications that need rigid document models. For example, if you were to exchange data between two applications, flexibility would not be your goal. In this case, you'd want to ensure that a given document adheres to a particular document model. Without these rules, who is to say which element structure is used?

Since the days of SGML, Document Type Definitions (DTDs) have provided the solution. When an application needed a strictly defined structure, DTDs were implemented to provide the rules. But as you'll learn, this is not always the case. XML Schema, as well as other schema languages, is primed and ready to share this responsibility. However, for legacy systems and those who are dealing with document-centric information, DTDs still enjoy widespread use. The role of DTDs has not been replaced completely.

XML DTD Components

DTDs allow you to place constraints on the element hierarchy of an XML document model as well as define loose content models for those elements. A DTD cannot specify the meaning of those elements or the datatypes of the data contained by the elements. This is indeed a shortcoming of XML DTDs—one that's addressed by XML Schema.

DTDs were originally designed with document-centric information in mind. XML has been adopted by the developers of e-commerce and business-to-business (B2B) applications, but its roots are not that data-centric. Therefore, it makes sense that DTDs focus on element hierarchy rather than on element datatypes.

In addition to working with elements, DTDs allow developers to specify attributes that can be associated with elements. Attributes provide additional information about the elements. In the following sections, we briefly cover the four distinct components that make up an XML DTD:

- Element type declarations
- Attribute-list declarations
- Notation declarations
- Entity declarations

Element Type Declarations

At the heart of any DTD are element type declarations. Every element in an XML document, if you expect the document to validate, must have a corresponding declaration. Each declaration provides the element name and content model:

```
<!ELEMENT element_name content_model>
```

The *element_name* is case sensitive and can be defined as any legal XML name. The *content_model* defines what the element can contain. For example, an element type declaration might restrict an element's content to data only, or it might allow several possible child elements. DTDs allow for four different content models:

- Element content model
- Mixed content model
- EMPTY content model
- ANY content model

In the following sections, we briefly touch on each content model.

Element Content Model

The element content model is used to define elements that can accept only other elements as content. For example, the following authors element can accept only an author child element:

```
<!ELEMENT authors (author)>
```

The parentheses are always used to contain the content model. The allowed child element is defined within the parentheses.

Element content models are used to define nesting relationships between elements. This is the key to defining a clear and concise structure for your data. Using the element content model, you can allow multiple child elements to occur, for example:

```
<!ELEMENT book (title, authors, pubDate, publisher, size,
    cover, topics, errata, description, website)>
```

In this case, the book element may contain one instance of each child element defined within the parentheses.

Defining Occurrences

DTDs allow you to loosely define the number of times a child element may be used in a content model. For example, you can require an element to occur at least once. Occurrence definitions are limited to the following options:

- Using the + occurrence indicator requires that a child occur once. The child element is also allowed to repeat:

```
<!ELEMENT authors (author+)>
```

- Using the ? occurrence indicator allows the child to occur once or not at all. The child element cannot repeat:

  ```
  <!ELEMENT book (title, authors, pubDate, publisher, size,
      errata?)>
  ```

- Using the * occurrence indicator allows the child to occur once, repeat, or not occur at all:

  ```
  <!ELEMENT authors (author*)>
  ```

- Not using an occurrence indicator requires that a child element occur once and only once:

  ```
  <!ELEMENT book (title, authors, pubDate)>
  ```

TIP

DTDs do not allow you to specify that a child element occurs exactly five times. When working with DTDs, some developers try to work around this looseness. For example, if you want to require the topic element to occur exactly three times, you could use the following element type declaration: <!ELEMENT topics (topic, topic, topic)>.

Defining Sequence

DTDs also allow you to require that child elements occur within a predefined order. For example, you can require that the title element occur before the authors element:

```
<!ELEMENT book (title, authors, pubDate)>
```

The comma connector is used to denote sequence.

Allowing Choices

If you want to allow for a choice, you can use the pipe bar (|) connector in place of the comma. For example, the following declaration requires that the document author make a choice between the pubDate element and the publisher element:

```
<!ELEMENT book (pubDate | publisher)>
```

Grouping

The element content model defines a pattern for the allowed child elements. Although using simple occurrence indicators and connectors may seem limiting, it's sometimes necessary to group more complex content models within a primary content model. You can accomplish this by using parentheses. For example, the following declaration allows for a rather complex content model:

```
<!ELEMENT book (title, author, (pubDate | publisher), description)>
```

Mixed Content Model

In document-centric documents, it's common to find an element that contains both character data and other elements. For example, the XHTML p (paragraph) element can contain character data in addition to other inline elements, such as the b (bold) or em (emphasis) element.

According to the XML 1.0 Specification, the mixed content model is used to define two different types of mixed content:

- Content that contains only character data
- Content that contains both character data and other child elements

If the content model allows for only character data, such as `<testId>1</testId>`, the declaration would be as follows:

```
<!ELEMENT testId (#PCDATA)>
```

However, if you want to allow a content model to contain character data and other child elements, you have to follow a strict syntax:

```
<!ELEMENT p (#PCDATA | b | em)*>
```

When you use truly mixed content, that content can contain both character data (#PCDATA) and other child elements (b and em). However, you're not allowed much control over occurrences or sequence. According to XML 1.0, mixed content models that allow for both data and child elements must be defined using the | connector and a trailing asterisk (*). Other than the asterisk defined outside of the parentheses, you're not allowed to use occurrence indicators. When defining a mixed content model, you must list #PCDATA first, followed by child elements in any order.

EMPTY Content Model

To refer to the EMPTY content model is a tad misleading considering it's used to define elements that cannot contain anything. In most cases, empty elements follow the typical empty element syntax (`<empty/>`); however, you can also use both the opening and closing tags (`<empty></empty>`). Regardless of how you decide to use these elements in your XML document, the declaration is the same:

```
<!ELEMENT cover EMPTY>
```

ANY Content Model

The ANY content model can be used if you want to allow for any type of content—any child elements or character data. The content model is not defined, and therefore, anything goes. However, any child elements used within the document must have corresponding element type declarations. In other words, undeclared elements are not allowed.

There are not many times you'll want to use this content model. After all, it runs contrary to the benefits of validation. However, if you're in the process of designing a DTD, there are times that you'll want to just check a section of it. To allow for this, you can use the ANY content model within declarations that you do not want to worry about just yet, as in the following example:

```
<!ELEMENT author ANY>
```

Attribute-List Declarations

Attributes, like elements, require the use of a declaration. Every attribute used must have a corresponding attribute-list declaration. A single attribute-list declaration can declare multiple attributes for an element type. However, if the same attribute is used for a different element type, you still have to include an additional attribute-list declaration for the second instance of the attribute. For example, the following XML document fragment would require an attribute-list declaration for each id attribute used (in bold) with a different element type:

```
<book isbn="0782128203" edition="1" cat="XML XHTML HTML"
    id="mxhtml01">
<title>Mastering XHTML</title>
<authors>
    <author>Ed Tittel</author>
    <author>Chelsea Valentine</author>
    <author>Lucinda Dykes</author>
    <author>Mary Burmeister</author>
</authors>
<pubDate year="2001"/>
<publisher>Sybex</publisher>
<size pp="1019"/>
<topics>
    <topic>XHTML</topic>
    <topic>HTML</topic>
    <topic>XML</topic>
    <topic>Web Design</topic>
</topics>
<errata id="mxhtml01"/>
<description>Your complete XHTML reference.</description>
</book>
```

Attribute-list declarations contain more information than their element type counterparts. For each attribute-list declaration, you must define the following information:

Element name   Defines the element with which the attribute is to be associated.

Attribute name   Defines the name for the attribute.

Datatype   Defines the datatype for the attribute value.

Default   Defines the occurrence of the attribute (required or optional), or defines a fixed or default value.

Each piece of information has its place in the attribute-list declaration:

```
<!ATTLIST element_name attribute_name datatype default_type>
```

Datatypes

For every attribute, you're required to define a datatype. However, DTDs do not allow for the type of datatyping that can be achieved using XML Schema. XML DTDs only allow for 10 different datatypes (whereas XML Schema allows for more than 40):

- CDATA contains character data or text.

- ID contains a unique name.

- IDREF references another element containing the same value identified as an ID.

- IDREFS contains a series of IDREFs delimited by white space.

- ENTITY contains a predefined external entity.

- ENTITIES contains a series of ENTITY names (predefined external entities) delimited by white space.

- NMTOKEN contains an XML NMTOKEN.

- NMTOKENS contains a series of NMTOKENs delimited by white space.

- NOTATION contains a notation (a description of how information should be processed).

- (*enumerated value*) contains a set of acceptable values.

If you're working with data-centric information—such as prices, quantity, or unique identifiers using a specific pattern—you won't find these datatypes very useful. We examine each datatype in the following sections.

CDATA

When you use the CDATA keyword, the attribute value can contain any text. *CDATA* stands for *character data*. It's the most general datatype, so using it is an easy and common way to define your attributes. For example, a cat (for *category*) attribute associated with a book element might be defined with a CDATA datatype:

```
<book cat="XML XHTML HTML">...</book>
```

The declaration for this markup could be as follows:

```
<!ELEMENT book (title, author, description)>
<!ATTLIST book cat CDATA #IMPLIED>
```

Using CDATA is common, but it doesn't allow you to say much about your attributes. For example, you would use the CDATA datatype to define all different types of data, such as prices, URLs, e-mail addresses, and text strings.

ID and *IDREF(S)*

The ID and IDREF datatypes work together. The ID datatype defines an attribute value that must be an XML name that is unique within a document instance. As you may have guessed, the ID datatype is used to assign unique identifiers to elements in your document model. Although it's common, ID attributes do not have to have the name id or ID. As a matter of fact, many developers use an id attribute defined with a CDATA datatype:

```
<!ATTLIST book id ID #IMPLIED>
```

WARNING   An ID attribute value must be an XML name, which means it may not begin with a number. There are a few solutions commonly implemented to get around this problem. First, you can prefix the number with an underscore (isbn="_0782128203"). Some developers don't use the ID datatype and instead use the CDATA datatype, which allows the value to remain a number (isbn="0782128203").

When working with the ID datatype, there are a few special considerations:

- Any given element type may only have one ID attribute type.
- An ID default type can only be #IMPLIED or #REQUIRED.
- The ID attribute value must be an XML name.

The IDREF(S) datatype is used in conjunction with the ID datatype as a way to cross-reference data or objects. The IDREF(S) attribute type must follow the same rules defined for the ID attribute type, with one additional rule: It can only reference ID attribute types that occur within the same XML document.

The IDREF/ID connection provides a simple inside-the-document linking mechanism in which every IDREF attribute is required to point to an ID attribute. You can declare an IDREF attribute type as follows:

```
<!ELEMENT book (title, author, description)>
<!ATTLIST book id ID #IMPLIED>

<!ELEMENT reference EMPTY>
<!ATTLIST reference idRef IDREF #REQUIRED>
```

To understand this example, take a look at Listing 4.1.

Listing 4.1   **An XML Document Using *ID* and *IDREF* Datatypes**

```
<?xml version="1.0" encoding="UTF-8"?>
<publications date="September 1, 2001">

<book isbn="0782128203" edition="1" cat="XML XHTML HTML"
    id="mxhtml01">
```

```
<title>Mastering XHTML</title>
<authors>
   <author>Ed Tittel</author>
   <author>Chelsea Valentine</author>
   <author>Lucinda Dykes</author>
   <author>Mary Burmeister</author>
</authors>
<pubDate year="2001"/>
<publisher>Sybex</publisher>
<size pp="1019"/>
<topics>
   <topic>XHTML</topic>
   <topic>HTML</topic>
   <topic>XML</topic>
   <topic>Web Design</topic>
</topics>
<errata code="mxhtml01"/>
<description>Newly revised and updated, Mastering XHTML is a
   complete guide to the markup language that is leading the
   world of Web development from HTML to XML. You know the
   dangers of being left behind in this field, and this book
   ensures that you aren't, teaching you step by step how to
   convert existing HTML sites to XHTML and how to build new
   sites using this specification. It's a great way to hone
   your current skills and acquire new ones.
</description>
</book>

<book isbn="0782128270" edition="1" cat="Java ECommerce XML"
   id="jdgexj01">
<title>Java Developer's Guide to E-Commerce with XML and JSP
   </title>
<authors>
   <author>William Brogden</author>
   <author>Chris Minnick</author>
</authors>
<pubDate year="2001"/>
<publisher>Sybex</publisher>
<size pp="464"/>
<topics>
   <topic>Java</topic>
   <topic>E-Commerce</topic>
   <topic>XML</topic>
</topics>
<errata code="jdgexj01"/>
<description>Your Java programming knowledge will go a long way
   toward building an effective e-commerce site. XML is the
   missing piece, and Java Developer's Guide to E-Commerce
   With XML and JSP gives you expert instruction in the
   techniques that unite these closely aligned technologies.
   Covering the latest Servlet and JSP APIs and the current
```

```
      XML standard, this book guides you through all the steps
      required to build and implement a cohesive, dynamic, and
      profitable site.
   </description>
   </book>

   <reviews>
      <review>
       <author>Amazon.com</author>
       <location url="http://www.amazon.com"/>
       <reference idRef="mxhtml01/">
      </review>
      <review>
       <author>Barnes and Noble</author>
       <location url="http://www.bn.com"/>
       <reference idRef="jdgexj01/">
      </review>
   </reviews>
   </publications>
```

In Listing 4.1, each book element is associated with a unique identifier (id="xhtml01"). Later in the document, we include a section on reviews of our books. Instead of identifying the book information all over again, we include an IDREF attribute that is defined as an IDREF datatype. The value of the IDREF attribute matches the corresponding book ID.

ID attributes are important whether you need to reference IDREF(S) or not because they give elements unique addresses. It's common practice to declare optional (using the #IMPLIED default type) ID attributes for many of elements in a document model—you never know when you might need one.

ENTITY(S)
An ENTITY datatype can accept a general entity name as a value. You'll have to declare the entity first, but after it's declared, you can use the entity as the attribute value. One common usage of this datatype is to refer to a document that cannot be parsed by an XML parser, such as a Microsoft Word document, an HTML file, or an image:

```
<!ATTLIST cover img ENTITY #IMPLIED>
```

In this example, we define an optional img attribute that can be used with the cover element type—this allows us to include an image of the book's cover art if we have one. Before you can use this entity, you must declare it first. For more information on entity declarations, see the section "Entities" later in this chapter.

NMTOKEN(S)
Name tokens (NMTOKEN) are similar to CDATA attribute types. As with CDATA, the value can be a character string; however, you're restricted in the characters you can use. With NMTOKEN(S),

you're only allowed to include any string of text consisting of letters, numbers, and a few special characters: period (.), underscore (_), dash (-), and a colon (:). We do not recommend using the colon because it's used for namespace prefixes. In addition, you cannot use white space characters within the NMTOKEN. You use NMTOKEN as follows:

```
<!ATTLIST book isbn NMTOKEN #REQUIRED>
```

You can include multiple name tokens separated by white space (for example, cat="XML XHTML HTML"); however, you must declare the attribute type as NMTOKENS, as in the following example:

```
<!ATTLIST book cat NMTOKENS #REQUIRED>
```

NOTATION

Notations refer to data that is not XML. This attribute type allows the author to declare that the element's content conforms to a declared notation. In other words, the attribute's value must be a notation (and you must use a notation declaration to declare that notation). A notation is a description of how information (that is not XML data) should be processed. We cover notations later in this chapter.

Enumeration

If you want to restrict the document author's attribute value choices to a short list, you use an enumerated attribute type. The enumerated type provides a choice of options:

```
<!ATTLIST pubDate year (1999 | 2000 | 2001) #REQUIRED>
```

When you define an enumerated list of options, the document author must select one of the defined options as the attribute value. If you choose to assign a default value, that value must be defined as a part of the enumerated list:

```
<!ATTLIST pubDate year (1999 | 2000 | 2001 | unknown) "unknown">
```

Default Types

For every attribute, you have to define a default type. You have four options to chose from:

#REQUIRED   When this keyword is used, the attribute is required:

```
<!ATTLIST element-name attribute-name datatype #REQUIRED>
```

#IMPLIED   When this keyword is used, the attribute is optional:

```
<!ATTLIST element-name attribute-name datatype #IMPLIED>
```

#FIXED   When this keyword is used, an additional value is also required. The attribute must always have the default value. If the attribute is not included, the value is assumed by the parser:

```
<!ATTLIST element-name attribute-name datatype #FIXED
    "fixed-value">
```

"value"   Instead of a keyword, you can insert a value in quotation marks. If the attribute is not used, the default value listed will be assumed by the parser. If the attribute is used and has another value, the default value is ignored:

```
<!ATTLIST element-name attribute-name datatype
    "default-value">
```

Multiple Attributes

A single *attribute-list declaration* can declare multiple attributes for a given element, which is why they are called attribute-list declarations. In most of the examples we've looked at so far, we only declared one attribute per element type. Here's an example of an element with multiple attributes:

```
<book isbn="0782128203" edition="1" cat="XML XHTML HTML"
    id="mxhtml01">
```

To create the attribute-list declaration for the collection of attributes associated with the preceding book element, all you need is this declaration:

```
<!ATTLIST book isbn     CDATA    #REQUIRED
               edition  CDATA    #REQUIRED
               cat      NMTOKENS #REQUIRED
               id       ID       #IMPLIED
>
```

Notations

XML does a superb job defining textual data because that's what it was created to do. However, as XML finds its way into all types of applications, it's being forced to handle non-XML data. For instance, if you were designing a Web-based application, you might be working with bitmap images, audio, and/or video files.

Notations were created as a way to identify non-XML data and to provide instructions on how to process the data. For example, to reference a Graphics Interchange Format (GIF) image, you not only reference the image, but you also tell the processor how to handle it. In this case, you tell the processor to pass it to a GIF viewer.

To include non-XML data, you need to declare a notation. Notation declarations use the following syntax:

```
<!NOTATION name SYSTEM/PUBLIC identifier>
```

The *name* is the name of the notation type, and the *identifier* is an external identifier that holds meaning for the XML processor. Let's take a look at a GIF image example. Consider the following markup, where the img attribute value is an entity that points to mxhtml.gif:

```
<cover img="mxhtml">
```

The following markup defines the notation declaration for the image:

```
<!NOTATION gif SYSTEM "image/gif">
```

If you want the processor to handle the image file, there's more to it than just defining a notation. The next step would be to define an entity that would reference the external file. We cover entities in the following section.

WARNING   The identifier must be recognized by the XML processor for the processor to know what to do. Unfortunately, no one has defined an external identifier scheme, which means there's not a convenient list of possible identifiers.

Entities

An *entity* is a placeholder for content. DTDs make ample use of entities and allow you to define and reuse information in both the DTD and in the XML document. After you define an entity, you can reference—or use—it as many times as you like throughout your document.

Entities serve many functions. One common function is to define data that you would like to use in multiple places. When you use an entity, the data is defined once and then referenced when needed, saving you a maintenance nightmare. Another common use for entities is to serve as a stand-in for reserved characters or for characters that do not appear on your keyboard.

As mentioned, when referencing non-XML data, such as an external image, you want to call on it with an entity reference and then reference that entity from within an attribute value. The notation is associated with an entity declaration, as in the following example:

```
<!NOTATION gif SYSTEM "image/gif">
<!ENTITY mxhtml SYSTEM "graphics/mxhtml.gif" NDATA gif>
```

Because entities serve a variety of functions, XML 1.0 defines several different types of entities, each with its own syntax and function. The different types of entities are based on the following categories:

Parsed vs. Unparsed   Entity content either can be parsed by an XML parser or, if it's not well-formed XML (think bitmap image), cannot be parsed by an XML parser.

General vs. Parameter   Every entity can be used either within the DTD subset (parameter) or within the XML document (general).

Internal vs. External   Every entity can either be defined within the entity declaration itself or can reference an external file that contains the entity.

Every entity has to fall into one of the options for each category. There are a few combinations that are not allowed, and when all is said and done, you're left with the following entity types:

- Internal parsed general (also known as an internal general entity)
- Internal parsed parameter (also known as an internal parameter entity)
- External parsed general
- External parsed parameter
- External unparsed general (also known as an unparsed entity)

In the following sections, we describe and define each allowed entity type.

Although each type of entity uses a syntax specific to its function, all entities follow a basic structure:

```
<!ENTITY entity-name "replacement-text">
<!ENTITY entity-name SYSTEM/PUBLIC "location-of-external-file">
```

TIP   If the same entity is declared more than once, the first declaration encountered is binding. This idea of a first-declaration-wins rule surprises many, but it works well in SGML, so its use is continued in XML. The practical effect is as follows: Because the internal subset of the DTD appears first, you can put entity declarations there to override those in the external part of the DTD.

Internal Parsed General

The *internal parsed general entity* is one of the simplest types of entities. All internal entities are parsed, which means that the XML processor must parse them as XML text. You're also likely to see them referred to as *internal general entities*—many people will leave out *parsed* because that's a requirement for all internal entities.

A general entity stores text for use within a document instance. In other words, a general entity acts as an abbreviation for commonly used text or text that is difficult (or tedious) to type. The internal part of an internal entity declaration indicates that the content of the parsed entity (replacement text) lies inside the document. The following are two examples of possible uses for internal general entities:

- As chunks of boilerplate text that you would rather store and manage in one place and that you're going to use in multiple documents. This approach saves time and bandwidth, in addition to making your data more manageable. Here is an example:

  ```
  <!ENTITY copyright "Copyright &copy; 2001, Sybex">
  ```

- As a uniform reference to URLs. Any XML document can contain many URLs. As we all know, URLs tend to move and can be painfully difficult to maintain. It's useful to use entities to help make this easier:

```
<!ENTITY url "http://www.sybex.com">
```

To declare an internal general entity, you would use the following syntax:

```
<!ENTITY entity-name "replacement-text">
<!ENTITY update "This document model was edited by
   Bill Brogden on 09.01.01">
```

In the preceding example, we created an entity called `update`. If Bill, or someone else, updates the XML document, he can change that information within the entity. Therefore, any document that references the DTD and calls on the `update` entity will know just when the document model was updated.

Because this entity is defined as a parsed entity, it cannot contain non-XML text. One of the advantages of using entity references is that, by storing the data in one location, it's easier to make changes to the text. Obviously, the benefit is increased exponentially when the entity reference is used in multiple documents.

Internal general entities can be referenced anywhere in the content of an element or attribute value, including an attribute default value (in the DTD). However, you can't just dump the name anywhere in the document and expect the processor to expand it for you. When you decide to reference an internal general entity, you must delimit it with an ampersand (&) and semicolon (;). In our previous example, we would use the entity in document markup like this:

```
<update>&update;</update>
```

There's one other way to use internal general entities, other than within the XML document: You can use an internal general entity inside a general entity reference, as in this example:

```
<!ENTITY contact "This book was edited by Mary Burmeister.
   Contact her at &email;">
```

This is allowed because the `email` entity that appears as a part of the `contact` entity will ultimately become part of the document's content. You can also use general entity references in other places in the DTD that ultimately become part of the document content (such as a default attribute value), but there are guidelines for their use:

- Internal general entity references cannot be circular. For example, you cannot declare the following two lines together:

```
<!ENTITY sybex "&copy; Sybex">
<!ENTITY copy "Copyright &sybex;">
```

In this case, both entities are defined using one another (they are circular).

- You cannot use internal general entity references to insert text within the DTD. For example, the following declarations are not valid:

```
<!ENTITY year "1999 | 2000 | 2001">
<!ELEMENT pubDate EMPTY>
<!ATTLIST pubDate year (&year;) #REQUIRED>
```

- The values defined as replacement text cannot contain the %, &, or " character. If you need to use one of these characters, you have to use general character references.

Listing 4.2 provides an example of an internal general entity.

Listing 4.2   **Using an Internal General Entity**

```
<!DOCTYPE publications [
    <!ENTITY % updatedtd SYSTEM "update.dtd">
    %updatedtd;

    <!ENTITY update "<update>
                        <author>Bill Brogden</author>
                        <date>September 18, 2001</date>
                        <documentation>Slight modifications to
                          document model</documentation>
                        </update>"
    >

<!ENTITY mxhtml SYSTEM "graphics/mxhtml.gif" NDATA gif>
<!ENTITY jdgexj SYSTEM "graphics/jdgexj.gif" NDATA gif>
<!ENTITY jdgsj SYSTEM "graphics/jdgsj.gif" NDATA gif>
<!NOTATION gif SYSTEM "image/gif">

<!ELEMENT publications (book+)>
<!ATTLIST publications xmlns CDATA #FIXED
"http://www.lanw.com/namespaces/pub">
<!ELEMENT book (title, authors, pubDate, publisher, size,
    cover?, topics, errata?, description, website?)>
<!ATTLIST book isbn CDATA #REQUIRED
                edition CDATA #REQUIRED
                cat CDATA #REQUIRED
                id CDATA #REQUIRED
>
<!ELEMENT authors (author+)>
<!ELEMENT size EMPTY>
<!ATTLIST size pp CDATA #REQUIRED>
<!ELEMENT cover EMPTY>
<!ATTLIST cover img ENTITY #REQUIRED>
<!ELEMENT topics (topic+)>
<!ELEMENT errata EMPTY>
```

```
<!ATTLIST errata code CDATA #REQUIRED>
<!ELEMENT pubDate EMPTY>
<!ATTLIST pubDate year CDATA #REQUIRED>
<!ELEMENT publisher (#PCDATA)>
<!ELEMENT description (#PCDATA)>
<!ELEMENT website (#PCDATA)>
<!ELEMENT title (#PCDATA)>
<!ELEMENT author (#PCDATA)>
<!ELEMENT topic (#PCDATA)>

]>

<publications xmlns="http://www.lanw.com/namespaces/pub">

<book isbn="0782128203" edition="1" cat="XML XHTML HTML"
    id="mxhtml01">
<title>Mastering XHTML</title>
<authors>
    <author>Ed Tittel</author>
    <author>Chelsea Valentine</author>
    <author>Lucinda Dykes</author>
    <author>Mary Burmeister</author>
</authors>
<pubDate year="2001"/>
<publisher>Sybex</publisher>

<size pp="1019"/>
<cover img="mxhtml"/>
<topics>
    <topic>XHTML</topic>
    <topic>HTML</topic>
    <topic>XML</topic>
    <topic>Web Design</topic>
</topics>
<errata code="mxhtml01"/>
<description>Newly revised and updated, Mastering XHTML is a
    complete guide to the markup language that is leading the
    world of Web development from HTML to XML. You know the
    dangers of being left behind in this field, and this book
    ensures that you aren't, teaching you step by step how to
    convert existing HTML sites to XHTML and how to build new
    sites using this specification. It's a great way to hone
    your current skills and acquire new ones.
</description>
</book>
<book>
…
</book>
&update;
</publications>
```

Internal Parsed Parameter

Internal parsed parameter entities (also known as internal parameter entities) are used to declare entities existing solely in the DTD. General entities are referenced inside the XML document, not in the DTD. (They can be used in the DTD as long as they're used within entity declarations that are intended to be used within the XML document.) Contrary to general entities, parameter entities are entities that are used solely within the DTD.

TIP   Internal parameter entities are declared and used with the DTD (either the internal or external subset). External parameter entities are used to link DTDs (their declaration references an external file with a URI). So how do you know which type of entity you are dealing with? If the entity declaration defines a Uniform Resource Identifier (URI), which points to an external resource, you know you're dealing with an external parameter entity.

Parameter entities are very similar to general entities. There are two distinctions in syntax that need to be made:

- Parameter entity references begin with a percent sign (%) instead of an ampersand (&).

- Parameter entity references can only be used in the DTD, not within the document.

An internal parameter entity follows this syntax model:

```
<!ENTITY % name "replacement-text">
```

You can also reference entity declarations in other DTD declarations. For example, the declaration on the first line could be referenced in another DTD declaration as shown on the second line:

```
<!ENTITY % head "h1, h2, h3, h4, h5, h6">
<!ELEMENT catalog (%head;)>
```

One of the strengths of using parameter entities is that you can reuse common lists of child elements or a group of common attributes. In our example, we can use the %head; entity every time we want to include the long list of h* children elements (h1, h2, h3, h4, h5, and h6). In other words, the larger the chunk of reusable data and the more you use the entity reference, the more useful the entity becomes. However, remember that you cannot use this entity within the document itself—this type is reserved for the DTD.

WARNING   You need to make sure that the entities are declared before you use them (order is important). For example, the following is not valid:

```
<!ELEMENT catalog (%head;)>
<!ENTITY % head "h1, h2, h3, h4, h5, h6">
```

Internal parameter entities can be used within declarations in the external subset; however, in the internal subset, internal parameter entity references can only be used outside declarations. For example, you can use the following markup in both the internal and external subsets:

```
<!ENTITY % date "<!ELEMENT date (#PCDATA)>">
%date;
```

This example may seem rather silly, but later in this chapter, we look at linking DTDs, which is done using this method, with a slight modification:

```
<!ENTITY % date SYSTEM "otherdtd.dtd">
    %date;
```

The following entity declarations can only be used in the external subset:

```
<!ELEMENT catalog (%head;)>
<!ENTITY % head "h1, h2, h3, h4, h5, h6">
```

Listing 4.3 provides an example of an internal parsed parameter entity.

Listing 4.3 **Using an Internal Parsed Parameter Entity**

```
<!ENTITY % inline "b | em | i | code">
<!ELEMENT update (author, date, documentation)>
<!ELEMENT author (#PCDATA | %inline;)*>
<!ELEMENT date (#PCDATA | %inline;)*>
<!ELEMENT documentation (#PCDATA | %inline;)*>
```

External Parsed General

Similar to internal general entities, external parsed general entities reference parseable XML data. Because external parsed general entities reference external files, they're useful for creating a common reference that can be shared among multiple documents.

There are two types of external parsed general entities: private and public. *Private external entities* are identified by the keyword SYSTEM and are intended for use by a single author or group of authors. *Public external entities* are identified by the keyword PUBLIC and are intended for more general use. Both follow a similar syntax:

```
<!ENTITY name SYSTEM "URI">
<!ENTITY name PUBLIC "public_id" "URI">
```

External entities are not without rules. References to parsed external entities cannot be made within the value of an attribute in case the character encoding of the entity is different from that of the main document.

WARNING A nonvalidating parser is not required to read and include the content of entities with external content.

Listing 4.4 illustrates an external parsed general entity.

Listing 4.4   **Using an External Parsed General Entity**

```
<!DOCTYPE publications [

<!ENTITY % updatedtd SYSTEM "update.dtd">
%updatedtd;
<!ENTITY update SYSTEM "update.xml">
<!ENTITY mxhtml SYSTEM "graphics/mxhtml.gif" NDATA gif>
<!ENTITY jdgexj SYSTEM "graphics/jdgexj.gif" NDATA gif>
<!ENTITY jdgsj SYSTEM "graphics/jdgsj.gif" NDATA gif>
<!NOTATION gif SYSTEM "image/gif">

<!ELEMENT publications (book+)>
<!ATTLIST publications xmlns CDATA #FIXED
    "http://www.lanw.com/namespaces/pub">
<!ELEMENT book (title, authors, pubDate, publisher, size,
    cover?, topics, errata?, description, website?)>
<!ATTLIST book isbn CDATA #REQUIRED
                edition CDATA #REQUIRED
                cat CDATA #REQUIRED
                id CDATA #REQUIRED
>
<!ELEMENT authors (author+)>
<!ELEMENT size EMPTY>
<!ATTLIST size pp CDATA #REQUIRED>
<!ELEMENT cover EMPTY>
<!ATTLIST cover img ENTITY #REQUIRED>
<!ELEMENT topics (topic+)>
<!ELEMENT errata EMPTY>
<!ATTLIST errata code CDATA #REQUIRED>
<!ELEMENT pubDate EMPTY>
<!ATTLIST pubDate year CDATA #REQUIRED>
<!ELEMENT publisher (#PCDATA)>
<!ELEMENT description (#PCDATA)>
<!ELEMENT website (#PCDATA)>
<!ELEMENT title (#PCDATA)>
<!ELEMENT author (#PCDATA)>
<!ELEMENT topic (#PCDATA)>

]>

<publications xmlns="http://www.lanw.com/namespaces/pub">

<book isbn="0782128203" edition="1" cat="XML XHTML HTML"
    id="mxhtml01">
<title>Mastering XHTML</title>
<authors>
    <author>Ed Tittel</author>
    <author>Chelsea Valentine</author>
```

```
    <author>Lucinda Dykes</author>
    <author>Mary Burmeister</author>
</authors>
<pubDate year="2001"/>
<publisher>Sybex</publisher>

<size pp="1019"/>
<cover img="mxhtml"/>
<topics>
    <topic>XHTML</topic>
    <topic>HTML</topic>
    <topic>XML</topic>
    <topic>Web Design</topic>
</topics>
<errata code="mxhtml01"/>
<description>...</description>
</book>
<book>
...
</book>
&update;
</publications>
```

External Parsed Parameter

Parameter entities are designed to improve DTD readability. All parameter entities can only be used within a DTD subset. In this case, the external parsed parameter entity is used to reference external files that contain the replacement text. As with internal parsed parameter entities, the declaration and entity reference use the % sign.

External parameter entity references are used to link external DTDs. To learn more about linking external DTD subsets, see the section "Modularizing Document Models" later in this chapter. There are two types of external entities: private and public. *Private external entities* are identified by the keyword SYSTEM and are intended for use by a single author or group of authors. *Public external entities* are identified by the keyword PUBLIC and are intended for general use. The syntax is as follows:

```
<!ENTITY % name SYSTEM "URI">
<!ENTITY % name PUBLIC "public_ID" "URI">
```

The external parsed parameter entity can be used within the DTD. As a matter of fact, it's common practice to reference the entity directly after its declaration. In the declaration, you reference the file that you want to include as part of the DTD. When you reference the entity, you're telling the processor to take a look in that file for additional declarations. This is how you can reference multiple external DTDs within a DTD, which is how you link DTDs. Keep in mind that when the processor expands the entity, the result must be well-formed DTD syntax.

Listing 4.5 illustrates an external parsed parameter entity.

Listing 4.5   **Using an External Parsed Parameter Entity**

```
<!DOCTYPE publications [

<!ENTITY % updatedtd SYSTEM "update.dtd">
%updatedtd;
<!ENTITY update "<update>
                    <author>Bill Brogden</author>
                    <date>September 18, 2001</date>
                    <documentation>Slight modifications to
                     document model</documentation>
                   </update>"
>

<!ENTITY mxhtml SYSTEM "graphics/mxhtml.gif" NDATA gif>
<!ENTITY jdgexj SYSTEM "graphics/jdgexj.gif" NDATA gif>
<!ENTITY jdgsj SYSTEM "graphics/jdgsj.gif" NDATA gif>
<!NOTATION gif SYSTEM "image/gif">

<!ELEMENT publications (book+)>
<!ATTLIST publications xmlns CDATA #FIXED
"http://www.lanw.com/namespaces/pub">
<!ELEMENT book (title, authors, pubDate, publisher, size,
    cover?, topics, errata?, description, website?)>
<!ATTLIST book isbn CDATA #REQUIRED
                edition CDATA #REQUIRED
                cat CDATA #REQUIRED
                id CDATA #REQUIRED
>
<!ELEMENT authors (author+)>
<!ELEMENT size EMPTY>
<!ATTLIST size pp CDATA #REQUIRED>
<!ELEMENT cover EMPTY>
<!ATTLIST cover img ENTITY #REQUIRED>
<!ELEMENT topics (topic+)>
<!ELEMENT errata EMPTY>
<!ATTLIST errata code CDATA #REQUIRED>
<!ELEMENT pubDate EMPTY>
<!ATTLIST pubDate year CDATA #REQUIRED>
<!ELEMENT publisher (#PCDATA)>
<!ELEMENT description (#PCDATA)>
<!ELEMENT website (#PCDATA)>
<!ELEMENT title (#PCDATA)>
<!ELEMENT author (#PCDATA)>
<!ELEMENT topic (#PCDATA)>

]>

<publications xmlns="http://www.lanw.com/namespaces/pub">
```

```
<book isbn="0782128203" edition="1" cat="XML XHTML HTML"
    id="mxhtml01">
<title>Mastering XHTML</title>
<authors>
    <author>Ed Tittel</author>
    <author>Chelsea Valentine</author>
    <author>Lucinda Dykes</author>
    <author>Mary Burmeister</author>
</authors>
<pubDate year="2001"/>
<publisher>Sybex</publisher>

<size pp="1019"/>
<cover img="mxhtml"/>
<topics>
    <topic>XHTML</topic>
    <topic>HTML</topic>
    <topic>XML</topic>
    <topic>Web Design</topic>
</topics>
<errata code="mxhtml01"/>
<description>…</description>
</book>
<book>
...
</book>
&update;
</publications>
```

External Unparsed General

As you already know, every XML entity can be either parsed or unparsed. All the ones that we've looked at so far have been parsed. The external unparsed general entity (also known as an unparsed entity) is actually the only type of entity that is not parsed by the XML proces sor. An unparsed entity allows you to reference external files that don't contain XML data, such as a graphic, sound, or other multimedia object. You can even use unparsed entities to embed an XML document if the document is in some unparseable representation—meaning that the document to be embedded does not adhere to the DTD. For example, you might want to include a shopping cart driven by its own XML document (and shopping elements) within an XML document. Instead of adding all the shopping elements to the DTD, you can reference that document as an external unparsed entity.

All unparsed entities are external because there's no way to express non-XML information internally in XML entity declarations. They are also general entities because it's forbidden (and senseless) to embed non-XML data in an XML DTD.

The syntax for an unparsed entity is specialized:

```
<!ENTITY name SYSTEM "URI" NDATA name>
```

Here's an example:

```
<!ENTITY mxhtml SYSTEM "graphics/mxhtml.gif" NDATA gif>
```

As with all external entity declarations, you can use either the SYSTEM or PUBLIC keyword. When you declare an unparsed entity, you also have to declare a notation to go with it that tells the processor how to handle the non-XML data. We discuss notation declarations in the next section.

You can pass these entities only within an attribute value in the XML document. Listing 4.6 illustrates external unparsed general entity.

Listing 4.6   **Using an External Unparsed General Entity**

```
<!DOCTYPE publications [

<!ENTITY % updatedtd SYSTEM "update.dtd">
%updatedtd;

<!ENTITY update "<update>
                    <author>Bill Brogden</author>
                    <date>September 18, 2001</date>
                    <documentation>Slight modifications to
                      document model</documentation>
                 </update>"
>
<!ENTITY mxhtml SYSTEM "graphics/mxhtml.gif" NDATA gif>
<!ENTITY jdgexj SYSTEM "graphics/jdgexj.gif" NDATA gif>
<!ENTITY jdgsj SYSTEM "graphics/jdgsj.gif" NDATA gif>

<!NOTATION gif SYSTEM "image/gif">

<!ELEMENT publications (book+)>
<!ATTLIST publications xmlns CDATA #FIXED
"http://www.lanw.com/namespaces/pub">
<!ELEMENT book (title, authors, pubDate, publisher, size,
   cover?, topics, errata?, description, website?)>
<!ATTLIST book isbn CDATA #REQUIRED
               edition CDATA #REQUIRED
               cat CDATA #REQUIRED
               id CDATA #REQUIRED
>
<!ELEMENT authors (author+)>
<!ELEMENT size EMPTY>
<!ATTLIST size pp CDATA #REQUIRED>
<!ELEMENT cover EMPTY>
<!ATTLIST cover img ENTITY #REQUIRED>
```

```
<!ELEMENT topics (topic+)>
<!ELEMENT errata EMPTY>
<!ATTLIST errata code CDATA #REQUIRED>
<!ELEMENT pubDate EMPTY>
<!ATTLIST pubDate year CDATA #REQUIRED>
<!ELEMENT publisher (#PCDATA)>
<!ELEMENT description (#PCDATA)>
<!ELEMENT website (#PCDATA)>
<!ELEMENT title (#PCDATA)>
<!ELEMENT author (#PCDATA)>
<!ELEMENT topic (#PCDATA)>

]>

<publications xmlns="http://www.lanw.com/namespaces/pub">

<book isbn="0782128203" edition="1" cat="XML XHTML HTML"
    id="mxhtml01">
<title>Mastering XHTML</title>
<authors>
    <author>Ed Tittel</author>
    <author>Chelsea Valentine</author>
    <author>Lucinda Dykes</author>
    <author>Mary Burmeister</author>
</authors>
<pubDate year="2001"/>
<publisher>Sybex</publisher>

<size pp="1019"/>
<cover img="mxhtml"/>
<topics>
    <topic>XHTML</topic>
    <topic>HTML</topic>
    <topic>XML</topic>
    <topic>Web Design</topic>
</topics>
<errata code="mxhtml01"/>
<description>…</description>
</book>
<book>

…
</book>
&update;
</publications>
```

Techniques for Designing a DTD Markup Model

DTDs define a vocabulary—a set of rules for your XML documents. DTDs have been around for about 20 years (used with SGML applications), and over those 20 years, many design techniques have been perfected. Some of these techniques, or tips, are obvious. For example, you'll want to keep your DTD subsets organized. This may seem like a given, but many newcomers are likely to define element type declarations in the order in which you expect them to be used. However, the emphasis of placement should be on grouping your declarations by function. These groupings can be separated logically with white space within a DTD subset, or they can be separated into their own DTD subsets.

Another simple, yet effective, tip is to use white space wisely. We highly recommend that you use white space throughout your content models to make them easier follow. For example, the following attribute-list declaration is difficult to follow:

```
<!ATTLIST book isbn CDATA #REQUIRED edition CDATA #REQUIRED
    cat NMTOKENS #REQUIRED id ID #IMPLIED>
```

However, by using white space, we can clearly, and quickly, identify each attribute:

```
<!ATTLIST book isbn     CDATA    #REQUIRED
               edition  CDATA    #REQUIRED
               cat      NMTOKENS #REQUIRED
               id       ID       #IMPLIED
>
```

There are other design tips and techniques that you need to be aware of if you plan to work with DTDs. We cover a few of these in the following sections.

Identifying Metadata

There are times when an element doesn't provide all the information needed for your data. Attributes allow you to associate metadata (e.g., a unique identifier or descriptive property) that describes additional information about your data. An attribute is commonly used to describe element behavior or to create a subtype. For example, the following book element contains four attributes:

```
<book isbn="0782128203" edition="1" cat="XML XHTML HTML"
    id="mxhtml01">
```

It's also common for elements to share the same metadata needs. For example, many vocabularies allow for an optional ID attribute for almost all elements. Within your own document model, you may have several elements that share common metadata needs. XHTML, for instance, defines several attributes (e.g., style, id, title, and class) that can be used with most of their elements. In our example, the id attribute is one that we want available to multiple elements in our document model. The attribute-list declaration for the attribute grouping for the book element is as follows:

```
<!ATTLIST book isbn    CDATA #REQUIRED
               edition CDATA #REQUIRED
               cat     CDATA #IMPLIED
               id      ID    #IMPLIED
>
```

Each time we wanted to define an id attribute for some element in our document model, we would have to introduce a new attribute-list declaration. Creating multiple attribute-list declarations to handle each id attribute for each element might quickly get out of hand. DTDs allow for the inclusion of parameter entities to help improve the readability and maintainability of your DTD. Instead of creating multiple declarations for the same attribute, we could define the following parameter entity:

```
<!ENTITY % commonatts "id ID #IMPLIED">
```

Now, every time we want to use the attribute, we can reference the parameter entity:

```
<!ATTLIST publications %commonatts;>
```

WARNING Parameter entities can only be referenced from within a declaration if they are defined and used in an external DTD subset.

Notations and Unparsed Data

Notations provide a formal mechanism for referencing unparseable data. If XML didn't allow you to mix textual data with other binary formats, it wouldn't be that helpful. With the current state of technology and media we, as developers, are constantly working with audio, video, graphics, and other file types. XML is not prepared to handle this type of information, but it's prepared to pass it on to a processor that *can* handle it.

A notation labels data and tells the XML processor what type of data is being defined. Notation declarations identify the name of the notation and an identifier, as follows:

```
<!NOTATION name identifier>
```

The *name* of the notation is defined by the developer and the *identifier* must have some meaning to the XML processor. The meaning of the identifier depends on the application that will handle it. In an ideal world, there would be a list of predefined identifiers for common file types. However, there's still debate about identifying external notation identifiers.

Notations are commonly used in conjunction with an unparsed external entity. The unparsed entity imports non-XML data. As you might remember, the declaration for an unparsed entity is rather lengthy:

```
<!ENTITY name SYSTEM "URI" NDATA name>
```

In the following DTD subset, we declare a two-notation declaration for a GIF file type using its MIME type as an identifier. A cover element is declared to be an empty element that contains one attribute, img, that references the unparsed entity:

```
<?xml version="1.0"?>
<!DOCTYPE graphic [
    <!ELEMENT graphic (cover)>
    <!ELEMENT cover EMPTY>
    <!ATTLIST cover img ENTITY #REQUIRED>
    <!NOTATION gif SYSTEM "image/gif">
    <!NOTATION jpeg SYSTEM "image/jpeg">
    <!ENTITY mxhtml SYSTEM "graphics/mxhtml.gif" NDATA gif>
]>
<graphic>
    <cover img="mxhtml"/>
</graphic>
```

When the XML processor comes across the mxhtml entity reference, it knows that it's not to be parsed (because of the NDATA). The XML processor then forgoes parsing and sends the data to the appropriate processor.

TIP   You do not have to include entity delimiters (& and ;) when referencing an entity from within an attribute value because the attribute datatype is already defined as an entity. Always pass unparsed entities through attribute values rather than as element content.

Notations don't provide specifics about nonparsed data handling. There's no way to predict how a processor might behave when it comes across an NDATA attribute. That is up to the application developer.

WARNING   If you expect your XML document to be processed by different programs, you have to be sure that each processor knows how to handle the notations defined. An alternative to working with notations would be to define a processing instruction to specify how to handle the non-XML data.

Reusing Data with Entities

DTDs allow you to create reusable chunks of data that can be referenced from within the DTD or XML document. This helps keep your XML documents clean and manageable. There are several ways to define your entities. For example, if you want to define a common header for all of your XML documents, you'll want to define an external entity that references an external file that contains the header information. On the other hand, if you want to create an entity to reference a common URL that's used throughout a specific document, it might be easier to define that entity internally.

TIP   XML Schema defines a mechanism that is analogous to general entities. The expectation is that other technologies will be used to fill the void. However, XML Schema allows developers to create definitions that can be reused throughout the DTD—similar to DTD parameter entities.

Modularizing Document Models

There are many advantages to be gained from modularizing your DTD. The most obvious is maintenance. Separating your DTD structure into pieces allows you to edit or update multiple sections at one time rather than having to wade through an entire DTD.

Another advantage is that using modules means that your DTD is configurable. Similar to how the W3C is handling the future of XHTML, separating DTD subsets by function allows you to mix and match the modules to configure your own document model.

There are two ways that XML 1.0 allows you to modularize your DTD:

- You can create separate DTD modules and link (import) them using external parameter entities.

- You can use conditional sections to mark DTD sections for inclusion or exclusion in the DTD.

In this section, we focus on using external parameter entities to import external DTD subsets.

There are many reasons you might want to break your DTD into manageable pieces. There are also cases in which you'll want to include DTD subsets from borrowed sources. For example, you may want to borrow from a few XHTML DTD subsets that define document structure and images, but you also want to use your very own group of elements.

When referencing an external parameter entity, the SYSTEM or PUBLIC identifier is used in the syntax:

```
<!ENTITY % name SYSTEM "URI">
<!ENTITY % name PUBLIC "public_ID" "URI">
```

To call on external DTD subsets, you must use a parameter entity reference (%name;). The interesting thing about importing DTDs is that you normally call on them directly after you define them:

```
<!ENTITY % images SYSTEM "images.dtd">
%images;
```

There are a few issues that you must consider when using this method to modularize your DTD, the most important of which is that when you call an external DTD subset, you're getting the entire set of declarations. You cannot be selective with the declarations you're getting. If this is a problem, you can redeclare elements to fit the desired document model. Although this was not what was intended, there's a first-read rule that requires the XML processor to use the first declaration found and discard any other declarations for the same element.

The XML processor is also required to concatenate all attribute-list declarations defined for a given element. This means that you can add additional attributes for an element if need be. As with element type declarations, if the same attribute name is declared twice for a given element, the first declaration found takes precedence.

This takes care of any declarations that we need to redefine. But, what if you need to delete a declaration from the imported set? This requires the use of conditional sections. However, the conditional section must be defined for a declaration before you can choose to exclude it. This means that if you're importing a DTD subset from a borrowed source and that source does not have conditional sections defined, you're out of luck.

DTDs and Namespaces

Namespaces, as you likely know, provide developers with a formal mechanism for resolving name conflicts while mixing XML vocabularies. For example, your document might contain a title element meant to contain book titles. At the same time, the document may contain the XHTML title element used to provide a title for the document. By associating each element with a different namespace, the processor recognizes a symbolic difference between the two.

XML Namespaces

For those of you who might not be familiar with XML namespaces, here's a quick crash course. An *XML namespace* is a special attribute used to uniquely identify a set of elements. The following syntax is used to define a namespace:

```
xmlns:prefix="namespaceURI"
```

Continued on next page

Also commonly referred to as a namespace declaration, this syntax is defined within an element, as in the following example:

```
<element xmlns:prefix="namespaceURI">
```

The parts of the namespace declaration are as follows:

- xmlns identifies the value as an XML namespace. It's required to declare a namespace and can be attached to any XML element.

- :prefix identifies a namespace prefix. It (including the colon) is only used if you're declaring a namespace prefix. If it's used, any element found in the document that uses the prefix (prefix:element) is then assumed to fall under the scope of the declared namespace.

- namespaceURI is the unique identifier. The value does not have to point to a Web resource; it's only a symbolic identifier. The value is required and must be defined within either single or double quotation marks.

There are two different ways you can define a namespace:

Default namespace   Defines a namespace using the xmlns attribute without a prefix, and all child elements are assumed to belong to the defined namespace.

Prefixed namespace   Defines a namespace using the xmlns attribute with a prefix. When the prefix is attached to an element, it's assumed to belong to that namespace.

Namespaces use the same syntax structure as attributes. For example, the following publications element contains both a version attribute and a default namespace:

```
<publications version="1.0"
    xmlns="http://www.lanw.com/namespaces/pub">
```

Whereas both xmlns and version may appear to be attributes, they're not. A namespace is of a different breed and serves a specific function. For this reason, it doesn't make sense to treat it as any old attribute. As a matter of fact, it would be wise to have a processor recognize the difference.

Namespaces were formally introduced by the W3C in January 1999—almost a year after XML 1.0 was introduced. According to the XML 1.0 Recommendation, namespaces don't exist. Because of this, DTDs are not namespace aware either, which means that you can use namespaces in both validating and nonvalidating XML documents. This can pose an interesting problem if you rely on DTD validation; however, you need to use namespaces to resolve naming conflicts. There are two solutions to this problem:

- Using a DTD, you can declare the namespace as an attribute, and be sure to qualify all element names with the prefix (if used)—for example, `<!ELEMENT pubs:title (#PCDATA)>`.

- You can opt to use a schema language rather than a DTD for validation. This is an option because XML Schema, as well as other schema languages, is namespace aware (see Chapter 6).

If you opt for the first option, there's some work that needs to be done: `xmlns` has to be declared as an attribute. When declaring the `xmlns` attribute, it's recommended that you fix the namespace value, as in this example:

```
<!ATTLIST publications xmlns CDATA #FIXED
    "http://www.lanw.com/namespaces/pub">
```

The element name must match the QName defined by the element type declaration. According to the Namespace Recommendation, `pubs:name` is the same as `name` (as long as both belong to the same namespace). The prefix is not formally a part of the element type name; it's only a reference to a namespace. However, because DTDs are not namespace aware, `pubs:name` is not the same as `name`. In this case, DTDs do not recognize the prefix as a separate entity; rather, they identify it as a part of the element type name.

Because DTDs do not recognize XML namespace prefixes, if used, the prefix must be defined as a part of the element or attribute name in the corresponding declaration. For example, if you want to use `pubs:title`, you have to use the following element type declaration:

```
<!ELEMENT pubs:title (#PCDATA)>
```

If you choose to use namespace prefixes, you'll have to define all element type and attribute-list declarations accordingly. This makes future modifications rather difficult. If you need to change the prefix used, you'll not only have to modify the XML document, but you'll also have to modify each individual declaration that references the prefix.

One way around this is to use parameter entities. Two steps are required to define parameter entities for a namespace prefix. The first step is to declare two entities to define the prefix and colon:

```
<!ENTITY % pubs_prefix "pubs">
<!ENTITY % colon ":">
```

The next step is to create entity declarations to define the QNames for any element type or attribute-list declarations that will need to use the prefix. Regrettably, you're unable to use the `pubs_prefix` and colon parameter entities directly within the element type or attribute-list declarations. If they're used, the XML parser will add extra space around the entities replacement text:

```
<!ENTITY % pubs_book "%pubs_prefix;%colon;name">
```

Now you're ready to use them within element type or attribute-list declarations.

WARNING   Parameter entities can only be referenced within another declaration if defined and used in the external DTD subset. This means that this solution won't work within an internal DTD subset.

Important XML DTDs

Many XML vocabularies are defined by a DTD. Unfortunately, there's not one site that has taken on the role of a standard DTD repository. There are, however, three Web sites that list some industry standard DTDs:

- www.schema.net
- www.xml.org
- www.biztalk.org

The W3C is another place to look for DTDs. Most XML vocabularies maintained by the W3C, such as Scalable Vector Graphics (SVG) or the Synchronized Multimedia Integration Language (SMIL), already have DTDs defined. The following lists some of the W3C standards that have accompanying DTDs:

- Extensible Hypertext Markup Language (XHTML)

    www.w3.org/TR/xhtml1/DTD/xhtml1-transitional.dtd

    www.w3.org/TR/xhtml1/DTD/xhtml1-strict.dtd

    www.w3.org/TR/xhtml1/DTD/xhtml1-frameset.dtd

- Mathematical Markup Language (MathML)

    www.w3.org/TR/MathML2/appendixa.html#parsing_dtd

- Scalable Vector Graphics (SVG)

    www.w3.org/TR/SVG/svgdtd.html

- Synchronized Multimedia Integration Language (SMIL)

    www.w3.org/TR/smil20/smil-DTD.html

Summary

For over 20 years, DTDs have been used to provide document models for SGML vocabularies. When XML was introduced, DTDs were introduced as an integral part of XML. As its only document modeling language, many legacy XML applications rely on DTDs for structure. Although this book focuses on XML Schema, we took a break and gave you an overview of DTDs in this chapter.

To clearly understand XML Schema, you need to understand XML DTDs. In this chapter, we defined the four important components of DTDs: notations, elements, attributes, and entities. Each component uses a declaration to define properties and characteristics—each with its own set of rules.

Although XML Schema allows you to define restrictions on datatypes, XML DTDs provide limited datatypes. Elements can only be defined as parsed character data, which is fine for document-centric data, but it isn't very useful when you want to designate items such as zip codes, product numbers, and telephone numbers. Attributes, on the other hand, provide some datatyping capabilities. This functionality is still limiting, however. There are only seven different datatypes that you can use to define items such as unique identifies, name tokens, and identifier references. The seven datatypes are CDATA, NMTOKEN(S), ENTITY (ENTITIES), NOTATION, ID, IDREF, and an enumerated value.

Structurally speaking, DTDs allow you to define fairly strict element content models. The design is fairly limiting; however, you can define the hierarchical structure of child elements as well as behavioral characteristics of each child.

DTDs are not going anywhere. Although XML needs a more complex and powerful document modeling language, it also needs a simple alternative. DTDs provide a simple approach that provides the foundation for a document's structure. You'll likely find yourself using XML with legacy applications or if you need to integrate data into an SGML application.

CHAPTER 5

Understanding XML Schema

- Introducing XML Schema terms and concepts

- Understanding XML Schema components

- Introducing XML Schema datatypes

- Understanding how XML namespaces fit in

- Introducing advanced XML Schema concepts

I t took a while for XML Schema to make it to the W3C Recommendation phase—the proposal was under development for over two years. With its release, however, came an essential component meant to help XML reach its full potential. With XML Schema, users can describe a document's structure as well as define datatypes for element and attribute content. Datatyping brings to XML document modeling an added functionality that increases a developer's ability to define electronic commerce systems, and it helps those using databases or needing to manipulate large volumes of data on the Web. In addition to datatypes, XML Schema is namespace aware and allows document authors to take advantage of namespace functionality.

The XML Schema language is defined by three separate specification documents. The first, XML Schema Part 1: Structures (the Structures document), defines constructs for describing the structure of XML documents. The second, XML Schema Part 2: Datatypes (the Datatypes document), defines a set of simple datatypes. And finally, the third, XML Schema Part 0: Primer, provides developers with a primer that explains what schemas are and how to build them.

This chapter is a starting point for understanding XML Schema. It's organized as an introduction to how the W3C's XML Schema language defines the mechanisms that allow developers to define document models and datatypes.

XML Schema Terms and Concepts

The term *schema* is commonly used in the database community and refers to the organization or structure for a database. When this term is used in the XML community, it refers to the structure (or model) of a class of documents. This model describes the hierarchy of elements and allowable content in a valid XML document. In other words, the schema defines constraints for an XML vocabulary. XML Schema is a formal definition for defining a schema for a class of XML documents.

The sheer volume of text involved in defining the XML Schema language can be overwhelming to an XML novice, or even to someone making the move from Document Type Definitions (DTDs) to XML Schema. To completely understand XML Schema, you have to be familiar with at least two specification documents (XML Schema Part 1: Structures and XML Schema Part 2: Datatypes), if not more. The following section is dedicated to introducing you to basic schema constructs and concepts.

Purpose and Requirements

XML is a self-describing language that provides developers with flexibility. However, too much flexibility can sometimes be detrimental for XML applications. In some cases, free-form

XML can be used (an XML document without a defined document model); however, defining strict document models that your XML documents must conform to can make them more useful. When you're designing XML applications, there are instances where validation is a must. For example, schema validation is helpful for organizing data and documents. You'll also find schemas necessary when supporting data interchange between different platform systems and services. These are among many scenarios that served as the primary motivation for a new validation model.

There were several application needs that developers wanted met but were not possible using DTDs. For example, developers wanted to be able to incorporate namespaces into their document models that would then provide better assurance in electronic commerce (e-commerce) transactions and greater security against unauthorized changes to validation rules. In addition, many developers needed the ability to define strict datatypes for attribute and element content to ensure data integrity before attempting to exchange that data.

As defined by the XML Schema Requirements document, the purpose of XML Schema is to provide an inventory of XML markup constructs with which to write schemas. XML Schema is expected to define a document model for a class of XML documents. XML Schema document models are designed to define the usage and relationships of various schema components, such as the following:

- Datatypes
- Elements and their content
- Attributes and their values
- Reusable components and their content
- Notations

In an effort to define a document model, the XML Schema Working Group was asked to address the following issues:

Structural schemas   The working group was expected to describe constructs for defining document models. These constructs are similar to those defined by DTDs in XML 1.0. The working group was expected to move beyond basic DTDs and define greater functionality, such as integration with namespaces and integration of primitive datatypes. These constraints are defined by XML Schema Part 1: Structures.

Primitive datatyping   This working group focused on allowing datatype definitions. This would allow developers to define constraints for integers, dates, and the like. These datatypes would be selected and defined based on experiences with Structured Query Language (SQL) and Java primitives. The constraints are defined by XML Schema Part 2: Datatypes.

Conformance   This working group was expected to define the relationship between the schema and the XML document instances. In addition, it was expected to define obligations for schema-aware processors. These constraints are defined by XML Schema Part I: Structures and XML Schema Part 2: Datatypes.

In the following subsections, we take a look at the design principles, usage scenarios, and requirements defined by the XML Schema Working Group in an effort to guide the creation of XML Schema.

Usage Scenarios

There are many reasons document authors are turning to XML Schema as their modeling language of choice. If you have a schema model, you can ensure that a document author follows it. This is important if you're defining an e-commerce application and you need to make sure that you receive exactly what you expect—nothing more and nothing less—when exchanging data. The schema model will also ensure that datatypes are followed, such as rounding all prices to the second decimal place, for example.

Another common usage for XML Schema is to ensure that your XML data follows the document model before the data is sent to a transformation tool. For example, you may need to exchange data with your parent company, and because your parent company uses a legacy document model, your company uses different labeling (bookPrice versus price). In this case, you would need to transform your data so it conforms to the parent company's document model. However, before sending your XML data to be transformed, you want to be sure that it's valid because one error could throw off the transformation process.

Another possible scenario is that you're asked to maintain a large collection of XML documents and then apply a style sheet to them to define the overall presentation (for example, for a CD-ROM or Web site). In this case, you need to make sure that each document follows the same document model. If one document uses a para instead of a p element (the latter of which the style sheet expects), the desired style may not be applied.

These are only a few scenarios that require the use of XML Schema (or a schema alternative). There are countless other scenarios that would warrant their use. The XML Schema Working Group carefully outlined several usage scenarios that it wanted to account for while designing XML Schema. As defined by the XML Schema Requirements document, the following usage scenarios were used to help shape and develop XML Schema:

- Publishing and syndication
- E-commerce transaction processing
- Supervisory control and data acquisition
- Traditional document authoring/editing governed by schema constraints

- Using schema to help query formulation and optimization
- Open and uniform transfer of data between applications, including databases
- Metadata interchange

Design Principles

The design principles outlined by the XML Schema Requirements document are fairly straightforward. XML Schema documents should be created so they are as follows:

- More expressive than XML DTDs
- Expressed in XML
- Self-describing
- Usable in a wide variety of applications that employ XML
- Straightforwardly usable on the Internet
- Optimized for interoperability
- Simple enough to implement with modest design and runtime resources
- Coordinated with relevant W3C specs, such as XML Information Set, XML Linking Language (XLink), Namespaces in XML, Document Object Model (DOM), the Hypertext Markup Language (HTML), and the Resource Description Framework (RDF) Schema.

Requirements

Before the participants of the XML Schema Working Group sat down to define XML Schema, they identified some key structural and datatype requirements. These requirements are defined in the following lists.

XML Schema has the following structural requirements (as stated by the W3C at www.w3 .org/TR/NOTE-xml-schema-req#Structural):

- Mechanisms for constraining document structure (namespaces, elements, and attributes) and content (datatypes, entities, and notations)
- Mechanisms to enable inheritance for element, attribute, and datatype definitions
- Mechanisms for URI reference to standard semantic understanding of a construct
- Mechanisms for embedded documentation
- Mechanisms for application-specific constraints and descriptions
- Mechanisms for addressing the evolution of schemata
- Mechanisms to enable integration of structural schemas with primitive datatypes

The datatype requirements as stated by the W3C at `www.w3.org/TR/NOTE-xml-schema-req#Datatype` are as follows:

- Provide for primitive datatyping, including byte, date, integer, sequence, and SQL and Java primitive datatypes.

- Define a type system that is adequate for import/export from database systems.

- Distinguish requirements relating to lexical data representation vs. those governing an underlying information set.

- Allow creation of user-derived datatypes, such as datatypes that are derived from an existing datatype and that may constrain some of its properties.

Here are the conformance requirements as stated by the W3C at `www.w3.org/TR/NOTE-xml-schema-req#Conformance`:

- Describe the responsibilities of conforming processors.

- Define the relationship between schemas and XML documents.

- Define the relationship between schema validity and XML validity.

- Define the relationship between schemas and XML DTDs and their information sets.

- Define the relationship among schemas, namespaces, and validity.

- Define a useful XML schema for XML schemas.

Basic Terminology

XML terminology is thrown around, sometimes recklessly, within the XML community. Understanding this terminology will help you understand conversations about XML a little more. Before we introduce XML Schema, you need to be familiar with a few terms defined by XML 1.0 (Second Edition) and the XML Schema languages.

Well Formed

A document is considered to be *well formed* if it meets all the well-formedness constraints defined by XML 1.0 (Second Edition). These constraints are as follows:

- The document contains one or more elements.

- The document consists of exactly one root element (also known as the document element).

- The name of an element's end tag matches the name defined in the start tag.

- No attribute may appear more than once within an element.

- Attribute values cannot contain a left-angle bracket (<).

- Elements delimited with start and end tags must nest properly within each other.

WARNING We have listed only those well-formedness constraints required for a free-form XML document (one without a DTD). There are approximately 10 other well-formedness constraints that define requirements for internal and external DTD subsets. Because we're not concerned with DTDs, we did not define these constraints.

Validity

According to the strict definition of *validity*, as defined by XML 1.0 (Second Edition), an XML document is valid if it has an associated document type (DOCTYPE) declaration and if the document complies with the constraints expressed in it. On a more general level, to say that an XML document is valid is to assume that it adheres to a defined model for a class of XML documents. In terms of XML Schema, *validity* means that an XML document conforms to the constraints expressed by the associated XML Schema documents.

TIP   A valid document does not ensure semantic perfection. Although XML Schema defines stricter constraints on element and attribute content than XML DTDs do, it cannot catch all errors. For example, you might define a price datatype that requires two decimal places. However, you might enter 1200.00 when you meant to enter 12.00 and the schema document wouldn't catch the error.

When dealing with validity, you need to keep in mind that there are three ways an XML document can exist:

- As a free-form, well-formed XML document that does not have DTD or schema associated to it

- As a well-formed and valid XML document, adhering to a DTD or schema

- As a well-formed document that is not valid because it does not conform to the constraints defined by the associated DTD or schema

XML Schema validity encompasses two separate but important functions:

Content model validity   Ensures that the element hierarchy and document structure are correct. Checks to make sure that elements are ordered and nested correctly.

Datatype validity   Ensures that element and attribute content adheres to the defined datatype. A datatype can define a scope for legal values as well as define a base type such as integer, decimal, or string.

Datatype

A broad definition of a *datatype* is a set of data with values that have predefined characteristics. Datatyping provides you with a way of assigning how the value associated with an element or attribute is to be represented, interpreted, or understood. Most datatypes devolve to a collection of so-called *data primitives*, which represent basic types to associate with values, including well-understood primitives such as integer, real number, character, string, and so forth.

According to the Datatypes specification, a datatype consists of a set of distinct values (value space), a set of lexical representations (lexical space), and a set of facets that characterize properties of the value space—individual values or lexical items. Datatypes are defined in greater detail later in this chapter.

Schema Component

A schema is said to be made up of *schema components*, which are the building blocks that make up the abstract data model of the schema. Element and attribute declarations, complex types, simple types, and notations are all examples of schema components.

XML Schema Structures

The XML Schema vocabulary is defined by XML Schema Part 1: Structures. The Structures document is burdened with defining the very nature of XML Schema and all of its components. In addition, the Structures document defines the vocabulary (elements and attributes) that can be used to define schema components that in turn make up the schema. In a nutshell, the Structures specification outlines constructs for defining, describing, and cataloging XML vocabularies for classes of XML documents.

This section is dedicated to introducing you to the Structures specification as well as the concepts defined by it. One of the best ways to understand the XML Schema language is to take a look at it. Therefore, the first thing we do is provide you with a brief example of a simple XML Schema document in Listing 5.1. Then in Listing 5.2, we show you an XML document instance that conforms to the schema defined in Listing 5.1.

Listing 5.1   XML Schema Document

```
<xsd:schema
    xmlns:xsd="http://www.w3.org/2001/XMLSchema"
    elementFormDefault="qualified"
    targetNamespace="http://www.lanw.com/namespaces/pub"
    xmlns="http://www.lanw.com/namespaces/pub">

<xsd:element name="publications">
    <xsd:complexType>
```

```
      <xsd:sequence>
        <xsd:element name="book" maxOccurs="unbounded">
          <xsd:complexType>
            <xsd:sequence>
             <xsd:element name="title" type="xsd:string"/>
             <xsd:element name="author" type="xsd:string"/>
             <xsd:element name="description" type="xsd:string"/>
            </xsd:sequence>
          </xsd:complexType>
        </xsd:element>
      </xsd:sequence>
    </xsd:complexType>
  </xsd:element>
</xsd:schema>
```

Listing 5.2   **XML Document Instance**

```
<?xml version="1.0"?>
<publications>
  <book>
    <title>Mastering XHTML</title>
    <author>Ed Tittel</author>
    <description>Newly revised and updated, Mastering XHTML
      is a complete guide to the markup language that is
      leading the world of Web development from HTML to
      XML.
    </description>
  </book>
  <book>
    <title>Java Developer's Guide to E-Commerce with
      XML and JSP</title>
    <author>William Brogden</author>
    <description>Covering the latest Servlet and JSP APIs
      and the current XML standard, this book guides you through
      all the steps required to build and implement a cohesive,
      dynamic, and profitable site.
    </description>
  </book>
</publications>
```

Before trying to understand each line of Listing 5.1, try to pick out constructs that make sense to you, such as one of the following two lines, for example:

```
<xsd:element name="publications">
<xsd:sequence>
```

Semantically these elements make sense. In Listing 5.1, element uses the name attribute to define an element name (publications). Then, the sequence element is a compositor that tells the processor that the child elements nested with the `sequence` element must occur in that order when used as a part of an XML document instance. There's much more to our example, but from the beginning, you should have some idea of what is going on in the schema document.

As we dive deeper into XML Schema, you'll have to be aware of a few distinctions about commonly used schema components. These distinctions are described in the following sections.

Definitions vs. Declarations

A *definition* describes a complex or simple type that either contains element or attribute declarations or references element or attribute declarations defined elsewhere in the document. A *declaration* defines an element or attribute, specifying the name and datatype for the component.

Here's a definition:

```
<xsd:complexType name="bookType">
  <xsd:sequence>
    <xsd:element name="title" type="xsd:string"/>
    <xsd:element name="author" type="xsd:string"/>
    <xsd:element name="description" type="xsd:string"/>
  </xsd:sequence>
</xsd:complexType>
```

TIP   Type definitions can define complex or simple types. In this case, we provide an example of a complex type definition.

Here's a declaration:

```
<xsd:element name="book">
  <xsd:complexType>
    <xsd:sequence>
      <xsd:element name="title" type="xsd:string"/>
      <xsd:element name="author" type="xsd:string"/>
      <xsd:element name="description" type="xsd:string"/>
    </xsd:sequence>
  </xsd:complexType>
</xsd:element>
```

Simple Type vs. Complex Type

A *simple type definition* constrains the text that is allowed to appear as content for an attribute value or text-only element without attributes. A *complex type definition* constrains the allowable content of elements. Both types govern possible attribute and child elements.

Here's a simple type definition:

```
<xsd:simpleType name="isbnType">
   <xsd:restriction base="xsd:string">
     <xsd:pattern value="[0-9]{10}"/>
   </xsd:restriction>
</xsd:simpleType>
```

Here's a complex type definition:

```
<xsd:complexType name="bookType">
   <xsd:sequence>
     <xsd:element name="title" type="xsd:string"/>
     <xsd:element name="author" type="xsd:string"/>
     <xsd:element name="description" type="xsd:string"/>
   </xsd:sequence>
</xsd:complexType>
```

Global vs. Local

Declarations and definitions can be declared globally or locally. A *globally defined component* is defined as a child of the schema element. A *locally defined component* (also known as *inline*) is defined as a child of another schema component.

A globally defined component would look like this:

```
<xsd:schema
      xmlns:xsd="http://www.w3.org/2001/XMLSchema"
      elementFormDefault="qualified"
      targetNamespace="http://www.lanw.com/namespaces/pub"
      xmlns="http://www.lanw.com/namespaces/pub">

<xsd:element name="publications">
   <xsd:complexType>
     <xsd:sequence>
       <xsd:element ref="book"/>
     </xsd:sequence>
   </xsd:complexType>
</xsd:element>

<xsd:element name="book" maxOccurs="unbounded">
   <xsd:complexType>
     <xsd:sequence>
        <xsd:element ref="title"/>
        <xsd:element ref="author"/>
        <xsd:element ref="description"/>
     </xsd:sequence>
   </xsd:complexType>
</xsd:element>
```

```
<xsd:element name="title" type="xsd:string"/>
<xsd:element name="author" type="xsd:string"/>
<xsd:element name="description" type="xsd:string"/>

</xsd:schema>
```

Here's an example of a locally defined component:

```
<xsd:schema
    xmlns:xsd="http://www.w3.org/2001/XMLSchema"
    elementFormDefault="qualified"
    targetNamespace="http://www.lanw.com/namespaces/pub"
    xmlns="http://www.lanw.com/namespaces/pub">

<xsd:element name="publications">
  <xsd:complexType>
    <xsd:sequence>
      <xsd:element name="book" maxOccurs="unbounded">
        <xsd:complexType>
         <xsd:sequence>
            <xsd:element name="title" type="xsd:string"/>
            <xsd:element name="author" type="xsd:string"/>
            <xsd:element name="description" type="xsd:string"/>
          </xsd:sequence>
        </xsd:complexType>
      </xsd:element>
    </xsd:sequence>
  </xsd:complexType>
</xsd:element>
</xsd:schema>
```

Schema Components

The Structures document defines the various schema components that make up a schema document. These components, such as type definitions and element declarations, make up the heart of the schema document. At the top level of any XML Schema document, a document author may define one of the five following basic schema components:

- Annotation
- Type definition
- Declaration
- Attribute group
- Model group

Figure 5.1 illustrates this relationship.

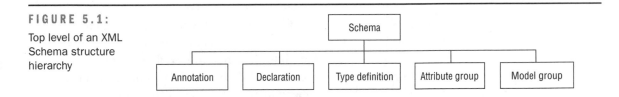

FIGURE 5.1:

Top level of an XML
Schema structure
hierarchy

Type Definitions

Type definitions are at the heart of many schema documents. There are two different types of definitions in addition to two different ways each type definition can be defined. We'll start with the two different types of definitions: simple and complex types (see Figure 5.2). Simple type definitions are used to define attributes and elements that can contain only data. Complex type definitions define content models for elements that may consist of elements and attributes.

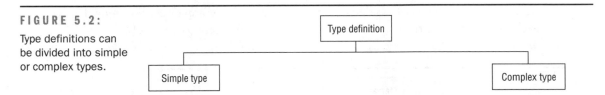

FIGURE 5.2:

Type definitions can
be divided into simple
or complex types.

You can define simple or complex types at the root level, in which case you must name them and reference them later (known as *named types*). Or, you can define them nested within other schema components (known as *anonymous types*). In this case, there's no need to reference them because they're defined as a part of the content model

Simple Types

Simple types are used to define all attributes and elements that contain only text and do not have attributes associated with them. When defining simple types, you can use XML Schema datatypes to restrict the text contained by the element or attribute. For example, you can require an attribute value to be an integer or date. You can even restrict that integer to consist of only three numbers. In addition to specifying simple restrictions on length, you can define patterns and other properties for your datatypes. This is done by using derivation techniques defined by the Structures document.

Simple datatypes are defined by derivation from other datatypes, either predefined and identified by the W3C XML Schema namespace or defined elsewhere in your schema. We discuss this topic in more detail later in this chapter and in Chapter 6.

Complex Types

An element is considered to be a *complex type* if it contains attribute or child elements. Complex types are used to define complex content models. For example, if you want to define a book element that contains `title` and `author` child elements, you would have to use a complex type definition. As with simple types, you can use derivation techniques to manipulate a complex type after it's defined. As the document author, you can restrict or extend a defined content model, or even substitute the model completely. We discuss this topic in more detail later in this chapter and in Chapter 6.

Declarations

The Structures document defines three types of declaration components: element, attribute, and notation. These three declarations are similar to those defined by XML 1.0.

Element Declarations

Element declarations define element names and types and can optionally define identity constraints. XML Schema allows document authors to define complex content models. However, it may take a little time to understand how to construct those models. Figure 5.3 illustrates allowable content within an element declaration.

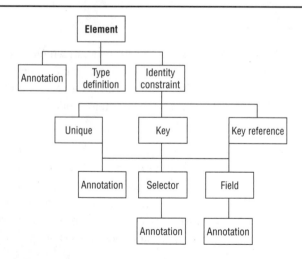

FIGURE 5.3:

Element declaration structure hierarchy

An element declaration may contain one of the following:

- An annotation to provide information for human or application consumption
- A type definition (simple or complex) to define allowable content and/or attributes
- An identity constraint to require uniqueness

There are a few ways you can declare an element:

- The element declaration can be defined globally at the top level of the schema document (see Figure 5.4).

- The element declaration can be defined locally within a complex type definition (see Figure 5.5). The complex type definition can be globally defined or defined within an element declaration.

FIGURE 5.4:

Declaration structure
hierarchy

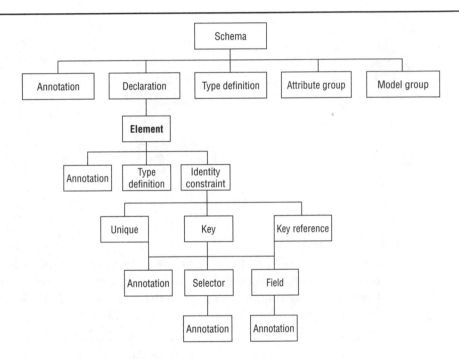

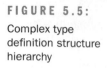

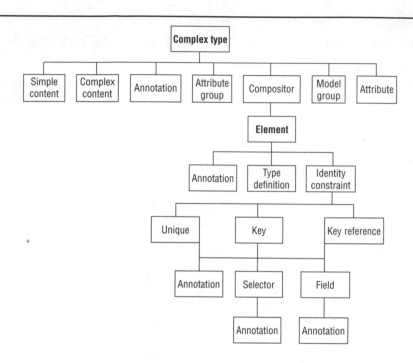

Attribute Declarations

An *attribute declaration* defines the attribute name, the simple type definition that specifies the datatype for the value or a built-in datatype, occurrence information, and (optionally) a default value. Document authors have access to the 44 built-in XML Schema datatypes and can develop their own. There are several ways an attribute declaration can be defined:

- Globally at the top level of the schema document as shown in Figure 5.6 (If declared globally, the declaration would have to be referenced from within a complex type definition.)

- Locally within a complex type definition that is defined globally as shown in Figure 5.7

- Locally within a complex type definition that is defined locally within an element declaration as shown in Figure 5.8

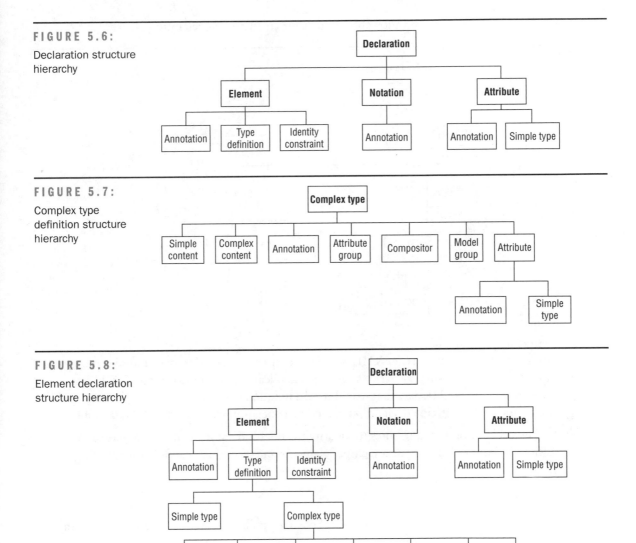

FIGURE 5.6:

Declaration structure hierarchy

FIGURE 5.7:

Complex type definition structure hierarchy

FIGURE 5.8:

Element declaration structure hierarchy

Attribute declarations contain one of the following:

- Annotation for human or application consumption.

- Simple type definition to define the datatype for the attribute. If a simple type is not defined locally, datatype information is defined using an attribute. That attribute value can define a built-in datatype or reference a simple type that is defined globally.

Figure 5.9 illustrates the allowable content for an attribute declaration.

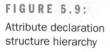

Attribute declaration
structure hierarchy

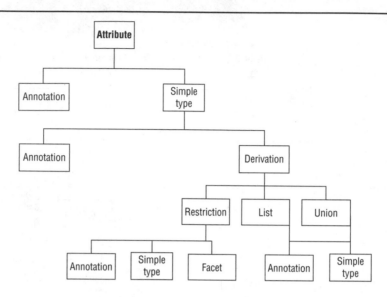

Notation Declarations

Similar to DTD notations, an XML notation component is used to declare links to external non-XML data and then associate an external application to handle the non-XML data. Examples of non-XML data that would need a notation declaration are image, audio, and sound files. The notation declaration is used in association with the NOTATION datatype.

The declaration uses attributes to identify the notation name, identifier, and external application. Notation declarations are empty elements and, therefore, cannot contain other schema components.

Working with Declarations

When you first begin to work with XML Schema, you'll realize that there are several ways you can define declarations:

- You can define elements and attributes as you need them, nesting the declarations within other element declarations (see "Inline Declarations").

- You can define declarations at the top level and reference them from within element declarations (see "Referencing Declarations").

- You can define named type definitions that are then referenced within element or attribute declarations (see "Named Types").

Inline Declarations

Inline declarations are defined locally within other schema components. For example, you can nest an element declaration within a complex type definition, which can also be nested within element declarations. Using this recursive behavior is a common method for defining elements. Attribute declarations can also be defined locally within a complex type definition. Listing 5.3 provides an example of inline element and attribute declarations.

Listing 5.3   An XML Schema Using Inline (or Local) Declarations

```
<xsd:schema
    xmlns:xsd="http://www.w3.org/2001/XMLSchema"
    elementFormDefault="qualified"
    targetNamespace="http://www.lanw.com/namespaces/pub"
    xmlns="http://www.lanw.com/namespaces/pub">

<xsd:element name="publications">
  <xsd:complexType>
    <xsd:sequence>
      <xsd:element name="book" maxOccurs="unbounded">
        <xsd:complexType>
          <xsd:sequence>
            <xsd:element name="title" type="xsd:string"/>
            <xsd:element name="author" type="xsd:string"/>
            <xsd:element name="description" type="xsd:string"/>
          </xsd:sequence>
          <xsd:attribute name="isbn" type="xsd:string"/>
        </xsd:complexType>
      </xsd:element>
    </xsd:sequence>
  </xsd:complexType>
</xsd:element>
</xsd:schema>
```

Referencing Declarations

If you defined your declarations globally, you can then reference them from within other complex or simple type definitions. This modular approach is a popular way to handle complex schema documents. When you modularize your complex definitions, they're easier to maintain and manipulate using derivation and substitution techniques. Listing 5.4 shows an element referencing globally defined declarations.

Listing 5.4   An XML Schema Document Referencing Globally Defined Declarations

```
<xsd:schema
    xmlns:xsd="http://www.w3.org/2001/XMLSchema"
    elementFormDefault="qualified"
    targetNamespace="http://www.lanw.com/namespaces/pub"
    xmlns="http://www.lanw.com/namespaces/pub">
```

```
<xsd:element name="publications">
  <xsd:complexType>
    <xsd:sequence>
      <xsd:element ref="book"/>
    </xsd:sequence>
  </xsd:complexType>
</xsd:element>

<xsd:element name="book" maxOccurs="unbounded">
  <xsd:complexType>
    <xsd:sequence>
      <xsd:element ref="title"/>
      <xsd:element ref="author"/>
      <xsd:element ref="description"/>
    </xsd:sequence>
    <xsd:attribute name="isbn" type="xsd:string"/>
  </xsd:complexType>
</xsd:element>

<xsd:element name="title" type="xsd:string"/>
<xsd:element name="author" type="xsd:string"/>
<xsd:element name="description" type="xsd:string"/>

</xsd:schema>
```

Named Types

The method of defining type definitions globally is also known as defining *named types* (because you name the type definition and then reference it later). Named types can be used like XML DTD parameter entities; you can define a content model or datatype and then reference that definition multiple times in the schema document. This approach is commonly used when working with complex datatypes or if you have content models that will be used more than once in the schema document. Listing 5.5 provides an example of named type definitions.

Listing 5.5   **An XML Schema Document Using Named Type Definitions**

```
<xsd:schema
    xmlns:xsd="http://www.w3.org/2001/XMLSchema"
    elementFormDefault="qualified"
    targetNamespace="http://www.lanw.com/namespaces/pub"
    xmlns="http://www.lanw.com/namespaces/pub">

<xsd:simpleType name="isbnType">
  <xsd:restriction base="xsd:string">
    <xsd:pattern value="[0-9]{10}"/>
  </xsd:restriction>
</xsd:simpleType>
```

```
<xsd:complexType name="pubType">
  <xsd:sequence>
    <xsd:element ref="book"/>
  </xsd:sequence>
</xsd:complexType>

<xsd:complexType name="bookType">
  <xsd:sequence>
    <xsd:element ref="title"/>
    <xsd:element ref="author"/>
    <xsd:element ref="description"/>
  </xsd:sequence>
</xsd:complexType>

<xsd:element name="publications" type="pubType"/>
<xsd:element name="book" type="bookType" maxOccurs="unbounded"/>
<xsd:element name="title" type="xsd:string"/>
<xsd:element name="author" type="xsd:string"/>
<xsd:element name="description" type="xsd:string"/>
</xsd:schema>
```

Attributes and Grouping

An *attribute group definition* is an association between a name and a set of attribute declarations, enabling reuse of the same set in several complex type definitions. This functionality is similar to using XML DTD parameter entities. There are many instances in which several attributes will be used in multiple content models. For example, the XHTML vocabulary allows attributes such as id, style, and title to be used with most of its elements. Instead of redefining these declarations, or even referencing these declarations in multiple places, you can define them as a group. Any content model that uses all three of these attributes can reference that group instead of having to reference each attribute individually, as shown here:

```
<xsd:attributeGroup name="commonAttributes">
  <xsd:attribute name="title" type="xsd:string"/>
  <xsd:attribute name="id" type="xsd:ID"/>
  <xsd:attribute name="style" type="xsd:string"/>
</xsd:attributeGroup>
```

Annotations

Annotations are helpful schema components because they provide formal definitions for information intended for humans or applications. Annotations can be defined at the top level, under the schema element, as well as within almost every other schema component. The annotation component may contain only two different elements (see Figure 5.10).

FIGURE 5.10:
The annotation
structure hierarchy

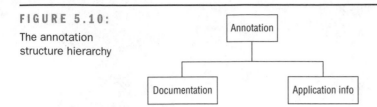

Although XML Schema defines these constructions, the specification does not define how this information should be interpreted. The following example contains an annotation meant for the document author, or any other two-legged creator who would need to use the schema document:

```
<xsd:element name="book">
   <xsd:annotation>
     <xsd:documentation xml:lang="en">
       Child elements content models defined using named
       complex types
     </xsd:documentation>
   </xsd:annotation>
   <xsd:complexType>
     <xsd:sequence>
       <xsd:element name="title" type="titleType"/>
       <xsd:element name="description" type="descType"/>
     </xsd:sequence>
   </xsd:complexType>
</xsd:element>
```

An Overview of XML Schema Datatypes

XML 1.0 DTDs allow for limited facilities for applying datatypes to document content. However, for many XML applications, a higher level of datatype checking is needed. Listing 5.6 defines an XML document that contains several values that would require strictly defined datatypes.

Listing 5.6   **A Schema Document That Uses Multiple Simple Type Definitions**

```
<xsd:schema
     xmlns:xsd="http://www.w3.org/2001/XMLSchema"
     elementFormDefault="qualified"
     targetNamespace="http://www.lanw.com/namespaces/pub"
     xmlns="http://www.lanw.com/namespaces/pub">

   <xsd:simpleType name="yearType">
     <xsd:restriction base="xsd:year"/>
   </xsd:simpleType>
```

```xml
<xsd:simpleType name="isbnType">
  <xsd:restriction base="xsd:string">
    <xsd:pattern value="[0-9]{10}"/>
  </xsd:restriction>
</xsd:simpleType>

<xsd:simpleType name="editionType">
  <xsd:restriction base="xsd:nonNegativeInteger">
    <xsd:minInclusive value="1"/>
    <xsd:maxInclusive value="10"/>
  </xsd:restriction>
</xsd:simpleType>

<xsd:simpleType name="ppType">
  <xsd:restriction base="xsd:nonNegativeInteger">
    <xsd:minInclusive value="1"/>
    <xsd:maxInclusive value="2000"/>
  </xsd:restriction>
</xsd:simpleType>

<xsd:element name="author" type="xsd:string"/>

<xsd:complexType name="authorsType">
  <xsd:sequence>
    <xsd:element ref="author" maxOccurs="5"/>
  </xsd:sequence>
</xsd:complexType>

<xsd:complexType name="bookType">
  <xsd:sequence>
    <xsd:element ref="title"/>
    <xsd:element name="authors" type="authorsType"/>
    <xsd:element name="pubDate" type="pubDateType"/>
    <xsd:element ref="publisher"/>
    <xsd:element name="size" type="sizeType"/>
    <xsd:element name="topics" type="topicsType"/>
    <xsd:element name="errata" type="errataType"
        minOccurs="0"/>
    <xsd:element ref="description"/>
    <xsd:element ref="website" minOccurs="0"/>
  </xsd:sequence>
  <xsd:attribute name="isbn" type="isbnType"
    use="required"/>
  <xsd:attribute name="edition" type="editionType"
    use="required"/>
  <xsd:attribute name="cat" type="xsd:NMTOKENS"
    use="required"/>
  <xsd:attribute name="id" type="xsd:ID"/>
</xsd:complexType>
```

```
<xsd:element name="description" type="xsd:string"/>

<xsd:complexType name="errataType">
  <xsd:attribute name="code" type="xsd:string" use="required"/>
</xsd:complexType>

<xsd:complexType name="pubDateType">
  <xsd:attribute name="year" type="xsd:string" use="required"/>
</xsd:complexType>

<xsd:element name="publications">
  <xsd:complexType>
    <xsd:sequence>
      <xsd:element name="book" type="bookType"
          maxOccurs="unbounded"/>
    </xsd:sequence>
  </xsd:complexType>
</xsd:element>

<xsd:element name="publisher" type="xsd:string"/>

<xsd:complexType name="sizeType">
  <xsd:attribute name="pp" type="ppType" use="required"/>
</xsd:complexType>

<xsd:element name="title" type="xsd:string"/>
<xsd:element name="topic" type="xsd:string"/>

<xsd:complexType name="topicsType">
  <xsd:sequence>
    <xsd:element ref="topic" maxOccurs="unbounded"/>
  </xsd:sequence>
</xsd:complexType>

  <xsd:element name="website" type="xsd:string"/>
</xsd:schema>
```

In Listing 5.6 there are four defined datatypes for the following attributes:

year   We use the built-in year datatype.

isbn   We derived our own datatype that defines a pattern for the ISBN.

edition   We restrict our datatype to only allow for an integer from 1 to 10.

pp   We restrict our datatype to only allow for an integer from 1 to 2000.

If we were to use XML 1.0 DTDs, we would not be able to express the necessary validity constraints for the content in attributes such as isbn, edition, and pp. However, XML Schema Part 2: Datatypes provides document authors with a robust, extensible datatype system for XML.

This datatype system is built on the idea of derivation. Beginning with one basic datatype, others are derived. In total, the Datatypes specification defines 44 built-in datatypes (datatypes that are *built into* the specification) that you can use. In addition to these built-in datatypes, you can derive your own datatypes using techniques such as restricting the datatype, extending the datatype, adding datatypes, or allowing a datatype to consist of a list of datatypes. Each of these techniques (restriction, extension, list, and union) is defined by the Structure document.

When we first think of datatypes, the assumption is that we're only talking about simple types (elements with text only or attribute values); however, the concept of datatyping applies to both simple and complex types. In the Datatypes specification, you'll find a discussion of simple types (working with complex types refers to working with content models and is covered in the Structures specification). One of the easiest ways to begin to understand XML Schema datatypes is to look at their type hierarchy.

Type Hierarchy

The *type hierarchy* identifies all 44 built-in datatypes and provides a road map for how each datatype was derived. All Schema datatypes (simple and complex) are derived from a root type. Figure 5.11 shows a snippet of the schema datatype hierarchy. In the figure, you should notice that a root type, anyType, is defined. When this type is used, it allows any content to appear. From anyType, the type hierarchy branches into simple types and complex types.

FIGURE 5.11:
XML Schema type
hierarchy

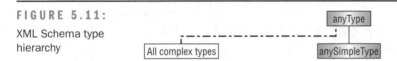

As covered previously in "Type Definitions," elements defined as simple types differ from complex types in that they cannot have child elements or attributes. In addition to text-only elements, attributes are always defined as simple types. On the other hand, only elements that may contain child elements and/or attributes are considered complex types. As you follow the type hierarchy, you'll notice that the root of all simple types is anySimpleType. Like anyType, this datatype can also be used. All 44 built-in simple types are derived from anySimpleType. You should note that each simple type is derived by restriction. None of the simple types is derived by extension; if you were to extend a simple type, you would, in theory, have to add a child element or attribute that contradicts the definition of a simple type.

If you need to use a datatype that is not defined by the specification, you have to derive your own. Figure 5.12 provides you with an illustration of the simple type definition component that is used to derive simple types. The only way to modify a built-in datatype is to restrict its content (restriction), permit a list of possible datatypes (list), or derive a new type that is based on the combination of other datatypes (union).

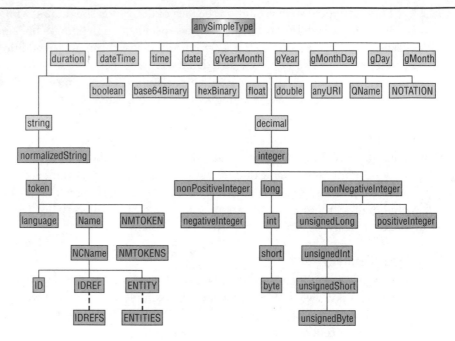

Datatype Properties

Every datatype is defined to consist of an ordered set of three properties: value space, lexical
space, and facets. Each of these helps constrain the possible content.

Value Space

The *value space* defines the allowable set of values for a given datatype. Each value in the
value space has at least one corresponding literal in the lexical space. For example, let's
assume the `street` element in the following markup is defined in a schema as a `string`
datatype (a *string* is a sequence of characters). For a `string` type, the value space and the lexical space are the same. `Main` is part of the value space for a `string` type (it's a group of four
characters) and `Main` is also the lexical representation—the string literal that represents the
value:

```
<!-- instance document -->
<street>Main</street>
```

The `total` element is defined as a `float` datatype in our hypothetical schema document:

```
<!-- instance document -->
<total>135000.00</total>
```

In this case, the representation of `total` is in string format, but the actual value is a numeric value that can be represented in many ways, including 135000, 135000.00, and 13.5E4. These three representations have the same numeric value but are three different literals from the float lexical space.

Lexical Space

The *lexical space* defines the set of valid literals for a given datatype. This is important because many values can oftentimes be expressed by multiple lexical representations. For example, 200.0 can also be expressed as 2.0e2.

Facets

Facets provide a set of defining aspects of a given datatype. If you want to define a minimum or maximum constraint, or if you need to restrict the length of a `string` datatype, you'll have to use a facet. There are two types of facets: fundamental and constraining:

Fundamental facets   Fundamental facets define the datatype that semantically characterizes the facet's value. The fundamental facets are as follows:

`equal`   Values with an `equal` facet can be compared and determined to be equal or not equal. For any values a and b in a value space, only one of the following is true: a=b or a!=b.

`ordered`   Values with an `ordered` facet have an ordered relationship with each other; for example, groups of numbers or groups of words that can be placed in an ordered sequence relative to each other have an `ordered` facet. The `ordered` facet can take the values `false` (not ordered), `partial`, or `total`.

`bounded`   Values with a `bounded` facet fit into a range of values with a specific lower and/or upper limit.

`cardinality`   The number of values in a value space can be `finite` or `countably infinite`.

`numeric`   Values can be classified as `numeric` (value="true") or nonnumeric (value="false").

Constraining (or nonfundamental) facets   *Constraining facets* are optional properties that constrain the permitted values of a datatype. The following are allowable constraining facets:

`length`   A nonnegative integer that defines the number of units of length. The units of length vary depending on the datatype. For example, for a `string` datatype, the units of length are measured in characters, whereas for a `hexBinary` datatype, units are measured in octets (8 bits) of binary data.

`minLength`   A nonnegative integer that defines the minimum number of units of length. The units of length vary depending on the datatype.

`maxLength`   A nonnegative integer that defines the maximum number of units of length. The units of length vary depending on the datatype.

`pattern`   Constrains the lexical space to literals that must match a defined pattern. The value must be a regular expression (defined in Chapter 7). For example, you can define a pattern for ISBNs. Using the `pattern` facet, the value could be defined as follows: `<xsd:pattern value="[0-9]{10}"/>`.

`enumeration`   Constrains the value of the datatype to a defined set of values. For example, an `importance` attribute can be limited to accepting only the value `high` or `low`.

`whiteSpace`   The value of this facet specifies how white space (tabs, line feeds, carriage returns, and spaces) is processed. The `whiteSpace` facet can accept only one of three values: `preserve`, `replace`, or `collapse`.

`maxInclusive`   Defines the inclusive upper bound for a datatype with the ordered property. Because it's inclusive, the defined value may be included within the value space. For example, you can define an upper bound of 100 for an integer datatype; in this case, the datatype may accept any integer less than or equal to 100.

`maxExclusive`   Defines the exclusive upper bound for a datatype with the ordered property. Because it's exclusive, the defined value may *not* be included within the value space. For example, you can define an upper bound of 100 for an integer datatype; in this case, the datatype may accept any integer less than 100.

`minInclusive`   Defines the inclusive lower bound for a datatype with the ordered property. Because it's inclusive, the defined value may be included within the value space. For example, you can define an upper bound of 10 for an integer datatype; in this case, the datatype may accept any integer greater than or equal to 10.

`minExclusive`   Defines the exclusive lower bound for a datatype with the ordered property. Because it's exclusive, the defined value may *not* be included within the value space. For example, you can define an upper bound of 10 for an integer datatype; in this case, the datatype may accept any integer greater than 10.

`totalDigits`   Defines the maximum number of digits allowable for a datatype derived from the `decimal` type.

`fractionDigits`   Defines the maximum number of digits allowable for the fractional part of a datatype derived from the `decimal` type.

Built-In and User-Derived

XML Schema provides document authors with a predefined set of datatypes, known as *built-in datatypes*. In addition to built-in datatypes, document authors may abstract their own datatype based on built-in types. User-derived datatypes provide an essential tool for constraining content for specific purposes.

Built-In

Built-in datatypes are already defined for you by the Datatypes specification. Figure 5.13 provides the type hierarchy for all built-in datatypes.

FIGURE 5.13:

XML Schema type hierarchy for built-in datatypes

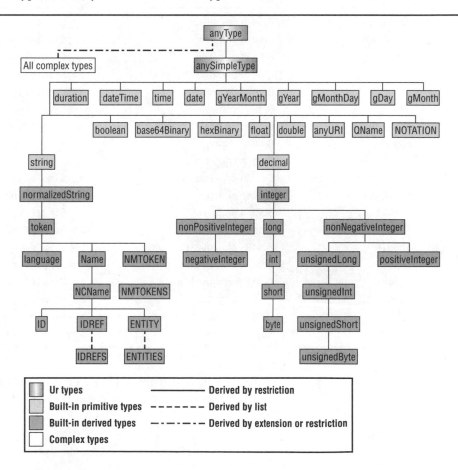

According to the Datatypes document, XML Schema allows for two basic types of built-in datatypes: primitive and derived. Although there's a clear distinction defined by the

Datatypes document, this distinction does not greatly affect how these datatypes may be used:

Primitive Primitive datatypes are those not defined in terms of other datatypes. Primitive datatypes are the basis for all other datatypes. The primitive datatypes are identified in Table 5.1. (See Chapter 7 for a more detailed list of these datatypes.)

TABLE 5.1: Primitive Datatypes

Type Name	Type	Derivation
duration	Built-in primitive	anySimpleType
dateTime	Built-in primitive	anySimpleType
time	Built-in primitive	anySimpleType
date	Built-in primitive	anySimpleType
gYearMonth	Built-in primitive	anySimpleType
gYear	Built-in primitive	anySimpleType
gMonthDay	Built-in primitive	anySimpleType
gDay	Built-in primitive	anySimpleType
gMonth	Built-in primitive	anySimpleType
boolean	Built-in primitive	anySimpleType
base64Binary	Built-in primitive	anySimpleType
hexBinary	Built-in primitive	anySimpleType
float	Built-in primitive	anySimpleType
double	Built-in primitive	anySimpleType
anyURI	Built-in primitive	anySimpleType
QName	Built-in primitive	anySimpleType
NOTATION	Built-in primitive	anySimpleType
string	Built-in primitive	anySimpleType
decimal	Built-in primitive	anySimpleType

Derived A derived datatype is one that is derived from a base type. The derived type inherits its value space from its base type and may also constrain the derived value space to be an explicit subset of the base type's value space. The predefined derived datatypes are identified in Table 5.2.

TABLE 5.2: Derived Datatypes

Type Name	Type	Derivation
integer	Built-in derived	decimal
token	Built-in derived	normalizedString
nonPositiveInteger	Built-in derived	integer
long	Built-in derived	integer
nonNegativeInteger	Built-in derived	integer
language	Built-in derived	token
Name	Built-in derived	token
NMTOKEN	Built-in derived	token
negativeInteger	Built-in derived	nonPositiveInteger
int	Built-in derived	long
unsignedLong	Built-in derived	nonNegativeInteger
positiveInteger	Built-in derived	nonNegativeInteger
NCName	Built-in derived	Name
NMTOKENS	Built-in derived	NMTOKEN
short	Built-in derived	int
unsignedInt	Built-in derived	unsignedLong
ID	Built-in derived	NCName
IDREF	Built-in derived	NCName
ENTITY	Built-in derived	NCName
byte	Built-in derived	short
unsignedShort	Built-in derived	unsignedInt
IDREFS	Built-in derived	IDREF
ENTITIES	Built-in derived	ENTITY
unsignedByte	Built-in derived	unsignedShort

User-Derived

Whereas the XML Schema specification offers you 44 datatypes, there will be occasions when you'll need to define your own datatypes. The only way to define your own datatype is to derive it using a predefined datatype as the base. There are three different ways a datatype can be derived:

Restriction   Uses facets to restrict the allowable content.

List   Derived datatype is a list of white-space-separated values of the base datatype.

Union   There are two or more base datatypes, and the value space–derived datatype is formed from the union of the value spaces of the base types.

Deriving datatypes is covered in more detail in the following section and in Chapter 7.

Datatype Categories

Datatypes in XML Schema are categorized into three groups called *characterization dichotomies*:

- Atomic vs. list vs. union datatypes
- Primitive vs. derived datatypes
- Built-in vs. user-derived datatypes

The definitions of these datatypes are specific to XML Schema and do not necessarily correspond exactly to the definition of these types in any other particular programming language.

Atomic

Atomic datatypes have a value that is considered indivisible and cannot be further broken down into other components. Atomic datatypes can be primitive or derived. All primitive datatypes are atomic.

List

List datatypes make up a group of defined, finite-length sequences of atomic values. The atomic datatype included in the definition of a list datatype is known as the `itemType` of that specific list datatype. List datatypes are always derived.

Union

Union datatypes are always derived from atomic or list datatypes and include the value spaces and lexical spaces of all the datatypes used to derive the union datatype. The datatypes in the group of datatypes included in a union datatype are known as the `memberTypes` of that specific union datatype.

We are now at the end of our introduction to XML Schema datatypes; however, there's much more to learn. Chapter 7 is dedicated to datatypes.

The Role of Namespaces

One of the more notable advantages to using XML Schema is that it's namespace aware. To take advantage of namespaces and XML Schema, you first need to understand the role of namespaces in XML.

Why Namespaces?

Namespaces were defined after XML 1.0 was formally presented to the public. After XML 1.0 was completed, the W3C set out to resolve a few problems, one of which dealt with naming conflicts. To understand the significance of this problem, first think about the future of the Web.

Shortly after the W3C introduced XML 1.0, an entire family of languages began to pop up, such as Mathematical Markup Language (MathML), Synchronized Multimedia Integration Language (SMIL), Scalable Vector Graphics (SVG), XLink, XForms, and the Extensible Hypertext Markup Language (XHTML). Instead of relying on one language to bear the burden of communicating on the Web, the idea was to present many languages that could work together. If functions were modularized, each language could do what it does best. The problem arises when a developer needs to use multiple vocabularies within the same application. For example, one might need to use SVG, SMIL, XHTML, and XForms for an interactive Web site. When mixing vocabularies, you have to have a way to distinguish between element types. Take the following example:

```
<html>
    <head>
        <title>Book List</title>
    </head>
    <body>
      <publications>
        <book>
          <title>Mastering XHTML</title>
          <author>Ed Tittel</author>
        </book>
        <book>
          <title>Java Developer's Guide to E-Commerce
           with XML and JSP</title>
          <author>William Brogden</author>
        </book>
      </publications>
    </body>
</html>
```

In this example, there's no way to distinguish between the two element types of the same name (`title`), even though they are semantically different.

A namespace solves this problem, providing a unique identifier for a collection of elements and/or attributes. The interesting thing about namespaces is that they're only symbolic references (the URL used typically doesn't point to anything specific). Listing 5.7 uses namespaces to resolve the name conflict in the preceding example.

Listing 5.7   An XML Document That Uses Default Namespaces

```
<html xmlns="http://www.w3.org/1999/xhtml">
    <head>
      <title>Book List</title>
    </head>
    <body>
      <publications xmlns="http://www.lanw.com/namespaces/pub">
```

```
      <book>
        <title>Mastering XHTML</title>
        <author>Ed Tittel</author>
      </book>
      <book>
        <title>Java Developer's Guide to E-Commerce
         with XML and JSP</title>
        <author>William Brogden</author>
      </book>
    </publications>
  </body>
</html>
```

All of the text in bold belongs to the publications namespace, http://www.lanw.com/ namespaces/pub, whereas all the XHTML elements belong to the XHTML namespace, http://www.w3.org/1999/xhtml.

Namespace URLs

Namespaces can confuse XML novices because the namespace names are URLs and therefore often mistaken for a Web address that points to some resource. However, XML namespace names are URLs that don't necessarily have to point to anything. Most times they don't, in fact. For example, if you visit the XSLT namespace, you would find a document that contains a single sentence: "This is the XSLT namespace." The unique identifier is meant to be symbolic; therefore, there's no need for a document to be defined. To help out those who are first learning about XML namespaces, the W3C commonly defines a resource for the namespace name; however, this is not required by the XML Namespace recommendation. URLs were selected for namespace names because they contain domain names that can work globally across the Internet and they are unique.

Declaring Namespaces

To declare a namespace, you need to be aware of the three possible parts of a namespace declaration:

- xmlns identifies the value as an XML namespace. This is required to declare a namespace and can be attached to any XML element.

- :*prefix* identifies a namespace prefix. It (including the colon) is only used if you're declaring a namespace prefix. If it's used, any element found in the document that uses the prefix (*prefix*:*element*) is then assumed to fall under the scope of the declared namespace.

- *namespaceURI* is the unique identifier. The value does not have to point to a Web resource; it's only a symbolic identifier. The value is required and must be defined within single or double quotation marks.

There are two different ways you can define a namespace:

Default namespace Defines a namespace using the `xmlns` attribute without a prefix, and all child elements are assumed to belong to the defined namespace.

Prefixed namespace Defines a namespace using the `xmlns` attribute with a prefix. When the prefix is attached to an element, it's assumed to belong to that namespace.

Listing 5.8 provides both an example of namespace defaulting and an example of namespace scoping (using a prefixed namespace).

Listing 5.8   **An XML Document That Uses Prefixed Namespaces**

```
<html xmlns="http://www.w3.org/1999/xhtml">
   <head>
     <title>Book List</title>
   </head>
   <body>
     <pub:publications
     xmlns:pub="http://www.lanw.com/namespaces/pub">
       <pub:book>
         <pub:title>Mastering XHTML</pub:title>
         <pub:author>Ed Tittel</pub:author>
       </pub:book>
       <pub:book>
         <pub:title>Java Developer's Guide to E-Commerce
           with XML and JSP</pub:title>
         <pub:author>William Brogden</pub:author>
       </pub:book>
     </pub:publications>
   </body>
</html>
```

XML Schema Namespaces

After you understand the basics behind XML namespaces, you're ready to face the three namespaces defined by XML Schema:

- XML Schema namespace is used for W3C XML Schema elements. You can define this namespace as a default namespace or with a prefix. The namespace URI is `http://www.w3.org/2001/XMLSchema`.

- XML Schema Datatype namespace is used to define built-in datatypes. The XML Schema namespace (`http://www.w3.org/2001/XMLSchema`) also defines built-in datatypes; therefore, it's not necessary to define it if you have defined the XML Schema namespace. The namespace URI is `http://www.w3.org/2001/XMLSchema-datatypes`.

- XML Schema instance namespace is used for W3C XML Schema attributes used in XML instance documents. The namespace is used to introduce `xsi:type`, `xsi:nil`, `xsi:schemaLocation`, and `xsi:noNamespaceSchemaLocation` attributes in instance documents. This namespace should be defined with an `xsi` prefix. The namespace URI is `http://www.w3.org/2001/XMLSchema-instance`.

The XML Schema namespace must be defined for a schema document. In addition, the XML Schema namespace must be used in the XML document instance when associating the schema. You'll learn more about these namespaces in Chapter 6.

Targeting Namespaces with XML Schema

If you want to use a namespace with your document instances, you have to define the namespace in your XML Schema document. To do this, you have to define a target namespace (`targetNamespace="http://www.yournamespace.com"`). The target namespace identifies the namespace to which the corresponding XML document should adhere. The following XML document uses a namespace (in bold):

```
<?xml version="1.0"?>
<publications xmlns="http://www.lanw.com/namespaces/pub">
   <book>
      <title>Mastering XHTML</title>
      <author>Ed Tittel</author>
   </book>
   <book>
      <title>Java Developer's Guide to E-Commerce with
        XML and JSP</title>
      <author>William Brogden</author>
   </book>
</publications>
```

XML Schema allows you to define a target namespace for any document that is to conform to the schema:

```
<schema targetNamespace="http://www.lanw.com/namespaces/pub">
...
</schema>
```

Identity Constraints

Whereas XML 1.0 allowed document authors to define an ID datatype for attribute values that, in turn, required the value to be unique to a document instance, XML Schema offers a more flexible and powerful mechanism for defining identity constraints. There are three different ways to define identity constraints using XML Schema:

- You can use the key and keyref elements to define relationships between elements. These are similar to the ID/IDREF connection; however, keys can be unique to a defined element set. XML Schema uses XPath expressions to identify an element set to which the key is required to be unique.

- You can use the unique element to specify that any attribute or element value must be unique within a defined scope. The unique element may contain a selector or field element. The selector element defines the element set for the uniqueness constraint. The field element is used to identify the attribute or element field relative to each selected element that has to be unique within the scope of the set of selected elements. Both the selector and field elements use an xpath attribute that contains an XPath expression.

- You can use an ID datatype. The ID datatype requires that the value be unique to the entire document instance. The IDREF datatype can be used to reference a defined ID.

To take advantage of XML Schema identity constraints, you need to understand the XPath language. XPath is a language that allows you to address into an XML document structure using a tree representation of your data—similar to the DOM. The tree representation of your data consists of nodes that you can then navigate. Figure 5.14 is a simplified tree representation of the XML document in Listing 5.9.

Listing 5.9 **The XML Document Used to Show a Simplified Tree Representation in Figure 5.14**

```
<review set="1">
  <question value="1">
    <body>Do you like cats?</body>
    <options>
      <option value="a">yes</option>
      <option value="b">no</option>
      <option value="c">maybe</option>
    </options>
  </question>
  <question value="1">
    <body>Do you like dogs?</body>
    <options>
      <option value="a">yes</option>
      <option value="b">no</option>
      <option value="c">maybe</option>
    </options>
  </question>
</review>
```

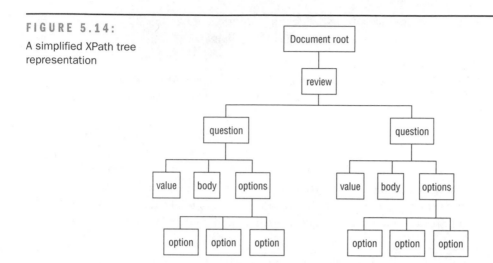

A simplified XPath tree representation

If you wanted to require that the value attribute is unique for every option element, you could use XPath to identify the options node set, in essence, requiring that the value of the value attribute be unique within each question element. This is a helpful tool for document modeling. With DTDs, you could only define identity constraints using IDs that had to be unique to the entire document instance, which doesn't give you much flexibility. By using XPath, you're able to identify node sets and therefore work on a modular level.

TIP   We take a closer look at XPath and identity constraints in Chapter 6.

Unique Values

In almost every document model, there's a need for identity constraints. Unique identifiers are found everywhere in data: ISBNs, Social Security numbers, product codes, and customer IDs. By enforcing unique values, you're able to check data integrity before sending that data to an application. If you're familiar with XML 1.0, you already know how to use an ID datatype. Although XML Schema supports this datatype (which is helpful for backward compatibility), it offers a more flexible model for defining uniqueness.

There are several disadvantages to using XML 1.0 IDs. To begin with, they only apply to attribute values. There's no way to define an element value as unique using XML 1.0. Second, the attribute value must then be unique to the entire document, and therefore, only one set of unique values is allowed, which would not be helpful when designing a document model for Listing 5.9. And finally, one of the most unnerving disadvantages is that XML 1.0

IDs cannot begin with a number and they cannot contain spaces. Because most unique identifiers begin with numbers, this last limitation was a hard one to swallow.

Using XML Schema identity constraints, you gain flexibility. For example, both element and attribute values can be defined to be unique. In addition, that unique value can be any datatype and therefore can begin with a number. And, as you know, the numbers don't have to be unique to the document instance. Instead, you can define a scope for unique value.

The unique element is used to require an element or attribute's value to be unique within a specified range. When using the unique element, you use XPath to identify the range (publications/book).

```
<xsd:unique name="bookID">
    <xsd:selector xpath="publications/book"/>
    <xsd:field xpath="@id"/>
</xsd:unique>
```

Key and Key References

Defining relationships is an important functionality, especially for those working with relational databases. XML Schema allows you to represent relationships using key and keyRef elements. These elements can also take advantage of XPath, thereby allowing you to specify the scope of a uniqueness constraint. The key element functions much like the unique element. The following shows how the key element is used:

```
<xsd:key name="bookKey">
    <xsd:selector xpath="publications/book"/>
    <xsd:field xpath="@id"/>
</xsd:key>

<xsd:keyref name="bookRef" refer="bookKey">
    <xsd:selector xpath="publications/review"/>
    <xsd:field xpath="book/@bookRef"/>
</xsd:keyref>
```

About Derivation and Substitution

XML Schema gets interesting when you're able to manipulate content models to tailor a particular application. Using derivation and substitution, you can redefine, append, and restrict content models to suit your needs. For example, you can add elements or attributes using the extension element, or you can eliminate elements using the restriction element. Derivation techniques apply to both simple and complex types.

Derivation

XML Schema introduces derivation to XML validation. *Derivation* allows you to derive new types by restricting or extending the type definition. Extension is only allowed for complex types.

With this new functionality, document authors are able to derive new types based on previously created types or ones that someone else may have defined. Deriving new types, whether they be simple or complex, is an improvement over having to use the static content models you could create using XML DTDs. XML Schema allows you to derive new complex and simple types.

Complex Types

You can constrain the element and/or attribute declarations of an existing type and therefore derive new content models based on previously defined models. The only two elements allowed for this type of derivation are `restriction` and `extension`. The `restriction` element contains an attribute that identifies the base type and contains the new content model definitions. In the following example, we have restricted a base type (`bookType`) and redefined its content model to only allow for one `title` element and one `author` element:

```
<xsd:complexType name="newBookType">
  <xsd:complexContent>
    <xsd:restriction base="bookType">
      <xsd:sequence>
        <xsd:element name="title" type="xsd:string"/>
        <xsd:element name="author" type="xsd:string"/>
      </xsd:sequence>
    </xsd:restriction>
  </xsd:complexContent>
</xsd:complexType>
```

Restriction is not the only way to derive new complex types; you can also extend content models using the `extension` element. Using the `extension` element, you can add an element and/or elements to an existing content model. In the following example, we add a `description` element and an `isbn` element:

```
<xsd:complexType name="newBookType">
  <xsd:complexContent>
    <xsd:extension base="bookType">
      <xsd:sequence>
        <xsd:element name="description" type="xsd:string"/>
        <xsd:element name="isbn" type="xsd:string"/>
      </xsd:sequence>
    </xsd:extension>
  </xsd:complexContent>
</xsd:complexType>
```

Simple Types

As with complex types, you can use derivation techniques to manipulate simple types. Using derivation, you can derive new simple types that serve as datatypes for content. Deriving simple types is not exactly the same as deriving complex types. One limitation is that you cannot extend a simple type. When deriving simple types, you can use one of the following elements: `restriction`, `list`, or `union`. Listing 5.10 provides an example of several derived simple types.

Listing 5.10   An XML Schema Document Using Derivation

```
<xsd:schema
    xmlns:xsd="http://www.w3.org/2001/XMLSchema"
    elementFormDefault="qualified"
    targetNamespace="http://www.lanw.com/namespaces/pub"
    xmlns="http://www.lanw.com/namespaces/pub">

  <xsd:simpleType name="yearType">
    <xsd:restriction base="xsd:year"/>
  </xsd:simpleType>

  <xsd:simpleType name="isbnType">
    <xsd:restriction base="xsd:string">
      <xsd:pattern value="[0-9]{10}"/>
    </xsd:restriction>
  </xsd:simpleType>

  <xsd:simpleType name="editionType">
    <xsd:restriction base="xsd:nonNegativeInteger">
      <xsd:minInclusive value="1"/>
      <xsd:maxInclusive value="10"/>
    </xsd:restriction>
  </xsd:simpleType>

  <xsd:simpleType name="ppType">
    <xsd:restriction base="xsd:nonNegativeInteger">
      <xsd:minInclusive value="1"/>
      <xsd:maxInclusive value="2000"/>
    </xsd:restriction>
  </xsd:simpleType>

  <xsd:element name="author" type="xsd:string"/>

  <xsd:complexType name="authorsType">
    <xsd:sequence>
      <xsd:element ref="author" maxOccurs="5"/>
    </xsd:sequence>
  </xsd:complexType>
```

```xsd
<xsd:complexType name="bookType">
  <xsd:sequence>
    <xsd:element ref="title"/>
    <xsd:element name="authors" type="authorsType"/>
    <xsd:element name="pubDate" type="pubDateType"/>
    <xsd:element ref="publisher"/>
    <xsd:element name="size" type="sizeType"/>
    <xsd:element name="topics" type="topicsType"/>
    <xsd:element name="errata" type="errataType"
      minOccurs="0"/>
    <xsd:element ref="description"/>
    <xsd:element ref="website" minOccurs="0"/>
  </xsd:sequence>
  <xsd:attribute name="isbn" type="isbnType"
    use="required"/>
  <xsd:attribute name="edition" type="editionType"
    use="required"/>
  <xsd:attribute name="cat" type="xsd:NMTOKENS"
    use="required"/>
  <xsd:attribute name="id" type="xsd:ID"/>
</xsd:complexType>

<xsd:element name="description" type="xsd:string"/>

<xsd:complexType name="errataType">
  <xsd:attribute name="code" type="xsd:string" use="required"/>
</xsd:complexType>

<xsd:complexType name="pubDateType">
  <xsd:attribute name="year" type="xsd:string" use="required"/>
</xsd:complexType>

<xsd:element name="publications">
  <xsd:complexType>
    <xsd:sequence>
      <xsd:element name="book" type="bookType"
        maxOccurs="unbounded"/>
    </xsd:sequence>
  </xsd:complexType>
</xsd:element>

<xsd:element name="publisher" type="xsd:string"/>

<xsd:complexType name="sizeType">
  <xsd:attribute name="pp" type="ppType" use="required"/>
</xsd:complexType>

<xsd:element name="title" type="xsd:string"/>
<xsd:element name="topic" type="xsd:string"/>

<xsd:complexType name="topicsType">
```

```
    <xsd:sequence>
      <xsd:element ref="topic" maxOccurs="unbounded"/>
    </xsd:sequence>
  </xsd:complexType>

  <xsd:element name="website" type="xsd:string"/>
</xsd:schema>
```

Restriction

The `restriction` element creates a datatype that is a subset of an existing type. You can apply a restriction using facets that limit properties of a datatype. For example, you can use the `maxLength` or `minLength` facets to define the maximum and minimum number of characters allowed for a given datatype. Each datatype has a specifically defined list of allowable facets. For example, you can't use the same facets for `integer` and `string` datatypes (facets are discussed in Chapter 7).

In the following example, we use the `pattern` facet to define the allowable pattern for an ISBN:

```
<xsd:simpleType name="isbnType">
  <xsd:restriction base="xsd:string">
    <xsd:pattern value="[0-9]{10}"/>
  </xsd:restriction>
</xsd:simpleType>
```

List

The `list` element creates a datatype that consists of a white-space-separated list of values. The `list` element uses an attribute to define the base type that is to be used for the list:

```
<xsd:simpleType name="isbnType">
  <xsd:restriction base="xsd:string">
    <xsd:pattern value="[0-9]{10}"/>
  </xsd:restriction>
</xsd:simpleType>

<xsd:simpleType name="isbnTypeList">
  <xsd:list itemType="isbnType"/>
</xsd:simpleType>
```

Union

The `union` element creates a datatype that is derived from multiple datatypes. The `union` element uses an attribute to define all base types participating in the union. Any of the defined base datatypes are allowed to be used. In the following example, the `oneType` and `twoType` datatypes are allowed:

```
<xsd:simpleType name="exampleTypeUnion">
  <xsd:union memberTypes="oneType twoType"/>
</xsd:simpleType>
```

Substitution

XML Schema supports substitution mechanisms that allow one group of elements to be replaced by another group of elements. This is especially helpful when you're working with a predefined XML Schema document. There are many instances in which you might want to redefine a content model, or even substitute the entire model with one of your own. Substitution is only defined for complex types. Listing 5.11 defines a schema document, but then at the end of that document, it defines a substitution group for the magType and bookType complex type definitions. The purpose of this was to define a general content model (title, author, and description) that can be used for both for the time being. Later, we can remove the substitution group and work with the more complex models.

Listing 5.11	An XML Schema Document Using Derivation

```
<xsd:schema
    xmlns:xsd="http://www.w3.org/2001/XMLSchema"
    elementFormDefault="qualified"
    targetNamespace="http://www.lanw.com/namespaces/pub"
    xmlns="http://www.lanw.com/namespaces/pub">

    <xsd:simpleType name="yearType">
      <xsd:restriction base="xsd:year"/>
    </xsd:simpleType>

    <xsd:simpleType name="isbnType">
      <xsd:restriction base="xsd:string">
        <xsd:pattern value="[0-9]{10}"/>
      </xsd:restriction>
    </xsd:simpleType>

    <xsd:simpleType name="editionType">
      <xsd:restriction base="xsd:nonNegativeInteger">
        <xsd:minInclusive value="1"/>
        <xsd:maxInclusive value="10"/>
      </xsd:restriction>
    </xsd:simpleType>

    <xsd:simpleType name="ppType">
      <xsd:restriction base="xsd:nonNegativeInteger">
        <xsd:minInclusive value="1"/>
        <xsd:maxInclusive value="2000"/>
      </xsd:restriction>
    </xsd:simpleType>

    <xsd:element name="author" type="xsd:string"/>

    <xsd:complexType name="authorsType">
      <xsd:sequence>
```

```xsd
      <xsd:element ref="author" maxOccurs="5"/>
    </xsd:sequence>
</xsd:complexType>

<xsd:complexType name="bookType">
  <xsd:sequence>
    <xsd:element ref="title"/>
    <xsd:element name="authors" type="authorsType"/>
    <xsd:element name="pubDate" type="pubDateType"/>
    <xsd:element ref="publisher"/>
    <xsd:element name="size" type="sizeType"/>
    <xsd:element name="topics" type="topicsType"/>
    <xsd:element name="errata" type="errataType"
      minOccurs="0"/>
    <xsd:element ref="description"/>
    <xsd:element ref="website" minOccurs="0"/>
  </xsd:sequence>
  <xsd:attribute name="isbn" type="isbnType"
    use="required"/>
  <xsd:attribute name="edition" type="editionType"
    use="required"/>
  <xsd:attribute name="cat" type="xsd:NMTOKENS"
    use="required"/>
  <xsd:attribute name="id" type="xsd:ID"/>
</xsd:complexType>

<xsd:complexType name="magType">
  <xsd:sequence>
    <xsd:element ref="title"/>
    <xsd:element name="authors" type="authorsType"/>
    <xsd:element name="pubDate" type="pubDateType"/>
    <xsd:element name="size" type="sizeType"/>
    <xsd:element name="topics" type="topicsType"/>
    <xsd:element ref="description"/>
  </xsd:sequence>
  <xsd:attribute name="publication" type="xsd:string"
    use="required"/>
  <xsd:attribute name="edition" type="editionType"
    use="required"/>
  <xsd:attribute name="cat" type="xsd:NMTOKENS"
    use="required"/>
  <xsd:attribute name="id" type="xsd:ID"/>
</xsd:complexType>

<xsd:element name="description" type="xsd:string"/>

<xsd:complexType name="errataType">
  <xsd:attribute name="code" type="xsd:string"
    use="required"/>
</xsd:complexType>
```

```xml
<xsd:complexType name="pubDateType">
  <xsd:attribute name="year" type="xsd:string"
    use="required"/>
</xsd:complexType>

<xsd:element name="publications">
  <xsd:complexType>
    <xsd:sequence>
      <xsd:element name="book" type="bookType"
        maxOccurs="unbounded"/>
      <xsd:element name="mag" type="magType"
        maxOccurs="unbounded"/>
    </xsd:sequence>
  </xsd:complexType>
</xsd:element>

<xsd:element name="publisher" type="xsd:string"/>

<xsd:complexType name="sizeType">
  <xsd:attribute name="pp" type="ppType" use="required"/>
</xsd:complexType>

<xsd:element name="title" type="xsd:string"/>
<xsd:element name="topic" type="xsd:string"/>

<xsd:complexType name="topicsType">
  <xsd:sequence>
    <xsd:element ref="topic" maxOccurs="unbounded"/>
  </xsd:sequence>
</xsd:complexType>

<xsd:element name="website" type="xsd:string"/>

<xsd:element name="book" type="bookType"
  substitutionGroup="genType"/>
<xsd:element name="mag" type="magType"
  substitutionGroup="genType"/>

<xsd:complexType name="genType">
  <xsd:sequence>
    <xsd:element ref="title"/>
    <xsd:element ref="author"/>
    <xsd:element ref="description"/>
  </xsd:sequence>
</xsd:complexType>
</xsd:schema>
```

Summary

XML Schema brings powerful validation to the world of XML. There are many reasons one would want to use XML Schema rather than an alternative validation tool. However, this chapter doesn't focus on why you might want to use XML Schema; it assumes you already do. In this chapter, we focus on the basic tenets of the language. There are a handful of constructs that developers must be familiar with if they want to take advantage of XML Schema. Once a developer has the basic concepts down (e.g., the difference between simple and complex types, how to derive simple and complex types, etc.), the rest will fall into place.

Understanding the XML Schema vocabulary is not the difficult part of mastering the language—it's conceptually understanding the language's functionality. There are some basic tenets that you must understand, and before you move on to the next chapter, please take a few moments to make sure that you have an understanding of the primary ones.

The XML Schema language is broken into two separate documents. The first one defines the XML Schema components. These components are introduced using the schema vocabulary. For example, the `element` element declares an element, and the `attribute` element declares an attribute. There are a variety of schema components defined, the most basic of which are listed here:

Type definitions   You can define two types of definitions: simple and complex.

Declarations   There are three types of declarations that you can define; these include element, attribute, and notation.

Annotations   You can add comments intended for humans or applications.

The XML Schema Datatypes document is the second part of the XML Schema language, and it defines the built-in datatypes that are predefined and ready for use. These datatypes serve as base types for any datatypes you might want to derive on your own. Although it's helpful to have 44 predefined datatypes, you'll undoubtedly want to derive your own. By using derivation, you can define patterns and limitations for your datatypes that will ensure data integrity and safeguard against errors. There are three ways you can derive datatypes: restriction, union, and list.

Not only can you derive simple types, but you can also use derivation to manipulate complex content models. Both derivation and substitution provide the document author with the flexibility to tailor any schema for a particular application. This is a great advantage that XML Schema enjoys over XML DTDs.

This is by no means the last stop. The next step to understanding the XML Schema language is to read Chapters 6 and 7. These two chapters make up the heart of the book because they define the XML Schema components and datatypes. With a firm understanding of the basic schema concepts, you're now ready for them.

CHAPTER 6

Understanding Schemas: Structures and Components

- Understanding the abstract data model

- Identifying the 13 schema components

- Working with element and attribute declarations

- Creating complex and simple type definitions

- Deriving simple type definitions

- Requiring uniqueness

- Examining the role of XML namespaces

This chapter examines XML Schema components and structures. The XML Schema Structures recommendation is defined in terms of an abstract data model that is based on information items defined by the XML Information Set (Infoset) recommendation. By identifying information items, the abstract data model has identified 13 different schema components. These components provide the foundation for the XML Schema vocabulary.

The rest of the vocabulary can be defined in terms of what can be contained within each schema component. There are several optional schema elements that can be used within key components. For example, within the annotation component, you can use a `documentation` or `appInfo` element.

In this chapter, we examine the abstract data model—components and all—and then move on to examine practical uses of the data model. In all, this chapter covers the bulk of the XML Schema Part 1: Structures Recommendation.

The Abstract Data Model

The concepts and definitions within XML Schema Part 1: Structures are defined in terms of information items (as defined by the XML Information Set, or Infoset). The Infoset provides a consistent set of definitions for use in other specifications, such as XML Schema, that need to refer to the information in a well-formed XML document. The Infoset identifies items that are deemed useful for other specifications as well as items that have an expected usefulness in future specifications.

In essence, XML Schema can be described in terms of an abstract data model based on the concept of information items. This is helpful for both applications and developers. By using the Infoset, XML Schema can strictly define the information that must be made available to XML Schema processors. This conceptual model is also a helpful tool for learning the XML Schema language.

The abstract data model is made up of 13 schema components, each of which has its own set of properties, validation rules, constraints on representation, and constraints on the components themselves.

Primary Schema Components

The primary schema components make up the bulk of the schema model. As you might guess, the primary components are based on type definitions and declarations, which are as follows:

- Simple type definitions
- Complex type definitions

- Attribute declarations
- Element declarations

Secondary Schema Components

The secondary schema components work with the primary components. Their roles span from allowing for reusable models to defining uniqueness. The following are the secondary schema components:

- Attribute group definitions
- Identity-constraint definitions
- Model group definitions
- Notation declarations

Helper Schema Components

Finally, the helper schema components are necessary to assist many of the primary schema components. To have a schema model, you must define declarations. The helper schema components are used to help the primary and secondary components. For example, annotations can be used to provide additional information about an element content model. You can also use wildcards as placeholders within an element content model. The helper schema components are as follows:

- Annotations
- Model groups
- Particles
- Wildcards
- Attribute uses

Schema Constraints and Validation Rules

XML allows for two different types of constraints for an XML document. The first type of constraint, *well-formedness*, is required for every XML document. Because XML Schema is an XML application, it too has to abide by well-formedness constraints. The second type of constraint, *validity*, identifies rules defined by a DTD. The XML Schema language has both a schema document and a DTD that govern XML Schema validity constraints.

XML Schema Constraints and Rules

The XML Schema specification provides four different types of normative statements about schema components, including statements about their representations in XML and their contribution to the validation of information items in the document instance:

Schema Component Constraint   Defines basic constraints on the schema components themselves. These constraints define conditions that the components must satisfy to be considered components.

Schema Representation Constraint   Defines constraints on the representation of schema components in XML beyond those expressed in the schema document that are used for the XML Schema vocabulary.

Validation Rule   Defines contributions to validation associated with schema components.

Schema Information Set Contribution   Defines augmentations to infosets expressed by schema components after validation.

XML Schema Components

In this section, we define each of the 13 different schema components as well as provide the following information:

Syntactical representation   We provide the basic syntactical representation for each component that defines allowable attributes.

Content model   Each schema component can accept a predefined list of elements that helps define component behavior. For example, the attribute declaration component can only accept a `simpleType` or `annotation` element as a child.

Restrictions   Each schema component has a set of restrictions that must be followed. For example, an element declaration component cannot name itself while referencing another declaration.

In the following sections, each schema component is defined and briefly explained. Later, in the section "Structuring Schemas," we cover more complicated and practical examples using these components. For now, we stick to the basics.

As we present each schema component, we also provide simple examples for illustration. For this section, all XML Schema examples will be defined in relation to the XML document shown in Listing 6.1.

⤵ **Listing 6.1** **XML Document Instance**

```xml
<?xml version="1.0" encoding="UTF-8"?>
<employees>
  <employee eid="p98145" dept="programming">
    <contact addInfo="contacts/98145.xml">
      <name>
        <firstName>Joe</firstName>
        <middleName int="B">Brian</middleName>
        <lastName>Smith</lastName>
      </name>
      <address>
        <street>611 Ridgewood Drive</street>
        <city>Denver</city>
        <state>Colorado</state>
        <zipcode>80210</zipcode>
      </address>
      <phone>
        <tel type="wk">303-4667339</tel>
        <tel type="hm">303-9842361</tel>
        <fax>303-4667357</fax>
      </phone>
      <email>JSmith@earthlink.net</email>
    </contact>
    <hireDate>1998-10-14</hireDate>
  </employee>
  <employee eid="t00022" dept="training">
    <contact addInfo="contacts/00022.xml">
      <name>
        <firstName>Sam</firstName>
        <middleName int="S">Stolte</middleName>
        <lastName>Williams</lastName>
      </name>
      <address>
        <street>2103 Steck Drive</street>
        <city>Austin</city>
        <state>Texas</state>
        <zipcode>78731</zipcode>
      </address>
      <phone>
        <tel type="wk">512-3467899</tel>
        <tel type="hm">512-4623356</tel>
        <fax>512-3465655</fax>
      </phone>
      <email>swilliams@verizon.net</email>
    </contact>
    <hireDate>2000-03-11</hireDate>
  </employee>
  <employee eid="p01164" dept="programming">
    <contact addInfo="contacts/01164.xml">
```

```
      <name>
        <firstName>Kate</firstName>
        <middleName int="S">Summer</middleName>
        <lastName>Carnes</lastName>
      </name>
      <address>
        <street>22 Jane Street</street>
        <city>New York</city>
        <state>New York</state>
        <zipcode>11238</zipcode>
      </address>
      <phone>
        <tel type="wk">212-4667339</tel>
        <tel type="hm">212-9842361</tel>
        <fax>212-4667357</fax>
      </phone>
      <email>kcarnes@earthlink.net</email>
    </contact>
    <hireDate>2001-08-28</hireDate>
  </employee>
</employees>
```

TIP   If you want to play around with these examples, be sure to visit the book's Web site. From there you can download the XML document instance and XML Schema document.

Element Declarations

Identified as primary schema components, element declarations are at the heart of your schema document. The element declaration defines the element name, content model, and allowable attributes as well as datatype and behavior for each element type.

The basic syntactical representation of an element declaration is as follows.

```
<element name="QName"
         ref="QName"
         type="QName"
         use="optional | prohibited | required"
         form="qualified | unqualified"
         id="ID"
         default="string"
         fixed="string"
>
    Content: (annotation?, ((simpleType | complexType)?,
      (unique | key | keyref)*))
</element>
```

A QName is a namespace-qualified name as defined in Namespaces in XML. It can consist of a simple name, an NCName (a nonqualified, or *noncolonized,* name), or a name with a prefix and colon. See Chapter 7 for more information.

Element declarations may be defined in the following ways:

- *An element may be named and defined globally.* The element declaration is then defined as an immediate child of the schema element. For our example, we've defined four elements— all globally. The employees element contains a complexType that allows for three child elements. Each of the three child elements is declared to contain a simple string datatype:

```
<xsd:schema
    targetNamespace=
    "http://www.technocoop.com/namespace/employees"
    xmlns="http://www.technocoop.com/namespace/employees"
    xmlns:xsd="http://www.w3.org/2001/XMLSchema"
    elementFormDefault="qualified">

    <xsd:element name="employees">
      <xsd:complexType>
        <xsd:sequence>
          <xsd:element ref="firstName"/>
          <xsd:element ref="middleName"/>
          <xsd:element ref="lastName"/>
        </xsd:sequence>
      </xsd:complexType>
    </xsd:element>
    <xsd:element name="firstName" type="xsd:string"/>
    <xsd:element name="middleName" type="xsd:string"/>
    <xsd:element name="lastName" type="xsd:string"/>

</xsd:schema>
```

- *An element may be named and defined locally.* The element is then defined as a child of the complexType element. When you use this approach, at least one declaration has to be defined globally. However, the rest of the elements may be declared locally within the initial declaration. In this case, the employees element is declared globally, and the other element declarations are defined as children of a complexType. The complexType element is required if you want to nest element declarations within each other:

```
<xsd:schema
    targetNamespace=
    "http://www.technocoop.com/namespace/employees"
    xmlns="http://www.technocoop.com/namespace/employees"
    xmlns:xsd="http://www.w3.org/2001/XMLSchema"
    elementFormDefault="qualified">
```

```
<xsd:element name="employees">
  <xsd:complexType>
    <xsd:sequence>
      <xsd:element name="firstName" type="xsd:string"/>
      <xsd:element name="middleName" type="xsd:string"/>
      <xsd:element name="lastName" type="xsd:string"/>
    </xsd:sequence>
  </xsd:complexType>
</xsd:element>

</xsd:schema>
```

TIP   Although the latter of the two preceding examples takes up fewer lines of markup, the first approach is better suited for complex schema models. The first approach allows for modularizing element declarations. Each approach is detailed in depth later in this chapter.

The element declaration component allows for the following elements to be defined within it:

- `complexType`

- `simpleType`

- Any of the identity constraints (`unique`, `key`, or `keyref`)

- `annotation`

There are several restrictions placed on using the element declaration component:

- The `default` and `fixed` attributes cannot both be present.

- If the element is declared locally within another schema component (other than the `schema element`), either the `ref` or `name` attribute must be used.

- If the `ref` attribute is used, only the `minOccurs`, `maxOccurs`, and `id` attributes are allowed in addition to the `ref` attribute.

- If the `ref` attribute is used, only the `annotation` element may be defined as a child of the declaration.

Attribute Declarations

The attribute declaration schema component is similar to the element declaration component. It can be defined globally as a child of the `schema` element, or it can be defined as a part of another schema component. The attribute declaration defines the attribute name, element association, datatype, behavior, and a default or fixed value.

There are some basic restrictions placed on attribute declarations. The first and foremost is that attribute values must always be defined as simple types. By nature, attribute values contain only text content (i.e., they cannot contain other child elements). Simple types are used to define text content. Another basic restriction is that the attribute order cannot be defined. Because XML doesn't allow you to define the order in which attributes occur within a given element, the attribute declaration component doesn't provide that functionality either.

The basic syntactical representation of an attribute declaration is as follows:

```
<attribute name="QName"
           ref="QName"
           type="QName"
           use="optional | prohibited | required"
           form="qualified | unqualified"
           id="ID"
           default="string"
           fixed="string"
           {any attributes with non-schema namespace}
>
    Content: (annotation?, (simpleType?))
</attribute>
```

None of the attributes previously defined is required; however, you must either name (name) the attribute or reference (ref) another attribute declaration. Without either of those values, your attribute declaration won't have any meaning to the processor.

Similar to element declarations, attribute declarations may be defined globally or locally. The following is an example of a globally defined attribute declaration:

```
<xsd:schema
    targetNamespace=
      "http://www.technocoop.com/namespace/employees"
    xmlns="http://www.technocoop.com/namespace/employees"
    xmlns:xsd="http://www.w3.org/2001/XMLSchema"
    elementFormDefault="qualified">

<xsd:attribute name="int" use="optional"
    type="xsd:string"/>

<xsd:element name="employees">
  <xsd:complexType>
    <xsd:sequence>
      <xsd:element name="firstName" type="xsd:string"/>
      <xsd:element name="middleName" type="xsd:string"/>
      <xsd:element name="lastName" type="xsd:string"/>
    </xsd:sequence>
```

```
      <xsd:attribute ref="int"/>
    </xsd:complexType>
  </xsd:element>
</xsd:schema>
```

In this case, the attribute declaration is referenced from within another schema component. If this is the case, the `ref` attribute is used to reference a predefined attribute declaration:

```
<xsd:attribute ref="int"/>
```

Attribute declarations may also be defined locally within the `complexType` element:

```
<xsd:schema
    targetNamespace=
      "http://www.technocoop.com/namespace/employees"
    xmlns="http://www.technocoop.com/namespace/employees"
    xmlns:xsd="http://www.w3.org/2001/XMLSchema"
    elementFormDefault="qualified">
    <xsd:element name="employees">
      <xsd:complexType>
        <xsd:sequence>
          <xsd:element name="firstName" type="xsd:string"/>
          <xsd:element name="middleName" type="xsd:string"/>
          <xsd:element name="lastName" type="xsd:string"/>
        </xsd:sequence>
        <xsd:attribute name="int" use="optional" type="xsd:string"/>
      </xsd:complexType>
    </xsd:element>
</xsd:schema>
```

Declaring elements and attributes globally allows you to reuse those components throughout the schema model. After they're declared locally, they're available only to that particular component.

One of the most important aspects of the attribute declaration component is its datatype information. The datatype of an attribute can be defined using a `type` attribute that references either a built-in datatype or a derived datatype defined elsewhere in the schema model. The following shows a reference to a built-in datatype:

```
<xsd:attribute name="dept" type="xsd:string" use="required"/>
```

If the `type` attribute is not used, the `simpleType` element can be used to derive a new datatype. In the following example, we use the built-in `string` datatype as our base type and enumeration facets to define possible attribute values:

```
<xsd:attribute name="dept" use="required">
    <xsd:simpleType>
      <xsd:restriction base="xsd:string">
        <xsd:enumeration value="management"/>
        <xsd:enumeration value="programming"/>
```

```
                <xsd:enumeration value="design"/>
                <xsd:enumeration value="training"/>
            </xsd:restriction>
        </xsd:simpleType>
    </xsd:attribute>
```

WARNING   When using the `simpleType` element, be sure to use both the opening and closing `attribute` tags.

The attribute declaration component allows for the following elements to be defined within it:

- `simpleType`
- `annotation`

There are several restrictions placed on using the attribute declaration component:

- You cannot use the `type` attribute within the declaration and also nest a `simpleType` element.

- You cannot define a default *and* fixed value for a given attribute.

- If you define a default value, as well as use the `use` attribute to define behavior, the value of the `use` attribute must be `optional`.

- You cannot define both the `ref` attribute and the `name` attribute for a given attribute.

- The value of the `name` attribute may not match `xmlns`.

Complex Type Definitions

Complex type definition components are used to define element content models that allow for attributes or child elements. The `complexType` element is used to mark the beginning and end of a content model. There are specific rules that you must follow when defining complex type definitions. We cover those rules shortly.

The basic syntactical representation of a complex type definition is as follows:

```
<complexType abstract="boolean"
            block="#all | List of
                    (extension | restriction)"
            final="#all | List of
                    (extension | restriction)"
            id="ID"
            mixed="boolean"
            name="NCName"
            {any attributes with non-schema namespace}
    >
```

```
    Content: (annotation?, (simpleContent | complexContent
      ((group | all | choice | sequence)?,
      ((attribute | attributeGroup)*, anyAttribute?))))
  </complexType>
```

Complex types can be defined both globally and locally. If defined globally, they can be referenced when needed. The advantage to defining global complex types is that they may be reused throughout the schema model (much like DTD parameter entities). The following illustrates a named complex type that is defined globally:

```
  <xsd:complexType name="contactType">
    <xsd:sequence>
      <xsd:element name="name" type="nameType"/>
      <xsd:element name="address" type="addressType"/>
      <xsd:element name="phone" type="phoneType"/>
      <xsd:element name="email" type="xsd:string"/>
    </xsd:sequence>
    <xsd:attribute name="addInfo" type="xsd:anyURI"
      use="required"/>
  </xsd:complexType>
```

After a complex type definition is defined, element declarations can reference that type:

```
  <xsd:element name="contact" type="contactType"/>
```

NOTE   Note the different values defined for the type attribute in the examples used in this section. XML Schema allows you to use one of the 44 built-in datatypes that are predefined by XML Schema (xsd:string), or you can create your own datatypes. We use the xsd: prefix with the string datatype because it belongs within the scope of the XML Schema namespace. When we define our own datatypes (nameType, addressType, phoneType, and contactType), the xsd: prefix is not used. In the preceding example, we're referencing datatypes from our own datatype library. To keep the example simple, we have not included the simple type definitions used to create those datatypes. We will cover that material in coming sections.

When complex type definitions are defined locally, the complexType element is defined as a child of element. In this case, the complex type is an anonymous type and the name attribute is not needed:

```
  <xsd:element name="contact">
    <xsd:complexType>
      <xsd:sequence>
        <xsd:element name="name" type="nameType"/>
        <xsd:element name="address" type="addressType"/>
        <xsd:element name="phone" type="phoneType"/>
        <xsd:element ref="email"/>
      </xsd:sequence>
```

```
        <xsd:attribute name="addInfo" type="xsd:anyURI"
          use="required"/>
      </xsd:complexType>
    </xsd:element>
```

WARNING The element declarations are never defined as immediate children of the comlexType element. They must be defined as children of a compositor element (all, sequence, or choice).

The complex type definition component allows for the following elements to be defined within it:

- simpleContent
- complexContent
- attribute
- attributeGroup
- anyAttribute
- Any of the compositors (all, choice, or sequence)
- group
- annotation

There are several restrictions placed on using the complex type definition component:

- If the base type definition is a simple type definition, the derivation method must be extension.
- Two or more attribute declarations cannot have identical names and target namespaces.
- Only one attribute declaration may exist that is derived from ID.

Attribute Group Definitions

Attribute group definition components allow you to group attribute declarations in one global definition that can be reused later. If a schema model uses a set of attributes for more than one element, it would be useful to define that set as an attribute group, the advantage being that the attributes would be defined once and then reused within content models.

The basic syntactical representation of an attribute group is as follows:

```
<attributeGroup id="ID"
                name="NCName"
                ref="QName"
                {any attributes with non-schema namespace}
```

```
    >
      Content: (annotation?,
        ((attribute | attributeGroup)*, anyAttribute?))
    </attributeGroup>
```

Attribute groups are similar to parameter entities used by DTDs. For example, you might want to define a set of common attributes that can be used with any element within your schema model:

```
<xsd:attributeGroup name="commonAtts">
  <xsd:attribute name="id" type="xsd:ID" use="required"/>
  <xsd:attribute name="title" type="xsd:string"
    use="required"/>
  <xsd:attribute name="style" type="xsd:string"
    use="required"/>
</xsd:attributeGroup>
```

The attribute group can then be reused in different content models, as shown here:

```
<xsd:element name="contact">
  <xsd:complexType>
    <xsd:sequence>
      <xsd:element name="name" type="nameType"/>
      <xsd:element name="address" type="addressType"/>
      <xsd:element name="phone" type="phoneType"/>
      <xsd:element ref="email"/>
    </xsd:sequence>
    <xsd:attribute name="addInfo" type="xsd:anyURI"
      use="required"/>
    <xsd:attributeGroup ref="commonAtts"/>
  </xsd:complexType>
</xsd:element>
```

TIP   Attribute declarations and attribute group definitions can be defined in any order because order is not significant.

The attribute group definition component allows the following elements to be defined within it:

- `attribute`
- `attributeGroup`
- `anyAttribute`
- `annotation`

Model Group Definitions

Like attribute group definitions, model group definitions allow you to define and reuse components. This time, you can define and reuse element declarations.

The basic syntactical representation of a model group definition is as follows:

```
<group name="NCName"
       ref="NCName"
       maxOccurs="nonNegativeInteger | unbounded"
       minOccurs="nonNegativeInteger"
       id="ID"
>
    Content: (annotation?, (all | choice | sequence))
</group>
```

There's only one attribute (name) that is used with the group element when it's being defined, and that attribute names the group. However, when the model group is used, you must use the ref attribute to reference the associated model group definition. Once the group is named, you can reference it throughout the schema model:

```
<xsd:group name="contactGroup">
   <xsd:sequence>
     <xsd:element name="name" type="nameType"/>
     <xsd:element name="address" type="addressType"/>
     <xsd:element name="phone" type="phoneType"/>
     <xsd:element ref="email"/>
   </xsd:sequence>
</xsd:group>

<xsd:element name="contact">
   <xsd:complexType>
     <xsd:group ref="contactGroup"/>
     <xsd:attribute name="addInfo" type="xsd:anyURI"
       use="required"/>
     <xsd:attributeGroup ref="commonAtts"/>
   </xsd:complexType>
</xsd:element>
```

The group element must contain a compositor that in turn contains the element declarations.

WARNING   When the model group is named, you cannot use the minOccurs or maxOccurs attributes.

The element schema component allows for the following elements to be defined within it:

- Any of the compositors (all, choice, or sequence)
- annotation

There are several restrictions placed on using the model group definition component:

- When the `name` attribute is used, you cannot use the `minOccurs` or `maxOccurs` attribute.
- Model group names must be unique within an XML Schema document.
- Model groups must include a compositor.

Particles

Particle components represent three different elements that allow `minOccurs` and `maxOccurs` attributes. Particles allow authors to define occurrence behavior. There are three elements that are considered particles:

- `element` (not immediately within `schema`)
- `group` (not immediately within `schema`)
- `any`

We do not define syntactical representations of these elements because they're covered in other component sections.

Wildcards

Wildcard components are used as placeholders that allow document instance authors to extend the instance document with elements not specified by the schema. For element declarations, the any element is used as a wildcard component. When a wildcard component is included in the schema model, the document instance is seen as extensible.

The basic syntactical representation of the `any` and `anyAttribute` elements is as follows:

```
<any id="ID"
     maxOccurs="nonNegativeInteger | unbounded"
     minOccurs="nonNegativeInteger"
     namespace="(##any | ##other) | List of
     (anyURI | (##targetNamespace | ##local))"
     processContents="lax | skip | strict"
     {any attributes with non-schema namespace}
>
   Content: (annotation?)
</any>

<anyAttribute
   id="ID"
   namespace="(##any | ##other) | List of
   (anyURI | (##targetNamespace | ##local))"
   processContents="lax | skip | strict"
   {any attributes with non-schema namespace}
```

```
>
  Content: (annotation?)
</anyAttribute>
```

The any and `anyAttribute` elements essentially provide document instance authors with the flexibility to extend the predefined document model. If you want to add a wildcard component to your schema model, it would be used in place of an element declaration:

```
<xsd:element name="contact">
   <xsd:complexType>
     <xsd:sequence>
       <xsd:any namespace="http://www.sybex.com" minOccurs="0"
         maxOccurs="unbounded" processContents="lax"/>
     </xsd:sequence>
   </xsd:complexType>
</xsd:element>
```

Later in this chapter, we cover working with wildcards and namespaces; however, we wanted to briefly introduce you the namespace attribute. The namespace attribute allows you to define to which namespace, if any, the new elements must belong. This still provides the schema author with an element of control over the allowable content. There are five possible values for the namespace attribute:

##any   The new elements can belong to any namespace.

##other   The new elements can belong to any namespace other than the target namespace defined by the schema model.

##targetNamespace   The new elements must belong to the target namespace defined by the schema model.

##local   The new elements cannot belong to any namespace.

anyURI   You can define a namespace URI to which the elements must belong.

Identity-Constraint Definitions

Identity-constraint definition components identify elements or attributes that must contain unique values within an XML schema or within a particular element set.

There are three primary categories for identity-constraint definitions:

Unique   The unique element requires uniqueness within a schema document or within a defined element set.

Key   The key element requires uniqueness as well as defines one end of a cross-reference.

Key reference   The keyRef element is used to reference a key.

The key and unique elements are quite similar in that they both require uniqueness. We define the syntactical representation for each element separately.

The basic syntactical representation of the unique element is as follows:

```
<unique id="ID"
        name="NCName"
        {any attributes with non-schema namespace}
>
    Content: (annotation?, (selector, field+))
</unique>
```

Here's the basic syntactical representation of the key element:

```
<key id="ID"
      name="NCName"
      {any attributes with non-schema namespace}
>
    Content: (annotation?, (selector, field+))
</key>
```

The basic syntactical representation of the keyRef element is as follows:

```
<keyref id="ID"
        name="NCName"
        refer="QName"
        {any attributes with non-schema namespace}
>
    Content: (annotation?, (selector, field+))
</keyref>
```

You can establish keys and uniqueness globally or within a node set. When you want to restrict uniqueness to a defined element set, you have to use the selector and field elements. The selector element identifies the node set, and the field element identifies the element or attribute that must be unique. XPath expressions are used to select an element or attribute. XPath expressions are based on the XPath data model that is famous for its interaction with the Extensible Stylesheet Language Transformations (XSLT).

TIP   To learn more about XPath expressions, see the XPath recommendation at www.w3.org/TR/xpath.

It's important to understand both the selector and field elements, so we include their syntactical representations as well:

```
<selector id="ID"
          xpath="XPath expression subset"
          {any attributes with non-schema namespace}
>
    Content: (annotation?)
</selector>
```

```
<field id="ID"
       xpath="XPath expression subset"
       {any attributes with non-schema namespace}
>
   Content: (annotation?)
</field>
```

The three primary identity-constraint components allow for the following elements to be defined:

- `selector`
- `field`
- `annotation`

In the following example, we introduce an `employees` element that may contain multiple `employee` elements. Following the `complexType` definition, we add an identity constraint that accomplishes the following:

- Uses the `xsd:selector` element to identify the node set to which the identity constraint will apply
- Uses the `xsd:field` element to identify the value that must be unique within the node set identified by the `xsd:selector` element

In this case, the `@eid` attribute value must be unique within the employee node set:

```
<xsd:element name="employees">
   <xsd:comlexType>
     <xsd:sequence>
       <xsd:element name="employee" type="employeeType"
          maxOccurs="unbounded"/>
     </xsd:sequence>
   </xsd:complexType>
   <xsd:unique name="employeeIdentificationNumber">
     <xsd:selector xpath="employee"/>
     <xsd:field xpath="@eid"/>
   </xsd:unique>
</xsd:element>
```

Notation Declarations

Notation declarations are components that mimic the functionality of DTD notation declarations. These components are used in conjunction with a NOTATION attribute to define the location of external non-XML data and then associate an external application to handle it.

The basic syntactical representation of a notation declaration is as follows:

```
<notation id="ID"
          name="NCName"
          public="anyURI"
          system="anyURI"
          {any attributes with non-schema namespace}
>
    Content: (annotation?)
</notation>
```

The notation component itself defines how to create the notation declaration, as in this example:

```
<xsd:notation name="gif" public="image/gif" system="GIFViewer.exe"/>
```

There's more to creating a notation than just defining a name and external application. The notation has to be associated with the data in question. To accomplish this, a derivative of the NOTATION datatype is used. In addition to the notation declaration, you have to define a simple type definition:

```
<xsd:simpleType name="imgType">
   <xsd:restriction base="xsd:NOTATION">
     <xsd:enumeration value="gif"/>
     <xsd:enumeration value="jpeg"/>
   </xsd:restriction>
</xsd:simpleType>

<xsd:notation name="gif" public="image/gif" system="GIFViewer.exe"/>
<xsd:notation name="jpeg" public="image/jpeg" system="JPEGViewer.exe"/>
```

> **WARNING** You must derive your own datatype using the NOTATION primitive type as the base. The NOTATION datatype may not be used directly in a schema model.

Annotations

The annotation component allows schema authors to provide additional information about the model. There are two allowable audiences for this information: humans and applications.

To define annotations for human consumption, you must use the following elements: annotation and documentation. This type of annotation is similar to using comments in XML 1.0. This type of schema component is meant to provide yourself and others with additional information about the purpose of the document or particular schema component. For example, you can add documentation about copyright or authoring information. You can also provide additional information about a particular content model. Suppose you intend to further modify a content model at a later date; you might want to include a comment to document your intention.

On the other hand, if you want to define annotations for application consumption, you must use the following elements: `annotation` and `appInfo`. The basic syntactical representation of an annotation is as follows:

```
<annotation id="ID"
            {any attributes with non-schema namespace}
>
    Content: (appInfo | documentation)*
</annotation>
```

Although XML Schema defines these constructions, the specification does not define how the information should be interpreted. The following example contains an annotation meant for the document author:

```
<xsd:element name="name">
   <xsd:annotation>
     <xsd:documentation xml:lang="en">
       Child element content models defined globally
     </xsd:documentation>
   </xsd:annotation>
   <xsd:complexType>
     <xsd:sequence>
       <xsd:element ref="firstName"/>
       <xsd:element ref="middleName"/>
       <xsd:element ref="lastName"/>
     </xsd:sequence>
   </xsd:complexType>
</xsd:element>
```

Simple Type Definitions

Simple type definition components are used to define datatype information for text content for both elements and attributes. A primary advantage of using XML Schema is its datatyping capabilities. Using the simple type definition component, you can use one of the 44 built-in datatypes or you can derive your own type libraries. When you derive your own datatypes, your options are fairly boundless. For example, you can use regular expressions to define patterns. These patterns allow you to define complex datatype scenarios.

The basic syntactical representation of a simple type definition is as follows:

```
<simpleType final="#all | (list | union | restriction)"
            id="ID"
            name="NCName"
            {any attributes with non-schema namespace}
>
    Content: (annotation?, (restriction | list | union))
</simpleType>
```

The simple type component may be defined globally, as a child of an attribute declaration, or within an element content model. Later in this chapter, we look at deriving simple types from built-in schema datatypes. Here's a simple example of allowing for an enumerated list of options for an attribute value:

```
<xsd:simpleType name="deptType">
  <xsd:restriction base="xsd:string">
    <xsd:enumeration value="management"/>
    <xsd:enumeration value="programming"/>
    <xsd:enumeration value="design"/>
    <xsd:enumeration value="training"/>
  </xsd:restriction>
</xsd:simpleType>
```

We can also define a pattern for element content that contains a phone number. In this case, we use a regular expression to define the pattern *xxx-xxxxxxx*:

```
<xsd:simpleType name="phoneType">
  <xsd:restriction base="xsd:string">
    <xsd:pattern value="[0-9]{3}-[0-9]{7}"/>
  </xsd:restriction>
</xsd:simpleType>
```

Using the similar simple type definition, we can define a pattern that can be used for zip codes:

```
<xsd:simpleType name="zipType">
  <xsd:restriction base="xsd:string">
    <xsd:pattern value="[0-9]{5}"/>
  </xsd:restriction>
</xsd:simpleType>
```

What you should notice is that in each of our examples, the simple type definition contains a `restriction` element. The `restriction` element is one of the allowable derivation methods that you can use to create your own datatypes. We cover other methods later in this chapter. After you've defined the derivation method, you use facets to define datatype behavior. For example, in the first example defined, we use the `enumeration` facet to provide an enumeration list of allowable elements. In following sections, we use the `pattern` facet to define the regular expression pattern that the datatype must follow. We take a closer look at patterns in Chapter 7.

Structuring Schemas

Obviously, there's more to XML Schema than the 13 defined schema components. To create a schema document, you must understand how these components work together. This section is dedicated to identifying common usage and properties of each component.

Working with Content Models

Earlier in this chapter, we looked at some basic content models defined using complex types and element declarations. In this section, we take a closer look at content models. When working with advanced content models, you can define reusable model groups, occurrence behavior, and different types of element content. This section is organized according to the following functions:

Compositors   You can use compositors to define behavior of child elements.

Occurrence behavior   You can use the `minOccurs` and `maxOccurs` attributes to define occurrence behavior.

Named content models   By defining content models at the top level of a schema document, you can reuse them throughout the schema document.

Element content and datatypes   There are four basic types of content models that an element may follow. We look at each of these standard content models as well as take a closer look at defining datatypes for nonelement content.

Compositors

Compositors are necessary elements that contain the actual element declarations. The `complexType` element cannot contain element declarations. Instead, it contains compositors that contain the element declarations. There are three compositors that you may use:

- `sequence`, which requires that content models follow the element sequence defined.

- `choice`, which requires that the document author makes a choice between defined options.

- `all`, which allows any of the element declarations to occur.

sequence

The `sequence` compositor allows you to require a sequence for child elements in a content model. For example, we might want to require that the content model for the `name` element contain `firstName`, `middleName`, and `lastName`—in that order:

```
<name>
    <firstName>Sam</firstName>
    <middleName>Stolte</middleName>
    <lastName>Williams</lastName>
</name>
```

To require that the child elements occur in that order, we would have to use the `sequence` compositor:

```
<xsd:element name="name">
    <xsd:complexType>
        <xsd:sequence>
```

```
        <xsd:element name="firstName" type="xsd:string"/>
        <xsd:element name="middleName" type="xsd:string"/>
        <xsd:element name="lastName" type="xsd:string"/>
      </xsd:sequence>
    </xsd:complexType>
  </xsd:element>
```

The `sequence` compositor can use the `minOccurs` or `maxOccurs` attribute to further define occurrence behavior. We cover these attributes shortly.

choice

The `choice` compositor is used much like the `sequence` element. In this case, the document author is given a choice between child elements. That choice can be made between 1, 2, or even 10 different element declarations.

For example, you might want to allow the `middleName` element to contain one of two child elements: `initial` or `name`. In this case, we allow for only one of these options:

```
<middleName>
    <initial>S</initial>
</middleName>
<middleName>
    <name>Stolte</name>
</middleName>
```

To allow for this content model, we would have to use the `choice` element:

```
<xsd:element name="middleName">
    <xsd:complexType>
      <xsd:choice>
        <xsd:element name="initial" type="xsd:string"/>
        <xsd:element name="name" type="xsd:string"/>
      </xsd:choice>
    </xsd:complexType>
  </xsd:element>
```

You can further express occurrence behavior by using the `minOccurs` and `maxOccurs` attributes with either the `choice` element or the element declarations themselves. For example, the following content models could be defined (note the `minOccurs` and `maxOccurs` attributes):

```
<xsd:element name="middleName">
    <xsd:complexType>
      <xsd:choice maxOccurs="2">
        <xsd:element name="initial" type="xsd:string"/>
        <xsd:element name="name" type="xsd:string"/>
      </xsd:choice>
    </xsd:complexType>
  </xsd:element>
```

In this example, we require that at least one of the child elements is used because, if the `minOccurs` attribute is not used, the default value of 1 is assumed. We also include the `maxOccurs` attribute to allow up to two choices to be made. The effect is that the document instance author can use both the `initial` and `name` elements but is only required to use one of them.

In this example, we add a `maxOccurs` attribute to the `initial` element declaration. In this case, it allows the document instance author to use the initial element twice:

```
<xsd:element name="middleName">
  <xsd:complexType>
    <xsd:choice>
      <xsd:element name="initial" type="xsd:string" maxOccurs="2"/>
      <xsd:element name="name" type="xsd:string"/>
    </xsd:choice>
  </xsd:complexType>
</xsd:element>
```

all

The `all` element is used to allow the document author to select any of the child elements defined. For example, the following content model allows the document author to choose one or multiple instances of the child elements declared:

```
<xsd:element name="name">
  <xsd:complexType>
    <xsd:all>
      <xsd:element name="firstName" type="xsd:string"/>
      <xsd:element name="middleName" type="xsd:string"/>
      <xsd:element name="lastName" type="xsd:string"/>
    </xsd:all>
  </xsd:complexType>
</xsd:element>
```

We don't recommend that you use this compositor often. The most common use of this element is while your schema model is in development, in which case you might want to fiddle with one part of the model but leave the other part alone for a while. In this case, you can use the `all` compositor for those content models that you're not ready to mess with yet.

Defining Occurrence

Two attributes control occurrence behavior: `minOccurs` and `maxOccurs`. These two attributes can be used separately or together to control element behavior.

Minimum Occurrences

The `minOccurs` attribute defines the minimum number of times an element or content model can occur. The default value for this attribute is 1. Therefore, if you do not specify a value, the element or content model must be used once.

You can use the `minOccurs` attribute with particle components, such as these:

- any
- group
- element
- choice
- sequence

TIP

You can also use `minOccurs` with the `all` element; however, its value can only be 0 or 1.

Using the XML Schema occurrence attributes is an improvement over using DTD occurrence indicators (*, +, and ?). For example, if you wanted to require at least six occurrences of the `employee` element, you would use the following markup:

```
<xsd:element name="employees">
   <xsd:complexType>
     <xsd:sequence>
       <xsd:element name="employee" type="employeeType" minOccurs="6"
         maxOccurs="unbounded"/>
     </xsd:sequence>
   </xsd:complexType>
</xsd:element>
```

Maximum Occurrences

The `maxOccurs` attribute defines the maximum number of occurrences for an element or content model. The default value for this attribute is 1.

For the value of `maxOccurs`, you can define a nonnegative integer, or you can use the value unbounded, which allows an unlimited number of occurrences.

You can use the `maxOccurs` attribute with particle components, such as these:

- any
- group
- element
- choice
- sequence

The `minOccurs` and `maxOccurs` attributes can be used with compositors, as well as element declarations, as shown in the following example:

```
<xsd:complexType name="nameType">
   <xsd:sequence maxOccurs="unbounded">
```

```
        <xsd:element name="firstName" type="xsd:string"/>
        <xsd:element name="middleName" type="xsd:string"/>
        <xsd:element name="lastName" type="xsd:string"/>
    </xsd:sequence>
  </xsd:complexType>
```

By adding the maxOccurs attribute, you allow for the following structure to occur in the document instance:

```
<firstName>Joe</firstName>
<middleName>Brian</middleName>
<lastName>Smith</lastName>

<firstName>Sam</firstName>
<middleName>Stolte</middleName>
<lastName>Williams</lastName>

<firstName>Kate</firstName>
<middleName>Summer</middleName>
<lastName>Carnes</lastName>
```

Named Content Models

Named content models, by way of complex type definitions, allow you to reuse, extend, or even restrict content models. Naming complex types is simple. The name attribute is used to define a name that can later be referenced; here's an example:

```
<xsd:complexType name="nameType">
    <xsd:sequence>
      <xsd:element ref="firstName"/>
      <xsd:element ref="middleName"/>
      <xsd:element ref="lastName"/>
    </xsd:sequence>
  </xsd:complexType>
```

Once the complex type is named, you can reference the named complex type definitions using the type attribute, as shown in this example:

```
<xsd:element name="name" type="nameType"/>
```

Element Content and Datatypes

All element content, unless otherwise defined, uses the anyType datatype found in the schema type hierarchy (for a closer look at the type hierarchy, see Chapter 5). The anyType datatype is found at the top of the datatype hierarchy and is the basis for all of the types. The anyType datatype allows for any content, including elements that are not declared as a part of the schema model.

Although `anyType` can be used, in most cases, we define a datatype (using the `type` attribute) for our elements instead. For elements, you'll want to define a content model containing child elements, use a built-in datatype for text content, or derive your own datatype for text content. The way element content is defined in XML Schema is similar to the way allowable content in DTDs is defined. As with DTDs, you can define content models as element content, text-only content, mixed content, EMPTY content, and ANY content:

Element content model   The element can contain child elements.

Text content model   The element can contain text only.

Mixed content model   The element can contain child elements and text.

EMPTY content model   The element does not contain child elements or text.

ANY content model   The element can contain any content.

Element Content

The element content model defines elements that can only contain other elements. For example, the `name` element contains only three child elements:

```
<name>
  <firstName>Joe</firstName>
  <middleName int="B">Brian</middleName>
  <lastName>Smith</lastName>
</name>
```

Element content is defined using a complex type definition. This can be done by either defining a named complex type that is later referenced or by including an anonymous complex type within the content model. Either way, a complex type definition must be used.

Compositors are used to define behavior for element content, and they contain the element declarations for the content model. There's not much to defining element content models. It can, however, get a bit tricky the more complex the content model. On a simple level, we can define a named complex type that will be used for the `name` element identified in the preceding example:

```
<xsd:complexType name="nameType">
  <xsd:sequence>
    <xsd:element ref="firstName"/>
    <xsd:element ref="middleName"/>
    <xsd:element ref="lastName"/>
  </xsd:sequence>
</xsd:complexType>
```

As we forge ahead with examples, be sure to notice the different techniques employed to define declarations and definitions. For example, in the preceding markup, we use a named complex type that is defined globally. The `sequence` element then contains element declaration references for global element declarations. In other examples, we'll use other techniques, such as anonymous simple and complex type definitions.

But what if you're defining a more complex structure? For example, you might want to allow the `contact` element to contain the `name`, `address`, and either the `phone` or `email` elements:

```
<contact addInfo="contacts/98145.xml">
   <name>
     <firstName>Joe</firstName>
     <middleName int="B">Brian</middleName>
     <lastName>Smith</lastName>
   </name>
   <address>
     <street>611 Ridgewood Drive</street>
     <city>Denver</city>
     <state>Colorado</state>
     <zipcode>80210</zipcode>
   </address>
   <email>JSmith@earthlink.net</email>
</contact>

<contact addInfo="contacts/00022.xml">
   <name>
     <firstName>Sam</firstName>
     <middleName int="S">Stolte</middleName>
     <lastName>Williams</lastName>
   </name>
   <address>
     <street>2103 Steck Drive</street>
     <city>Austin</city>
     <state>Texas</state>
     <zipcode>78731</zipcode>
   </address>
   <phone>
     <tel type="wk">512-3467899</tel>
     <tel type="hm">512-4623356</tel>
     <fax>512-3465655</fax>
   </phone>
</contact>
```

In this example, the document instance uses two different content models for the `contact` element. To allow for this variation, we could use the following complex type definition:

```
<xsd:complexType name="contactType">
   <xsd:sequence>
     <xsd:element ref="name"/>
```

```
      <xsd:element ref="address"/>
      <xsd:choice>
        <xsd:element ref="phone"/>
        <xsd:element ref="email"/>
      </xsd:choice>
    </xsd:sequence>
  </xsd:complexType>
```

NOTE Note that the element declarations are referencing globally declared elements not contained within our example.

In this instance, we require that the document instance author use either the phone or email element.

Text

There are two ways to define text-only content. First, you can use a built-in datatype within the element declaration:

```
<xsd:element name="tel" type="xsd:string"/>
```

However, if you want to derive your own datatype, you have to use the simpleContent element. When deriving your own element datatype, either you can define a complex type that will be used later or you can define an element declaration that uses an anonymous type.

Here's a named complex type definition:

```
<xsd:complexType name="telType">
  <xsd:simpleContent>
    <xsd:restriction base="xsd:string">
      <xsd:pattern value="[0-9]{3}-[0-9]{7}"/>
    </xsd:restriction>
  </xsd:simpleContent>
</xsd:complexType>
```

Here's an anonymous type definition:

```
<xsd:element name="tel">
  <xsd:complexType>
    <xsd:simpleContent>
      <xsd:restriction base="xsd:string">
        <xsd:pattern value="[0-9]{3}-[0-9]{7}"/>
      </xsd:restriction>
    </xsd:simpleContent>
  </xsd:complexType>
</xsd:element>
```

Elements that contain text only can also contain attributes. The attribute declaration would be contained by the restriction element, as in this example:

```
<xsd:complexType name="telType">
  <xsd:simpleContent>
```

```
      <xsd:restriction base="xsd:string">
        <xsd:pattern value="[0-9]{3}-[0-9]{7}"/>
        <xsd:attribute name="type" use="required">
          <xsd:simpleType>
            <xsd:restriction base="xsd:NMTOKEN">
              <xsd:enumeration value="hm"/>
              <xsd:enumeration value="wk"/>
            </xsd:restriction>
          </xsd:simpleType>
        </xsd:attribute>
      </xsd:restriction>
    </xsd:simpleContent>
  </xsd:complexType>
```

Mixed Content

When an element contains both child elements and character data, it follows the mixed content model. This content model is used mostly with document-centric information; for example, when the document calls for paragraphs of text. In the following example, we use a `message` element that contains both text and other child elements:

```
<message>The project team consisted of <projectLead>Sam</projectLead>,
    <projectMember>Kate</projectMember>, and <projectMember>Joe</projectMember>.
    The project was successful and marked the beginning of a
    relationship with <client>Williams and Sons Publishing<client>. All
    project evaluations will be submitted one week from today.</message>
```

The declaration that should be used to define a mixed content model is as follows:

```
<xsd:element name="message">
  <xsd:complexType mixed="true">
    <xsd:sequence>
      <xsd:element name="projectMember" type="xsd:string"/>
      <xsd:element name="projectLead" type="xsd:string"/>
      <xsd:element name="client" type="xsd:string"/>
    </xsd:sequence>
  </xsd:complexType>
</xsd:element>
```

In this example, we introduce a `mixed` attribute to the `complexType` element. If you're introducing a mixed content model (elements and text), you have to use this attribute.

EMPTY

If an element does not contain any character data, it's considered empty. Empty elements are placeholders, commonly used to mark locations or embed objects. These empty elements can accept attributes. For example, the HTML `img` element is an empty element used to embed a graphics file. If you want to use an empty element to act as a placeholder, you would use the following element declaration:

```
<xsd:element name="mark">
   <xsd:complexType/>
</xsd:element>
```

However, many times you'll want to use attributes with empty elements. In the previous section, we used a message element that contained a mixture of child elements and character data. The child elements contained within the message element identified data that pertained to employees involved in the project. Instead of introducing new elements that contain string datatypes, we could use empty elements that reference employee data, as in the following markup, for example:

```
<message>The project team consisted of <staff eidRef="p98145"/>,
   <staff eidRef="t00022"/>, and <staff eidRef="p01164"/>. The project was
   successful and marked the beginning of a relationship with
   <client>Williams and Sons Publishing<client>. All project
   evaluations will be submitted one week from today.
</message>
```

In this case, we want to define an element type declaration that uses a complexType element that contains an attribute declaration (or you could do it with a named complex type definition). There are two ways you can define the complex type: as an anonymous definition (see the following example) or as a named complex type. If no content model is defined, as in the following example, the processor knows that the element should be empty:

```
<xsd:element name="staff">
   <xsd:complexType>
     <xsd:attribute name="eidRef" type="xsd:int"/>
   </xsd:complexType>
   <xsd:keyRef name="employeeIdentificationNumberRef">
     <xsd:selector xpath="message/staff"/>
     <xsd:field xpath="@eidRef"/>
   </xsd:keyRef>
</xsd:element>
```

In this example, we create an empty element that uses an attribute to reference an employee identification number. We also use the keyRef element to establish a relationship with the employee ID that was defined as a key elsewhere in the document (keys are discussed in detail later in this chapter).

If you want to create a simple empty element (one that might be used as a placeholder), you can do so as follows:

```
<xsd:element name="staff">
   <xsd:complexType/>
</xsd:element>
```

When you want to use the `staff` element, you can use it as an empty element or as an element with no content:

```
<staff/>
<staff></staff>
```

ANY

Much as the DTD does with the `ANY` keyword, XML Schema provides schema authors with a mechanism that allows for any content, as well as any attribute, to be used within an element.

To allow for any content to be used within an element, you have to use the any element:

```
<xsd:element name="contact">
  <xsd:complexType mixed="true">
    <xsd:sequence>
      <xsd:any maxOccurs="unbounded" processContents="skip"/>
    </xsd:sequence>
  </xsd:complexType>
</xsd:element>
```

The `processContents` attribute defines whether validation of any of the elements used is necessary. The `processContents` attribute values are defined as follows:

- `strict`, which is the default and means validation is required and a declaration must be found.

- `skip`, which means no validation necessary; the element must simply be well formed.

- `lax`, which means the element is validated if possible.

In the preceding example, we use the `skip` value. In this case, the processor will not attempt to validate the contents of the `contact` element. The only requirement is that the `contact` element is well formed.

When using the any element, we can also use a `namespace` attribute to define namespace behavior for any child elements:

```
namespace="(##any | ##other) | List of (anyURI |
   (##targetNamespace | ##local))"
```

The `namespace` attribute values are defined as follows:

- `##any`, which means the content may belong to any namespace.

- `##other`, which means the content may belong to any namespace other than the target namespace.

- `##targetNamespace`, which means the element belongs to the target namespace.

- `##local`, which means the element doesn't belong to any namespace. Otherwise, you can include the URI of a namespace.

- *anyURI*, which means a single namespace or a white-space-separated list of namespaces can be specified.

Creating and Using Model Groups

Compositors are used within complex type definitions as containers of element declarations. If you plan on reusing a content model, you might want to consider creating a model group that contains the compositor(s) and element declarations. The group element is used to define a model group component, as follows:

```
<xsd:group base="nameGroup">
   <xsd:sequence>
      <xsd:element name="firstName" type="xsd:string"/>
      <xsd:element name="lastName" type="xsd:string"/>
   </xsd:sequence>
<xsd:group>
```

The named model group is defined globally and then referenced later using a group element with a ref attribute. The group element may contain one of the three compositors: sequence, choice, or all. The compositors then contain element declarations.

Reusing Model Groups

After you've created the model groups, you're ready to use (and reuse) them. To use a defined model group, you use the group element with a ref attribute as follows:

```
<xsd:element name="staffName">
   <xsd:complexType>
      <xsd:group ref="nameGroup"/>
   </xsd:complexType>
</xsd:element>

<xsd:element name="clientName">
   <xsd:complexType>
      <xsd:group ref="nameGroup"/>
   </xsd:complexType>
</xsd:element>
```

In this example, we've created two elements that will use the same content model:

```
<staffName>
   <firstName>...</firstName>
   <lastName>...</lastName>
</staffName>
<clientName>
   <firstName>...</firstName>
   <lastName>...</lastName>
</clientName>
```

You can also build upon group models within a content model. For example, we might want to include some additional information for the staffName element. In the following element declaration, we add a middleName element to the content model:

```
<xsd:element name="staffName">
   <xsd:complexType>
```

```
    <xsd:sequence>
      <xsd:group ref="nameGroup"/>
      <xsd:element name="middleName" type="xsd:string"/>
    </xsd:sequence>
  </xsd:complexType>
</xsd:element>
```

Occurrence Behavior and Model Groups

The group element can also accept the minOccurs and maxOccurs attributes. This allows the model group to repeat within a given element content model. The key is that these attributes can be used only when referencing the model group—they cannot be used when the group is being defined globally. Here's how you would use these attributes:

```
<xsd:group ref="nameGroup" maxOccurs="unbounded"/>
```

Declaring Attributes

Working with simple attribute declarations that use built-in datatypes is easy. These declarations may be defined locally or globally and are defined as empty elements requiring the use of only a few attributes. When you decide you're ready to derive your own datatypes for attribute values, the declarations become a little trickier. Before we dive into the complicated end, we cover the basics of declaring attributes.

Going Global or Local

Like element declarations, attributes can be defined locally or globally. If they're defined globally, you use the name attribute to name them and then you reference them later, as shown here:

```
<xsd:attribute name="eidRef" type="xsd:int"/>

<xsd:element name="staff">
  <xsd:complexType>
    <xsd:attribute ref="eidRef"/>
  </xsd:complexType>
  <xsd:keyRef name="employeeIdentificationNumberRef">
    <xsd:selector xpath="message/staff"/>
    <xsd:field xpath="@eidRef"/>
  </xsd:keyRef>
</xsd:element>
```

However, you can also define the attribute locally:

```
<xsd:element name="staff">
  <xsd:complexType>
    <xsd:attribute name="eidRef" type="xsd:int"/>
  </xsd:complexType>
```

```
    <xsd:keyRef name="employeeIdentificationNumberRef">
      <xsd:selector xpath="message/staff"/>
      <xsd:field xpath="@eidRef"/>
    </xsd:keyRef>
  </xsd:element>
```

In both of these examples, we define attributes that use built-in datatypes. If you want to derive your own datatype, you have to use the `simpleType` element. This element can be nested within the attribute declaration, or it can be defined globally and then referenced using the `type` attribute.

The following shows the `simpleType` element defined locally:

```
<xsd:attribute name="dept" use="required">
  <xsd:simpleType>
    <xsd:restriction base="xsd:string">
      <xsd:enumeration value="management"/>
      <xsd:enumeration value="programming"/>
      <xsd:enumeration value="design"/>
      <xsd:enumeration value="training"/>
    </xsd:restriction>
  </xsd:simpleType>
</xsd:attribute>
```

This example shows the `simpleType` element defined globally:

```
<xsd:attribute name="dept" use="required" type="deptType"/>

<xsd:simpleType name="deptType">
  <xsd:restriction base="xsd:string">
    <xsd:enumeration value="management"/>
    <xsd:enumeration value="programming"/>
    <xsd:enumeration value="design"/>
    <xsd:enumeration value="training"/>
  </xsd:restriction>
</xsd:simpleType>
```

We take a closer look at deriving simple types later in this chapter.

Attribute Behavior

XML Schema allows schema authors to define how an attribute must be used. For example, the schema model can require the use of an attribute, or it can allow that attribute to be optional. This functionality mimics DTD keywords such as #IMPLIED, #REQUIRED, and #FIXED. For XML Schema, you add the `use` attribute and choose one of its three values:

- `optional`, which means the attribute is not required.
- `prohibited`, which means the attribute cannot be used.
- `required`, which means the attribute is required.

Defining Default and Fixed Values

You can also provide a fixed or default value. To do this, you have to use either the `fixed` or `default` attribute, as shown here:

```
<xsd:attribute name="version" fixed="1.0" use="required"/>
<xsd:attribute name="version" default="1.0" type="xsd:string"/>
```

The value of both the `fixed` and `default` attributes would be used in the document instance. In the first example, the `version` attribute is required and therefore must be used. The value of the `version` attribute must be `1.0`. In the second example, the `version` attribute has a default value assigned. If the attribute is not used in the document instance, the default value of `1.0` is assumed.

Defining Attribute Groups

Similar to defining model groups for element content models, you can group attribute declarations. Grouped attributes mimic DTD parameter entities. An attribute group allows you to define a collection of common attributes that you want to reuse. Once they're defined as a group, all you have to do is reference that group.

The first step is to name the attribute group and define its contents, as shown in this example:

```
<xsd:attributeGroup name="commonAttributes">
   <xsd:attribute name="title" type="xsd:string"/>
   <xsd:attribute name="id" type="xsd:ID"/>
   <xsd:attribute name="style" type="xsd:string"/>
</xsd:attributeGroup>
```

After the attribute group is defined, you can use it within anonymous or named complex type definitions, as follows:

```
<xsd:complexType name="messageType">
   <xsd:sequence>
     <xsd:element name="to" type="xsd:string"/>
     <xsd:element name="from" type="xsd:string"/>
     <xsd:element name="text" type="xsd:string"/>
   </xsd:sequence>
   <xsd:attributeGroup ref="commonAttributes"/>
</xsd:complexType>
```

You can also build on attribute groups from within a content model:

```
<xsd:complexType name="messageType">
   <xsd:sequence>
     <xsd:element name="to" type="xsd:string"/>
     <xsd:element name="from" type="xsd:string"/>
     <xsd:element name="text" type="xsd:string"/>
```

```
        </xsd:sequence>
        <xsd:attributeGroup ref="commonAttributes"/>
        <xsd:attribute name="priority" type="priorityType"/>
    </xsd:complexType>
```

Deriving Complex and Simple Types

XML Schema allows you to derive new complex and simple types. To do so, you must identify a base type and then alter it to produce a new type. The Structures document identifies four types of derivation:

- `restriction`, which identifies an existing base type and uses facets to restrict its content.

- `extension`, which identifies an existing base type and adds to it.

- `list`, which identifies an existing base type that the user can the list as a value.

- `union`, which identifies existing base types that can be combined to define a new type.

These four derivation methods cannot always be used. When deriving simple types, you can only use the `restriction`, `list`, and `union` methods. The `extension` method is not allowed. When deriving complex types, you can only use the `restriction` and `extension` methods.

Deriving Complex Types

If you want to derive a new datatype for element content, you cannot simply use the `restriction` or `extension` element within the complex type. First you have to define the content of a complex type as simple or complex content. Complex types can be defined in one of two ways: as containing complex content or as containing simple content. Both types allow attributes; however, the allowable content differs:

- Simple content is used to define elements that contain text-only content.

- Complex content is used to define elements that contain child elements.

In other words, the main difference between the two categories is that simple content does not allow child elements. To designate the content as either simple or complex, you have to use the `simpleContent` or `complexContent` element, respectively. After you've used one of these elements, you're ready to add the `restriction` or `extension` element.

If you're not deriving a new type, you do not have to use the `simpleContent` or `complexContent` element. Those elements are only used when deriving new types.

Deriving by Extension

When you use the `extension` element, you're adding to a type definition. For example, you might want to add an attribute to `middleNameType`:

```
<xsd:complexType name="middleNameTypeExtended">
    <xsd:simpleContent>
```

```
    <xsd:extension base="middleNameType">
      <xsd:attribute name="initial" type="xsd:string"/>
    </xsd:extension>
  </xsd:simpleContent>
</xsd:complexType>
```

To use this new type, you can define it within an element declaration:

```
<xsd:element name="middleName" type="middleNameTypeExtended"/>
```

Now, when you use the middleName element in the document instance, you have to use the initial attribute, which was added to the complex type definition as an extension:

```
<middleName initial="S">
```

You can also add elements to an existing complex type. We can create a complex definition that allows for three elements, for example:

```
<xsd:complexType name="employeeType">
  <xsd:sequence>
    <xsd:element name="name" type="nameType"/>
    <xsd:element name="contact" type="contactType"/>
  </xsd:sequence>
</xsd:complexType>
```

From this base type, we want to add another child element. In this case, we start with a complex type definition for employeeType. Using another complex type definition, we add the new element:

```
<xsd:complexType name="employeeTypeExtension">
  <xsd:complexContent>
    <xsd:extension base="employeeType">
      <xsd:sequence>
        <xsd:element name="name" type="nameType"/>
      </xsd:sequence>
    </xsd:extension>
  </xsd:complexContent>
</xsd:complexType>
```

In this example, we complete several steps. First, we name the new complex type. Next, we define it as complex content because we're working with child elements. We then use the extension element to add the new element and identify the base type for that extension. Now, we are ready to use the new type:

```
<xsd:element name="employee" type="employeeTypeExtension"/>
```

Deriving by Restriction

There are two different ways you can work with the restriction element. First, you can work with complex content models. In this case, you might want to allow a content model to use only two of the three child elements defined. When you want to restrict an element content model, you do so using the `complexContent` element within a `complexType` element:

```
<xsd:complexType name="nameType">
    <xsd:sequence>
      <xsd:element name="firstName" type="xsd:string"/>
      <xsd:element name="middleName" type="xsd:string"/>
      <xsd:element name="lastName" type="xsd:string"/>
    </xsd:sequence>
</xsd:complexType>

<xsd:complexType name="nameTypeRestricted">
    <xsd:complexContent>
      <xsd:restriction base="nameType">
        <xsd:sequence>
          <xsd:element name="firstName" type="xsd:string"/>
          <xsd:element name="lastName" type="xsd:string"/>
        </xsd:sequence>
      </xsd:restriction>
    </xsd:complexContent>
</xsd:complexType>
```

In this example, we first create a complex type definition called `nameType`. Then we derive a new type from `nameType`. The second complex type definition (`nameTypeRestricted`) uses `nameType` as the base. The new complex type uses a similar sequence of child elements; however, this time we eliminate the `middleName` element, thereby providing a more restricted content model.

TIP   You can also derive simple types using the `restriction` element. This is covered in the following sections.

Deriving New Simple Types

Deriving simple types is similar to deriving complex types, except you can use only the following derivation methods:

- `restriction`
- `list`
- `union`

The most common simple type derivation method is the `restriction` method.

Restriction

You can use the `restriction` method to derive new datatypes for text-only content. In other words, you can also use the `restriction` method for simple type definitions. For example, you might want to define a specific pattern for telephone numbers that require a hyphen between the area code and the telephone number. When using the `restriction` method to modify simple type definitions, you have to define a base type and then use facets to restrict its contents. Essentially, the `restriction` element creates a datatype that is a subset of an existing type. You can apply a restriction using facets that limit properties of a datatype. For example, you can use the `maxLength` and `minLength` facets to define the maximum and minimum number of characters allowed for a given datatype. Each datatype has a specifically defined list of allowable facets.

TIP   Remember that simple type definitions can be used for both element and attribute content as long as it's text only. All the examples in this section can be used to constrain datatypes for elements or attributes.

There are 12 possible constraining facets:

`enumeration`

`fractionDigits`

`length`

`maxExclusive`

`maxInclusive`

`maxLength`

`minExclusive`

`minInclusive`

`minLength`

`pattern`

`totalDigits`

`whiteSpace`

In this section, we focus on simple type definitions. Both elements and attributes with text-only contents are defined with simple types. These simple types can be used for attribute or element datatypes. We provide a brief description of each facet in this section, along with examples of each one:

`enumeration`   Constrains the value of the datatype to a defined set of values. For example, a simple type definition can define a named datatype (`dayType`) that allows for one of the seven days of the week as its value:

```
<xsd:simpleType name="dayType">
   <xsd:restriction base="xsd:string">
```

```
            <xsd:enumeration value="Monday"/>
            <xsd:enumeration value="Tuesday"/>
            <xsd:enumeration value="Wednesday"/>
            <xsd:enumeration value="Thursday"/>
            <xsd:enumeration value="Friday"/>
            <xsd:enumeration value="Saturday"/>
            <xsd:enumeration value="Sunday"/>
        </xsd:restriction>
    </xsd:simpleType>
```

`fractionDigits`   Defines the maximum number of digits allowable for the fractional part of a datatype derived from `decimal`:

```
<xsd:simpleType name="numericType">
    <xsd:restriction base="xsd:decimal">
        <xsd:totalDigits value="10"/>
        <xsd:fractionDigits value="3"/>
    </xsd:restriction>
</xsd:simpleType>
```

`length`   Defines the number of units of length using a nonnegative integer. The units of length vary depending on the datatype. For example, for a `string` datatype, the units of length are measured in characters, whereas for a `hexBinary` datatype, units are measured in octets (8 bits) of binary data. In this example, we set the number of characters for the `isbn-Type` element to 10:

```
<xsd:simpleType name="isbnType">
    <xsd:restriction base="string">
        <xsd:length value="10" fixed="true"/>
    </xsd:restriction>
</xsd:simpleType>
```

`maxExclusive`   Defines the exclusive upper bound for a datatype with the ordered property. Because it's exclusive, the defined value may *not* be included within the value space. For example, you can define an upper bound of 100 for an integer datatype; in this case, the datatype may accept any integer less than 100:

```
<xsd:simpleType name="upperType">
    <xsd:restriction base="integer">
        <xsd:maxExclusive value="101"/>
    </xsd:restriction>
</xsd:simpleType>
```

`maxInclusive`   Defines the inclusive upper bound for a datatype with the ordered property. Because it's inclusive, the defined value may be included within the value space. For example, you can define an upper bound of 100 for an integer datatype; in this case, the datatype may accept any integer less than or equal to 100:

```
<xsd:simpleType name="editionType">
    <xsd:restriction base="xsd:nonNegativeInteger">
        <xsd:minInclusive value="1"/>
        <xsd:maxInclusive value="10"/>
    </xsd:restriction>
</xsd:simpleType>
```

`maxLength`   Defines the maximum number of units of length using a nonnegative integer. The units of length vary depending on the datatype. Here's an example of `maxLength`:

```
<xsd:element name="myString">
    <xsd:simpleType>
        <xsd:restriction base="xsd:normalizedString">
            <xsd:maxLength value="10"/>
        </xsd:restriction>
    </xsd:simpleType>
</xsd:element>
```

`minExclusive`   Defines the exclusive lower bound for a datatype with the ordered property. Because it's exclusive, the defined value may *not* be included within the value space. You can define a lower bound of 10 for an integer datatype; in this case, the datatype may accept any integer greater than 10:

```
<xsd:simpleType name="lowerType">
    <xsd:restriction base="xsd:integer">
        <xsd:minExclusive value="99"/>
    </xsd:restriction>
</xsd:simpleType>
```

`minInclusive`   Defines the inclusive lower bound for a datatype with the ordered property. Because it's inclusive, the defined value may be included within the value space. For example, you can define a lower bound of 10 for an integer datatype; in this case, the datatype may accept any integer greater than or equal to 10:

```
<xsd:simpleType name="editionType">
    <xsd:restriction base="xsd:nonNegativeInteger">
        <xsd:minInclusive value="1"/>
        <xsd:maxInclusive value="10"/>
    </xsd:restriction>
</xsd:simpleType>
```

`minLength`   Defines the minimum number of units of length using a nonnegative integer. The units of length vary depending on the datatype. Here's an example of `minLength`:

```
<xsd:simpleType name="productCodeType">
    <xsd:restriction base="xsd:string">
```

```
        <xsd:minLength value="5"/>
    </xsd:restriction>
</xsd:simpleType>
```

pattern Constrains the lexical space to literals that must match a defined pattern. The value must be a regular expression (defined in Chapter 7). For example, you can define a pattern for ISBNs. Using the **pattern** facet, you could define the value as follows:

```
<xsd:simpleType name="isbnType">
    <xsd:restriction base="xsd:string">
        <xsd:pattern value="[0-9]{10}"/>
    </xsd:restriction>
</xsd:simpleType>
```

totalDigits Defines the maximum number of digits allowable for a datatype derived from decimal; here's an example:

```
<xsd:element name="money">
    <xsd:simpleConent>
        <xsd:restriction base="xsd:decimal">
            <xsd:totalDigits value="4"/>
            <xsd:fractionDigits value="2"/>
        </xsd:restriction>
    </xsd:simpleContent>
</xsd:element>
```

whiteSpace Specifies how white space (tabs, line feeds, carriage returns, and spaces) is processed. The **whiteSpace** facet can accept only three values: **preserve**, **replace**, or **collapse**. Here is an example of **whiteSpace**:

```
<xsd:simpleType name="token">
    <xsd:restriction base="xsd:normalizedString">
        <xsd:whiteSpace value="collapse"/>
    </xsd:restriction>
</xsd:simpleType>
```

TIP   To learn more about facets, see Chapter 7.

List

The **list** element creates a datatype that consists of a white-space-separated list of values. The **list** element uses an attribute to define the base type to be used for the list, as shown in this example:

```
<xsd:simpleType name="numericDayList">
    <xds:list itemType="xsd:decimal"/>
</xsd:simpleType>
```

Using the list derivation method is quite simple. The steps involved are as follows:

1. Define a name for the simple type (remember, this method can be used only with simple type definitions).

2. Include the `list` element.

3. Use the `itemType` attribute to identify the datatype that will be used for the list.

When the new simple type is used in the document instance, a white-space-separated list of the datatype may be used:

```
<day>1 2 3 4 5 6 7</day>
```

Union

The `union` element creates a datatype that is derived from multiple datatypes. The `union` element uses an attribute to define all base types participating in the union. Any of the defined base datatypes are allowed. In the following example, the first and second datatypes are allowed:

```
<xsd:simpleType name="exampleTypeUnion">
   <xsd:union memberTypes="first second"/>
</xsd:simpleType>
```

The base types of `union`, `first`, and `second` are known as the member types. To take a closer look at how to work with unions, consider the following example:

```
<day>M T W Th F S Su</day>
<day>1 2 3 4 5 6 7</day>
```

In this example, the `day` element contains two different datatypes. One is a decimal and the other can be defined using the `enumeration` facet. You should also notice that each element consists of a white-space-separated list of datatypes. In this scenario, we will have to use both the `union` and `list` derivation methods.

First, we want to define the simple type definition for the enumerated values (M, T, W, Th, F, S, Su):

```
<xsd:simpleType name="alphaDayType">
   <xsd:restriction base="xsd:string">
     <xsd:enumeration value="M"/>
     <xsd:enumeration value="T"/>
     <xsd:enumeration value="W"/>
     <xsd:enumeration value="Th"/>
     <xsd:enumeration value="F"/>
     <xsd:enumeration value="S"/>
     <xsd:enumeration value="Su"/>
   </xsd:restriction>
</xsd:simpleType>
```

Next, we want to define simple types using the list derivation method:

```
<xsd:simpleType name="alphaDayTypeList">
   <xsd:list itemType="alphaDayType"/>
</xsd:simpleType>
<xsd:simpleType name="numericDayTypeList">
   <xsd:list itemType="xsd:decimal"/>
</xsd:simpleType>
```

The final step is to define the union:

```
<xsd:simpleType name="unionDayType">
   <xsd:union memberTypes="alphaDayTypeList numberDayTypeList"/>
</xsd:simpleType>
```

These four simple type definitions defined in this section work together to allow for either datatype to be used within the day element.

Working with Namespaces

XML Schema offers flexible namespace support. This support allows you to use both pre-fixed and default namespaces in document instances as well as use elements and attributes from other namespaces. As a matter of fact, you can even include elements from unknown namespaces. This is a significant advantage over using XML DTDs.

There are three XML Schema namespaces that you should be familiar with:

- The XML Schema namespace used for W3C XML Schema elements. You can define this namespace as a default namespace or with a prefix. The namespace URI is `http://www.w3.org/2001/XMLSchema`.

- The XML Schema Datatype namespace specifies the use of built-in datatypes. The XML Schema namespace (`http://www.w3.org/2001/XMLSchema`) also specifies the use of built-in datatypes; therefore, it's not necessary to use the XML Schema datatype namespace if you've defined the XML Schema namespace. The namespace URI is `http://www.w3.org/2001/XMLSchema-datatypes`.

- The XML Schema instance namespace used for W3C XML Schema attributes used in XML instance documents. The namespace is used to introduce `xsi:type`, `xsi:nil`, `xsi:schemaLocation`, and `xsi:noNamespaceSchemaLocation` attributes in instance documents. This namespace should be defined with an `xsi` prefix. The namespace URI is `http://www.w3.org/2001/XMLSchema-instance`.

Targeting Namespaces

If you want to use a namespace with your document instances, you have to define that namespace in your XML Schema document. To do so, you have to define a target namespace (`targetNamespace="http://www.yournamespace.com"`). The target namespace identifies the namespace to which the corresponding XML document should adhere. The following XML document uses a namespace (in bold):

```
<?xml version="1.0" encoding="UTF-8"?>
<employees xmlns="http://www.lanw.com/namespaces/employee">
    <employee eid="p98145" dept="programming">
      <contact addInfo="contacts/98145.xml">
        <name>
          <firstName>Joe</firstName>
          <middleName int="B">Brian</middleName>
          <lastName>Smith</lastName>
        </name>
        <address>
          <street>611 Ridgewood Drive</street>
          <city>Denver</city>
          <state>Colorado</state>
          <zipcode>80210</zipcode>
        </address>
        <phone>
          <tel type="wk">303-4667339</tel>
          <tel type="hm">303-9842361</tel>
          <fax>303-4667357</fax>
        </phone>
        <email>JSmith@earthlink.net</email>
      </contact>
      <hireDate>1998-10-14</hireDate>
    </employee>
    <employee eid="t00022" dept="training">
      ...
    </employee>
    <employee eid="p01164" dept="programming">
      ...
    </employee>
</employees>
```

XML Schema allows you to define a target namespace for any document that is to conform to the schema, as shown in this example:

```
<schema
    targetNamespace="http://www.lanw.com/namespaces/employee">
  ...
</schema>
```

Document Models without a Namespace

There are times when you won't want to use a namespace for the document instance, in which case you just have to omit the `targetNamespace` attribute, as we do in this example:

```
<xsd:schema xmlns:xsd="http://www.w3.org/2001/XMLSchema">
  <xsd:element name="employee">
    <xsd:complexType>
      <xsd:sequence>
        <xsd:element name="name" type="xsd:string"/>
        <xsd:element name="email" type="xsd:string"/>
        <xsd:element name="hireDate" type="xsd:string"/>
      </xsd:sequence>
    </xsd:complexType>
  </xsd:element>
</xsd:schema>
```

The document instance that could be created would not contain a namespace:

```
<?xml version="1.0"?>
<employee
    xmlns:xsi="http://www.w3.org/2001/XMLSchema-instance"
    xsi:noNamespaceSchemaLocation="employee.xsd">
    <name>Joe Smith</name>
    <email>JSmith@earthlink.net</email>
    <hireDate>1998-10-14</hireDate>
</employee>
```

Because the document instance does not define a namespace, `noNamespaceSchemaLocation` is used to point to the schema document. To use schema instance attributes, you have to define the schema instance namespace (`http://www.w3.org/2001/XMLSchema-instance`). It's common practice to do so using the `xsi` prefix.

TIP   If your schema model calls for a namespace, the document instance will use the `schemaLocation` attribute rather than the `noNamespaceSchemaLocation` attribute to point to the schema document.

Document Models with a Namespace

As you already know, the `targetNamespace` is used to define a namespace for the document model. It's added to the `schema` root element. The value of that attribute is the namespace that must be used for the document instance, as this example shows:

```
<xsd:schema
    xmlns:xsd="http://www.w3.org/2001/XMLSchema"
    targetNamespace="http://www.lanw.com/namespaces/employee"
    xmlns="http://www.lanw.com/namespaces/employee">
    <xsd:element name="employee">
```

```
      <xsd:complexType>
        <xsd:sequence>
          <xsd:element name="name" type="xsd:string"/>
          <xsd:element name="email" type="xsd:string"/>
          <xsd:element name="hireDate" type="xsd:string"/>
        </xsd:sequence>
      </xsd:complexType>
    </xsd:element>
  </xsd:schema>
```

In this example, we've added two new attributes to the schema root element. The first is the `targetNamespace` attribute, which is to be used in the document instances. The second attribute defines a default namespace for the schema document. Any element or attribute used, or referenced (`ref="hireDate"`), would belong to this namespace. This is necessary because we've defined a target namespace for the new vocabulary we're creating. No matter where we use that vocabulary (in a document instance, or even within the schema document), we have to define its namespace.

There's one rule that you must understand when working with namespaces and XML Schema: Elements declared globally must be qualified, whereas, unless specified, elements declared locally must not be qualified.

If we were to define the following schema vocabulary, notice that there's one global element declaration that contains three local element declarations:

```
<xsd:schema
    xmlns:xsd="http://www.w3.org/2001/XMLSchema"
    targetNamespace="http://www.lanw.com/namespaces/employee"
    xmlns="http://www.lanw.com/namespaces/employee">
    <xsd:element name="employee">
      <xsd:complexType>
        <xsd:sequence>
          <xsd:element name="name" type="xsd:string"/>
          <xsd:element name="email" type="xsd:string"/>
          <xsd:element name="hireDate" type="xsd:string"/>
        </xsd:sequence>
      </xsd:complexType>
    </xsd:element>
  </xsd:schema>
```

According to XML Schema, global declarations must be qualified (if a target namespace is declared) within the document instance. However, locally declared elements do not have to be qualified. Therefore, the following document instance would also be valid:

```
<?xml version="1.0"?>
<em:employee
    xmlns:em="http://www.lanw.com/namespaces/employee"
```

```
xmlns:xsi="http://www.w3.org/2001/XMLSchema-instance"
xsi:schemaLocation="http://www.lanw.com/namespaces/employee employee.xsd">
<name>Joe Smith</name>
<email>JSmith@earthlink.net</email>
<hireDate>1998-10-14</hireDate>
</em:employee>
```

You might be tempted to define a default namespace within the employee element, as follows:

```
<employee
   xmlns="http://www.lanw.com/namespaces/employee"
   xmlns:xsi="http://www.w3.org/2001/XMLSchema-instance"
   xsi:schemaLocation="http://www.lanw.com/namespaces/employee employee.xsd">
```

However, that would not be valid because the local declarations cannot be declared. To better understand how namespaces and XML Schema work together, you need to understand how XML Schema treats namespace qualification.

Namespace Qualification

When working with namespaces, the schema author must decide whether the namespace of each element and attribute should be hidden or exposed in the document instance. To do this, you set the value of the elementFormDefault and attributeFormDefault attributes as a part of the schema element:

```
elementFormDefault="qualified | unqualified"
attributeFormDefault="qualified | unqualified"
```

elementFormDefault

By setting the elementFormDefault attribute, you can require the document instance to expose or hide namespace qualifications. If elementFormDefault is set to unqualified (which is also the default), the document instance may hide all namespace qualifications. This only applies to those elements that are defined locally. Therefore, all globally declared elements would have to be qualified in the document instance:

```
<?xml version="1.0"?>
<em:employee
   xmlns:em="http://www.lanw.com/namespaces/employee"
   xmlns:xsi="http://www.w3.org/2001/XMLSchema-instance"
   xsi:schemaLocation="http://www.lanw.com/namespaces/employee employee.xsd">
   <name>Joe Smith</name>
   <email>JSmith@earthlink.net</email>
   <hireDate>1998-10-14</hireDate>
</em:employee>
```

On the other hand, if you use `elementFormDefault="qualified"`, the namespace of each element would have to be exposed in document instances:

```
<?xml version="1.0"?>
<em:employee
    xmlns:em="http://www.lanw.com/namespaces/employee"
    xmlns:xsi="http://www.w3.org/2001/XMLSchema-instance"
    xsi:schemaLocation="http://www.lanw.com/namespaces/employee employee.xsd">
    <em:name>Joe Smith</em:name>
    <em:email>JSmith@earthlink.net</em:email>
    <em:hireDate>1998-10-14</em:hireDate>
</em:employee>
```

In this case, each element is explicitly qualified. All elements, whether declared locally or globally, are qualified.

TIP   We take a closer look at qualifying namespaces in Chapter 8.

attributeFormDefault

The `attributeFormDefault` attribute works much like its `elementFormDefault` counterpart. The main difference is that in this case, we're dealing with attributes. Let's take the example from the previous section and add a couple of attributes to the `employee` element:

```
<xsd:schema
    xmlns:xsd="http://www.w3.org/2001/XMLSchema"
    targetNamespace="http://www.lanw.com/namespaces/employee"
    xmlns="http://www.lanw.com/namespaces/employee">
    <xsd:element name="employee">
      <xsd:complexType>
        <xsd:sequence>
          <xsd:element name="name" type="xsd:string"/>
          <xsd:element name="email" type="xsd:string"/>
          <xsd:element name="hireDate" type="xsd:string"/>
        </xsd:sequence>
        <xsd:attribute name="dept" type="xsd:string"/>
        <xsd:attribute name="client" type="xsd:string"/>
      </xsd:complexType>
    </xsd:element>
</xsd:schema>
```

Now we want to add the `elementFormDefault` and `attributeFormDefault` attributes to the schema element:

```
<xsd:schema
    xmlns:xsd="http://www.w3.org/2001/XMLSchema"
    targetNamespace="http://www.lanw.com/namespaces/employee"
```

```
       xmlns="http://www.lanw.com/namespaces/employee"
       elementFormDefault="qualified"
       attributeFormDefault="qualified">
       <xsd:element name="employee">
         <xsd:complexType>
           <xsd:sequence>
             <xsd:element name="name" type="xsd:string"/>
             <xsd:element name="email" type="xsd:string"/>
             <xsd:element name="hireDate" type="xsd:string"/>
           </xsd:sequence>
           <xsd:attribute name="dept" type="xsd:string"/>
           <xsd:attribute name="client" type="xsd:string"/>
         </xsd:complexType>
       </xsd:element>
     </xsd:schema>
```

We have set both attributes to qualified; therefore, all elements and attributes in our instance document must be qualified, as follows:

```
<em:employee
    xmlns:em="http://www.lanw.com/namespaces/employee"
    xmlns:xsi="http://www.w3.org/2001/XMLSchema-instance"
    xsi:schemaLocation="http://www.lanw.com/namespaces/employee employee.xsd"
    em:dept="programming"
    em:client="Smith and Co">
    <em:name>Joe Smith</em:name>
    <em:email>JSmith@earthlink.net</em:email>
    <em:hireDate>1998-10-14</em:hireDate>
</em:employee>
```

If we set elementFormDefault to qualified and omit attributeFormDefault (remembering its default value is unqualified), we could use the following document instance:

```
<em:employee
    xmlns:em="http://www.lanw.com/namespaces/employee"
    xmlns:xsi="http://www.w3.org/2001/XMLSchema-instance"
    xsi:schemaLocation="http://www.lanw.com/namespaces/employee employee.xsd"
    dept="programming"
    client="Smith and Co">
    <em:name>Joe Smith</em:name>
    <em:email>JSmith@earthlink.net</em:email>
    <em:hireDate>1998-10-14</em:hireDate>
</em:employee>
```

The only difference is that we've omitted the associated namespace prefix (em) from the attribute names.

Summary

The XML Schema vocabulary is divided into 13 components. Each of these components has an important role within the schema model. The first part of this chapter focused on defining these components, and the second part focused on using them. It's important that you have a firm understanding of some of the primary components.

The element declaration component is used to declare all elements for your vocabulary. Element declarations can be declared globally or locally. When it's defined, the element declaration can be defined as an empty element (using the `type` attribute to define a preexisting datatype) or it can contain a complex type definition that defines a more complex content model.

The next logical component to look at would be the complex type definition. As with many schema components, the complex type definition can be defined locally or globally. When it's defined globally, the component can be reused throughout the document—saving time and space. Within a complex type definition, you'll find the element content model. Depending on the type of content, you'll use the `simpleContent` element, the `complexContent` element, or a compositor.

Attribute declarations are similar to element declarations in that they can be defined locally or globally. They can be defined as empty elements (using the `type` attribute to reference a preexisting datatype) or they can contain simple type definitions.

If you want to work with text-only content and you want to derive your own datatypes for that content, you have to use the simple type definition component. This component can be used for both elements and attributes as long as you're only dealing with text. The simple type definitions allow you to derive new datatypes using the `restriction`, `list`, and `union` derivation techniques.

These four components (element declarations, attribute declarations, simple type definitions, and complex type definitions) make up the bulk of any schema document. However, there are other helper components that exist to make your schema document more flexible, efficient, and usable. For example, you can use model and attribute groups to define reusable chunks of information. You can also use particles to define occurrence behavior for your elements. To summarize, you can use the following components within a schema model:

- Element declaration
- Attribute declaration
- Simple type definition
- Complex type definition
- Model group

- Attribute group
- Particle
- Wildcards
- Identify-constraint definition
- Notation declaration
- Annotations

CHAPTER 7

Understanding Schema Datatypes

- Introducing datatype concepts and terminology

- Understanding the role of datatypes in schemas

- Understanding datatype dichotomies

- Examining built-in, primitive, and derived datatypes

- Using datatypes in schemas

- Working with datatype restrictions and constraints

The W3C XML Schema Part 2: Datatypes Recommendation expands and extends the types of data that can be contained in an XML element or attribute through a structured system of built-in and user-derived datatypes.

DTDs mainly use one datatype—the text string. There are a few provisions for constraining the contents of a text string with DTDs, but the choices are very limited. You cannot specify numeric datatypes (for example, dates or times) in a DTD, but it can easily be done in a schema. Most of the traditional programming language datatypes (string, numeric, date/time, and structural) are included in XML Schema datatypes, and inheritance of datatypes is also supported. Sources of the datatypes in XML Schema include Java, Structured Query Language (SQL), ISO/IEC 11404 language-independent datatypes, and the Extensible Markup Language (XML) 1.0.

Datatypes offer a means to validate information content, such as making sure that the content of a phone number element is a specific number of digits and does not include letters or other characters. Datatypes can also be used to transfer information to and from databases.

Introducing Datatype Concepts and Terminology

Datatypes in XML Schema are composed of three parts:

- A *value space*, which is the set of values for a specific datatype
- A *lexical space*, which is the set of valid literals, also known as *lexical representations*, for a specific datatype
- A set of *facets*, which is the aspects that define a datatype

Each value in the value space has at least one corresponding literal in the lexical space. For example, let's assume the street element in the following markup is defined in a schema as a string datatype (a *string* is a sequence of characters). For a string type, the value space and the lexical space are the same. Main is part of the value space for a string type (it's a group of four characters) and Main is also the lexical representation—the string literal that represents the value:

```
<!-- instance document -->
<street>Main</street>
```

The total element is defined as a float datatype in our hypothetical schema document:

```
<!-- instance document -->
<total>135000.00</total>
```

In this case, the representation of total is in string format, but the actual value is a numeric value that can be represented in many ways, including 135000, 135000.00, and 13.5E4. These three representations have the same numeric value but are three different literals from the float lexical space.

TIP   The W3C XML Schema specification also defines a *canonical lexical representation,* which is the subset of literals for a given datatype that corresponds one to one to the values in the value space—there's only one canonical lexical representation for any particular value in a value space.

Facets determine the value space and properties of a datatype. There are two types of facets:

- *Fundamental* facets, which define a datatype

- *Nonfundamental*, or *constraining*, facets, which limit the range of possible values for a datatype

There are five fundamental facets:

equal   Values with an equal facet can be compared and determined to be equal or not equal. For any values *a* and *b* in a value space, only one of the following is true: *a=b* or *a!=b*.

ordered   Values with an ordered facet have an ordered relationship with each other; for example, groups of numbers or groups of words that can be placed in an ordered sequence relative to each other have ordered relationships. The ordered facet can take the values false (not ordered), partial, or total.

bounded   Values with a bounded facet fit into a range of values with a specific lower and/or upper limit.

cardinality   The number of values in a value space can be classified as finite (value="finite") or countably infinite (value="countably infinite").

numeric   Values can be classified as numeric (value="true") or nonnumeric (value="false").

TIP   For more details on partial and total ordering, see the ordered facet definitions in Section 4.2.2 of the XML Schema Part 2: Datatypes Recommendation at www.w3.org/TR/xmlschema-2/.

Every XML schema datatype has at least three fundamental facets: equal, cardinality, and numeric. Datatypes may also have constraining facets that limit both their value space and their lexical space.

There are twelve constraining facets:

length   length is the number of units of length. The value must be a nonnegative integer, but the units vary depending on the datatype:

- Characters are used for the string datatype.

- Octets (8 bits) of binary data are used for the hexBinary datatype.

- Octets of binary data are used for the base64Binary datatype.

- The number of list items is used for the list datatype.

WARNING   If length is specified for a datatype, neither minLength nor maxLength can be specified for that datatype.

maxLength   maxLength is the maximum number of units of length.

minLength   minLength is the minimum number of units of length.

pattern   A pattern is a *regular expression* (a sequence of characters). A lexical representation has a valid pattern facet if the lexical representation is among the character sequences specified by the value of the regular expression.

Regular expressions in schema are similar to regular expressions in the Perl programming language. For more details on regular expressions in schema, see Appendix F, XML Schema Part 2: Datatypes at www.w3.org/TR/xmlschema-2/#regexs. For more information on using regular expressions in schema documents and an applet to test regular expression code against a sample regular expression, see "Regular Expressions" by Daniel Potter at www.xfront.org/xml-schema/.

enumeration   enumeration specifies a set of valid values for a value space.

whiteSpace   The value of this facet specifies how white space (tabs, line feeds, carriage returns, and spaces) is processed. A whiteSpace facet can have one of three values:

- preserve (No modification is done.)

- replace (Tabs, line feeds, and carriage returns are replaced with spaces.)

- collapse (After tabs, line feeds, and carriage returns are replaced with spaces, sequences of spaces are collapsed to a single space and leading and trailing spaces are removed.)

maxInclusive   maxInclusive is the upper bound for a range of values in a value space. This value is included in the range.

`maxExclusive`   `maxExclusive` is the upper bound for a range of values in a value space. This value is not included in the range; only values up to this limit are included.

`minInclusive`   `minInclusive` is the lower bound for a range of values in a value space. This value is included in the range.

`minExclusive`   `minExclusive` is the lower bound for a range of values in a value space. This value is not included in the range; only values down to this limit are included.

You do not have to use the same type of bound for each end of a range; for example, it's valid to use a `minInclusive` facet with a `maxExclusive` facet.

`totalDigits`   `totalDigits` is a facet used with datatypes derived from the `decimal` type. `totalDigits` sets the maximum number of digits in the entire number, and its value must be a positive integer.

`fractionDigits`   `fractionDigits` is a facet used with datatypes derived from the `decimal` type. `fractionDigits` sets the maximum number of digits in the fractional part of the number, and its value must be a nonnegative integer.

We explore schema datatypes further, including definitions and examples of each of the 44 built-in XML schema datatypes, later in this chapter in the sections "Understanding Datatype Dichotomies," "Built-In Datatypes," "Primitive Datatypes," and "Derived Datatypes."

The Role of Datatypes in Schemas

The use of XML in data interchange necessitates an expanded and extensible system of datatypes. To validate data, a more extensive content specification is required so an XML processor can distinguish between, for example, a date and a Uniform Resource Locator (URL). Both are text strings, in the broadest definition of a string, but without a more comprehensive typing system for data, it's difficult for an application to correctly differentiate between them and, in addition, determine if the specific content is valid for that type.

The February 1999 W3C note on XML Schema requirements documents the agreed-upon requirements for the development of a schema language. Datatype requirements are an integral part of this document and include the following areas in which expanded and extensible datatypes are beneficial:

- E-commerce transactions
- Network data and message exchange
- Document development, such as technical manuals
- Database queries

- Uniform data transfer between applications, including databases
- Metadata exchange
- Information distribution through publishing

TIP   See "XML Schema Requirements: W3C Note 15 February 1999" at www.w3.org/TR/ 1999/NOTE-xml-schema-req-19990215 for additional information on the development of a schema language.

Datatypes also offer the opportunity for much more specific searching of Web documents than is currently possible with text-based searches. Text-based searching has become increasingly difficult and less useful with the massive number of documents currently on the Web. Schema-based XML documents could allow type-based searching, such as searching by date or by product number, for example.

The ability to use multiple namespaces in a single document allows the use of multiple schemas in one document, promotes sharing and reuse of schema information, and promotes the development of standardized schemas for certain types of information, such as phone numbers, e-mail addresses, mailing addresses, and credit card information. In addition, user-derived datatypes provide a way to extend schemas to meet the needs of application development and decrease the need for applications to provide their own methods of data checking and validation.

Understanding Datatype Dichotomies

Datatypes in XML Schema are categorized into three groups called *characterization dichotomies*:

- Atomic vs. list vs. union datatypes
- Primitive vs. derived datatypes
- Built-in vs. user-derived datatypes

These definitions are specific to XML Schema and do not necessarily correspond exactly to the definition of these types in any particular programming language.

Atomic, List, and Union Datatypes

The first group of datatype dichotomies includes the atomic, list, and union datatypes. Definitions for the value spaces and lexical spaces for these three datatypes are shown in Table 7.1.

TABLE 7.1: Atomic, List, and Union Datatypes

Datatype	value space	lexical space
Atomic	"Atomic" values that cannot be further divided	Literals specific to the datatype
List	Finite-length sequences of atomic values	White-space-separated sequence of literals
Union	Union of the value spaces of its member types	Union of the lexical spaces of its member types

Atomic datatypes have values that are considered indivisible and cannot be further broken down into component parts. Atomic datatypes can be primitive or derived (see Table 7.2 in the next section, "Primitive and Derived Datatypes"). The following are examples of atomic datatypes:

```
<!-- instance document -->
<myAtom>45988</myAtom>
<myAtom2>a string of characters</myAtom2>
```

The first is an `integer` (an atomic derived type from the `float` primitive type), and the second is a `string` (an atomic primitive type).

List datatypes make up a group of defined, finite-length sequences of atomic values. The atomic datatype included in the definition of a list datatype is known as the `itemType` of that specific list datatype. List datatypes are always derived and can include the following constraining facets:

- `length` (unit of length is number of list items)
- `maxlength`
- `minLength`
- `enumeration`
- `pattern`
- `whiteSpace` (`collapse` is the fixed value)

If a list datatype is derived from an atomic datatype that allows white space, such as a `string`, the list items will be automatically separated at the white space boundaries. Therefore, white space can't be included in any individual list item value. In the following example, the length of the list is five:

```
<!-- schema -->
<simpleType name="myLuckyNumbers">
    <list itemType="decimal"/>
</simpleType>
```

```
<!-- instance document -->
<numbers xsi:type="myLuckyNumbers"> 3 7 13 17 21.5 </numbers>
```

In this example, the length of our list is also five:

```
<!-- schema -->
<simpleType name="myString">
   <list itemType="string"/>
</simpleType>
<!-- instance document -->
<string_list xsi:type="myString">
   This string is a list
</string_list>
```

As you can see, a list is not a useful datatype for manipulating sentences, paragraphs, or any text grouping.

Union datatypes are always derived from atomic or list datatypes and include the value spaces and lexical spaces of all the datatypes used to derive the union datatype. The datatypes in the group of datatypes included in a union datatype are known as the memberTypes of that specific union datatype.

When the values of a union datatype are validated, they're validated in the order in which they're defined in the union datatype definition until a match is found:

```
<!-- schema -->
<xsd:element name="dog">
   <xsd:simpleType>
     <xsd:union>
       <xsd:simpleType>
       <xsd:restriction base="nonNegativeInteger"/>
     </xsd:simpleType>
       <xsd:simpleType>
        <xsd:restriction base="string"/>
       </xsd:simpleType>
     </xsd:union>
   </xsd:simpleType>
 </xsd:element>
<!-- instance document -->
<dog>15</dog>
<dog>hound</dog>
```

The first instance of the dog element validates as a nonnegative integer, and the second instance validates as a string.

Primitive and Derived Datatypes

The second group of datatype dichotomies includes primitive and derived datatypes. The definitions of these types are shown in Table 7.2.

TABLE 7.2: Primitive and Derived Datatypes

datatype	definition
Primitive	Not derived or defined based on other datatypes
anySimpleType	Base type of all primitive types
Derived	Derived and defined based on other datatypes

XML Schema includes 19 primitive datatypes. They are the base types for all other XML datatypes and can't be broken into smaller components. The section "Primitive Datatypes" later in this chapter includes definitions and examples of these 19 datatypes.

The XML Schema specification also includes a datatype named anySimpleType, which is the base type for all primitive types. anySimpleType is the simple version of the Ur-type definition. For more information on the Ur-type, see Chapter 6. The value space for anySimpleType is the union of the value spaces of all primitive datatypes.

XML Schema also includes 25 built-in derived datatypes. Derived datatypes are defined in terms of a base type and can be built in or user derived. The section "Derived Datatypes" later in this chapter includes definitions and examples of the 25 built-in derived datatypes.

Built-In and User-Derived Datatypes

The XML Schema Recommendation specifies 44 built-in datatypes, including both primitive and derived datatypes. The derived datatypes include built-in derived types and user-derived types. There's no fundamental difference between these two types of derived datatypes—the built-in derived types are simply common types provided by the W3C Recommendation. Schema designers are free to derive their own types using the format for user-derived types.

User-derived types and built-in derived types are constructed using simple type definitions and one of the following three methods:

Restriction   The restriction method specifies values for zero or more constraining facets in order to limit the value space and/or the lexical space to a subset of the base type. In this example, the string type has been restricted to five valid values:

```
<!-- schema -->
<xsd:element name="grades">
  <xsd:simpleType>
    <xsd:restriction base="xsd:string">
      <xsd:enumeration value="A"/>
      <xsd:enumeration value="B"/>
      <xsd:enumeration value="C"/>
      <xsd:enumeration value="D"/>
      <xsd:enumeration value="F"/>
```

```
        </xsd:restriction>
      </xsd:simpleType>
    </xsd:element>
```

List   The list method uses a finite sequence of itemType attributes to derive a new type. The value of the itemType attribute is the base datatype that is used to derive a new type:

```
<!-- schema -->
<simpleType name="websafe_hex">
    <list itemType="string"/>
</simpleType>
<!-- instance document -->
<color xsi:type="websafe_hex"> 00 33 66 99 cc ff</color>
```

Union   The union method joins the value spaces and lexical spaces of one or more datatypes to derive a new type:

```
<!-- schema -->
<xsd:element name="recipe">
    <xsd:simpleType>
      <xsd:union>
        <xsd:simpleType>
         <xsd:restriction base="decimal"/>
        </xsd:simpleType>
        <xsd:simpleType>
          <xsd:restriction base="string"/>
        </xsd:simpleType>
      </xsd:union>
    </xsd:simpleType>
</xsd:element>
<!-- instance document -->
<recipe>1.5</recipe>
<recipe>cups</recipe>
```

TIP	For more information on simple type definitions, see Chapter 6.

Built-In Datatypes

Built-in datatypes are defined in the W3C Schema for Datatype Definitions and include primitive and derived types. Table 7.3 illustrates the hierarchy of the built-in schema datatypes.

TABLE 7.3: Hierarchy of Built-In Datatypes

Level	Type Name	Type	Derivation
1	anyType	Ur type	Base type for all XML Schema datatypes
2	anySimpleType	Ur type	anyType
2	All complex types	Complex types	anyType
3	duration	Built-in primitive	anySimpleType
3	dateTime	Built-in primitive	anySimpleType
3	time	Built-in primitive	anySimpleType
3	date	Built-in primitive	anySimpleType
3	gYearMonth	Built-in primitive	anySimpleType
3	gYear	Built-in primitive	anySimpleType
3	gMonthDay	Built-in primitive	anySimpleType
3	gDay	Built-in primitive	anySimpleType
3	gMonth	Built-in primitive	anySimpleType
3	boolean	Built-in primitive	anySimpleType
3	base64Binary	Built-in primitive	anySimpleType
3	hexBinary	Built-in primitive	anySimpleType
3	float	Built-in primitive	anySimpleType
3	double	Built-in primitive	anySimpleType
3	anyURI	Built-in primitive	anySimpleType
3	QName	Built-in primitive	anySimpleType
3	NOTATION	Built-in primitive	anySimpleType
3	string	Built-in primitive	anySimpleType
3	decimal	Built-in primitive	anySimpleType
4	normalizedString	Built-in derived	string
4	integer	Built-in derived	decimal
5	token	Built-in derived	normalizedString
5	nonPositiveInteger	Built-in derived	integer
5	long	Built-in derived	integer
5	nonNegativeInteger	Built-in derived	integer
6	language	Built-in derived	token
6	Name	Built-in derived	token
6	NMTOKEN	Built-in derived	token
6	negativeInteger	Built-in derived	nonPositiveInteger
6	int	Built-in derived	long
6	unsignedLong	Built-in derived	nonNegativeInteger

Continued on next page

TABLE 7.3 CONTINUED: Hierarchy of Built-In Datatypes

Level	Type Name	Type	Derivation
6	positiveInteger	Built-in derived	nonNegativeInteger
7	NCName	Built-in derived	Name
7	NMTOKENS	Built-in derived	NMTOKEN
7	short	Built-in derived	int
7	unsignedInt	Built-in derived	unsignedLong
8	ID	Built-in derived	NCName
8	IDREF	Built-in derived	NCName
8	ENTITY	Built-in derived	NCName
8	byte	Built-in derived	short
8	unsignedShort	Built-in derived	unsignedInt
9	IDREFS	Built-in derived	IDREF
9	ENTITIES	Built-in derived	ENTITY
9	unsignedByte	Built-in derived	unsignedShort

The level number (in the first column) is provided only as a guide to the hierarchy. It's not a part of the datatype information itself and is not part of the W3C specification.

Figure 7.1 shows a graphic presentation of the built-in datatype hierarchy. This diagram is reproduced from the "Built-In Datatypes" section of the W3C Schema Recommendation at www.w3.org/TR/xmlschema-2/#built-in-datatypes. The schema definition of each datatype can be found in the W3C Schema for Datatype Definitions at www.w3.org/TR/xmlschema-2/#schema.

The built-in datatypes are designed to be used with the XML Schema specification as well as other XML specifications. When using built-in datatypes with schemas, the namespace is http://www.w3.org/2001/XMLSchema. When using built-in datatypes with other XML specifications, the namespace is http://www.w3.org/2001/XMLSchema-datatypes.

FIGURE 7.1:

A graphic presentation of the built-in datatype hierarchy

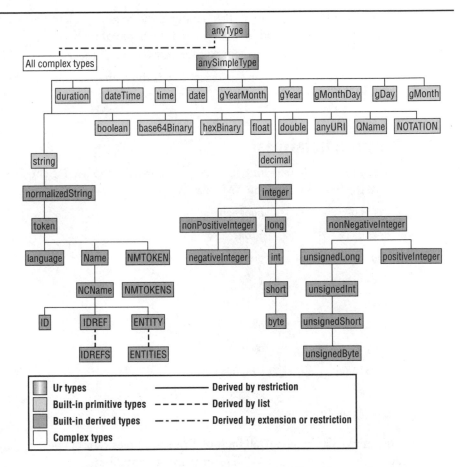

Each of these built-in datatypes can be referenced with a URI. To address a datatype, a facet, or a facet within a datatype, follow these steps:

1. Start with the base URI, which is the XML Schema namespace:

   ```
   http://www.w3.org/2001/XMLSchema
   ```

2. Add a fragment identifier.

   - To address a datatype, the fragment identifier is the name of the datatype:

     ```
     http://www.w3.org/2001/XMLSchema#float
     ```

   - To address a facet, the fragment identifier is the name of the facet:

     ```
     http://www.w3.org/2001/XMLSchema#pattern
     ```

- To address a facet within a datatype, the fragment identifier is the name of the datatype followed by a period and the name of the facet:

  `http://www.w3.org/2001/XMLSchema#string.pattern`

User-derived datatypes are associated with the namespace of the schema in which they're defined rather than with the XML Schema namespace.

Primitive Datatypes

There are 19 built-in primitive datatypes defined in the XML Schema specification. These 19 are the base for all of the XML datatypes:

string	boolean
decimal	float
double	duration
dateTime	time
date	gYearMonth
gYear	gMonthDay
gDay	gMonth
hexBinary	base64Binary
anyURI	QName
NOTATION	

Primitive datatypes are all built in. Primitive types cannot contain elements or attributes, but they can be used as a value in an element or attribute.

string   The string datatype represents a finite-length sequence of characters. Each character has a corresponding *Universal Character Set (UCS)* code point, which is an integer. The value space and the lexical space of a string are the same.

The only built-in type derived from string is the normalizedString type.

Facets	Name	Value
Fundamental	bounded	false
	cardinality	countably infinite
	numeric	false
	ordered	false

Facets	Name	Value
Constraining	length	
	maxLength	
	enumeration	
	minLength	
	pattern	
	whiteSpace	

```
<!-- schema -->
<xsd:element name="myString" type="xsd:string"/>
<!-- instance document -->
<myString>This is a simple string literal</myString>
```

boolean   The boolean datatype is used for binary logic (true/false). The lexical space is {true,false} and {1,0}. Either true or 1 may be used for a true value, and either false or 0 may be used for a false value.

No built-in datatypes are derived from boolean.

Facets	Name	Value
Fundamental	bounded	false
	cardinality	finite
	numeric	false
	ordered	false
Constraining	pattern	
	whiteSpace	

```
<!-- schema -->
<xsd:element name="choose" default="true" type="xsd:boolean"/>
<!-- instance document, using default value -->
<choose/>
<!-- instance document, not using default value -->
<choose>false</choose>
```

decimal   The decimal datatype represents a finite-length sequence of digits separated by a period. The facet totalDigits (value must be a positive integer) can be used to set the maximum number of digits in the entire number, and the facet fractionDigits (value must be a nonnegative integer) can be used to set the maximum number of digits in the fractional part of the number. Leading and trailing zeroes are optional. An optional leading + or - sign is also allowed. If no leading sign is used, it's assumed to be +.

The integer datatype is derived from the decimal type.

Facets	Name	Value
Fundamental	bounded	false
	cardinality	countably infinite
	numeric	true
	ordered	total
Constraining	totalDigits	
	pattern	
	enumeration	
	maxInclusive	
	minInclusive	
	fractionDigits	
	whiteSpace	
	maxExclusive	
	minExclusive	

```
<!-- schema -->
<xsd:element name="money">
   <xsd:simpleType>
     <xsd:restriction base="xsd:decimal">
       <xsd:totalDigits value="4"/>
       <xsd:fractionDigits value="2"/>
     </xsd:restriction>
   </xsd:simpleType>
</xsd:element>
<!-- instance document -->
<money>14.98</money>
```

In this example, the money element is constrained by the totalDigits and fractionDigits facets.

float   The float datatype represents a 32-bit, single-precision Institute of Electrical and Electronics Engineers (IEEE) floating-point number. The value space includes values in the range $m \times 2^e$, where m is an integer whose absolute value is less than 2^{24} and e is an integer between −149 and 104 inclusive. The lexical space is a *mantissa* (decimal number) optionally followed by E (or e) followed by an `integer` exponent, such as 13.57E15. `float` can take many forms; for example, all of these are floating point numbers: 12, –56.78, 3.79e25, 99.95. There are five special values for `float`: `positive zero`, `negative zero`, `positive infinity`, `negative infinity`, and `not-a-number`. The lexical representations are 0, -0, INF, -INF, and NaN.

No built-in datatypes are derived from `float`.

Facets	Name	Value
Fundamental	bounded	true
	cardinality	finite
	numeric	true
	ordered	total
Constraining	pattern	
	whiteSpace	
	maxInclusive	
	minInclusive	
	enumeration	
	maxExclusive	
	minExclusive	

```
<!-- schema -->
<xsd:element name="charge">
   <xsd:simpleType>
     <xsd:restriction base="xsd:float">
       <xsd:minExclusive value="1.00"/>
       <xsd:maxExlusive value="100.00"/>
     </xsd:restriction>
   </xsd:simpleType>
</xsd:element>
<!-- instance document -->
<charge>19.99</charge>
```

`double`   The `double` datatype represents a 64-bit, double-precision IEEE floating-point number. The value space includes values in the range $m \times 2^e$, where m is an integer whose absolute value is less than 2^{53} and e is an integer between –1075 and 970 inclusive. The lexical space is the same as that for the `float` datatype, a mantissa followed by an optional exponent. Like `float`, `double` includes the five special values of 0, -0, INF, -INF, and NaN.

No built-in datatypes are derived from `double`.

Facets	Name	Value
Fundamental	bounded	true
	cardinality	finite
	numeric	true
	ordered	total
Constraining	pattern	
	whiteSpace	
	maxInclusive	
	minInclusive	
	enumeration	
	maxExclusive	
	minExclusive	

```
<!-- schema -->
<xsd:element name="myDouble" type="xsd:double"/>
<!-- instance document -->
<myDouble>-133.459e-12</myDouble>
```

duration   The `duration` datatype represents a duration. The value space can include six components in this order: year, month, day, hour, minute, and second. The lexical space is the extended format P*n*Y*n*M*n*DT*n*H*n*M*n*S:

- P = period (required)
- *n*Y = number of years
- *n*M = number of months
- *n*D = number of days
- T = date/time separator (can be omitted if all time items are excluded)
- *n*H = number of hours
- *n*M = number of minutes
- *n*S = number of seconds (can include decimal digits)

Any value that is zero may be omitted, but at least one number and its designator must be included in the lexical representation. Duration may be preceded by an optional minus sign (-) to indicate a negative duration.

No built-in datatypes are derived from duration.

Facets	Name	Value
Fundamental	bounded	false
	cardinality	countably infinite
	numeric	false
	ordered	partial
Constraining	pattern	
	whiteSpace	
	maxInclusive	
	minInclusive	
	enumeration	
	maxExclusive	
	minExclusive	

```
<!-- schema -->
<xsd:element name="vacation">
   <xsd:simpleType>
     <xsd:restriction base="xsd:duration">
       <xsd:pattern value="P\d+D\d+H\d+M\d+S"/>
     </xsd:restriction>
   </xsd:simpleType>
</xsd:element>
<!-- instance document -->
<vacation>P10D2H30M45S</vacation>
```

In this example, a pattern facet is specified as a restriction of the duration type. The pattern is P*n*D*n*H*n*M*n*S, or number of days, hours, minutes, and seconds. The value represented in the instance document is a period of 10 days, 2 hours, 30 minutes, and 45 seconds. In a regular expression, \d specifies one or more digits and + specifies the content to follow; for example, \d+D specifies any digit followed by D.

dateTime   The dateTime datatype represents a specific time and date. The value space is the ISO 8601 *Combinations of date and time of day* values. The lexical representation is the format *CCYY-MM-DD*T*hh*:*mm*:*ss*, which corresponds to the following:

- *CC* = century
- *YY* = year

- *MM* = month
- *DD* = day
- T = date/time separator
- *hh* = hour
- *mm* = minute
- *ss* = second

This format may be followed by Z to indicate *UTC (Coordinated Universal Time)* or followed by a + or - and the difference represented as *hh*:*mm* to indicate the time zone from UTC.

Leading zeros are required if *CCYY* would be less than four digits; otherwise, leading zeros are prohibited. The other fields must have two digits or use leading zeros. An optional - may be used to indicate a negative number.

No built-in datatypes are derived from dateTime.

Facets	Name	Value
Fundamental	bounded	false
	cardinality	countably infinite
	numeric	false
	ordered	partial
Constraining	pattern	
	whiteSpace	
	maxInclusive	
	minInclusive	
	enumeration	
	maxExclusive	
	minExclusive	

```
<!-- schema -->
<xsd:element name="time_of_birth">
   <xsd:simpleType>
     <xsd:restriction base="xsd:dateTime">
       <xsd:enumeration value="1950-06-25T04:15:00"/>
       <xsd:enumeration value="1988-12-14T21:30:05"/>
     </xsd:restriction>
   </xsd:simpleType>
</xsd:element>
```

```
<!-- instance document -->
<time_of_birth>1950-06-25T04:15:00</time_of_birth>
```

time   The time datatype represents a specific time that recurs every day. The value space is the ISO 8601 *time of day* values. The lexical space is the same as the time portion of the dateTime lexical space, *hh:mm:ss*, with an optional time zone specification.

No built-in datatypes are derived from time.

Facets	Name	Value
Fundamental	bounded	false
	cardinality	countably infinite
	numeric	false
	ordered	partial
Constraining	pattern	
	whiteSpace	
	maxInclusive	
	minInclusive	
	enumeration	
	maxExclusive	
	minExclusive	

```
<!-- schema -->
<xsd:element name="meeting" type="xsd:time"/>
<!-- instance document -->
<meeting>10:30:00Z</meeting>
```

date   The date datatype represents a calendar date. The value space is the Gregorian calendar dates defined in ISO 8601. The lexical space is the same as the date portion of the dateTime lexical space, *CCYY-MM-DD*, with an optional time zone specification.

No built-in datatypes are derived from date.

Facets	Name	Value
Fundamental	bounded	false
	cardinality	countably infinite
	numeric	false
	ordered	partial

Facets	Name	Value
Constraining	pattern	
	whiteSpace	
	maxInclusive	
	minInclusive	
	enumeration	
	maxExclusive	
	minExclusive	

```
<!-- schema -->
<xsd:element name="anniversary" type="xsd:date"/>
<!-- instance document -->
<anniversary>1960-07-15</anniversary>
```

gYearMonth   The gYearMonth datatype represents a specific Gregorian month in a specific Gregorian year. The value space is the Gregorian calendar months in ISO 8601. The lexical representation is *CCYY-MM*, with an optional time zone indicator.

No built-in datatypes are derived from gYearMonth.

Facets	Name	Value
Fundamental	bounded	false
	cardinality	countably infinite
	numeric	false
	ordered	partial
Constraining	pattern	
	whiteSpace	
	maxInclusive	
	minInclusive	
	enumeration	
	maxExclusive	
	minExclusive	

```
<!-- schema -->
<xsd:element name="graduation" type="xsd:gYearMonth"/>
<!-- instance document -->
<graduation>1996-05Z</graduation>
```

gYear   The gYear datatype represents a Gregorian year. The value space is the Gregorian calendar years in ISO 8601. The lexical space is *CCYY*, with an optional time zone indicator.

No built-in datatypes are derived from gYear.

Facets	Name	Value
Fundamental	bounded	false
	cardinality	countably infinite
	numeric	false
	ordered	partial
Constraining	pattern	
	whiteSpace	
	maxInclusive	
	minInclusive	
	enumeration	
	maxExclusive	
	minExclusive	

```
<!-- schema -->
<xsd:element name="interval">
   <xsd:simpleType>
     <xsd:restriction base="xsd:gYear">
       <xsd:minInclusive value="1776"/>
       <xsd:maxInclusive value="1976"/>
     </xsd:restriction>
   </xsd:simpleType>
</xsd:element>
<!-- instance document -->
<interval>1842</interval>
```

gMonthDay   The gMonthDay datatype represents a Gregorian date that recurs yearly. The value space is the set of *calendar dates* in ISO 8601. The lexical space is *--MM-DD*, with an optional time zone indicator.

No built-in datatypes are derived from gMonthDay.

Facets	Name	Value
Fundamental	bounded	false
	cardinality	countably infinite
	numeric	false
	ordered	partial
Constraining	pattern	
	whiteSpace	
	maxInclusive	
	minInclusive	
	enumeration	
	maxExclusive	
	minExclusive	

```
<!-- schema -->
<xsd:element name="birthday" type="xsd:gMonthDay"/>
<!-- instance document -->
<birthday>--10-25</birthday>
```

gDay   The gDay datatype represents a day of the month that recurs. The value space is the set of calendar dates in ISO 8601. The lexical space is ---*DD*, with an optional time zone indicator.

No built-in datatypes are derived from gDay.

Facets	Name	Value
Fundamental	bounded	false
	cardinality	countably infinite
	numeric	false
	ordered	partial
Constraining	pattern	
	whiteSpace	
	maxInclusive	
	minInclusive	

```
enumeration

maxExclusive

minExclusive
```

```
<!-- schema -->
<xsd:element name="checkpoint" type="xsd:gDay"/>
<!-- instance document -->
<checkpoint>---15</checkpoint>
```

gMonth   The gMonth datatype represents a Gregorian month that recurs every year. The value space is the set of calendar months in ISO 8601. The lexical space is *--MM--*, with an optional time zone indicator.

No built-in datatypes are derived from gMonth.

Facets	Name	Value
Fundamental	bounded	false
	cardinality	countably infinite
	numeric	false
	ordered	partial
Constraining	pattern	
	whiteSpace	
	maxInclusive	
	minInclusive	
	enumeration	
	maxExclusive	
	minExclusive	

```
<!-- schema -->
<xsd:element name="school_starts" type="xsd:gMonth"/>
<!-- instance document -->
<school_starts>--09--</school_starts>
```

hexBinary   The hexBinary datatype represents hex-encoded binary data. The value space is finite-length sequences of binary octets. The lexical space is hexadecimal digits corresponding to the octet code. For example, 008F is hex encoding for binary 00010111.

No built-in datatypes are derived from hexBinary.

Facets	Name	Value
Fundamental	bounded	false
	cardinality	countably infinite
	numeric	false
	ordered	false
Constraining	length	
	maxLength	
	enumeration	
	minLength	
	pattern	
	whiteSpace	

```
<!-- schema -->
<xsd:element name="hex1" type="xsd:hexBinary"/>
<!-- instance document -->
<hex1>FFCC9E</hex1>
```

base64Binary   The base64Binary datatype represents base64-encoded binary data. The value space is finite-length sequences of binary octets. The lexical space is base64 digits corresponding to the octet code. For example, ABCD is base64 encoding for binary 00010111. The binary stream is encoded using the Base64 Content-Transfer-Encoding.

For more details on base64 Content-Transfer-Encoding and the base64 alphabet, see Section 6.8 of RFC 2045 at www.ietf.org/rfc/rfc2045.txt.

No built-in datatypes are derived from base64Binary.

Facets	Name	Value
Fundamental	bounded	false
	cardinality	countably infinite
	numeric	false
	ordered	false

Facets	Name	Value
Constraining	length	
	maxLength	
	enumeration	
	minLength	
	pattern	
	whiteSpace	

```
<!-- schema -->
<xsd:element name="binaryto64" type="xsd:base64Binary"/>
<!-- instance document -->
<binaryto64>AC2xaQ</binaryto64>
```

anyURI   The anyURI datatype represents a URI reference. The value can be absolute or relative and may have an optional fragment identifier. Mapping from anyURI values to URIs is defined in the XLink specification, Section 5.4 at www.w3.org/TR/2000/PR-xlink-20001220. The lexical space is a finite-length sequence of characters, which results in strings that are legal URIs after applying the algorithm from Section 5.4 of the XLink Recommendation.

No built-in datatypes are derived from anyURI.

Facets	Name	Value
Fundamental	bounded	false
	cardinality	countably infinite
	numeric	false
	ordered	false
Constraining	length	
	maxLength	
	enumeration	
	minLength	
	pattern	
	whiteSpace	

```
<!-- schema -->
<xsd:element name="address">
   <xsd:simpleType>
```

```
        <xsd:restriction base="xsd:anyURI">
          <xsd:enumeration value=
          "http://www.w3.org/TR/2000/PR-xlink-20001220/"/>
          <xsd:enumeration value=
           "http://www.w3.org/TR/xmlschema-2/"/>
        </xsd:restriction>
      </xsd:simpleType>
</xsd:element>
<!-- instance document -->
<address>http://www.w3.org/TR/xmlschema-2/</address>
```

QName   The QName datatype represents a namespace-qualified name as defined in Namespaces in XML (www.w3.org/TR/1999/REC-xml-names-19990114/). A namespace-qualified name consists of a namespace prefix (which is associated with a namespace URI reference in a namespace declaration), the namespace delimiter character (:), and then a local name (which is a name of an element with an NCName datatype). NCName datatypes are covered in the following section, "Derived Datatypes." The lexical space is the set of strings that match the QName format.

Facets	Name	Value
Fundamental	bounded	false
	cardinality	countably infinite
	numeric	false
	ordered	false
Constraining	length	
	maxLength	
	enumeration	
	minLength	
	pattern	
	whiteSpace	

In this example, rr is the namespace prefix, and track_number is the name of an element with an NCName datatype.

```
<!-- instance document -->
<xmlns:rr="http://railroads.com/schema">
<!-- the "track_number" element's namespace is
   http://railroads.com/schema -->
<rr:track_number>15546</rr:track_number>
```

NOTATION   The NOTATION datatype represents the NOTATION attribute type of XML 1.0 Second Edition. The value space depends on the specific instance document and must match the notation name in the schema declaration. The lexical space is all the notation names declared in the schema.

WARNING   To ensure compatibility with XML 1.0, NOTATION should only be used on attributes. An enumeration facet value is required in order to use NOTATION in a schema.

No built-in datatypes are derived from NOTATION.

Facets	Name	Value
Fundamental	bounded	false
	cardinality	countably infinite
	numeric	false
	ordered	false
Constraining	length	
	maxLength	
	enumeration	
	minLength	
	pattern	
	whiteSpace	

```
<!-- schema -->
 <xsd:notation name="swf" public="image/swf"
   system="SWF_viewer.exe"/>
<xsd:element name="myAnimation">
   <xsd:complexType>
    <xsd:complexContent>
      <xsd:extension base="xsd:anyType">
        <xsd:attribute name="note" type="notationType"/>
      </xsd:extension>
    </xsd:complexContent>
   </xsd:complexType>
</xsd:element>
<xsd:simpleType name="notationType">
   <xsd:restriction base="xsd:NOTATION">
     <xsd:enumeration value="swf"/>
     <xsd:enumeration value="fla"/>
```

```
    </xsd:restriction>
</xsd:simpleType>
<!-- instance document -->
<myAnimation note="swf">Schema Lesson</myAnimation>
```

Derived Datatypes

There are 25 built-in derived datatypes defined in the XML Schema specification. Derived datatypes can contain element or mixed content and can have attributes.

The 25 derived datatypes are as follows:

normalizedString	token
language	NMTOKEN
NMTOKENS	Name
NCName	ID
IDREF	IDREFS
ENTITY	ENTITIES
integer	nonPositiveInteger
negativeInteger	long
int	short
byte	nonNegativeInteger
unsignedLong	unsignedInt
unsignedShort	unsignedByte
positiveInteger	

Derived datatypes are derived from an existing datatype known as a *base type*. New derived types can originate from either a primitive type or another derived type. The constraining facets are used to define the derived type. The fundamental facets for a derived datatype are the same as those of the base type.

normalizedString   The normalizedString datatype is derived from the string type. It represents strings that do *not* contain carriage returns, line feeds, or tab characters. The value space and the lexical space are the same—the set of strings that do not contain these characters.

The token type is derived from normalizedString.

Facets	Name
Constraining	length
	maxLength
	enumeration
	minLength
	pattern
	whiteSpace

The normalizedString type is derived by using a whiteSpace value of replace, which replaces tabs, line feeds, and carriage returns with spaces.

```
<!-- schema -->
<xsd:element name="myString">
   <xsd:simpleType>
     <xsd:restriction base="xsd:normalizedString">
       <xsd:maxLength value="50"/>
     </xsd:restriction>
   </xsd:simpleType>
</xsd:element>
<!-- instance document -->
<myString>Here's one. </myString>
```

In this example, the normalizedString type is further constrained to a maxLength value of 50.

token   The token datatype is derived from the normalizedString type. It represents strings that do *not* contain the following:

- Carriage return, line feed, or tab characters

- Leading or trailing spaces

- Internal sequences of two or more spaces

The value space and the lexical space are the same—the set of strings that do not contain these characters or specified spaces.

Three built-in datatypes are derived from token: language, NMTOKEN, and Name.

Facets	Name
Constraining	length
	maxLength
	enumeration
	minLength
	pattern
	whiteSpace

The token type is derived by using a whiteSpace value of collapse. After tabs, line feeds, and carriage returns are replaced with spaces, sequences of spaces are collapsed to a single space and leading and trailing spaces are removed.

```
<!-- schema -->
<xsd:element name="label" type="xsd:token"/>
<!-- instance document -->
<label>This is a token string</label>
```

language   The language datatype is derived from the token type. The language type represents language identifiers as defined by RFC 1766 and included in XML 1.0 Second Edition. The value space and the lexical space are the same—the set of strings that are valid language identifiers.

No built-in datatypes are derived from language.

Facets	Name
Constraining	length
	maxLength
	enumeration
	minLength
	pattern
	whiteSpace

The language type is derived from token by using a pattern facet. The pattern, a regular expression, is shown in the following sample, adapted from the W3C Schema for Datatype Definitions:

```
<!-- schema -->
<xsd:simpleType>
  <xsd:restriction base="xsd:token">
    <xsd:pattern value="([a-zA-Z]{2}|[iI]-[a-zA-Z]+|[xX]-
    [a-zA-Z]{1,8})(-[a-zA-Z]{1,8})*"/>
  </xsd:restriction>
</xsd:simpleType>
```

We can further restrict this type using enumeration, as shown in the following sample:

```
<!-- schema -->
<xsd:element name="language_native">
  <xsd:simpleType>
    <xsd:restriction base="xsd:language">
      <xsd:enumeration value="de"/>
      <xsd:enumeration value="fr"/>
      <xsd:enumeration value="en-GB"/>
      <xsd:enumeration value="en-US"/>
    </xsd:restriction>
  </xsd:simpleType>
</xsd:element>
<!-- instance document -->
<language_native>fr</language_native>
```

In this example, we have restricted the language choices to German, French, English-GreatBritain, and English-US.

NMTOKEN   The NMTOKEN datatype is derived from the token type. It represents the NMTOKEN attribute type in XML 1.0 Second Edition. NMTOKEN must use XML NameChar characters, which include any Unicode letters and digits and any of four punctuation characters: underscore (_), colon (:), hyphen (-), and period (.). Unlike with ID, any of these characters may be used in the first character position. NMTOKEN values may not contain any white space.

WARNING   To ensure compatibility with XML 1.0, NMTOKEN should only be used on attributes.

The NMTOKENS datatype is derived from NMTOKEN.

Facets	Name
Constraining	length
	maxLength
	enumeration
	minLength
	pattern
	whiteSpace

The NMTOKEN type is derived from token by using a pattern facet (\c+).

```
<!-- schema -->
<xsd:element name="title">
   <xsd:complexType>
      <xsd:complexContent>
        <xsd:extension base="xsd:anyType">
        <xsd:attribute name="degree" type="xsd:NMTOKEN"/>
        </xsd:extension>
      </xsd:complexContent>
   </xsd:complexType>
</xsd:element>
<!-- instance document -->
<title degree="MS">Mister</title>
```

NMTOKENS   The NMTOKENS datatype is derived from the NMTOKEN type. It represents the NMTOKENS attribute type of XML 1.0 Second Edition. The value space is the set of finite-, nonzero-length sequences of values for NMTOKENS datatypes. The lexical space is the set of white-space-separated lists of values for NMTOKENS datatypes.

WARNING   To ensure compatibility with XML 1.0, NMTOKENS should only be used on attributes.

No built-in datatypes are derived from NMTOKENS.

Facets	Name
Constraining	length
	maxLength
	whiteSpace
	minLength
	enumeration

The NMTOKENS type is derived from NMTOKEN by using a list with the itemType value NMTOKEN and a minLength facet value of 1.

```
<!-- schema -->
…
<xsd:attribute name="degree" type="xsd:NMTOKENS"/>
…
<!-- instance document -->
<title degree="BA MS">Mister</title>
```

Name   The Name datatype is derived from the token type. It represents XML names. The value space and the lexical space are the same—the set of strings that match an XML name as defined in Namespaces in XML (www.w3.org/TR/1999/REC-xml-names-19990114).

For more information on the rules and structure of XML names, see the article "The Naming of Parts" by John Simpson at www.xml.com/pub/a/2001/07/25/namingparts.html.

The NCName datatype is derived from the Name type.

Facets	Name
Constraining	length
	maxLength
	enumeration
	minLength
	pattern
	whiteSpace

The Name type is derived from token by using a pattern facet (\i\c*).

```
<!-- instance document -->
<names xmlns="http://www.mycompany.org/schemas/e-commerce"
xmlns:market="http://www.mycompany.org/schemas/market">
<market:group>Alpha</market:group>
```

In this example, market:group is a namespace-qualified name.

NCName   The NCName datatype is derived from the name type. It represents a nonqualified, or *noncolonized* name. The value space and the lexical space are the same—the set of strings that match a nonqualified name as defined in Namespaces in XML (www.w3.org/TR/1999/REC-xml-names-19990114/).

Three built-in datatypes are derived from NCName: ID, IDREF, and ENTITY.

Facets	Name
Constraining	length
	maxLength
	enumeration
	minLength
	pattern
	whiteSpace

NCName is derived from Name by using a pattern facet ([\i-[:]][\c-[:]]*).

```
<!-- schema -->
<xsd:element name="group" type="xsd:NCName"/>
<!-- instance document -->
<group>Alpha</group>
```

ID   The ID datatype is derived from the NCName type. It represents the ID attribute type of XML 1.0 Second Edition. The value space and the lexical space are the same—the set of all strings, which conforms to the NCName string guidelines in Namespaces in XML (www.w3.org/TR/1999/REC-xml-names-19990114/).

ID is a unique identifier and may be used only once in an instance document.

WARNING   To ensure compatibility with XML 1.0, ID should only be used on attributes.

No built-in datatypes are derived from ID.

Facets	Name
Constraining	length
	maxLength
	enumeration
	minLength
	pattern
	whiteSpace

ID is derived from NCName by simple restriction.

```
<!-- schema -->
<xsd:element name="bank">
    <xsd:complexType>
      <xsd:complexContent>
        <xsd:extension base="xsd:anyType">
        <xsd:attribute name="degree" type="xsd:ID"/>
        </xsd:extension>
      </xsd:complexContent>
    </xsd:complexType>
</xsd:element>
<!-- instance document -->
<bank branch="412x">Northern</bank>
```

IDREF   The IDREF datatype is derived from the NCName type. It represents the IDREF attribute type of XML 1.0 Second Edition. IDREF refers to an element or attribute of type ID in the same instance document, and the value for IDREF must match a value for ID in the same instance document. The value space and the lexical space are the same—the set of all strings that conform to the NCName string guidelines in Namespaces in XML (www.w3.org/TR/1999/REC-xml-names-19990114/).

WARNING   To ensure compatibility with XML 1.0, IDREF should only be used on attributes.

The IDREFS datatype is derived from IDREF.

Facets	Name
Constraining	length
	maxLength
	enumeration
	minLength
	pattern
	whiteSpace

IDREF is derived from NCName by simple restriction.

```
<!-- schema -->
<xsd:element name="bank">
    <xsd:complexType>
      <xsd:complexContent>
        <xsd:extension base="xsd:anyType">
```

```
        <xsd:attribute name="branch" type="xsd:ID"/>
      </xsd:extension>
    </xsd:complexContent>
  </xsd:complexType>
</xsd:element>
<xsd:element name="city">
  <xsd:complexType>
    <xsd:complexContent>
      <xsd:extension base="xsd:anyType">
      <xsd:attribute name="branch_division"
        type="xsd:IDREF"/>
      </xsd:extension>
    </xsd:complexContent>
  </xsd:complexType>
</xsd:element>
<!-- instance document -->
<bank branch="412x">Northern</bank>
<city branch_division="412x">Chicago</city>
```

IDREFS   The IDREFS datatype is derived from the IDREF type. It represents the IDREFS attribute of XML 1.0 Second Edition. The value space is the set of finite-, nonzero-length sequences of IDREF values. The lexical space is the white-space-separated list of IDREF values.

WARNING To ensure compatibility with XML 1.0, IDREFS should only be used on attributes.

No built-in datatype is derived from IDREFS.

Facets	Name
Constraining	length
	maxLength
	whiteSpace
	minLength
	enumeration

IDREFS is derived from IDREF by using a list with the itemType value IDREF and a minLength facet value of 1.

```
<!-- schema -->
<xsd:complexType name="bankref">
  <xsd:sequence>
    <xsd:element name="bank" minOccurs="0"
      maxOccurs="unbounded">
      <xsd:complexType>
        <xsd:complexContent>
```

```
            <xsd:extension base="xsd:anyType">
              <xsd:attribute name="branch" type="xsd:ID"/>
            </xsd:extension>
          </xsd:complexContent>
        </xsd:complexType>
      </xsd:element>
    </xsd:sequence>
  </xsd:complexType>
  <xsd:element name="city">
    <xsd:complexType>
      <xsd:complexContent>
        <xsd:extension base="xsd:anyType">
          <xsd:attribute name="branch_division"
            type="xsd:IDREFS"/>
        </xsd:extension>
      </xsd:complexContent>
    </xsd:complexType>
  </xsd:element>
  <!-- instance document -->
  <bank branch="412x">Northern</bank>
  <bank branch="513a">Central</bank>
  <bank branch="793c">Southern</bank>
  <city branch_division="412x 513a 793c">Chicago</city>
```

ENTITY   The ENTITY datatype is derived from the NCName type. It represents the ENTITY attribute type of XML 1.0 Second Edition. The value space and the lexical space are the same—the set of strings that match a nonqualified name as defined in Namespaces in XML (www.w3.org/TR/1999/REC-xml-names-19990114) and have been declared an unparsed entity. The value of ENTITY must match an unparsed entity name declaration in a notation element in the schema.

WARNING   To ensure compatibility with XML 1.0, ENTITY should only be used on attributes.

The ENTITIES built-in datatype is derived from ENTITY.

Facets	Name
Constraining	length
	maxLength
	enumeration
	minLength
	pattern
	whiteSpace

ENTITY is derived from NCName by simple restriction.

```
<!-- schema -->
<xsd:notation name="jpg" public="image/jpg"
    system="JPG_viewer.exe"/>
<xsd:complexType name="entityref">
    <xsd:sequence>
      <xsd:element name="picture">
        <xsd:complexType>
          <xsd:complexContent>
            <xsd:extension base="xsd:anyType">
              <xsd:attribute name="image"type="xsd:ENTITY"/>
            </xsd:extension>
          </xsd:complexContent>
        </xsd:complexType>
      </xsd:element>
    </xsd:sequence>
</xsd:complexType>
<!-- instance document -->
<picture image="jpg">Brochure</picture>
```

ENTITIES   The ENTITIES datatype is derived from the ENTITY type. It represents the ENTITIES attribute type of XML 1.0 Second Edition. The value space is the set of finite-, nonzero-length sequences of entities. The lexical space is the white-space-separated list of entities. The value of ENTITIES must match the set of unparsed entity names declared in notation elements in the schema.

WARNING To ensure compatibility with XML 1.0, ENTITIES should only be used on attributes.

No built-in datatypes are derived from ENTITIES.

Facets	Name
Constraining	length
	maxLength
	whiteSpace
	minLength
	enumeration

ENTITIES is derived from ENTITY by using a list with the itemType value ENTITY and a minLength facet value of 1.

```
<!-- schema -->
<xsd:notation name="jpg" public="image/jpg" system="JPG_viewer.exe"/>
```

```
<xsd:notation name="gif" public="image/gif" system="GIF_viewer.exe"/>
<xsd:notation name="png" public="image/png" system="PNG_viewer.exe"/>
<xsd:complexType name="entityref">
   <xsd:sequence>
     <xsd:element name="gallery">
       <xsd:complexType>
         <xsd:complexContent>
           <xsd:extension base="xsd:anyType">
             <xsd:attribute name="images" type="imageTypes"/>
           </xsd:extension>
         </xsd:complexContent>
       </xsd:complexType>
     </xsd:element>
   </xsd:sequence>
</xsd:complexType>
<xsd:element name="gallery">
   <xsd:complexType>
     <xsd:complexContent>
       <xsd:extension base="xsd:anyType">
         <xsd:attribute name="images" type="imageTypes"/>
       </xsd:extension>
     </xsd:complexContent>
   </xsd:complexType>
</xsd:element>
<xsd:simpleType name="imageTypes">
   <xsd:restriction base="xsd:ENTITIES">
     <xsd:enumeration value="jpg"/>
     <xsd:enumeration value="gif"/>
     <xsd:enumeration value="png"/>
   </xsd:restriction>
</xsd:simpleType>
<!-- instance document -->

<gallery images="jpg gif png">Online_Brochure</gallery>
```

integer   The integer datatype is derived from the decimal type. It represents the mathe-matical concept of integers. The value space is the infinite set of positive and negative inte-gers. The lexical space is the finite-length sequence of decimal digits with an optional leading + or -.

Three built-in datatypes are derived from integer: nonPositiveInteger, long, and non-NegativeInteger.

Facets	Name
Constraining	totalDigits
	pattern
	enumeration
	maxInclusive
	minInclusive
	fractionDigits
	whiteSpace
	maxExclusive
	minExclusive

The integer type is derived by using a fractionDigits value of 0.

```
<!-- instance document -->
<myInteger>1</myInteger>
<myInteger>-35</myInteger>
<myInteger>+678432</myInteger>
<myInteger>5001182828293</myInteger>
```

nonPositiveInteger   The nonPositiveInteger datatype is derived from the integer type. The value space is the infinite set of integers less than and including zero. The lexical space is a finite-length sequence of decimal digits preceded by a -.

The negativeInteger datatype is derived from nonPositiveInteger.

Facets	Name
Constraining	totalDigits
	pattern
	enumeration
	maxInclusive
	minInclusive
	fractionDigits
	whiteSpace
	maxExclusive
	minExclusive

The nonPositiveInteger type is derived by using a maxInclusive value of 0.

```
<!-- schema -->
<xsd:simpleType name="BC">
   <xsd:restriction base="xsd:nonPositiveInteger">
     <xsd:minInclusive value="unbounded"/>
     <xsd:maxInclusive value="-2001"/>
   </xsd:restriction>
</xsd:simpleType>
<!-- instance document -->
<BC>-5365</BC>
```

negativeInteger   The negativeInteger datatype is derived from the nonPositiveInteger type. The value space is the infinite set of integer values less than or equal to –1. The lexical space is a finite-length sequence of decimal digits preceded by a -.

No built-in datatypes are derived from negativeInteger.

Facets	Name
Constraining	totalDigits
	pattern
	enumeration
	maxInclusive
	minInclusive
	fractionDigits
	whiteSpace
	maxExclusive
	minExclusive

The negativeInteger type is derived by using a maxInclusive value of -1.

```
<!-- schema -->
<xsd:simpleType name="neg_2">
   <xsd:restriction base="xsd:negativeInteger">
     <xsd:pattern value="-\d{2}"/>
   </xsd:restriction>
</xsd:simpleType>
<!-- instance document -->
<neg_2>-49</neg_2>
```

In this example, `negativeInteger` is restricted to the set of two-digit negative integers. The `pattern` facet is `-\d{2}`, which constrains the set to numbers starting with - and containing exactly two `{2}` digits (`\d`).

`long`   The `long` datatype is derived from the `integer` type. The value space is integer values from –9223372036854775808 up to and including 9223372036854775807. The lexical space is a finite-length sequence of decimal digits with an optional leading - or +.

The `int` datatype is derived from `long`.

Facets	Name
Constraining	totalDigits
	pattern
	enumeration
	maxInclusive
	minInclusive
	fractionDigits
	whiteSpace
	maxExclusive
	minExclusive

The `long` type is derived by using a `maxInclusive` value of 9223372036854775807 and a `minInclusive` value of -9223372036854775808.

```
<!-- schema -->
<xsd:element name="bignumbers">
<xsd:simpleType>
   <xsd:restriction base="xsd:long">
     <xsd:enumeration value="2177483647"/>
     <xsd:enumeration value="-2177483647"/>
   </xsd:restriction>
</xsd:simpleType>
</xsd:element>
<!-- instance document -->
<bignumbers>2177483647</bignumbers>
```

`int`   The `int` datatype is derived from the `long` type. The value space is integer values from –2147483648 up to and including 2147483647. The lexical space is a finite-length sequence of decimal digits with an optional leading - or +.

The short datatype is derived from `int`.

Facets	Name
Constraining	totalDigits
	pattern
	enumeration
	maxInclusive
	minInclusive
	fractionDigits
	whiteSpace
	maxExclusive
	minExclusive

The `int` type is derived by using a `maxInclusive` value of 2147483647 and a `minInclusive` value of -2147483648.

```
<!-- schema -->
<xsd:element name="ninedigits">
   <xsd:simpleType>
     <xsd:restriction base="xsd:int">
       <xsd:totalDigits value="9"/>
     </xsd:restriction>
   </xsd:simpleType>
</xsd:element>
<!-- instance document -->
<ninedigits>217748364</ninedigits>
```

In this example, the total number of digits is restricted to nine by using the `totalDigits` facet with a value of 9. The same result could be obtained by using a `pattern` facet with a value of `\d{0,9}`, which specifies a sequence of zero to nine digits, as shown in the following example:

```
<!-- schema -->
<xsd:element name="ninedigits">
   <xsd:simpleType>
     <xsd:restriction base="xsd:int">
       <xsd:pattern value="\d{0,9}"/>
     </xsd:restriction>
   </xsd:simpleType>
</xsd:element>
<!-- instance document -->
<ninedigits>217748364</ninedigits>
```

short   The short datatype is derived from the int type. The value space is integer values from –32768 up to and including 32767. The lexical space is a finite-length sequence of decimal digits with an optional leading - or +.

The byte datatype is derived from short.

Facets	Name
Constraining	totalDigits
	pattern
	enumeration
	maxInclusive
	minInclusive
	fractionDigits
	whiteSpace
	maxExclusive
	minExclusive

The short type is derived by using a maxInclusive value of 32767 and a minInclusive value of -32768.

```
<!-- schema -->
<xsd:complexType name="shortlist">
  <xsd:sequence>
    <xsd:element name="to_do" minOccurs="0"
      maxOccurs="unbounded">
      <xsd:complexType>
        <xsd:complexContent>
          <xsd:extension base="xsd:anyType">
            <xsd:attribute name="recur" type="xsd:short"/>
          </xsd:extension>
        </xsd:complexContent>
      </xsd:complexType>
    </xsd:element>
  </xsd:sequence>
</xsd:complexType>
<!-- instance document -->
<to_do recur="365">wake up</to_do>
<to_do recur="365">brush teeth</to_do>
<to_do recur="250">go to office</to_do>
```

byte The byte datatype is derived from the short type. The value space is integer values from –128 up to and including 127. The lexical space is a finite-length sequence of decimal digits with an optional leading - or +.

No built-in datatypes are derived from byte.

Facets	Name
Constraining	totalDigits
	pattern
	enumeration
	maxInclusive
	minInclusive
	fractionDigits
	whiteSpace
	maxExclusive
	minExclusive

The byte type is derived by using a maxInclusive value of 127 and a minInclusive value of -128.

```
<!-- schema -->
<xsd:complexType name="myBytes">
  <xsd:choice>
    <xsd:element name="byte1" type="xsd:byte"/>
    <xsd:element name="byte2" type="xsd:byte"/>
    <xsd:element name="byte3" type="xsd:byte"/>
  </xsd:choice>
</xsd:complexType>
<!-- instance document -->
<byte2>55</byte2>
```

nonNegativeInteger The nonNegativeInteger datatype is derived from the integer type. The value space is the infinite set of integers greater than or equal to zero. The lexical space is a finite-length sequence of decimal digits with an optional leading - or +.

Two datatypes are derived from `nonNegativeInteger`: `unsignedLong` and `positiveInteger`.

Facets	Name
Constraining	totalDigits
	pattern
	enumeration
	maxInclusive
	minInclusive
	fractionDigits
	whiteSpace
	maxExclusive
	minExclusive

The `nonNegativeInteger` type is derived by using a `minInclusive` value of 0.

```
<!-- schema -->
<xsd:element name="bank_balance"
    type="xsd:nonNegativeInteger"/>
<!-- instance document -->
<bank_balance>32</bank_balance>
```

unsignedLong   The `unsignedLong` datatype is derived from the `nonNegativeInteger` type. The value space is the set of integers greater than or equal to 0 and less than or equal to 18446744073709551615. The lexical space is a finite-length sequence of decimal digits.

The `unsignedInt` datatype is derived from `unsignedLong`.

Facets	Name
Constraining	totalDigits
	pattern
	enumeration
	maxInclusive
	minInclusive
	fractionDigits
	whiteSpace
	maxExclusive
	minExclusive

The `unsignedLong` type is derived by using a `maxInclusive` value of 18446744073709551615.

```
<!-- schema -->
<xsd:simpleType name="distance_sun">
   <xsd:restriction base="xsd:unsignedLong">
     <xsd:pattern value="\d{8}"/>
   </xsd:restriction>
</xsd:simpleType>
<!-- instance document -->
<distance_sun>93000000</distance_sun>
```

`unsignedInt` The `unsignedInt` datatype is derived from the `unsignedLong` type. The value space is the set of integers greater than or equal to 0 and less than or equal to 4294967295. The lexical space is a finite-length sequence of decimal digits.

The `unsignedShort` datatype is derived from `unsignedInt`.

Facets	Name
Constraining	totalDigits
	pattern
	enumeration
	maxInclusive
	minInclusive
	fractionDigits
	whiteSpace
	maxExclusive
	minExclusive

The `unsignedInt` type is derived by using a `maxInclusive` value of 4294967295.

```
<!-- schema -->
<xsd:simpleType name="grains_of_sand">
   <xsd:restriction base="xsd:unsignedInt">
     <xsd:maxInclusive value="4000000000"/>
   </xsd:restriction>
</xsd:simpleType>
<!-- instance document -->
<grains_of_sand>4000000000</grains_of_sand >
```

unsignedShort   The `unsignedShort` datatype is derived from the `unsignedInt` type. The value space is the set of integers greater than or equal to 0 and less than or equal to 65535. The lexical space is a finite-length sequence of decimal digits.

The `unsignedByte` datatype is derived from `unsignedShort`.

Facets	Name
Constraining	totalDigits
	pattern
	enumeration
	maxInclusive
	minInclusive
	fractionDigits
	whiteSpace
	maxExclusive
	minExclusive

The `unsignedShort` type is derived by using a `maxInclusive` value of 65535.

```
<!-- schema -->
<xsd:element name="shortstop">
  <xsd:simpleType>
    <xsd:restriction base="xsd:unsignedShort">
      <xsd:enumeration value="15515"/>
      <xsd:enumeration value="38860"/>
    </xsd:restriction>
  </xsd:simpleType>
</xsd:element>
<!-- instance document -->
<shortstop>38860</shortstop>
```

unsignedByte   The `unsignedByte` datatype is derived from the `unsignedShort` type. The value space is the set of integers greater than or equal to 0 and less than or equal to 255. The lexical space is a finite-length sequence of decimal digits.

No built-in datatypes are derived from `unsignedByte`.

Facets	Name
Constraining	totalDigits
	pattern

Facets	Name
	enumeration
	maxInclusive
	minInclusive
	fractionDigits
	whiteSpace
	maxExclusive
	minExclusive

The unsignedByte type is derived by using a maxInclusive value of 255.

```
<!-- schema -->
<xsd:complexType name="RGB">
   <xsd:sequence>
     <xsd:element name="red" type="xsd:unsignedByte"/>
     <xsd:element name="green" type="xsd:unsignedByte"/>
     <xsd:element name="blue" type="xsd:unsignedByte"/>
   </xsd:sequence>
</xsd:complexType>
<!-- instance document -->
<red>33</red>
<green>255</green>
<blue>99</blue>
```

positiveInteger   The positiveInteger datatype is derived from the nonNegativeInteger type. The value space is the infinite set of integers greater than or equal to 1. The lexical space is a finite-length sequence of decimal digits with an optional leading +.

No built-in datatypes are derived from positiveInteger.

Facets	Name
Constraining	totalDigits
	pattern
	enumeration
	maxInclusive
	minInclusive
	fractionDigits
	whiteSpace
	maxExclusive
	minExclusive

The positiveInteger type is derived by using a minInclusive value of 1.

```
<!-- schema -->
<xsd:complexType name="record_sets">
   <xsd:sequence>
      <xsd:element name="record" minOccurs="0"
        maxOccurs="unbounded">
        <xsd:simpleType>
           <xsd:restriction base="xsd:positiveInteger">
              <xsd:pattern value="555\d{3}"/>
           </xsd:restriction>
        </xsd:simpleType>
      </xsd:element>
   </xsd:sequence>
</xsd:complexType>
<!-- instance document -->
<record>555158</record>
<record>555687</record>
<record>555736</record>
```

Using Datatypes in Schemas

The use of datatypes in schemas depends on the types of data content that will be included in the instance document. Several types of information content are particularly well suited to schema datatypes, such as order forms, catalogs, contact data, and e-commerce applications.

In this section, we review a schema designed for an initial contact form. This schema needs to include several different datatypes for managing different types of content, such as date, address, phone numbers, and e-mail addresses.

The contact schema (contact.xsd) shown in Listing 7.1 includes 11 elements and several different datatypes. Here's an explanation of the markup shown in Listing 7.1:

1. There are five simple string datatypes with no constraints: first_name, last_name, street_address, city, and state.

```
<xsd:complexType name="addressType">
   <xsd:sequence>
     <xsd:element name="first_name" type="xsd:string"/>
     <xsd:element name="last_name" type="xsd:string"/>
     <xsd:element name="street_address" type="xsd:string"/>
     <xsd:element name="city" type="xsd:string"/>
     <xsd:element name="state" type="xsd:string"/>
   </xsd:sequence>
</xsd:complexType>
```

These simple strings do not include any further restrictions and are joined together as a sequence in a `complexType` element named `addressType`.

2. An element declaration followed by a simple type definition with a restriction on the pattern facet is used for `zipcode`. The pattern definition is five digits followed by an optional group of a hyphen and four additional digits for extended zip codes.

```
<xsd:element name="zipcode"/>
<xsd:simpleType name="zipcodeType">
   <xsd:restriction base="xsd:string">
     <xsd:pattern value="\d{5}(-\d{4})?"/>
   </xsd:restriction>
</xsd:simpleType>
```

3. An element declaration followed by a simple type definition with a restriction on the pattern facet is used for `phone_work`. The pattern definition is three digits followed by a hyphen and an additional seven digits.

```
<xsd:element name="phone_work"/>
<xsd:simpleType name="phoneType">
   <xsd:restriction base="xsd:string">
   <xsd:pattern value="\d{3}-\d{7}"/>
   </xsd:restriction>
</xsd:simpleType?>
```

4. The `phoneType` definition is then used in the element declarations for `phone_home` and `fax`, which are joined in a sequence in the `complexType` element named `phone`.

```
<xsd:complexType name="phone">
   <xsd:sequence>
     <xsd:element name="phone_home" type="phoneType"/>
     <xsd:element name="fax" type="phoneType"/>
   </xsd:sequence>
</xsd:complexType>
```

5. An element declaration followed by a simple type definition with a restriction on the pattern facet is used for `email`. The pattern definition is any character one or more times, followed by @, then any character one or more times.

```
<xsd:element name="email"/>
<xsd:simpleType name="emailType">
   <xsd:restriction base="xsd:string">
     <xsd:pattern value=".+@.+"/>
   </xsd:restriction>
</xsd:simpleType>
```

6. A simple element declaration using the built-in `date` type is used for `contact_date`. The format for the `date` type is *CCYY-MM-DD*, with an optional time zone specification.

```
<xsd:element name="contact_date" type="xsd:date"/>
```

The complete markup for the contact schema is shown in Listing 7.1.

Listing 7.1   **Contact Information (*contact.xsd*)**

```xml
<?xml version="1.0" encoding="UTF-8"?>
<xsd:schema targetNamespace="http://www.mycompany.com/schemas"
    xmlns:xsd="http://www.w3.org/2001/XMLSchema"
    xmlns="http://www.mycompany.com/schemas"
    elementFormDefault="qualified"
    attributeFormDefault="unqualified">
<xsd:element name="contact" type="addressType">
    <xsd:annotation>
      <xsd:documentation>This document is designed as a format
      for using contact data. The author is Lucinda
      Dykes.</xsd:documentation>
    </xsd:annotation>
</xsd:element>
<xsd:complexType name="addressType">
    <xsd:sequence>
      <xsd:element name="first_name" type="xsd:string"/>
      <xsd:element name="last_name" type="xsd:string"/>
      <xsd:element name="street_address" type="xsd:string"/>
      <xsd:element name="city" type="xsd:string"/>
      <xsd:element name="state" type="xsd:string"/>
    </xsd:sequence>
</xsd:complexType>
<xsd:element name="zipcode"/>
<xsd:simpleType name="zipcodeType">
    <xsd:restriction base="xsd:string">
      <xsd:pattern value="\d{5}(-\d{4})?"/>
    </xsd:restriction>
</xsd:simpleType>
<xsd:element name="phone_work"/>
<xsd:simpleType name="phoneType">
    <xsd:restriction base="xsd:string">
      <xsd:pattern value="\d{3}-\d{7}"/>
    </xsd:restriction>
</xsd:simpleType>
<xsd:complexType name="phone">
    <xsd:sequence>
      <xsd:element name="phone_home" type="phoneType"/>
      <xsd:element name="fax" type="phoneType"/>
    </xsd:sequence>
</xsd:complexType>
<xsd:element name="email"/>
<xsd:simpleType name="emailType">
    <xsd:restriction base="xsd:string">
      <xsd:pattern value=".+@.+"/>
    </xsd:restriction>
</xsd:simpleType>
<xsd:element name="contact_date" type="xsd:date"/>
</xsd:schema>
```

Working with Datatype Restrictions and Constraints

The W3C XML Schema Recommendation includes several constraints and restrictions on datatype definitions.

Simple type definitions are used to define the value space and the lexical space of datatypes through the use of fundamental and constraining facets. Datatypes have a unique name (assigned by the simple type definition) and a target namespace. The identifying name must be unique within a schema.

There are additional constraints on using simple type definitions to derive datatypes:

- When using a list element, an itemType attribute or a simpleType child may be present, but not both.

- When using a restriction element, a base attribute or a simpleType child may be present, but not both.

- When using a union element, a memberTypes attribute must be nonempty or there must be at least one simpleType child.

There are also several constraints on the value space of derived datatypes, as outlined in Table 7.4.

TABLE 7.4 : Derived Datatype Constraints

Variety	Value Space of Derived Datatype
Atomic	Subset of the value space of the base type.
List	Sequence of values from the value space of the base type (itemType); base type must be atomic or union.
Union	Union of the value spaces of each base type (memberTypes); only pattern and enumeration facets may be used to derive the new datatype.

In addition, there are restrictions on the constraining facets for each datatype. If the variety is list, only length, minLength, maxLength, pattern, enumeration, and whiteSpace may be used. If the variety is union, only pattern and enumeration may be used. If the variety is atomic, the allowable constraining facets depend on the base type. See the sections "Primitive Datatypes" and "Derived Datatypes" earlier in this chapter for a list of the valid constraining facets for each base type and "Constraints on Simple Type Definition Schema Components," Part 4.1.5 of the XML Schema Part 2: Datatypes Recommendation at www.w3.org/TR/xmlschema-2.

Datatypes in XML Schema are extremely powerful and offer new ways to describe XML elements and attributes with more precision than is possible with DTDs. Derivation of new datatypes is a structured and straightforward approach to extending the usefulness of XML in describing and using data.

Summary

The W3C XML Schema Recommendation includes more datatypes than any other schema language. In addition to the 44 built-in primitive and derived datatypes, XML Schema also offers schema designers the ability to create user-derived datatypes. These user-derived datatypes can be specifically designed for the types of data in the XML instance documents that will be validated against the XML Schema documents.

The constraining facets used in XML Schema datatypes give the schema designer the means to create very specific datatypes. For example, the `pattern` facet and the support for regular expressions facilitates designing user-derived types, which are extremely useful for validating data content such as phone numbers or e-mail addresses.

Other schema languages, covered in detail in Chapter 12, offer a variety of datatypes, and some of these languages can use XML Schema datatypes. However, no other language allows reusable user-derived datatypes. In XML Schema, user-derived datatypes are given a type name by the schema designer. This type name can be reused when defining other elements and attributes without having to redefine the specifications of the type.

Although the XML Schema Recommendation does not include support for co-constraints, such as element A can be present only if element B is also present, it does support the inclusion of Schematron code (covered in detail in Chapter 12) within an XML Schema document. This feature extends the capabilities of XML Schema by allowing strong datatypes and co-constraints to be included in a single XML Schema. It's very likely that other support for co-constraints may be included in future versions of the XML Schema Recommendations.

The strong support for datatypes makes XML Schema extremely useful for validating data-oriented XML instance documents, although XML Schema can also be used to validate document-oriented XML instance documents. For more information on the difference between data-oriented and document-oriented XML documents, see Section 1.1 of the XML Schema: Part 2: Datatypes Recommendation (`www.w3.org/TR/xmlschema-2/#Intro`).

CHAPTER 8

Designing XML Schema Documents

- Naming markup

- Modularizing your document model

- Making decisions about content models

- Working with namespaces

As you begin to dig deeper and deeper into XML Schema, you might realize that there are several ways to use the language. Developing useful and efficient schema documents takes some careful planning. One of the benefits of XML Schema is its flexibility and power; however, if you're unaware of the best way to wield that power, your schema design will suffer.

One complaint about the XML Schema standard is its complexity. Although it's complex because it was designed to be both flexible and powerful, this complexity does pose a problem for schema designers. When entering the designing phase, there are several decisions you have to make. For example, when modularizing your schema documents, which method do you use to reference the other modules (`redefine`, `include`, or `import`)? When is it best to create a named `complexType` definition rather than an element declaration? Should you use `elementFormDefault` to expose or hide namespaces? These, among many other questions, are answered in this chapter.

The participants of the XML-DEV mailing list have struggled with XML Schema design decisions for some time now. As an outgrowth from those struggles and discussions, Roger Costello has put together a summary titled "XML Schema: Best Practices." This summary can be found on his Web site at `www.xfront.com/BestPractices.html`. The xFront.com Web site contains material sponsored by The MITRE Corporation. In the following sections, we provide you with a summary of these findings, in addition to some of our own.

A Debt of Gratitude

As we stated in the introduction, much of the material in this chapter is based on discussions found on the XML-DEV mailing list. During these discussions, many developers went back and forth on schema design and implementation issues. These discussions continue.

We would like to take a moment to thank MITRE, Roger Costello, and the other discussion participants. Our thanks go out to the following people:

- Roger Costello
- Curt Arnold
- Len Bullard
- Mary Pulvermacher
- Paul Spencer
- Rick Jelliffe
- Caroline Clewlow
- Jon Cleaver

- Francis Norton
- Eddie Robertsson
- Jeff Rafter
- Ronald Bourret
- Toivo Lainevool
- Eric van der Vlist
- Martin Bryan
- Sam Hunting
- Tom Passin
- Mike Ripley
- John Schlesinger
- Richard Lanyon
- Ajay Sanghi
- Tom Gavin
- Robin Cover
- Clark Evans
- Dan Vint
- Henry Thompson
- Christian Nentwich
- Tim Bray
- Jeff Greif
- Caroline Weller

What Name Should You Give Your Elements and Attributes?

Naming is an important concept that is commonly overlooked. Naming your markup is the first step to creating efficient, usable schemas. Although this may seem like an obvious observation, there are several concepts that govern a well-named vocabulary that XML designers should be aware of:

- Element and attribute names should be semantic.
- The vocabulary should follow consistent naming conventions.

- Acronyms and abbreviations should be used responsibly.
- Regional labeling should be taken into account.
- Industry labeling may be used when applicable.

We discuss these concepts in more detail in the following sections.

Semantics

When defining element names, keep semantics in mind. The label defined for an element or attribute name should easily identify the data contained within it. For example, `employees` is more descriptive than `people`, `email` is more descriptive than `contact`, and `hireDate` is more descriptive than `hire`.

On that same note, don't be too descriptive. Element names should be short and concise. For example, `employeeHireDate` is a bit long. If `hireDate` is nested within an `employee` element, as shown in the following markup, the relationship is already established and there's no reason to restate it within the element name:

```
<employee>
    <hireDate>08-01-2001</hireDate>
</employee>
```

Element and attribute names should be thoughtfully planned out before you design a document model. If you keep them short, concise, and descriptive, you'll be on the right track.

Consistent Naming Conventions

Many times, one-word element names are not descriptive enough. In many cases, we need to use two words to semantically describe element or attribute content. There have been several naming conventions adopted by the XML community. Many developers use one of the following:

```
bookTitle
book-title
book.title
book_title
```

TIP   Some developers may choose to initial-cap the beginning of the element name while keeping with one of the four structures defined.

There's no great advantage to using one of the four conventions defined. In our mind, `bookTitle` is easier to write. Searching for the period, hyphen, or underscore can take a split second longer. However, the decision is largely based on personal preference.

Whatever the decision may be, one thing must be true: you must stick with a particular naming convention for the entire document. Switching naming conventions is not only confusing but can also add a heavy maintenance price tag. Keep the naming conventions consistent and simple. For example, the following markup is *not* recommended:

```
<employee>
  <firstName>Sam</firstName>
  <last_name>Williams</last_name>
  <hire-date>08-01-2001</hire-date>
</employee>
```

Acronyms and Abbreviations

Acronyms and abbreviations can make labeling easy, save time and space, and improve readability as long as you use them responsibly. For example, if you want to include employee social security numbers, you can use the abbreviation *SSN*. There are several standard abbreviations and acronyms and their use is recommended. On the other hand, creating new abbreviations—for example, bt for bookTitle—may not be useful. Keep users in mind. If your document model will be used by others, they may not recognize your abbreviations and your document model will be useless to them.

Regional and Industry Labeling

Be aware of the semantics surrounding a given word. For example, *tick* can be used a variety of ways, as a verb or a noun, for example, and both forms have several meanings. Keep your users in mind and avoid using regionally specific terminology.

In addition to being sensitive to regional labeling, you need to be aware of industry labeling. Many industries have established a common nomenclature. If this is the case, feel free to use those labels. For example, for a book catalog, we could use *ISBN* (which stands for International Standard Book Number) as an identifier for each book.

Should You Modularize Your Schema?

When developing a complex document model, it's important to create a clear conceptual standard for organizing it. Using a modular approach breaks the document model into multiple *modules*, or *building blocks*. When combined, the modules provide the complete framework for the document model.

XML Schema supports this design approach and, in many cases, encourages it. There are several advantages to adopting a modular approach:

- It allows developers to reuse schema components.

- It allows developers to use other developers' schemas.

- It reduces the complexity of schemas.

- It supports object-oriented design principles.

- It allows developers to create their own type libraries.

- It eases development, testing, and maintainability.

Once you decide to adopt this approach, you'll have to decide how to combine the modules when needed. XML Schema provides three primary methods (elements) for combining modules: `import`, `include`, and `redefine`.

import

If you wish to use schema modules that belong to different namespaces, you have to use the `import` element to combine the modules. For example, you could use any of the core XHTML modules as well as your own schema module. The resulting document instance would use XHTML document structure elements while embedding your vocabulary within the XHTML body element.

TIP   Use the `import` element when you use schema modules that belong to different namespaces. If you're only using modules that belong to the same schema, you can use the `include` or `redefine` element. The advantages are defined in the following sections.

When pulling in definitions and declarations from an external schema, you'll likely have to work with multiple namespaces. By using the `import` element, you can identify the schema location as well as the namespace for the new schema document, as shown in Listing 8.1.

Listing 8.1   **Using the *import* Element**

```
<xsd:schema
    xmlns:xsd="http://www.w3.org/2001/XMLSchema"
    elementFormDefault="qualified"
    targetNamespace="http://www.lanw.com/namespaces/pub"
    xmlns="http://www.lanw.com/namespaces/pub">

<xsd:import
    schemaLocation="http://www.lanw.com/schema/structure.xsd"
    namespace="http://www.lanw.com/namespaces/structure"/>
<xsd:include
    schemaLocation="http://www.lanw.com/namespaces/
    typeLibrary.xsd"/>

    <xsd:element name="publications">
      <xsd:complexType>
```

```
        <xsd:sequence>
          <xsd:element name="book" maxOccurs="unbounded">
            <xsd:complexType>
              <xsd:sequence>
               <xsd:element name="title" type="xsd:string"/>
               <xsd:element name="contact" type="contactType"/>
               <xsd:element name="errata" type="errataType"
                  minOccurs="0"/>
              </xsd:sequence>
              <xsd:attributeGroup ref="bookAttributes"/>
            </xsd:complexType>
          </xsd:element>
        </xsd:sequence>
      </xsd:complexType>
    </xsd:element>

    <xsd:attributeGroup name="bookAttributes">
      <xsd:attribute name="isbn" type="isbnType"
        use="required"/>
      <xsd:attribute name="edition" type="editionType"
        use="required"/>
      <xsd:attribute name="cat" type="xsd:NMTOKENS"
        use="required"/>
      <xsd:attribute name="id" type="xsd:ID"/>
    </xsd:attributeGroup>
  </xsd:schema>
```

What's important to grasp from Listing 8.1 is that the publication elements belong to their own namespace (`http://www.lanw.com/namespaces/pub`), whereas the structure elements belong to a different namespace (`http://www.lanw.com/namespaces/structure`). This allows the document instance to consist of both defined namespaces. Because we have set `element-FormDefault="qualified"`, our document instance must expose the namespaces.

redefine

If you need to incorporate *and* modify modules that belong to the same document model, and therefore the same namespace, you have to use the `redefine` element. Both schema documents must use the same target namespace.

TIP   Use the `redefine` element when you're using and modifying schema modules that belong to the same namespace or do not have a namespace defined.

The primary advantage to using this method is that you can modify declarations and definitions, thereby providing support for evolution and versioning. This method was designed to provide a declarative and modular approach to schema modification, with functionality no different except in scope from what would be achieved by wholesale text copying and redefinition by editing. One warning found in the Structures specification document is that there are no guarantees that redefinitions are side-effect free. That is to say, there may be unexpected impacts on other type definitions that are based on the redefined one, even to the extent that some such definitions become ill formed.

If you use the redefine element, you have two options for the target namespace usage:

- The schema document must have the same target namespace as the redefined schema document.

- The redefined schema document does not define a target namespace, in which case, the redefined schema document adopts the primary schema document's target namespace.

When you use the redefine element, you're restricted in the following ways:

- Type definitions must use themselves as their base type definition.

- Attribute group definitions and model group definitions must be supersets or subsets of their original definitions, either by including exactly one reference to themselves or by containing only (possibly restricted) components, which appear in a corresponding way in the redefined components.

In Listing 8.2, we added the contactType definition from typeLibrary.xsd and then modified it using the redefine element. In this case, we've extended that type to include an editor child element. Doing this allows us to customize applications rather than having to create different modules for each possible scenario.

Listing 8.2   Redefining a Type

```
<xsd:schema
    xmlns:xsd="http://www.w3.org/2001/XMLSchema"
    elementFormDefault="qualified"
    targetNamespace="http://www.lanw.com/namespaces/pub"
    xmlns="http://www.lanw.com/namespaces/pub">

<xsd:redefine
    schemaLocation="http://www.lanw.com/schema/typeLibrary.xsd">
    <xsd:complexType name="contactType">
      <xsd:complexContent>
        <xsd:extension base="contactType">
          <xsd:element name="editor" type="xsd:string"/>
        </xsd:extension>
      </xsd:complexContent>
    </xsd:complexType>
</xsd:redefine>

    <xsd:element name="publications">
```

```
<xsd:complexType>
  <xsd:sequence>
    <xsd:element name="book" maxOccurs="unbounded">
        <xsd:complexType>
          <xsd:sequence>
           <xsd:element name="title" type="xsd:string"/>
           <xsd:element name="contact" type="contactType"/>
            <xsd:element name="errata" type="errataType"
               minOccurs="0"/>
          </xsd:sequence>
          <xsd:attributeGroup ref="bookAttributes"/>
        </xsd:complexType>
    </xsd:element>
  </xsd:sequence>
</xsd:complexType>
</xsd:element>

<xsd:attributeGroup name="bookAttributes">
  <xsd:attribute name="isbn" type="isbnType"
    use="required"/>
  <xsd:attribute name="edition" type="editionType"
    use="required"/>
  <xsd:attribute name="cat" type="xsd:NMTOKENS"
    use="required"/>
  <xsd:attribute name="id" type="xsd:ID"/>
</xsd:attributeGroup>
</xsd:schema>
```

include

One a smaller scale, you might not need to reference modules from different vocabularies or to redefine a module of your own. Instead, you just want to combine modules that belong to the same namespace. For this method, you'll want to use the `include` element. It can be used only when the same target namespace is assumed, as in, for example, the following situations:

- When the schema document must have the same target namespace as the redefined schema document.

- When the redefined schema document does not define a target namespace, in which case, the included module adopts the primary schema document's target namespace.

TIP   Use the `include` element when you use schema modules that belong to the same namespace or do not have a namespace defined.

In Listing 8.3, we simply include the definitions and declarations as if they were already defined within the same schema document.

Listing 8.3   **Including the Definitions and Declarations**

```
<xsd:schema
    xmlns:xsd="http://www.w3.org/2001/XMLSchema"
    elementFormDefault="qualified"
    targetNamespace="http://www.lanw.com/namespaces/pub"
    xmlns="http://www.lanw.com/namespaces/pub">

    <xsd:include
      schemaLocation="http://www.lanw.com/schema/
        typeLibrary.xsd"/>
    <xsd:element name="publications">
      <xsd:complexType>
        <xsd:sequence>
          <xsd:element name="book" maxOccurs="unbounded">
            <xsd:complexType>
              <xsd:sequence>
               <xsd:element name="title" type="xsd:string"/>
               <xsd:element name="contact" type="contactType"/>
                <xsd:element name="errata" type="errataType"
                   minOccurs="0"/>
              </xsd:sequence>
              <xsd:attributeGroup ref="bookAttributes"/>
            </xsd:complexType>
          </xsd:element>
        </xsd:sequence>
      </xsd:complexType>
    </xsd:element>

    <xsd:attributeGroup name="bookAttributes">
      <xsd:attribute name="isbn" type="isbnType"
        use="required"/>
      <xsd:attribute name="edition" type="editionType"
        use="required"/>
      <xsd:attribute name="cat" type="xsd:NMTOKENS"
        use="required"/>
      <xsd:attribute name="id" type="xsd:ID"/>
    </xsd:attributeGroup>
</xsd:schema>
```

Content Models

Designing content models can be complex. As stated in the introduction of this chapter, there are many options available to the schema designer and each option has its own set of advantages and disadvantages. To create flexible and usable content models, you have to be familiar with each option available to you and its corresponding strengths and weaknesses. In the following sections, we identify possible decisions you'll have to make as a schema designer and provide you with a road map for making those decisions.

First, we'd like to identify the questions you're likely to ask yourself along the way:

- *Is it best to define a sequence or a choice?* There are several compositors you can use to define content model behavior. The two most common are the `sequence` and `choice` elements.

- *Do I define components locally or globally?* You have the option to define element and attribute declarations, as well as simple and complex type definitions, globally (as a child of the schema element) or locally (nested within another schema component).

- *Do I use named type definitions or declarations?* You have the option to define named type definitions and then reference them later or create element declarations that contain the type definition.

- *What is the best way to define extensibility?* You can provide extensibility by using the `extension` or any element.

Is It Best to Define a Sequence or Choice?

As the designer, one of the many decisions you'll have to make about your content model is which compositor to use. There are a few at your disposal: `all`, `sequence`, and `choice`. Before you think of the different types of compositors, take a second to think about the different types of data. Several questions come to mind:

- Does your data require many child elements?

- How will those child elements be used?

- Will a defined order help establish a pattern for a content model?

- Will a defined order hinder the usage of an element?

Let's take a second to think about a couple of XHTML elements:

The paragraph element   The paragraph (p) element can contain other elements as well as text. If you define the order for allowable child elements, you would hinder its usage. For example, the document model has to allow any number of child elements (such as em, b, and i) to occur in any order within the p element:

```
<p>The <b>paragraph</b> element may contain all sorts
   of other elements, such as the <em>emphasis</em>
   and the <i>italics</i> elements.</p>
```

The table element   The `table` element can contain several elements, such as `caption`, `thead`, `tbody`, `tfoot`, and `tr`. Structure is essential in XHTML tables. For example, an XHTML processor expects to read the table caption before the table head:

```
<table>
    <caption>Employee Data</caption>
    <thead>...</thead>
    <tbody>...</tbody>
</table>
```

The table row element   The table row (`tr`) element can only contain either the `td` element or the `th` element. In this case, the author must make a choice between the two. The following markup shows the correct usage of these elements:

```
<tr>
    <th>Name</th>
    <th>Hire Date</th>
</tr>
<tr>
    <td>Sam Williams</td>
    <td>08-01-2001</td>
</tr>
<tr>
    <td>Karl Lundin</td>
    <td>08-15-2001</td>
</tr>
```

If you think about the three elements defined previously, you'll see that they all have different needs:

- The `p` element needs an open-ended content model, one that allows for many different child elements (`all`).

- The `table` element requires a defined sequence of elements (`sequence`).

- The `tr` element requires the author to choose between two elements (`choice`).

We discuss these options in more detail in the following sections.

The *all* Element

The `all` element allows for a loosely defined structure. When the `all` compositor is used, the contents may occur in any order, as in this example:

```
<xsd:element name="book">
    <xsd:complexType>
        <xsd:all>
            <xsd:element name="title" type="xsd:string"/>
            <xsd:element name="editor" type="contactType"/>
            <xsd:element name="author" type="errataType"
```

```
            minOccurs="0"/>
        </xsd:all>
      </xsd:complexType>
   </xsd:element>
```

The `all` compositor method allows the document author (not the schema author) to decide the order of elements. By adding `minOccurs="0"`, you effectively create an open-ended model that allows any of the possible elements to occur in any order.

The only other way to allow for this type of flexibility is to define all the possible content models using the `choice` compositor; however, that would result in a long and complicated schema with many `choice` compositors defined to govern one content model.

There's only one reason to use the `all` compositor: if you need to allow for different possible combinations of element content. Many document-centric models might be prone to follow this approach.

When you use the `all` compositor, you have to be aware of what you're allowing. The schema document enforces little to no structure for the content model, meaning that the document author can create various model structures:

```
<book>
    <title>...</title>
    <editor>...</editor>
    <author>...</author>
</book>
<book>
    <author>...</author>
    <title>...</title>
    <editor>...</editor>
</book>
<book>
    <editor>...</editor>
    <author>...</author>
    <title>...</title>
</book>
```

If you need, or want, to establish a pattern for a content model, `all` should not be your choice.

The *sequence* Element

The `sequence` compositor is the most commonly used compositor. When used, the `sequence` element defines a strict structural hierarchy. For a given content model, `sequence` defines the order in which child elements may occur, as in this example:

```
<xsd:element name="book">
    <xsd:complexType>
```

```
    <xsd:sequence>
      <xsd:element name="title" type="xsd:string"/>
      <xsd:element name="editor" type="contactType"/>
      <xsd:element name="author" type="xsd:string"
        minOccurs="0"/>
    </xsd:sequence>
  </xsd:complexType>
</xsd:element>
```

When the book element is used in a document instance, the content model must follow the sequence defined by the complexType element, as shown here:

```
<book>
   <title>...</title>
   <editor>...</editor>
   <author>...</author>
</book>
```

The advantage of this approach is structure. When elements follow a similar structure, they create an intuitive pattern that is easier for both humans and processors to understand. When you enforce similar components to follow a similar structure, you add to the efficiency of your schema document. For example, if you were to define contact information for an employee, you would want to enforce the content model defined:

```
<contact>
   <tel type="hm">212-5447688</tel>
   <tel type="wk">212-5552232</tel>
   <email>joesmith@domain.com</email>
</contact>
```

If you were to allow document authors to use different structures for each contact element, the instance document would not be as readable. You might also have to prepare the processing application to handle the different models. For example, the following markup shows inconsistent content model sequences:

```
<contact>
   <tel type="hm">512-4742288</tel>
   <email>janecarnes@domain.com</email>
   <tel type="wk">512-3389822</tel>
</contact>
<contact>
   <tel type="hm">212-5447688</tel>
   <tel type="wk">212-5552232</tel>
   <email>joesmith@domain.com</email>
</contact>
<contact>
   <email>johnwilliams@domain.com</email>
   <tel type="hm">212-3987348</tel>
   <tel type="wk">212-3988661</tel>
</contact>
```

The disadvantage of this approach is the same as the advantage: structure. Once you have defined a structural model using the `sequence` element, the document author has no choice but to stick with it. This requires the schema author to do some forward thinking. Be sure to anticipate any possible content models before deciding on the `sequence` compositor.

The *choice* Element

The third compositor allows document authors to make a choice. By allowing options, you provide flexibility within a content model. For example, if you want to include contact information for a customer, you can request either an e-mail address or a telephone number:

```
<customer>
    <email>janecarnes@domain.com</email>
</customer>
<customer>
    <tel>512-3389822</tel>
</customer>
```

The `choice` element allows schema authors to enumerate the allowable choices and should be used when the schema author wants to provide an either/or choice, as in this example:

```
<xsd:element name="customer">
    <xsd:complexType>
      <xsd:choice>
        <xsd:element name="email" type="xsd:string"/>
        <xsd:element name="tel" type="xsd:string"/>
      </xsd:choice>
    </xsd:complexType>
</xsd:element>
```

The benefit of this approach is that, although you offer flexibility to the document instance author, you also limit that flexibility by supplying the enumerated list of options, which helps prevent the schema document from becoming too complicated.

Recommendation

In this case, there's no explicit recommendation. The decision depends on the type of content model you're creating. One thing you should keep in mind is that you can also define occurrence behavior for each of the compositors using the `minOccurs` and `maxOccurs` attributes. By defining this behavior, we can make our examples either more flexible or more rigid depending on the attribute used.

Do I Define Components Locally or Globally?

Schema documents can be riddled with complexity. The question is, How can you simplify complexity while taking advantage of XML Schema's flexibility? One of the first design issues a schema author must face is whether to define components locally or globally. A schema component is global if it's defined as an immediate child of the schema element, and it's local if it's not an immediate child of the schema element.

There are three common approaches to answering the question, How can you simplify complexity while taking advantage of XML Schema's flexibility? They are as follows:

Salami Slice design   Define global element declarations that are later referenced.

Venetian Blind design   Define global complex type and simple type definitions that are named and later referenced.

Russian Doll design   Nest the local element declaration within other schema component.

Each approach has its own set of characteristics, advantages, and disadvantages. In the following sections, we examine each approach.

Salami Slice Design

Many developers take a modular approach by defining global element declarations. When this is done, those declarations are later referenced within other complex type definitions. When you break element declarations into separate components, they become easier to maintain and manipulate using derivation and substitution techniques, as shown in Listing 8.4.

Listing 8.4   The Salami Slice Design

```
<xsd:schema
    xmlns:xsd="http://www.w3.org/2001/XMLSchema"
    elementFormDefault="qualified"
    targetNamespace="http://www.lanw.com/namespaces/pub"
    xmlns="http://www.lanw.com/namespaces/pub">

<xsd:element name="publications">
   <xsd:complexType>
     <xsd:sequence>
       <xsd:element ref="book"/>
     </xsd:sequence>
   </xsd:complexType>
</xsd:element>

<xsd:element name="book" maxOccurs="unbounded">
   <xsd:complexType>
     <xsd:sequence>
        <xsd:element ref="title"/>
        <xsd:element ref="author"/>
        <xsd:element ref="description"/>
```

```
        </xsd:sequence>
        <xsd:attribute name="isbn" type="xsd:string"/>
     </xsd:complexType>
  </xsd:element>

  <xsd:element name="title" type="xsd:string"/>
  <xsd:element name="author" type="xsd:string"/>
  <xsd:element name="description" type="xsd:string"/>

  </xsd:schema>
```

The Salami Slice design and the Russian Doll design take the opposite approaches. In Listing 8.4, we define all declarations globally (producing *slices* that can be reused). The benefit of this approach is component reuse and repurpose. Once each component is declared globally, they're pieced together later to make up content models.

There are several definable characteristics for the Salami Slice design:

Reusable content   Each element declaration is visible to other schemas and to other schema components, which allows other content models to reuse the globally declared elements.

Global scope   All element declarations have global scope, and therefore, all namespaces for declared elements must be exposed. Regardless of the value of `elementFormDefault`, globally defined elements cannot hide their namespaces.

Verbose   When separate schema components are used on a global level, all declarations are exposed and clearly visible.

Coupled   When external declarations are referenced, the components become interconnected. If you make changes to a content model, it might affect other content models as well.

Russian Doll Design

The Russian Doll design (shown in Listing 8.5) uses inline declarations that are defined locally within other schema components. For example, you can nest an element declaration within a complex type definition, which can also be nested within element declarations. Using this recursive behavior is a common method for defining compact element declaration components. Attribute declarations can also be defined locally within a complex type definition.

Listing 8.5   The Russian Doll Design

```
<xsd:schema
    xmlns:xsd="http://www.w3.org/2001/XMLSchema"
    elementFormDefault="qualified"
    targetNamespace="http://www.lanw.com/namespaces/pub"
    xmlns="http://www.lanw.com/namespaces/pub">
```

```
<xsd:element name="publications">
  <xsd:complexType>
    <xsd:sequence>
      <xsd:element name="book" maxOccurs="unbounded">
        <xsd:complexType>
          <xsd:sequence>
            <xsd:element name="title" type="xsd:string"/>
            <xsd:element name="author" type="xsd:string"/>
            <xsd:element name="description" type="xsd:string"/>
          </xsd:sequence>
          <xsd:attribute name="isbn" type="xsd:string"/>
        </xsd:complexType>
      </xsd:element>
    </xsd:sequence>
  </xsd:complexType>
</xsd:element>
</xsd:schema>
```

What you should notice is that the Russian Doll design is more compact than the Salami Slice design. You should also notice that the nested elements are not defined globally and, therefore, document instance authors can hide their namespaces. There are several definable characteristics for the Russian Doll design:

Not reusable   Because declarations are defined locally as a part of another content model, they are not reusable.

Localized scope   Because several element declarations are defined locally (nested within other schema components), they are localized and therefore the namespaces for them can be hidden in instance documents using `elementFormDefault="unqualified"`.

Compact   All declarations are defined within the same schema component and defined as a single unit. This is in contrast to how elements are declared using the Salami Slice design.

Decoupled   Because all declarations are nested within a single component, that component is self-contained and therefore doesn't interact with other components, which means that changes to the component will have little impact on other schema components. This allows for element substitution.

Venetian Blind Design

The Venetian Blind design (shown in Listing 8.6) works similarly to the Salami Slice design in that it also modularizes components. However, in this case, we're working with named type definitions on a global level rather than with element declarations. The main advantage to using named type definitions is that you can maximize reuse of schema components. Using the same document model, we can define named complex types on a global level.

Listing 8.6   **The Venetian Blind Design**

```
<xsd:schema
   xmlns:xsd="http://www.w3.org/2001/XMLSchema"
   elementFormDefault="qualified"
   targetNamespace="http://www.lanw.com/namespaces/pub"
   xmlns="http://www.lanw.com/namespaces/pub">

   <xsd:complexType name="pubType>
      <xsd:sequence>
         <xsd:element name="book" type="bookType"/>
      </xsd:sequence>
   </xsd:complexType>

   <xsd:complexType name="bookType">
      <xsd:sequence>
         <xsd:element name="title" type="xsd:string"/>
         <xsd:element name="author" type="xsd:string"/>
         <xsd:element name="description" type="xsd:string"/>
      </xsd:sequence>
      <xsd:attribute name="isbn" type="xsd:string"/>
   </xsd:complexType>

<xsd:element name="publications" type="pubType"/>

</xsd:schema>
```

There are two main benefits to using this design method. We already hinted at the first one: reuse. This benefit is similar to that of the Salami Slice design. At the same time, with the Venetian Blind model, you also gain the added benefit of localizing namespaces. This benefit is similar to the benefit you get with the Russian Doll design. By using the element-FormDefault attribute, you can hide or expose namespaces. In our example, we have required that the namespace be exposed in the document instance. However, by changing the attribute value to unqualified, we can hide (or localize) the namespace in document instances. The Venetian Blind model allows for both localizing namespaces and component reuse.

There are several definable characteristics for the Venetian Blind design:

Maximum reuse   All complex and simple type definitions that are defined globally can be reused.

Localized   Because element declarations are nested within named types, you increase the potential for namespace hiding.

Easy exposure switching   You can use the `elementFormDefault` attribute to turn namespace localization on or off.

Coupled   When you use globally defined named types that are later referenced, the components become interconnected.

Recommendation

Each design model offers its own set of advantages and disadvantages. If you're working with multiple namespaces in the document instance, you might not want to use the Salami Slice design because it requires namespaces to be exposed. On the other hand, you might rely on element substitution to manipulate content models. In that case, you'll have to use the Salami Slice design.

There seems to be clear-cut suggestions for when to use each design model:

Venetian Blind design   When your goal is flexibility with namespace exposure and where component reuse is important

Salami Slice design   When your goal is to allow for element substitution and namespace exposure is not an issue

Russian Doll design   When your goal is to minimize schema size and coupling of components is of utmost concern

Do I Use Named Type Definitions or Declarations?

When should an item be declared as an element and when should it be defined as a type? This question is a little easier to tackle than the preceding one. There are a few advantages types enjoy over element declarations. We'll look at each approach in the following sections.

Element Declaration

Elements can be declared globally (Salami Slice design) or locally (Russian Doll design). First, let's look at an element declaration:

```
<xsd:element name="book">
  <xsd:complexType>
    <xsd:sequence>
      <xsd:element ref="title"/>
      <xsd:element ref="author"/>
      <xsd:element ref="description"/>
    </xsd:sequence>
  </xsd:complexType>
</xsd:element>
```

Element declarations have the following definable characteristics:

Allow for element substitution   To use element substitution, you must define the element with an element declaration.

Allow for localized or global scope   Element declarations can be defined locally or globally. If they're declared globally, `elementFormDefault` cannot turn namespace exposure on or off and namespaces must always be exposed. However, if they're defined locally, namespaces are hidden.

Do not encourage reuse   Locally declared elements cannot be reused. Globally declared elements can be reused. It's better to use types if your goal is reuse.

Named Type Definition

The method of defining type definitions globally is also known as defining named types (because you name the type definition and then reference it later). Named types can be used like XML DTD parameter entities; you can define a content model or datatype and then reference that definition multiple times in the schema document. This approach is commonly used when working with complex datatypes or if you have content models that will be used more than once in the schema document. For example, the following complex type definition can be reused throughout the schema document:

```
<xsd:complexType name="bookType">
  <xsd:sequence>
    <xsd:element ref="title"/>
    <xsd:element ref="author"/>
    <xsd:element ref="description"/>
  </xsd:sequence>
</xsd:complexType>
```

Named type definitions have the following definable characteristics:

Do not allow for element substitution   To use element substitution, you must define the element with an element declaration. You cannot use type definitions.

Allow for localized scope   When complex type definitions are defined globally, you can take advantage of the `elementFormDefault` attribute and can therefore turn namespace exposure on or off.

Maximum reuse   They offer flexible, reusable components.

Recommendation

There's not a clear-cut answer to the question, Do I use named type definitions or declarations? To explore your choices, we evaluate the following possible scenarios:

- Reuse content (winner: named type definition)
- Allow for nillable content (winner: named type definition)
- Element substitution desired (winner: element declaration)
- If none of the preceding scenarios matters (winner: named type definition)

Reuse Content

If your primary goal in your schema design is to allow for the reuse of content models, you'll want to define a named type definition that can then be reused:

```
<xsd:complexType name="pubType">
  <xsd:complexType>
    <xsd:sequence>
      <xsd:element name="title" type="xsd:string"/>
      <xsd:element name="desc" type="xsd:string"/>
    </xsd:sequence>
  </xsd:complexType>
</xsd:complexType>
…
<xsd:element name="book" type="pubType"/>
<xsd:element name="magazine" type="pubType"/>
```

In this example, we've defined two types of publications: book and magazine. We want both to use the same content model, so we can define a complex type that we later reuse for both elements.

Allow for Nillable Content

When you're developing a content model that you want to be nillable sometimes but not always, you have to use a named type definition. Your first thought might be to add a nillable attribute to the element declaration and be done with it. However, you cannot reuse an element declaration and add nillability. For example, the following is *not* allowed:

```
<xsd:element name="book">
  …
</xsd:element>
<xsd:element ref="book" nillable="true"/>
```

The ref and nillable attributes are mutually exclusive, and therefore, you cannot use both of them at the same time. The only way to accomplish the dynamic morphing capability is by defining book as a type and reusing it as an element, as shown here:

```
<xsd:complexType name="bookType">
  …
</xsd:complexType>
```

```
<xsd:element name="book" nillable="true" type="bookType"/>
...
<xsd:element name="book" type="bookType"/>
```

Element Substitution Desired

There are two ways you can provide document instance authors with a choice: You can use the choice compositor when defining the element content model or you can allow for element substitution. In this case, we would like to enable instance document authors to use different elements interchangeably (for example, we might want to allow book, publication, and title to be used interchangeably):

```
<book>
...
</book>
...

<publication>
...
</publication>
...

<title>
...
</title >
```

To allow for this substitution capability, we have to declare book, publication, and title as elements *and* as members of substitutionGroup:

```
<xsd:element name="book">
...
</xsd:element>
<xsd:element name="publication" substitutionGroup="book"/>
<xsd:element name="title" substitutionGroup="book"/>
```

If None of the Preceding Matters

If none of the preceding scenarios is applicable and you don't have any compelling reasons to use a type or declaration, you should opt for a type. An element can always be created from a type, whereas the inverse is not allowed. For example, you can create a bookType:

```
<xsd:complexType name="bookType">
...
</xsd:complexType>
```

Later, you could create a book element from that type:

```
<xsd:element name="book" type="bookType"/>
```

You can use the same name for element declarations and complex type definitions. In the previous example, we could name the complex type and the element declaration book.

Namespaces

As the schema designer, you have to be aware of how to use XML namespaces within the schema document as well as how namespaces will be used in document instances. XML Schema provides several options for both scenarios. In this section, we focus on resolving the following two issues:

XML namespaces in the schema document   The schema document must reference the XML Schema namespaces in addition to an optional target namespace. As the developer, you must decide how to define both of these namespaces (either as the default or with namespace prefixes).

XML namespaces in the document instance   Within the schema document, you can define how namespaces should be used in document instances. For example, you can require that all elements be qualified, or you can allow some elements to be unqualified. This is an important issue when working with multiple schema modules.

Defining Default Namespaces

When creating an XML Schema document, on most occasions, there are at least two namespaces you need to define:

- The XML Schema namespace (`http://www.w3.org/2001/XMLSchema`)
- The target namespace for your document model

As the designer, you can choose to define either (or none) of these namespaces as the default. This section focuses on making that decision.

Using XML Schema as the Default Namespace

In this scenario, we define the XML Schema namespace as the default and qualify all references to components that fall within the scope of the target namespace. Listing 8.7 provides an example of this scenario.

Listing 8.7   **Defining the XML Schema Namespace as the Default**

```
<?xml version="1.0"?>
<schema xmlns="http://www.w3.org/2001/XMLSchema"
    targetNamespace="http://www.lanw.com/namespaces/pub"
```

```
  xmlns:pub="http://www.lanw.com/namespaces/pub"
  elementFormDefault="qualified">
  <include schemaLocation="book.xsd"/>
  <element name="products">
    <complexType>
      <sequence>
        <element name="publications">
          <complexType>
            <sequence>
              <element ref="pub:book" maxOccurs="unbounded"/>
            </sequence>
          </complexType>
        </element>
      </sequence>
    </complexType>
  </element>
</schema>
```

In this case, we use the XML Schema namespace as the default. Because it's defined as the default, we don't have to use any prefixes with the schema elements (`schema`, `include`, `element`, `sequence`, and `complexType`). We also use the `include` element to pull in components from another schema document. The tricky part comes when you define a `target namespace`, which defines the namespace for the document instance. Once an element is declared, anytime it's used, it must fall within the scope of that target namespace. In this case, the book element is declared in the `book.xsd` schema document and then referred to (used) later in the schema document. Because it must fall within the scope of the target namespace, if we want to use it, we have to add the namespace to our schema document. To do this, we define a namespace in our document that has the same value as the target namespace. Any references (using the ref attribute) to components in the target namespace (`products`, `publications`, `book`, etc.) are explicitly qualified with `pub`.

The advantage to this approach is that it keeps your schema design clean. Using the *xsd* prefix can clutter a schema document. On the other hand, for first-time schema designers, using namespace qualifiers for referenced elements is many times confusing. For example, the first line can be easier to understand than the second:

```
<element ref="pub:book"/>
<xsd:element ref="book"/>
```

Using *targetNamespace* as the Default Namespace

Another option is to make the target namespace the default namespace and explicitly qualify all components from the XML Schema namespace. This approach is similar to our previous scenario; however, in this case, the schema vocabulary uses the prefix, as shown in Listing 8.8.

Listing 8.8   *targetNamespace* as the Default Namespace

```
<?xml version="1.0"?>
<xsd:schema xmlns:xsd="http://www.w3.org/2001/XMLSchema"
    targetNamespace="http://www.lanw.com/namespaces/pub"
    xmlns="http://www.lanw.com/namespaces/pub"
    elementFormDefault="qualified">

    <xsd:include schemaLocation="book.xsd"/>
    <xsd:element name="products">
      <xsd:complexType>
        <xsd:sequence>
          <xsd:element name="publications">
            <xsd:complexType>
              <xsd:sequence>
                <xsd:element ref="book" maxOccurs="unbounded"/>
              </xsd:sequence>
            </xsd:complexType>
          </xsd:element>
        </xsd:sequence>
      </xsd:complexType>
    </xsd:element>
</xsd:schema>
```

In this example, the target namespace is also defined as the default namespace. This means that any references to components in the target namespace don't have to be namespace qualified.

As you might assume, the advantage of this approach is the opposite of the disadvantage of the previously defined approach. This design is easier for novices to understand. On the other hand, the design can be rather cluttered with tons of namespace qualifiers; therefore, readability suffers.

Defining Both with Prefixes

Your other option is to not use a default namespace at all. Instead, you would define both namespaces with prefixes, as shown in Listing 8.9.

Listing 8.9   Defining Both Namespaces with Prefixes

```
<?xml version="1.0"?>
<xsd:schema xmlns:xsd="http://www.w3.org/2001/XMLSchema"
    targetNamespace="http://www.lanw.com/namespaces/pub"
    xmlns:pub="http://www.lanw.com/namespaces/pub"
    elementFormDefault="qualified">
    <xsd:include schemaLocation="book.xsd"/>
    <xsd:element name="products">
```

```
    <xsd:complexType>
      <xsd:sequence>
        <xsd:element name="publications">
          <xsd:complexType>
            <xsd:sequence>
              <xsd:element ref="pub:book"
                maxOccurs="unbounded"/>
            </xsd:sequence>
          </xsd:complexType>
        </xsd:element>
      </xsd:sequence>
    </xsd:complexType>
  </xsd:element>
</xsd:schema>
```

In this example, everything is qualified with a namespace prefix. The advantage to this approach is that nothing is implied—everything is explicitly stated. However, it unnecessarily clutters a schema document. There's really no compelling reason this design approach should be adopted—unless you need to explicitly state all namespace associations.

Recommendation

A true benefit does not exist that warrants a real recommendation. Much of your decision is left up to personal preference. If you're a novice or you're using example documents for training purposes, we recommend that you qualify the XML Schema namespace and use a default target namespace.

Hiding or Exposing Namespaces

The questions here are as follows:

- When should a schema be designed to hide (localize) namespaces within the schema?

- When should it be designed to expose namespaces in instance documents?

The more complicated the schema, the more complicated the issue of namespace qualification. On many occasions, a schema document will use multiple schema modules.

When working with multiple schema documents, and possibly multiple namespaces, the schema author must decide whether the namespace of each element should be hidden or exposed in the document instance. To do this, you set the value of the `elementFormDefault` attribute as a part of the `schema` element. The possible values are listed here:

- `elementFormDefault="unqualified"`, which means the namespaces will be hidden (localized) within the schema

- `elementFormDefault="qualified"`, which means the namespaces will be exposed in instance documents

elementFormDefault="unqualified"

When you set the `elementFormDefault` attribute to `unqualified`, the document instance might hide all namespace qualifications. This applies only to those elements that are not defined globally. That means that at least the root element would have to be qualified; however, its children don't, as shown here:

```
<pub:products xmlns:pub="http://www.lanw.com/namespaces/pub"
    xmlns:xsi="http://www.w3.org/2001/XMLSchema-instance"
    xsi:schemaLocation="http://www.lanw.com/namespaces/
       pubpublications.xsd>
    <publications type="fiction">
      <book>...</book>
      <book>...</book>
      <book>...</book>
    </publications>
    <publications type="nonfiction"
      <book>...</book>
      <book>...</book>
      <book>...</book>
    </publications>
</pub:products>
```

The advantage to this approach is that the document instance is less cluttered and, therefore, more readable. Another benefit is that users aren't aware that multiple schemas were used.

elementFormDefault="qualified"

When you use `elementFormDefault="qualified"`, the namespace of each element would have to be exposed in document instances:

```
<pub:products xmlns:pub="http://www.lanw.com/namespaces/pub"
    xmlns:xsi="http://www.w3.org/2001/XMLSchema-instance"
    xsi:schemaLocation="http://www.lanw.com/namespaces/
       pubpublications.xsd>
    <pub:publications type="fiction">
      <pub:book>...</pub:book>
      <pub:book>...</pub:book>
      <pub:book>...</pub:book>
    </pub:publications>
    <pub:publications type="nonfiction"
      <pub:book>...</pub:book>
      <pub:book>...</pub:book>
      <pub:book>...</pub:book>
    </pub:publications>
</pub:products>
```

In this case, each element is explicitly qualified. The result of this approach is that users know that multiple schemas were used for the document model; however, the document is also cluttered. There are some reasons you would want users to see the namespaces. First, you might want credit for the document model. For example, if we wanted to include books from other publishers, we might use their schema model that defined their namespace. The document instance might then read like this:

```
<pub:publications type="sybex">
    <sybex:book>...</sybex:book>
    <sybex:book>...</sybex:book>
    <sybex:book>...</sybex:book>
</pub:publications>
```

Each schema document used should have the same value for `elementFormDefault`. The `elementFormDefault` attribute applies only to the schema that it's in. It does not apply to schemas that it includes or imports. Consequently, if you want to hide namespaces, all schemas involved must have `elementFormDefault="unqualified"` set for each schema document. The inverse is true as well. If you want to expose namespaces, all schemas documents must have `elementFormDefault="qualified"` set.

You can define some schema documents with `elementFormDefault="qualified"` and others with `elementFormDefault="unqualified"`. The document instance would then consist of some qualified elements and others would not be qualified. This is legal.

One advantage of setting `elementFormDefault="qualified"` is that it forces document instances to preserve namespace qualification, which in effect provides your company with recognition—yet another compelling reason to expose namespaces. If the namespace is required for processing, by hiding it, you're forcing the processing application to go to the schema to look up this information, costing you processing time.

WARNING   Globally defined elements must be qualified in the document instance.

Recommendation

There's not clear-cut advantage to either approach. What we recommend is that you create two versions of the schema documents: one that exposes namespaces and one that hides them. If you also take steps to follow the Venetian Blind design (not using global element declarations), you can use the `elementFormDefault` attribute as a switch to turn namespace exposure on and off.

You hide namespaces for the following reasons:

To provide simplicity   Hiding namespaces helps to create simple and readable documents.

When additional information is not needed   Namespaces can provide additional information about a component, but if that is not needed, you should examine whether namespace qualification is necessary.

You expose namespaces for the following reasons:

To provide recognition   When recognition is important and information is necessary for document instance users

To avoid naming conflicts   If document instances will use the same element names that have different semantics attached

Summary

This chapter addressed many questions you're likely to face as you begin to create complex schema models. In reaction to the DTD's inability to satisfy designers' needs, XML Schema was designed to allow for complex content models and datatyping. For many reasons, the result was a modeling language that allows for flexibility in design. One of the complaints lodged against XML Schema is that it's too complex (and flexible) for the average developer. This chapter attacked that problem head on and answered many design-related questions.

As developers continue to work with this emerging technology, they'll undoubtedly find additional "best practices" that are applicable. Much of the information in this chapter was based on an ongoing conversation hosted by the XML-DEV mailing list on this very topic. If you're interested in learning more, or even joining this conversation, visit www.xfront.com.

There are many choices available to you as schema designers. As you forge ahead, keep the following design principles in mind:

- Element and attribute names should be semantic.

- The vocabulary should follow consistent naming conventions.

- Acronyms and abbreviations should be used responsibly.

- Regional labeling should be taken into account.

- Industry labeling may be used when applicable.

- Use the import element when you use schema modules that belong to different namespaces.

- Use the redefine element when you use and modify schema modules that belong to the same namespace or do not have a namespace defined.

- Use the include element when you use schema modules that belong to the same namespace or do not have a namespace defined.

- Use the Venetian Blind design when your goal is flexibility with namespace exposure and component reuse is important.

- Use the Salami Slice design when your goal is to allow for element substitution and namespace exposure is not an issue.

- Use the Russian Doll design when your goal is to minimize schema size and coupling of components is of utmost concern.

- Use named type definitions when your goal is to reuse content or to allow for nillable content.

- Use element declarations when element substitution is needed.

- Localize namespaces if you need to provide simplicity or namespaces are not needed to add additional information to a document instance.

- Expose namespaces to provide recognition for the authors of a schema model or when you need to avoid naming conflicts in document instances.

If you keep these design tips in mind when designing schema models, you'll be better equipped to create usable and efficient schema models.

CHAPTER 9

Converting DTDs to Schemas

- Defining uniqueness

- Dealing with entities

- Working with namespaces

- Using XML Spy

- Highlighting other conversion tools

XML Schema has taken center stage in the XML community as the long-awaited answer to many shortcomings found in XML DTDs. When XML 1.0 was first released, it was based upon the Standard Generalized Markup Language (SGML), which has a strong history with document-centric information. DTDs served SGML well and have served XML well (in the beginning). However, XML is expected to take data exchange and e-commerce to a new level. To do this, it needs a strong validation tool capable of keeping up with data-centric information.

It's expected that many XML developers will look toward XML Schema to provide the answer to their validation needs. This is not to say that XML DTDs will cease to be used. Their use will continue, but it is expected to be isolated to legacy applications, in addition to applications that need to be SGML compliant.

In this move to adopt XML Schema, you might be faced with the task of converting old XML DTDs to comply with the XML Schema model. Rest assured, there are tools out there that will do most of the work for you; however, no matter which tool you use, you'll have to do some refining on your own. You'll be expected to understand how to identify which pieces need refining and how to make the necessary changes to take full advantage of XML Schema. This chapter is dedicated to preparing you to make those decisions.

Declaring Elements and Attributes

One of the easiest parts of converting your DTD to an XML Schema is working with the elements and attributes. Luckily, the easiest part is also the first step in understanding how to convert an XML DTD subset into an XML Schema document. The following two sections cover converting both element and attribute declarations.

Element Declarations

DTD element type declarations allow for several different content model constraints. XML Schema offers similar, and sometimes enhanced, functionality. Table 9.1 provides a rundown of how they compare.

TABLE 9.1: DTD and XML Schema Features

DTD Concept	DTD Syntax	XML Schema Equivalent
element type declaration	`<!ELEMENT book (content model)>`	`<xsd:element name="book">` *...content model...* `</xsd:element>`

Continued on next page

TABLE 9.1 CONTINUED: DTD and XML Schema Features

DTD Concept	DTD Syntax	XML Schema Equivalent
Mixed content models (#PCDATA only)	`<!ELEMENT title (#PCDATA)>`	`<xsd:element name="title" type="xsd:string"/>`

Mixed content models	`<!ELEMENT description (#PCDATA | bold)*>`	`<xsd:element name="description">`
		`  <xsd:complexType mixed="true">`
		`    <xsd:sequence>`
		`      <xsd:element name="bold"`
		`        type="xsd:string"/>`
		`    </xsd:sequence>`
		`  </xsd:complexType>`
		`</xsd:element>`

ANY content model	`<!ELEMENT book ANY>`	`<element name="book">`
		`  <complexType>`
		`    <sequence>`
		`    <any minOccurs="1"`
		`      maxOccurs="unbounded"`
		`      processContents="skip"/>`
		`    </sequence>`
		`  </complexType>`
		`</element>`

EMPTY content model	`<!ELEMENT img EMPTY>`	`<xsd:element name="img">`
		`  <xsd:complexType/>`
		`</xsd:element>`

, (sequence connector)	`<!ELEMENT book (title, description)>`	`<xsd:element name="book">`
		`  <xsd:complexType>`
		`    <xsd:sequence>`
		`      <xsd:element name="title"`
		`        type="xsd:string "/>`
		`      <xsd:element`
		`        name="description"`
		`        type="xsd:string"/>`
		`    </xsd:sequence>`
		`  </xsd:complexType>`
		`</xsd:element>`

| (choice connector)	`<!ELEMENT content (description | review)>`	`<xsd:element name="content">`
		`  <xsd:complexType>`
		`    <xsd:choice>`
		`      <xsd:element`
		`        name="description"`
		`        type="xsd:string"/>`
		`      <xsd:element`
		`        name="review"`
		`        type="xsd:string"/>`
		`    </xsd:choice>`
		`  </xsd:complexType>`
		`</xsd:element>`

Continued on next page

TABLE 9.1 CONTINUED: DTD and XML Schema Features

DTD Concept	DTD Syntax	XML Schema Equivalent

? (optional occurrence indicator)	`<!ELEMENT book (edition?, title)>`	`<xsd:element name="book">`
		`  <xsd:complexType>`
		`    <xsd:sequence>`
		`      <xsd:element name="edition"`
		`      type="xsd:string"`
		`      minOccurs="0"`
		`      maxOccurs="1"/>`
		`      <xsd:element name="title"`
		`      type="xsd:string"/>`
		`    </xsd:sequence>`
		`  </xsd:complexType>`
		`</xsd:element>`

+ (required and repeatable occurrence indicator)	`<!ELEMENT book (title, description+)>`	`<xsd:element name="book">`
		`  <xsd:complexType>`
		`   <xsd:sequence>`
		`      <xsd:element name="title"`
		`      type="xsd:string"/>`
		`      <xsd:element`
		`      name="description"`
		`      type="xsd:string"`
		`      minOccurs="1"`
		`      maxOccurs="unbounded"/>`
		`    </xsd:sequence>`
		`  </xsd:complexType>`
		`</xsd:element>`

* (optional and repeatable occurrence indicator)	`<!ELEMENT book (title, description*)>`	`<xsd:element name="book">`
		`  <xsd:complexType>`
		`    <xsd:sequence>`
		`      <xsd:element name="title"`
		`      type="xsd:string"/>`
		`      <xsd:element`
		`      name="description"`
		`      type="meta.content"`
		`      minOccurs="0"`
		`      maxOccurs="unbounded"/>`
		`    </xsd:sequence>`
		`  </xsd:complexType>`
		`</xsd:element>`

Continued on next page

TABLE 9.1 CONTINUED: DTD and XML Schema Features

DTD Concept	DTD Syntax	XML Schema Equivalent

( ) (grouping)	`<!ELEMENT book (title,`
	`(description |`
	`review))>`
		`<xsd:element name="book">`
		`<xsd:complexType>`
		` <xsd:sequence>`
		`   <xsd:element name="title"`
		`   type="xsd:string"/>`
		`   <xsd:group   ref="content"/>`
		` </xsd:sequence>`
		`</xsd:complexType>`
		`</xsd:element>`
		`<xsd:group name="content">`
		` <xsd:choice>`
		`   <xsd:element`
		`   name="description"`
		`   type="xsd:string"/>`
		`   <xsd:element name="review"`
		`   type="xsd:string"/>`
		` </xsd:choice>`
		`</xsd:group>`

Many of the equivalent mechanisms are easy to grasp. For example, if you want to insist that the content model for book consists of a title element followed by a description element (sequence), you use the sequence element:

```
<xsd:element name="book">
   <xsd:complexType>
     <xsd:sequence>
       <xsd:element name="title" type="xsd:string"/>
       <xsd:element name="description" type="xsd:string"/>
     </xsd:sequence>
   </xsd:complexType>
</xsd:element>
```

Most comparisons are similarly easy to understand, but if you don't understand schema concepts, they're covered in Chapters 6 and 7.

A common question when creating XML Schema element declarations is whether the item should be declared as an element or as a type (and then referenced). There's an advantage to defining types and then referencing them rather than directly declaring an item as an element. If you use the type method, other elements can use that type, or you can easily create new elements based on that type. This is not to say that you should always use the type method. If you know that the element will only be defined once, or that it contains only character data, you should declare the element.

If you elect to define an element declaration, the complex type would be nested within the element declaration.

```
<xsd:element name="book">
   <xsd:complexType>

      ...

   </xsd:complexType>
</xsd:element>
```

If you choose to define a complex type definition, you need to reference that type from within an element declaration:

```
<xsd:complexType name="bookType">

   ...

</xsd:complexType>
<xsd:element name="book" type="bookType"/>
```

TIP   The value of the complexType name attribute can be the same as the name of the element. In our examples, however, we avoid using the same name to make the distinction clear.

In addition to deciding between defining a type definition versus defining an element declaration, you have to decide if you should use local or global element declarations.

Element declarations are said to be global if they're defined as immediate children of the schema element. If they're nested within other elements, they're local. In discussions on the XML Dev mailing list, several solutions have been presented. To summarize, the consensus is that there are three basic models for element declarations:

- Russian Doll
- Salami Slice
- Venetian Blind

We discuss these in more detail in the following sections.

Russian Doll Design

In the Russian Doll design, the element declarations are nested within other element declarations; therefore, the structure of the element declaration mirrors the instance document structure:

```
<xsd:element name="book">
   <xsd:complexType>
     <xsd:sequence>
       <xsd:element name="title" type="xsd:string"/>
       <xsd:element name="author" type="xsd:string"/>
       <xsd:element name="description" type="xsd:string"/>
     </xsd:sequence>
   </xsd:complexType>
</xsd:element>
```

Salami Slice Design

Each element declaration in the Salami Slice design is defined globally and therefore referenced from within other complex types. In this case, each declaration is defined individually and then assembled into a defined structure using the `ref` attribute:

```
<xsd:element name="title" type="xsd:string"/>
<xsd:element name="author" type="xsd:string"/>
<xsd:element name="description" type="xsd:string"/>
<xsd:element name="Book">
   <xsd:complexType>
     <xsd:sequence>
      <xsd:element ref="title"/>
        <xsd:element ref="author"/>
        <xsd:element ref="description"/>
     </xsd:sequence>
   </xsd:complexType>
</xsd:element>
```

Venetian Blind Design

The Venetian Blind design is similar to the Salami Slice design; each item is defined globally as its own individual component. The difference here is that instead of declaring elements globally, we're defining global complex types that we will then use in an element declaration:

```
<xsd:complexType name="bookType">
   <xsd:sequence>
     <xsd:element name="title" type="xsd:string"/>
     <xsd:element name="author" type="xsd:string"/>
     <xsd:element name="author" type="xsd:string"/>
   </xsd:sequence>
</xsd:complexType>
<xsd:element name="book" type="bookType"/>
```

There's no clear-cut answer to which is the best of the three designs. There are many factors that impact your design decision. Chapter 8 takes a more in-depth look at making these design decisions. For our examples, we use a combination of these design models.

As an example, we've converted an XML DTD subset to an XML Schema document. Listing 9.1 provides the initial XML DTD, and Listing 9.2 provides the XML Schema equivalent.

Listing 9.1   **An XML External DTD Subset**

```
<?xml version="1.0" encoding="UTF-8"?>
<!NOTATION gif SYSTEM "image/gif">
<!ENTITY mxhtml SYSTEM "graphics/mxhtml.gif" NDATA gif>
```

```
<!ENTITY jdgexj SYSTEM "graphics/jdgexj.gif" NDATA gif>
<!ENTITY jdgsj SYSTEM "graphics/jdgsj.gif" NDATA gif>
<!ELEMENT publications (book+)>
<!ATTLIST publications xmlns CDATA #FIXED
    "http://www.lanw.com/namespaces/pub">
<!ELEMENT book (title, authors, pubDate, publisher, size,
    cover?, topics, errata?, description, website?)>
<!ATTLIST book
        isbn CDATA #REQUIRED
        edition CDATA #REQUIRED
        cat NMTOKENS #REQUIRED
        id ID #IMPLIED
>
<!ELEMENT authors (author+)>
<!ATTLIST size pp CDATA #REQUIRED>
<!ELEMENT size EMPTY>
<!ELEMENT cover EMPTY>
<!ATTLIST cover img ENTITY #REQUIRED>
<!ELEMENT topics (topic+)>
<!ELEMENT errata EMPTY>
<!ATTLIST errata code CDATA #REQUIRED>
<!ELEMENT title (#PCDATA)>
<!ELEMENT pubDate EMPTY>
<!ATTLIST pubDate year CDATA #REQUIRED>
<!ELEMENT publisher (#PCDATA)>
<!ELEMENT description (#PCDATA)>
<!ELEMENT website (#PCDATA)>
<!ELEMENT author (#PCDATA)>
<!ELEMENT topic (#PCDATA)>
```

Listing 9.2   **An XML Schema Document Using Global *simpleType* and *complexType* Declarations**

```
<xsd:schema
    xmlns:xsd="http://www.w3.org/2000/10/XMLSchema"
    elementFormDefault="qualified"
    targetNamespace="http://www.lanw.com/namespaces/pub"
    xmlns="http://www.lanw.com/namespaces/pub">
    <xsd:simpleType name="yearType">
      <xsd:restriction base="xsd:year"/>
    </xsd:simpleType>

    <xsd:simpleType name="isbnType">
      <xsd:restriction base="xsd:string">
        <xsd:pattern value="[0-9]{10}"/>
      </xsd:restriction>
    </xsd:simpleType>

    <xsd:simpleType name="imageType">
      <xsd:restriction base="xsd:NOTATION">
        <xsd:enumeration value="gif"/>
```

```
      </xsd:restriction>
    </xsd:simpleType>

    <xsd:simpleType name="editionType">
      <xsd:restriction base="xsd:nonNegativeInteger">
        <xsd:minInclusive value="1"/>
        <xsd:maxInclusive value="10"/>
      </xsd:restriction>
    </xsd:simpleType>

    <xsd:simpleType name="ppType">
      <xsd:restriction base="xsd:nonNegativeInteger">
        <xsd:minInclusive value="1"/>
        <xsd:maxInclusive value="2000"/>
      </xsd:restriction>
    </xsd:simpleType>

    <xsd:element name="author" type="xsd:string"/>

    <xsd:complexType name="authorsType">
      <xsd:sequence>
        <xsd:element ref="author" maxOccurs="5"/>
      </xsd:sequence>
    </xsd:complexType>

    <xsd:complexType name="bookType">
      <xsd:sequence>
        <xsd:element ref="title"/>
        <xsd:element name="authors" type="authorsType"/>
        <xsd:element name="pubDate" type="pubDateType"/>
        <xsd:element ref="publisher"/>
        <xsd:element name="size" type="sizeType"/>
        <xsd:element name="cover" type="coverType"
          minOccurs="0"/>
        <xsd:element name="topics" type="topicsType"/>
        <xsd:element name="errata" type="errataType"
          minOccurs="0"/>
        <xsd:element ref="description"/>
        <xsd:element ref="website" minOccurs="0"/>
      </xsd:sequence>
      <xsd:attribute name="isbn" type="isbnType"
        use="required"/>
      <xsd:attribute name="edition" type="editionType"
        use="required"/>
      <xsd:attribute name="cat" type="xsd:NMTOKENS"
        use="required"/>
      <xsd:attribute name="id" type="xsd:ID"/>
    </xsd:complexType>

    <xsd:complexType name="coverType">
      <xsd:simpleContent>
```

```xsd
      <xsd:extension base="xsd:hexBinary">
        <xsd:attribute name="imgType" type="imageType"
          use="required"/>
      </xsd:extension>
    </xsd:simpleContent>
  </xsd:complexType>

<xsd:element name="description" type="xsd:string"/>

<xsd:complexType name="errataType">
  <xsd:attribute name="code" type="xsd:string"
    use="required"/>
</xsd:complexType>

<xsd:complexType name="pubDateType">
  <xsd:attribute name="year" type="xsd:string"
    use="required"/>
</xsd:complexType>

<xsd:element name="publications">
  <xsd:complexType>
    <xsd:sequence>
      <xsd:element name="book" type="bookType"
        maxOccurs="unbounded"/>
    </xsd:sequence>
  </xsd:complexType>
</xsd:element>

<xsd:element name="publisher" type="xsd:string"/>

<xsd:complexType name="sizeType">
  <xsd:attribute name="pp" type="ppType" use="required"/>
</xsd:complexType>

<xsd:element name="title" type="xsd:string"/>
<xsd:element name="topic" type="xsd:string"/>

<xsd:complexType name="topicsType">
  <xsd:sequence>
    <xsd:element ref="topic" maxOccurs="unbounded"/>
  </xsd:sequence>
</xsd:complexType>

<xsd:element name="website" type="xsd:string"/>

<xsd:notation name="gif" public="image/gif"
  system="viewer.exe"/>
</xsd:schema>
```

Attribute Declarations

Converting attribute-list declarations is quite similar to converting element type declarations. The significant difference between XML DTD and XML Schema attributes is their use of datatypes. Whereas XML DTDs only allow for 10 attribute datatypes, XML Schema allows for 44-plus datatypes, including mechanisms for creating your own datatypes. Chapter 6 is devoted entirely to datatypes, so we won't cover them here. However, if you want to convert your DTD to a schema, we strongly recommend that you take advantage of datatyping.

XML Schema allows for similar functionality as offered by DTDs. In addition, XML Schema offers even more flexibility in defining occurrence and datatypes. Table 9.2 provides a rundown of how they compare.

TABLE 9.2: DTD and XML Schema Features

DTD Concept	DTD Syntax	XML Schema Equivalent

attribute-list declarations	`<!ATTLIST img src CDATA #REQUIRED>`	`<xsd:element name="img">`
		` <xsd:complexType>`
		`  <xsd:attribute`
		`   name="src"`
		`   type="`
		`   xsd:uriReference"`
		`   use="required"/>`
		` </xsd:complexType>`
		`</xsd:element>`

Multiple attribute-list declarations	`<!ATTLIST img src CDATA #REQUIRED alt CDATA #REQUIRED>`	Not supported in the strict sense; however, you can define a group of attributes that can then be referenced from within content models:
		`<xsd:element name"img">`
		` <xsd:complexType>`
		`  <xsd:attributeGroup`
		`   ref="imageType"/>`
		` </xsd:complexType>`
		`<xsd:element>`
		
		`<xsd:attributeGroup`
		` name="imageType">`
		` <xsd:attribute name="src"`
		`  type="xsd:uriReference"`
		`  use="required"/>`
		` <xsd:attribute name="alt"`
		`  type="xsd:string"`
		`  use="required"/>`
		`</xsd:attributeGroup>`

Continued on next page

TABLE 9.2 CONTINUED: DTD and XML Schema Features

DTD Concept	DTD Syntax	XML Schema Equivalent
Attribute default value	`<!ATTLIST book author CDATA "unknown">`	`<xsd:attlist name="author" default="unknown"/>`
Required attribute (#REQUIRED)	`<!ATTLIST img src CDATA #REQUIRED>`	`<xsd:attribute name="src" type="xsd:uriReference" use="required"/>`
Optional attribute (#IMPLIED)	`<!ATTLIST img width CDATA #IMPLIED>`	`<xsd:attribute name="width" type="xsd:number" use="optional"/>`
Fixed attribute (#FIXED)	`<!ATTLIST book-list version CDATA #FIXED "1.0">`	`<xsd:attribute name="version" type="xsd:number" fixed="1.0"/>`

For an example, we've converted an XML DTD subset to an XML Schema document. Listing 9.3 provides the initial XML DTD, and Listing 9.4 provides the XML Schema equivalent.

Listing 9.3   **The XML External DTD Subset**

```
<?xml version="1.0" encoding="UTF-8"?>
<!NOTATION gif SYSTEM "image/gif">
<!ENTITY mxhtml SYSTEM "graphics/mxhtml.gif" NDATA gif>
<!ENTITY jdgexj SYSTEM "graphics/jdgexj.gif" NDATA gif>
<!ENTITY jdgsj SYSTEM "graphics/jdgsj.gif" NDATA gif>
<!ELEMENT publications (book+)>
<!ATTLIST publications xmlns CDATA #FIXED
    "http://www.lanw.com/namespaces/pub">
<!ELEMENT book (title, authors, pubDate, publisher, size,
    cover?, topics, errata?, description, website?)>
<!ATTLIST book
        isbn CDATA #REQUIRED
        edition CDATA #REQUIRED
        cat NMTOKENS #REQUIRED
        id ID #IMPLIED
>
<!ELEMENT authors (author+)>
<!ATTLIST size pp CDATA #REQUIRED>
<!ELEMENT size EMPTY>
<!ELEMENT cover EMPTY>
<!ATTLIST cover img ENTITY #REQUIRED>
<!ELEMENT topics (topic+)>
<!ELEMENT errata EMPTY>
```

```
<!ATTLIST errata code CDATA #REQUIRED>
<!ELEMENT title (#PCDATA)>
<!ELEMENT pubDate EMPTY>
<!ATTLIST pubDate year CDATA #REQUIRED>
<!ELEMENT publisher (#PCDATA)>
<!ELEMENT description (#PCDATA)>
<!ELEMENT website (#PCDATA)>
<!ELEMENT author (#PCDATA)>
<!ELEMENT topic (#PCDATA)>
```

Listing 9.4   XML Schema Document (Equivalent to XML External DTD Subset in Listing 9.3)

```
<xsd:schema
    xmlns:xsd="http://www.w3.org/2000/10/XMLSchema"
    elementFormDefault="qualified"
    targetNamespace="http://www.lanw.com/namespaces/pub"
    xmlns="http://www.lanw.com/namespaces/pub">
    <xsd:simpleType name="yearType">
      <xsd:restriction base="xsd:year"/>
    </xsd:simpleType>

    <xsd:simpleType name="isbnType">
      <xsd:restriction base="xsd:string">
        <xsd:pattern value="[0-9]{10}"/>
      </xsd:restriction>
    </xsd:simpleType>

    <xsd:simpleType name="imageType">
      <xsd:restriction base="xsd:NOTATION">
        <xsd:enumeration value="gif"/>
      </xsd:restriction>
    </xsd:simpleType>

    <xsd:simpleType name="editionType">
      <xsd:restriction base="xsd:nonNegativeInteger">
        <xsd:minInclusive value="1"/>
        <xsd:maxInclusive value="10"/>
      </xsd:restriction>
    </xsd:simpleType>

    <xsd:simpleType name="ppType">
      <xsd:restriction base="xsd:nonNegativeInteger">
        <xsd:minInclusive value="1"/>
        <xsd:maxInclusive value="2000"/>
      </xsd:restriction>
    </xsd:simpleType>

    <xsd:element name="author" type="xsd:string"/>

    <xsd:complexType name="authorsType">
      <xsd:sequence>
        <xsd:element ref="author" maxOccurs="5"/>
```

```
    </xsd:sequence>
  </xsd:complexType>

  <xsd:complexType name="bookType">
    <xsd:sequence>
      <xsd:element ref="title"/>
      <xsd:element name="authors" type="authorsType"/>
      <xsd:element name="pubDate" type="pubDateType"/>
      <xsd:element ref="publisher"/>
      <xsd:element name="size" type="sizeType"/>
      <xsd:element name="cover" type="coverType"
        minOccurs="0"/>
      <xsd:element name="topics" type="topicsType"/>
      <xsd:element name="errata" type="errataType"
        minOccurs="0"/>
      <xsd:element ref="description"/>
      <xsd:element ref="website" minOccurs="0"/>
    </xsd:sequence>
    <xsd:attribute name="isbn" type="isbnType"
      use="required"/>
    <xsd:attribute name="edition" type="editionType"
      use="required"/>
    <xsd:attribute name="cat" type="xsd:NMTOKENS"
      use="required"/>
    <xsd:attribute name="id" type="xsd:ID"/>
  </xsd:complexType>

  <xsd:complexType name="coverType">
    <xsd:simpleContent>
    <xsd:extension base="xsd:hexBinary">
      <xsd:attribute name="imgType" type="imageType"
        use="required"/>
    </xsd:extension>
    </xsd:simpleContent>
  </xsd:complexType>

  <xsd:element name="description" type="xsd:string"/>

  <xsd:complexType name="errataType">
    <xsd:attribute name="code" type="xsd:string"
      use="required"/>
  </xsd:complexType>

  <xsd:complexType name="pubDateType">
    <xsd:attribute name="year" type="xsd:string"
      use="required"/>
  </xsd:complexType>

  <xsd:element name="publications">
    <xsd:complexType>
      <xsd:sequence>
```

```
        <xsd:element name="book" type="bookType"
           maxOccurs="unbounded"/>
      </xsd:sequence>
    </xsd:complexType>
  </xsd:element>

  <xsd:element name="publisher" type="xsd:string"/>

  <xsd:complexType name="sizeType">
    <xsd:attribute name="pp" type="ppType" use="required"/>
  </xsd:complexType>

  <xsd:element name="title" type="xsd:string"/>
  <xsd:element name="topic" type="xsd:string"/>

  <xsd:complexType name="topicsType">
    <xsd:sequence>
      <xsd:element ref="topic" maxOccurs="unbounded"/>
    </xsd:sequence>
  </xsd:complexType>

  <xsd:element name="website" type="xsd:string"/>

  <xsd:notation name="gif" public="image/gif"
     system="viewer.exe"/>
</xsd:schema>
```

Of IDs and Keys

Whereas XML DTDs allow only one way to define uniqueness, using an ID attribute datatype, XML Schema provides several mechanisms:

- ID (and IDREF, IDREFS) datatype. The ID datatype requires that the value be unique to the entire document instance. The IDREF datatype allows you to reference a defined ID.

- The key and keyref elements allow you to define relationships between elements. Similar to the ID/IDREF connection, however, is that keys can be unique to a defined element set. XML Schema uses XPath expressions to identify an element set to which the key is required to be unique.

- The unique element allows you to specify that any attribute or element value must be unique within a defined scope. The unique element may contain a selector or field element. The selector element defines the element set for the uniqueness constraint. The field element is used to identify the attribute or element field relative to each selected element that has to be unique within the scope of the set of selected elements. Both the selector and field elements use an xpath attribute that contains an XPath expression.

One drawback to using XML DTD ID datatypes is that they have to be unique to the entire document. There are many cases in which you might need an element or attribute to be unique within the scope of an element set rather than the entire document. For example, in the following document instance (Listing 9.5), we want the value attributes of the option element to be unique only within the scope of the options element.

Listing 9.5   **Unique *value* attributes**

```
<?xml version="1.0"?>
<Title>Java 2 Exam Prep Test A</Title>
<ModuleID>1</ModuleID>
<question value="1" topic="primitive values" difficulty="0">
<body>Which of these attempts to assign a value to a byte
    primitive variable is out of the byte range?</body>
<options>
<option value="a"><![CDATA[byte b = (byte) 255; ]]></option>
<option value="b"><![CDATA[byte b = (byte) 128 ; ]]></option>
<option value="c"><![CDATA[byte b = (byte) -128 ; ]]></option>
<option value="d"><![CDATA[byte b = (byte) 127 ; ]]></option>
</options>
</question>
<question value="2" topic="package and import" difficulty="0">
<body>Let's suppose you're writing a utility class and your
company's policy is to keep utility classes in a package named
"conglomo.util" - select the correct code fragment to start a
class file for a class that uses classes in the java.awt and
java.util standard library packages.<br/>
    fragment A<br/>
      package java.conglomo.util<br/>
      import java.awt.*<br/>
      import java.util.*<br/>
    fragment B.<br/>
      package conglomo.util ;<br/>
      import java.awt.* ;<br/>
      import java.util.* ;<br/>
    fragment C.<br/>
      import java.awt.* ;<br/>
      import java.util.* ;<br/>
      import conglomo.util.* ;<br/>
</body>
<option value="a">Code Fragment A</option>
<option value="b">Code Fragment B</option>
<option value="c">Code Fragment C</option>
</question>
```

If the value attribute was declared as an ID datatype, the parser would find an error because each value value is not unique to the entire document.

As defined in Chapter 4, the ID and IDREF datatypes work together to cross-reference data. The ID datatype defines an attribute value that must be an XML name that is unique within a document instance. It's used to assign unique identifiers to elements in your document model, as in the following:

```
<!ATTLIST book id ID #IMPLIED>
```

When working with the ID datatype, there are a few special considerations:

- Any given element type may only have one ID attribute type.

- An ID default type can only be #IMPLIED or #REQUIRED.

- The ID attribute value must be an XML name.

The IDREF(S) datatype is used in conjunction with the ID datatype as a way to cross-reference data or objects. The IDREF(S) attribute type must follow the same rules defined for the ID attribute type, with one additional rule: it can only reference ID attribute types that occur within the same XML document.

The IDREF/ID connection provides a simple inside-the-document linking mechanism in which every IDREF attribute is required to point to an ID attribute. You can declare an IDREF attribute type as follows:

```
<!ELEMENT book (title, author, description)>
<!ATTLIST book id ID #IMPLIED>
<!ELEMENT reference EMPTY>
<!ATTLIST reference id IDREF #REQUIRED>
```

There are a few problems with DTD ID and IDREF datatypes. To begin with, ID datatypes must be unique to the entire document. That means you have no way to define unique identifiers for a defined element set. In addition, ID and IDREF datatypes cannot begin with an integer. Many unique identifiers that come to mind are social security numbers, ISBNs, or product numbers. In most cases, unique identifiers are defined as a number. That is not allowed by XML 1.0 DTDs.

XML Schema also allows for ID and IDREF datatypes. Both the ID and IDREF schema datatypes are equivalent to the ID attribute datatype. The ID and IDREF datatypes are derived from the NCName type, which represents the ID attribute type of XML 1.0 Second Edition. The value space and the lexical space are the same—the set of all strings that conform to the NCName string guidelines in Namespaces in XML (this means that they cannot begin with a digit). As with XML DTD ID datatypes, a schema ID datatype must be unique to the entire document instance. In addition, an element may have only one ID attribute. Schema IDREF datatypes also follow the same rules as XML DTD IDREF datatypes.

In our example, we keep with the XML Schema ID datatype; therefore, we don't go on to define the key, keyref, or unique elements. Definitions and examples for each of these elements can be found in Chapter 6.

With the specifics defined, it's time to convert our XML internal DTD subset to an XML Schema. In our XML document (Listing 9.6), we declare the id attribute as the ID datatype.

Listing 9.6   **An XML External DTD Subset with *ID* Attribute Datatypes**

```
<?xml version="1.0" encoding="UTF-8"?>
<!NOTATION gif SYSTEM "image/gif">
<!ENTITY mxhtml SYSTEM "graphics/mxhtml.gif" NDATA gif>
<!ENTITY jdgexj SYSTEM "graphics/jdgexj.gif" NDATA gif>
<!ENTITY jdgsj SYSTEM "graphics/jdgsj.gif" NDATA gif>
<!ATTLIST publications xmlns CDATA #FIXED
   "http://www.lanw.com/namespaces/pub">
<!ELEMENT publications (book+)>
<!ELEMENT book (title, authors, pubDate, publisher,
   size, cover?, topics, errata?, description, website?)>
<!ATTLIST book
         isbn CDATA #REQUIRED
         edition CDATA #REQUIRED
         cat NMTOKENS #REQUIRED
         id ID #IMPLIED
>
<!ELEMENT authors (author+)>
<!ATTLIST size pp CDATA #REQUIRED>
<!ELEMENT size EMPTY>
<!ELEMENT cover EMPTY>
<!ATTLIST cover img ENTITY #REQUIRED>
<!ELEMENT topics (topic+)>
<!ELEMENT errata EMPTY>
<!ATTLIST errata code CDATA #REQUIRED>
<!ELEMENT title (#PCDATA)>
<!ELEMENT pubDate EMPTY>
<!ATTLIST pubDate year CDATA #REQUIRED>
<!ELEMENT publisher (#PCDATA)>
<!ELEMENT description (#PCDATA)>
<!ELEMENT website (#PCDATA)>
<!ELEMENT author (#PCDATA)>
<!ELEMENT topic (#PCDATA)>
```

Listing 9.7 shows a complexType that contains an attribute that is declared as an ID datatype.

Listing 9.7   An XML Schema Using the *ID* Datatype

```
<xsd:complexType name="bookType">
  <xsd:sequence>
    <xsd:element ref="title"/>
    <xsd:element name="authors" type="authorsType"/>
    <xsd:element name="pubDate" type="pubDateType"/>
    <xsd:element ref="publisher"/>
    <xsd:element name="size" type="sizeType"/>
    <xsd:element name="cover" type="coverType" minOccurs="0"/>
    <xsd:element name="topics" type="topicsType"/>
    <xsd:element name="errata" type="errataType"
      minOccurs="0"/>
    <xsd:element ref="description"/>
    <xsd:element ref="website" minOccurs="0"/>
  </xsd:sequence>
    <xsd:attribute name="isbn" type="isbnType"
      use="required"/>
    <xsd:attribute name="edition" type="editionType"
      use="required"/>
    <xsd:attribute name="cat" type="xsd:NMTOKENS"
      use="required"/>
    <xsd:attribute name="id" type="xsd:ID"/>
</xsd:complexType>
```

Working with Entities

Working with entities is an interesting thorn in the side of developers when they are converting an XML DTD to an XML Schema. XML Schema does not define an equivalent for XML DTD general entities. For example, you can't define a schema equivalent for the following DTD declarations:

```
<!ENTITY copy "Copyright 2001">
<!ENTITY baseurl "http://www.sybex.com/">
```

This is only to say that you cannot achieve the same functionality using XML Schema. There are other ways to import other data or define reusable data sources. However, XML Schema is not one of them.

WARNING   There's currently no support for named character entity references (as used in XHTML) within XML Schema.

On the other hand, XML Schema does allow you to mimic the behavior of parameter entities. A direct equivalent of XML DTD parameter entities is not defined, but other formal mechanisms are in place to allow for similar functionality.

The example we've used throughout this chapter (and most of this book) does not use parameter entities; therefore, we've borrowed an example from the XHTML DTD. In the XHTML DTD, there's an `html.content` parameter entity defined that contains a content model for the `html` element declaration:

```
<ENTITY % html.content "(head+,body+)">
```

If you want to reproduce this functionality in an XML Schema, you use a `group` element:

```
<xsd:group name="html.content">
   <xsd:sequence>
     <xsd:element ref="head" minOccurs="1">
     <xsd:element ref="body" minOccurs="1">
   </xsd:sequence>
</xsd:group>
```

You could also define the content model as its own complex type (using the `complexType` element):

```
<xsd:complexType name="html.content">
   <xsd:sequence>
     <xsd:element ref="head" minOccurs="1">
     <xsd:element ref="body" minOccurs="1">
   </xsd:sequence>
</xsd:complexType>
```

Defining complex types that can then be reused will prove an invaluable resource when creating well-designed XML Schemas. As you might have already noticed, XML Schema can get cumbersome. In length alone, an XML Schema document can be a lot to handle. When you're working with multiple schemas, or defining a complex schema for your document model, it makes sense to take advantage of type definitions. If any content model might be reused, we recommend defining a complex type, even if there's only a chance that it might be reused. After the complex type is created, it can be referenced throughout the schema document as many times as you like.

Namespaces

DTDs are not namespace aware. This can pose an interesting problem if you rely on DTD validation; however, you need to use namespaces to resolve naming conflicts. If you're using a DTD, it's difficult to anticipate how a namespace might be used. For example, will the document author want to use a namespace prefix or a default namespace for the document instance? Because DTDs are not namespace aware, the DTD views the namespace as any old attribute, and it must be declared as such. If you want to allow for namespace prefixes, you have to hand-code them as a part of the element names in each and every element type declaration. This can be a tedious and cumbersome process—one of the reasons we like working with XML Schema.

Because DTDs do not recognize XML namespace prefixes, a prefix, if used, must be defined as a part of the element or attribute name in the corresponding declaration. For example, if you want to use `pubs:title`, you have to use the following element type declaration:

```
<!ELEMENT pubs:title (#PCDATA)>
```

If you choose to use namespace prefixes, you'll have to define all element type and attribute-list declarations accordingly. This makes future modifications rather difficult. If you need to change the prefix used, not only do you have to modify the XML document, you also have to modify each declaration that references the prefix.

TIP You can use parameter entities to allow for an easier way for future modification to the prefix, but the solution is still cumbersome. There are two steps for defining parameter entities for a namespace. For more information on this process, see Chapter 4.

Listing 9.8 defines an example DTD subset that assumes the document author will be using a default namespace for each document instance.

Listing 9.8   **An XML External DTD Subset Allowing for a Default Namespace**

```
<?xml version="1.0" encoding="UTF-8"?>
<!NOTATION gif SYSTEM "image/gif">
<!ENTITY mxhtml SYSTEM "graphics/mxhtml.gif" NDATA gif>
<!ENTITY jdgexj SYSTEM "graphics/jdgexj.gif" NDATA gif>
<!ENTITY jdgsj SYSTEM "graphics/jdgsj.gif" NDATA gif>
<!ATTLIST publications xmlns CDATA #FIXED
   "http://www.lanw.com/namespaces/pub">
<!ELEMENT publications (book+)>
<!ELEMENT book (title, authors, pubDate, publisher, size,
   cover?, topics, errata?, description, website?)>
<!ATTLIST book
         isbn CDATA #REQUIRED
         edition CDATA #REQUIRED
         cat NMTOKENS #REQUIRED
         id ID #IMPLIED
>
<!ELEMENT authors (author+)>
<!ATTLIST size pp CDATA #REQUIRED>
<!ELEMENT size EMPTY>
<!ELEMENT cover EMPTY>
<!ATTLIST cover img ENTITY #REQUIRED>
```

```
<!ELEMENT topics (topic+)>
<!ELEMENT errata EMPTY>
<!ATTLIST errata code CDATA #REQUIRED>
<!ELEMENT title (#PCDATA)>
<!ELEMENT pubDate EMPTY>
<!ATTLIST pubDate year CDATA #REQUIRED>
<!ELEMENT publisher (#PCDATA)>
<!ELEMENT description (#PCDATA)>
<!ELEMENT website (#PCDATA)>
<!ELEMENT author (#PCDATA)>
<!ELEMENT topic (#PCDATA)>
```

Now, what if the document author wants to use a prefixed namespace? The answer is that you must have a completely different DTD subset defined. Listing 9.9 defines an external subset that assumes the document author will want to use a namespace prefix.

Listing 9.9　　　**An XML External DTD Subset Allowing for a Prefix Namespace**

```
<?xml version="1.0" encoding="UTF-8"?>
<!NOTATION gif SYSTEM "image/gif">
<!ENTITY mxhtml SYSTEM "graphics/mxhtml.gif" NDATA gif>
<!ENTITY jdgexj SYSTEM "graphics/jdgexj.gif" NDATA gif>
<!ENTITY jdgsj SYSTEM "graphics/jdgsj.gif" NDATA gif>
<!ATTLIST pubs:publications xmlns:pubs CDATA #FIXED
    "http://www.lanw.com/namespaces/pub">
<!ELEMENT pubs:publications (pubs:book+)>
<!ELEMENT pubs:book (pubs:title, pubs:authors, pubs:pubDate,
    pubs:publisher, pubs:size, pubs:cover?, pubs:topics,
    pubs:errata?, pubs:description, pubs:website?)>
<!ATTLIST pubs:book
          isbn CDATA #REQUIRED
          edition CDATA #REQUIRED
          cat NMTOKENS #REQUIRED
          id ID #IMPLIED
>
<!ELEMENT pubs:authors (pubs:author+)>
<!ATTLIST pubs:size pp CDATA #REQUIRED>
<!ELEMENT pubs:size EMPTY>
<!ELEMENT pubs:cover EMPTY>
<!ATTLIST pubs:cover img ENTITY #REQUIRED>
<!ELEMENT pubs:topics (pubs:topic+)>
<!ELEMENT pubs:errata EMPTY>
<!ATTLIST pubs:errata code CDATA #REQUIRED>
<!ELEMENT pubs:title (#PCDATA)>
<!ELEMENT pubs:pubDate EMPTY>
<!ATTLIST pubs:pubDate year CDATA #REQUIRED>
<!ELEMENT pubs:publisher (#PCDATA)>
<!ELEMENT pubs:description (#PCDATA)>
<!ELEMENT pubs:website (#PCDATA)>
<!ELEMENT pubs:author (#PCDATA)>
<!ELEMENT pubs:topic (#PCDATA)>
```

We understand that this is a lot of typing. And moreover, you have no way of anticipating how someone might want to use your namespace. If you choose to convert either of the DTDs, the same schema document will be produced (Listing 9.10).

Listing 9.10   An XML Schema Document

```
<xsd:schema
    xmlns:xsd="http://www.w3.org/2000/10/XMLSchema"
    elementFormDefault="qualified"
    targetNamespace="http://www.lanw.com/namespaces/pub"
    xmlns="http://www.lanw.com/namespaces/pub">

    <xsd:simpleType name="yearType">
      <xsd:restriction base="xsd:year"/>
    </xsd:simpleType>

    <xsd:simpleType name="isbnType">
      <xsd:restriction base="xsd:string">
        <xsd:pattern value="[0-9]{10}"/>
      </xsd:restriction>
    </xsd:simpleType>

    <xsd:simpleType name="imageType">
      <xsd:restriction base="xsd:NOTATION">
        <xsd:enumeration value="gif"/>
      </xsd:restriction>
    </xsd:simpleType>

    <xsd:simpleType name="editionType">
      <xsd:restriction base="xsd:nonNegativeInteger">
        <xsd:minInclusive value="1"/>
        <xsd:maxInclusive value="10"/>
      </xsd:restriction>
    </xsd:simpleType>

    <xsd:simpleType name="ppType">
      <xsd:restriction base="xsd:nonNegativeInteger">
        <xsd:minInclusive value="1"/>
        <xsd:maxInclusive value="2000"/>
      </xsd:restriction>
    </xsd:simpleType>

    <xsd:element name="author" type="xsd:string"/>

    <xsd:complexType name="authorsType">
      <xsd:sequence>
        <xsd:element ref="author" maxOccurs="5"/>
      </xsd:sequence>
    </xsd:complexType>
```

```
<xsd:complexType name="bookType">
  <xsd:sequence>
    <xsd:element ref="title"/>
    <xsd:element name="authors" type="authorsType"/>
    <xsd:element name="pubDate" type="pubDateType"/>
    <xsd:element ref="publisher"/>
    <xsd:element name="size" type="sizeType"/>
    <xsd:element name="cover" type="coverType"
      minOccurs="0"/>
    <xsd:element name="topics" type="topicsType"/>
    <xsd:element name="errata" type="errataType"
      minOccurs="0"/>
    <xsd:element ref="description"/>
    <xsd:element ref="website" minOccurs="0"/>
  </xsd:sequence>
  <xsd:attribute name="isbn" type="isbnType"
    use="required"/>
  <xsd:attribute name="edition" type="editionType"
    use="required"/>
  <xsd:attribute name="cat" type="xsd:NMTOKENS"
    use="required"/>
  <xsd:attribute name="id" type="xsd:ID"/>
</xsd:complexType>

<xsd:complexType name="coverType">
  <xsd:simpleContent>
  <xsd:extension base="xsd:hexBinary">
  <xsd:attribute name="imgType" type="imageType"
  use="required"/>
  </xsd:extension>
  </xsd:simpleContent>
</xsd:complexType>

<xsd:element name="description" type="xsd:string"/>

<xsd:complexType name="errataType">
  <xsd:attribute name="code" type="xsd:string"
    use="required"/>
</xsd:complexType>

<xsd:complexType name="pubDateType">
  <xsd:attribute name="year" type="xsd:string"
    use="required"/>
</xsd:complexType>

<xsd:element name="publications">
  <xsd:complexType>
    <xsd:sequence>
      <xsd:element name="book" type="bookType"
        maxOccurs="unbounded"/>
    </xsd:sequence>
```

```
      </xsd:complexType>
    </xsd:element>

    <xsd:element name="publisher" type="xsd:string"/>

    <xsd:complexType name="sizeType">
      <xsd:attribute name="pp" type="ppType"
        use="required"/>
    </xsd:complexType>

    <xsd:element name="title" type="xsd:string"/>
    <xsd:element name="topic" type="xsd:string"/>

    <xsd:complexType name="topicsType">
      <xsd:sequence>
        <xsd:element ref="topic" maxOccurs="unbounded"/>
      </xsd:sequence>
    </xsd:complexType>

    <xsd:element name="website" type="xsd:string"/>

    <xsd:notation name="gif" public="image/gif"
      system="viewer.exe"/>
  </xsd:schema>
```

Non-XML Data

Notations provide a formal mechanism for referencing unparseable data. A notation labels data and tells the XML processor what type of data is being defined. DTD notation declarations define the name of the notation and an identifier:

```
<!NOTATION name identifier>
```

The name of the notation is defined by the developer. The identifier must have some meaning to the XML processor. The meaning depends on the application that will handle it. In an ideal world, there would be a list of predefined identifiers for common file types. However, there's still debate about identifying external notation identifiers.

If you're using an XML DTD, notations are used in conjunction with an unparsed external entity. The unparsed entity imports non-XML data:

```
<!ENTITY name SYSTEM "URI" NDATA name>
```

In the following DTD subset, we declare a two-notation declaration for a GIF file type using its MIME types as an identifier. A cover element is declared to be an empty element that contains one attribute, img, that references the unparsed entity:

```
<?xml version="1.0"?>
<!DOCTYPE graphic [
```

```
    <!ELEMENT graphic (cover)>
    <!ELEMENT cover EMPTY>
    <!ATTLIST cover img ENTITY #REQUIRED>
    <!NOTATION gif SYSTEM "image/gif">
    <!NOTATION jpeg SYSTEM "image/jpeg">
    <!ENTITY mxhtml "graphics/mxhtml.gif" NDATA gif>
]>
<graphic>
    <cover img="mxhtml"/>
</graphic>
```

When the XML processor comes across the mxhtml entity reference and knows that it's not to be parsed (because of the NDATA), it then forgoes parsing and sends the data to the appropriate processor.

Notations don't provide specifics about nonparsed data handling. There's no way to predict how a processor might behave when it comes across an NDATA attribute. That is left to the hands of the application developer.

XML Schema is not that much different. If you want to allow for non-XML data in your document model, you have to use a notation declaration. The good news is that you no longer have to declare an external entity as well. The notation declaration provides the element name and a public and system identifier and, therefore, serves the same purpose as the DTD notation declaration:

```
<xsd:notation name="jpeg" public="image/jpeg" system="viewer.exe"/>
```

To associate the notation declaration to a given attribute value, you must use the NOTATION datatype. There's one restriction, however, and that is that you cannot directly use it. Instead, you have to derive a datatype from the NOTATION datatype:

```
<xsd:notation name="gif" public="image/gif"
    system="viewer.exe"/>
<xsd:notation name="jpeg" public="image/jpeg"
    system="viewer.exe"/>
<xsd:notation name="png" public="image/png"
    system="viewer.exe"/>

<xsd:simpleType name="imageType">
  <xsd:restriction base="xsd:NOTATION">
    <xsd:enumeration value="gif"/>
    <xsd:enumeration value="jpeg"/>
    <xsd:enumeration value="png"/>
  </xsd:restriction>
</xsd:simpleType>
```

Listing 9.11 illustrates how a DTD subset might use declarations to allow for non-XML data to be referenced.

Listing 9.11   **An XML External DTD Subset Using Notation Declarations**

```
<?xml version="1.0" encoding="UTF-8"?>
<!NOTATION gif SYSTEM "image/gif">
<!ENTITY mxhtml SYSTEM "graphics/mxhtml.gif" NDATA gif>
<!ENTITY jdgexj SYSTEM "graphics/jdgexj.gif" NDATA gif>
<!ENTITY jdgsj SYSTEM "graphics/jdgsj.gif" NDATA gif>
<!ATTLIST publications xmlns CDATA #FIXED
    "http://www.lanw.com/namespaces/pub">
<!ELEMENT publications (book+)>
<!ELEMENT book (title, authors, pubDate, publisher, size,
    cover?, topics, errata?, description, website?)>
<!ATTLIST book
          isbn CDATA #REQUIRED
          edition CDATA #REQUIRED
          cat NMTOKENS #REQUIRED
          id ID #IMPLIED
>
<!ELEMENT authors (author+)>
<!ATTLIST size pp CDATA #REQUIRED>
<!ELEMENT size EMPTY>
<!ELEMENT cover EMPTY>
<!ATTLIST cover img ENTITY #REQUIRED>
<!ELEMENT topics (topic+)>
<!ELEMENT errata EMPTY>
<!ATTLIST errata code CDATA #REQUIRED>
<!ELEMENT title (#PCDATA)>
<!ELEMENT pubDate EMPTY>
<!ATTLIST pubDate year CDATA #REQUIRED>
<!ELEMENT publisher (#PCDATA)>
<!ELEMENT description (#PCDATA)>
<!ELEMENT website (#PCDATA)>
<!ELEMENT author (#PCDATA)>
<!ELEMENT topic (#PCDATA)>
```

Listing 9.12 shows the XML Schema equivalent.

Listing 9.12   **Equivalent XML Schema Document Using Notation Declarations**

```
<xsd:schema
    xmlns:xsd="http://www.w3.org/2000/10/XMLSchema"
    elementFormDefault="qualified"
    targetNamespace="http://www.lanw.com/namespaces/pub"
    xmlns="http://www.lanw.com/namespaces/pub">

    <xsd:simpleType name="yearType">
      <xsd:restriction base="xsd:year"/>
    </xsd:simpleType>
```

```
<xsd:simpleType name="isbnType">
  <xsd:restriction base="xsd:string">
    <xsd:pattern value="[0-9]{10}"/>
  </xsd:restriction>
</xsd:simpleType>

<xsd:simpleType name="imageType">
  <xsd:restriction base="xsd:NOTATION">
    <xsd:enumeration value="gif"/>
  </xsd:restriction>
</xsd:simpleType>

<xsd:simpleType name="editionType">
  <xsd:restriction base="xsd:nonNegativeInteger">
    <xsd:minInclusive value="1"/>
    <xsd:maxInclusive value="10"/>
  </xsd:restriction>
</xsd:simpleType>

<xsd:simpleType name="ppType">
  <xsd:restriction base="xsd:nonNegativeInteger">
    <xsd:minInclusive value="1"/>
    <xsd:maxInclusive value="2000"/>
  </xsd:restriction>
</xsd:simpleType>

<xsd:element name="author" type="xsd:string"/>

<xsd:complexType name="authorsType">
  <xsd:sequence>
    <xsd:element ref="author" maxOccurs="5"/>
  </xsd:sequence>
</xsd:complexType>

<xsd:complexType name="bookType">
  <xsd:sequence>
    <xsd:element ref="title"/>
    <xsd:element name="authors" type="authorsType"/>
    <xsd:element name="pubDate" type="pubDateType"/>
    <xsd:element ref="publisher"/>
    <xsd:element name="size" type="sizeType"/>
    <xsd:element name="cover" type="coverType"
      minOccurs="0"/>
    <xsd:element name="topics" type="topicsType"/>
    <xsd:element name="errata" type="errataType"
      minOccurs="0"/>
    <xsd:element ref="description"/>
    <xsd:element ref="website" minOccurs="0"/>
  </xsd:sequence>
  <xsd:attribute name="isbn" type="isbnType"
    use="required"/>
```

```
    <xsd:attribute name="edition" type="editionType"
      use="required"/>
    <xsd:attribute name="cat" type="xsd:NMTOKENS"
      use="required"/>
    <xsd:attribute name="id" type="xsd:ID"/>
</xsd:complexType>

<xsd:complexType name="coverType">
  <xsd:simpleContent>
  <xsd:extension base="xsd:hexBinary">
  <xsd:attribute name="imgType" type="imageType"
  use="required"/>
  </xsd:extension>
  </xsd:simpleContent>
</xsd:complexType>

<xsd:element name="description" type="xsd:string"/>

<xsd:complexType name="errataType">
  <xsd:attribute name="code" type="xsd:string"
    use="required"/>
</xsd:complexType>

<xsd:complexType name="pubDateType">
  <xsd:attribute name="year" type="xsd:string"
    use="required"/>
</xsd:complexType>

<xsd:element name="publications">
  <xsd:complexType>
    <xsd:sequence>
      <xsd:element name="book" type="bookType"
        maxOccurs="unbounded"/>
    </xsd:sequence>
  </xsd:complexType>
</xsd:element>

<xsd:element name="publisher" type="xsd:string"/>

<xsd:complexType name="sizeType">
  <xsd:attribute name="pp" type="ppType" use="required"/>
</xsd:complexType>

<xsd:element name="title" type="xsd:string"/>
<xsd:element name="topic" type="xsd:string"/>

<xsd:complexType name="topicsType">
  <xsd:sequence>
    <xsd:element ref="topic" maxOccurs="unbounded"/>
  </xsd:sequence>
</xsd:complexType>

<xsd:element name="website" type="xsd:string"/>
```

```
<xsd:notation name="gif" public="image/gif"
    system="viewer.exe"/>
</xsd:schema>
```

Working with XML Spy

XML Spy is an XML editor that supports multiple schema dialects. It also includes a handy tool for easily converting any document model to any of the following models:

- BizTalk Schema
- Document Content Descriptions (DCDs)
- DTD
- W3C Schema
- XML-Data

You can download a trial version of XML Spy at www.xmlspy.com/download.html.

To convert your document model, complete the following steps from within XML Spy:

1. Open the existing schema or DTD.

2. Select Convert DTD/Schema from the DTD/Schema drop-down menu to launch the Convert DTD/Schema dialog box (shown in Figure 9.1).

FIGURE 9.1:

The Convert DTD/Schema dialog box in XML Spy

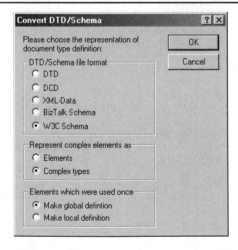

3. Select the desired document model and click OK.

If you select W3C Schema, you also have to specify how to represent complex elements (as elements or as defined complex types) and how to define elements only used once (globally or locally). In our example, we selected Complex Types and Make Global Definition.

TIP

We avoided the use of namespaces to simplify the example. In Listing 9.15, however, we added namespace references.

Listing 9.13 provides an example XML DTD subset that will be converted using XML Spy.

Listing 9.13   **An Original XML External DTD Subset**

```
<?xml version="1.0" encoding="UTF-8"?>
<!NOTATION gif SYSTEM "image/gif">
<!ENTITY mxhtml SYSTEM "graphics/mxhtml.gif" NDATA gif>
<!ENTITY jdgexj SYSTEM "graphics/jdgexj.gif" NDATA gif>
<!ENTITY jdgsj SYSTEM "graphics/jdgsj.gif" NDATA gif>
<!ATTLIST publications xmlns CDATA #FIXED
    "http://www.lanw.com/namespaces/pub">
<!ELEMENT publications (book+)>
<!ELEMENT book (title, authors, pubDate, publisher, size,
    cover?, topics, errata?, description, website?)>
<!ATTLIST book
          isbn CDATA #REQUIRED
          edition CDATA #REQUIRED
          cat NMTOKENS #REQUIRED
          id ID #IMPLIED
>
<!ELEMENT authors (author+)>
<!ATTLIST size pp CDATA #REQUIRED>
<!ELEMENT size EMPTY>
<!ELEMENT cover EMPTY>
<!ATTLIST cover img ENTITY #REQUIRED>
<!ELEMENT topics (topic+)>
<!ELEMENT errata EMPTY>
<!ATTLIST errata code CDATA #REQUIRED>
<!ELEMENT title (#PCDATA)>
<!ELEMENT pubDate EMPTY>
<!ATTLIST pubDate year CDATA #REQUIRED>
<!ELEMENT publisher (#PCDATA)>
<!ELEMENT description (#PCDATA)>
<!ELEMENT website (#PCDATA)>
<!ELEMENT author (#PCDATA)>
<!ELEMENT topic (#PCDATA)>
```

XML Spy converts this subset and produces an almost-perfect XML Schema document (Listing 9.14). However, there are many relationships and definitions that are assumed based on limited information. For example, XML Spy converts declarations defined to handle our binary image files (notation declarations and attribute-list declarations with associated entity declarations) literally, whereas there's no longer a need for an ENTITY attribute datatype.

XML Spy is only a tool and cannot interpret all intended usages. It's also important that you closely scrutinize your new generated XML Schema document. There may be many ways to improve upon the new document model. For example, in the DTD subset, we define the isbn attribute as a CDATA datatype. In the generated XML Schema document, the datatype has been converted to a string datatype. Now that we're using XML Schema, we'd rather define a more accurate datatype that allows for only a 10-digit nonnegative integer. To accommodate our new datatype, we either have to define it by hand or use XML Spy to insert it. Either way, don't expect XML Spy to generate complex datatypes based solely on a DTD subset. Listing 9.14 shows the XML Schema document generated by XML Spy.

Listing 9.14   **An XML Schema Document Generated by XML Spy 3.5**

```xml
<?xml version="1.0" encoding="UTF-8"?>
<!-- edited with XML Spy v3.5 NT (http://www.xmlspy.com)
   by Chelsea Valentine (LANWrights) -->
<!--W3C Schema generated by XML Spy v3.5 NT
   (http://www.xmlspy.com)-->
<xsd:schema xmlns:xsd="http://www.w3.org/2000/10/XMLSchema"
            elementFormDefault="qualified">
  <xsd:element name="author" type="xsd:string"/>
    <xsd:complexType name="authorsType">
      <xsd:sequence>
        <xsd:element ref="author"
                       maxOccurs="unbounded"/>
      </xsd:sequence>
  </xsd:complexType>
  <xsd:complexType name="bookType">
    <xsd:sequence>
      <xsd:element ref="title"/>
      <xsd:element name="authors"
                     type="authorsType"/>
      <xsd:element name="pubDate"
                     type="pubDateType"/>
      <xsd:element ref="publisher"/>
      <xsd:element name="size" type="sizeType"/>
      <xsd:element name="cover"
                     type="coverType"
                     minOccurs="0"/>
      <xsd:element name="topics"
                     type="topicsType"/>
      <xsd:element name="errata"
                     type="errataType"
                     minOccurs="0"/>
      <xsd:element ref="description"/>
```

```xml
      <xsd:element ref="website"
                   minOccurs="0"/>
  </xsd:sequence>
  <xsd:attribute name="isbn"
                 type="xsd:string"
                 use="required"/>
  <xsd:attribute name="edition"
                 type="xsd:string"
                 use="required"/>
  <xsd:attribute name="cat"
                 type="xsd:NMTOKENS"
                 use="required"/>
  <xsd:attribute name="id"
                 type="xsd:ID"/>
</xsd:complexType>
<xsd:complexType name="coverType">
  <xsd:attribute name="img"
                 type="xsd:ENTITY" use="required"/>
</xsd:complexType>
<xsd:element name="description"
             type="xsd:string"/>
<xsd:complexType name="errataType">
  <xsd:attribute name="code"
                 type="xsd:string"
                 use="required"/>
</xsd:complexType>
<xsd:complexType name="pubDateType">
  <xsd:attribute name="year"
                 type="xsd:string"
                 use="required"/>
</xsd:complexType>
<xsd:element name="publications">
  <xsd:complexType>
    <xsd:sequence>
      <xsd:element name="book"
                   type="bookType" maxOccurs="unbounded"/>
    </xsd:sequence>
  </xsd:complexType>
</xsd:element>
<xsd:element name="publisher"
             type="xsd:string"/>
<xsd:complexType name="sizeType">
  <xsd:attribute name="pp"
                 type="xsd:string"
                 use="required"/>
</xsd:complexType>
<xsd:element name="title"
             type="xsd:string"/>
<xsd:element name="topic"
             type="xsd:string"/>
<xsd:complexType name="topicsType">
```

```
      <xsd:sequence>
        <xsd:element ref="topic"
                     maxOccurs="unbounded"/>
      </xsd:sequence>
    </xsd:complexType>
    <xsd:element name="website"
                 type="xsd:string"/>
    <xsd:notation name="gif"
                  system="image/gif"/>
  </xsd:schema>
```

As stated previously, there are several ways we might want to enhance the generated XML Schema document. Listing 9.15 highlights a few items that we wanted to change in our document (changes in bold).

Listing 9.15   **A Modified XML Schema Document**

```
<xsd:schema
   xmlns:xsd="http://www.w3.org/2000/10/XMLSchema"
   elementFormDefault="qualified"
   targetNamespace="http://www.lanw.com/namespaces/pub"
   xmlns="http://www.lanw.com/namespaces/pub">

   <xsd:simpleType name="yearType">
     <xsd:restriction base="xsd:year"/>
   </xsd:simpleType>

   <xsd:simpleType name="isbnType">
     <xsd:restriction base="xsd:string">
       <xsd:pattern value="[0-9]{10}"/>
     </xsd:restriction>
   </xsd:simpleType>

   <xsd:simpleType name="imageType">
     <xsd:restriction base="xsd:NOTATION">
       <xsd:enumeration value="gif"/>
     </xsd:restriction>
   </xsd:simpleType>

   <xsd:simpleType name="editionType">
     <xsd:restriction base="xsd:nonNegativeInteger">
       <xsd:minInclusive value="1"/>
       <xsd:maxInclusive value="10"/>
     </xsd:restriction>
   </xsd:simpleType>

   <xsd:simpleType name="ppType">
     <xsd:restriction base="xsd:nonNegativeInteger">
       <xsd:minInclusive value="1"/>
```

```
      <xsd:maxInclusive value="2000"/>
   </xsd:restriction>
</xsd:simpleType>

<xsd:element name="author" type="xsd:string"/>

<xsd:complexType name="authorsType">
   <xsd:sequence>
      <xsd:element ref="author" maxOccurs="5"/>
   </xsd:sequence>
</xsd:complexType>

<xsd:complexType name="bookType">
   <xsd:sequence>
      <xsd:element ref="title"/>
      <xsd:element name="authors" type="authorsType"/>
      <xsd:element name="pubDate" type="pubDateType"/>
      <xsd:element ref="publisher"/>
      <xsd:element name="size" type="sizeType"/>
      <xsd:element name="cover" type="coverType"
         minOccurs="0"/>
      <xsd:element name="topics" type="topicsType"/>
      <xsd:element name="errata" type="errataType"
         minOccurs="0"/>
      <xsd:element ref="description"/>
      <xsd:element ref="website" minOccurs="0"/>
   </xsd:sequence>
   <xsd:attribute name="isbn" type="isbnType"
      use="required"/>
   <xsd:attribute name="edition" type="editionType"
      use="required"/>
   <xsd:attribute name="cat" type="xsd:NMTOKENS"
      use="required"/>
   <xsd:attribute name="id" type="xsd:ID"/>
</xsd:complexType>

<xsd:complexType name="coverType">
   <xsd:simpleContent>
   <xsd:extension base="xsd:hexBinary">
   <xsd:attribute name="imgType" type="imageType"
   use="required"/>
   </xsd:extension>
   </xsd:simpleContent>
</xsd:complexType>

<xsd:element name="description" type="xsd:string"/>

<xsd:complexType name="errataType">
   <xsd:attribute name="code" type="xsd:string"
      use="required"/>
</xsd:complexType>
```

```
<xsd:complexType name="pubDateType">
  <xsd:attribute name="year" type="xsd:string"
    use="required"/>
</xsd:complexType>

<xsd:element name="publications">
  <xsd:complexType>
    <xsd:sequence>
      <xsd:element name="book" type="bookType"
        maxOccurs="unbounded"/>
    </xsd:sequence>
  </xsd:complexType>
</xsd:element>

<xsd:element name="publisher" type="xsd:string"/>

<xsd:complexType name="sizeType">
  <xsd:attribute name="pp" type="ppType" use="required"/>
</xsd:complexType>

<xsd:element name="title" type="xsd:string"/>
<xsd:element name="topic" type="xsd:string"/>

<xsd:complexType name="topicsType">
  <xsd:sequence>
    <xsd:element ref="topic" maxOccurs="unbounded"/>
  </xsd:sequence>
</xsd:complexType>

<xsd:element name="website" type="xsd:string"/>

<xsd:notation name="gif" public="image/gif"
    system="viewer.exe"/>
</xsd:schema>
```

Other DTD-to-Schema Conversion Tools

XML Spy is not the only tool available that supports DTD-to-schema conversion. In this section, we highlight three additional tools you should take a look at. In addition to these three tools, we also recommend that you keep your eyes peeled. As schema languages gain more attention in the XML community (and we expect they will), you're likely to see more conversion tools on the market. To keep up with XML-related software, visit www .xmlsoftware.com.

Turbo XML

A wonderful alternative to XML Spy is Turbo XML. Similar to XML Spy, Turbo XML provides facilities for creating, validating, converting, and managing XML Schemas, XML files, and DTDs. When deciding what tool to choose for our validation needs for the creation of examples defined in this book, it was a toss-up between XML Spy and Turbo XML. We recommend giving Turbo XML a try.

Here are some of the features that make Turbo XML so great:

- Creates, converts, and validates schema dialects
- Supports DTD, XML-Data Reduced (XDR), Schema for Object-Oriented XML (SOX) v.2, REgular LAnguage description for XML (RELAX), and XML Schema
- Provides graphical representation of schemas and DTDs
- Imports data structures and documents
- Provides comprehensive schema documentation and reporting using notes
- Allows for opening from and saving to URLs
- Creates schema-aware XML documents
- Supports Extensible Stylesheet Language Transformations (XSLT)
- Provides a highly intuitive graphical interface for the design and navigation of long or complex XML business documents

In addition to these features, Turbo XML provides enhanced management facilities that allow you to manage just about any XML project.

You can find Turbo XML at `www.tibco.com/products/extensibility/solutions/turbo_xml.html`.

dtd2xs

This no-frills, easy-to-use tool allows you to translate a DTD into an XML Schema. dtd2xs is not an authoring tool like XML Spy and Turbo XML. The dtd2xs translator maps meaningful DTD entities onto XML Schema constructs (`simpleType`, `attributeGroup`, `group`). It also maps DTD comments onto XML Schema documentation constructs. There's not much else to say about this lightweight translator. If all you need to do is convert your DTD to an XML Schema, you might want to skip the bulky tools and opt for this simple translator.

You can download this tool at `http://puvogel.informatik.med.uni-giessen.de/dtd2xs/`.

DTD2RELAX

We know this chapter covers converting XML DTDs to XML Schema; however, while we're on the topic of converting from one document model to another, we wanted to mention a handy tool that allows you to convert XML DTDs to RELAX modules. You can use this lightweight tool both from the command line and through a GUI. To learn more about RELAX, see Chapter 12.

TIP   RELAX is in the process of evolving, and the newest generation is being called RELAX NG. Read more about this evolution in Chapter 12.

You can find DTD2RELAX at `www.horobi.com/Projects/RELAX/Archive/DTD2RELAX.html`.

Summary

XML DTDs were created from a document perspective, and for this reason, DTDs have begun to grow out of their usefulness in the enterprise space. This should come as no surprise because DTDs are not good at viewing XML document instances from a data and type perspective. Within this new space—of e-commerce and B2B transactions—data models depend on typed data such as order number, product pricing, and employee identification. This type of data model is not easily defined by a DTD.

As developers, you're likely to face this type of data when designing an XML application. When designing your data model, you'll be faced with the decision of selecting the appropriate tool. There are many options to choose from: Microsoft's XDR, Schematron, RELAX NG, DTDs, or XML Schema (just to name a few of the more popular).

You're also likely to face legacy applications that were created using DTDs. In this case, you'll have to ask yourself if you need to update or modify your data model. This decision is largely based on the type of data you're working with. Document-centric data, most of what is found on the Web, can use a DTD for its data model. If all you need to do is design a document structure that allows for paragraphs, abstracts, and other text-related elements, DTDs can provide a simple and easy solution. However, if your data consists of product numbers and prices, you most likely want to take advantage of XML Schema.

In this chapter, we focused on converting legacy DTD models to follow the new and improved XML Schema model. This is a tricky task at times. Although there are some obvious DTD-to-schema equivalents (allowing for choice within a content model, or defining occurrences for an element), there are DTD components that cannot be replicated (general entities). In addition, there are some schema components that you might want to introduce that you could not use with XML DTDs (complex datatyping). Although we couldn't provide you with an answer to every solution, we hope that you walk away from this chapter with a better understanding of how you might begin the conversion process. Chapters 6 and 7 undoubtedly shed more light on complex XML Schema scenarios.

CHAPTER 10

Important XML Schemas

- Understanding Schema for Schemas

- Understanding Schema for Datatype Definitions

- Examining other standard XML Schemas

- Exploring interesting non-standard XML Schemas

The W3C XML Schema Recommendation includes two schema documents that define the structures and datatypes of the XML Schema language: Schema for Schemas (Appendix A of XML Schema Part 1: Structures) and Schema for Datatype Definitions (Appendix A of XML Schema Part 2: Datatypes). Schemas are also included in other W3C documents, such as the Synchronized Multimedia Integration Language (SMIL) Recommendation and the Modularization of XHTML in XML Schema Working Draft.

An assortment of public schemas is available in schema registries and repositories. The two largest and most general registries and repositories are the XML.org Registry operated by the Organization for the Advancement of Structured Information Standards (OASIS) at www.xml.org/xml/registry.jsp and Microsoft's BizTalk.org repository at www.biztalk.org. Both sites include sample schemas from a wide range of different types of industries.

Understanding Schema for Schemas

Schema for Schemas, the schema document in Appendix A of XML Schema Part I: Structures, is an XML document that defines the basic framework and components of XML Schema. It describes and details the structure, meaning, and relationships of these components, including datatypes, elements, attributes, values, and default values. It's used to create vocabularies for XML documents.

The Schema for Schemas definitions depend on four other W3C documents:

- The Schema for Datatype Definitions at www.w3.org/TR/xmlschema-2/#schema specifies datatypes for elements and attributes. It's discussed in the next section of this chapter.

- The XML Information Set (Infoset) is an abstract data set that specifies the definitions of a well-formed XML document. It can be viewed at www.w3.org/TR/2001/REC-xml-infoset-20011024.

- Namespaces in XML at www.w3.org/TR/1999/REC-xml-names-19990114 provides a means to qualify XML elements and attributes by associating them with a namespace.

- The XML Path Language (XPath) provides a method to address parts of an XML document, as well as ways to manipulate strings, numbers, and Booleans. It's available at www.w3.org/TR/1999/REC-xpath-19991116.

TIP   Schema for Schemas is available at www.w3.org/TR/2001/REC-xmlschema-1-20010502/#normative-schemaSchema.

XML Schema elements, attributes, groups, and language types are named and defined in Schema for Schemas. As detailed in Chapter 6, XML Schema is defined in an abstract data model that is made up of 13 schema components divided into 3 groups. We'll briefly review each component as well as the important features of how they're defined by the Schema for Schemas. An understanding of these components is essential to a basic understanding of schema structure and function. These components can be used in any schema. You can reference Schema for Schemas by using the Schema for Schemas namespace: `http://www.w3.org/2001/XMLSchema`.

The first group of schema components is called primary components and includes the following:

Simple type definitions   Contain only character data and cannot contain other elements or attributes.

Complex type definitions   Contain other elements or attributes.

Element declarations   Include many properties. A name is required, but most other properties are optional. If an optional property is not present in the declaration, it's assumed to have a value of `absent`. The following table shows the element declaration's properties and descriptions.

Property	Description
Abstract	If `true`, can be used as a placeholder for a substitution group. Optional.
Annotation	Information about an element or its content. Optional.
Identity constraints	Constrains content to be unique. Optional.
Name	An NCName. Required.
Nillable	If `true`, can be valid with no content, even if not defined as empty. Optional.
Scope	Global or local (defined in the context of the schema).
Substitution group	Elements that can be substituted for an abstract element. Optional.
Target namespace	Target namespace of the parent `schema` element, if present.
Type	Datatype, simple type, complex type, or anonymous type (no type specified).
Value constraint	`default` or `fixed`. Optional.

Attribute declarations   Attributes can also include many properties (shown in the following table). A name is required, but most other properties are optional.

Property	Description
Annotation	Information about an attribute or its content. Optional.
Name	An NCName. Required.
Target namespace	Target namespace of the parent schema element, if present, and if attribute is qualified.
Type	Datatype.
Value constraint	default or fixed. Optional.

The second group of schema components is called secondary components and includes the following:

Attribute group definitions   A set of attribute declarations that is defined as a group and incorporated as a group in a complex type definition. A name is required.

```
<xsd:attributeGroup name="GroupN">
   <xsd:attribute name="Member1" type="xsd:string"/>
   ...
</xsd:attributeGroup>
<xsd:complexType name="sales">
   ...
   <xsd:attributeGroup ref="GroupN"/>
</xsd:complexType>
```

Identity-constraint definitions   There are three identity constraints that can be used in a schema:

- unique indicates that a character name must be unique.
- key is similar to unique, but the value can be referenced.
- keyref defines a reference to a key.

A name is required.

Model group definitions   A model group definition references a model group by assigning it a name. See *Model groups* in the next group of schema components.

Notation declarations   Notation declarations are used to include URI references to content or applications available within the user's system (SYSTEM) or online (PUBLIC). A name is required.

The final group of schema components is the helper components. Helper components, listed here, are used as a part of other components:

Annotations   Provide information about a schema component. There are two different ways they can be used:

- documentation provides additional information to the schema user.
- appInfo is application information for processing.

Model groups   A collection of element declarations or references that is grouped using a *compositor*. A name is required. There are three compositors used in a schema:

- sequence groups elements in a defined order.
- choice defines a choice between several elements or groups.
- all groups elements, but they can be in any order.

Here's an example of the sequence compositor:

```
<xsd:sequence>
    <xsd:element ref="top"/>
    <xsd:element ref="bottom"/>
    <xsd:element ref="left"/>
    <xsd:element ref="right"/>
</xsd:sequence>
```

Particles   An element declaration, a model group, or a wildcard combined with a value for minOccurs and/or maxOccurs to control occurrence.

Wildcards   A wildcard, specified by using any, is a special type of particle for validating an attribute or element dependent on the namespace name but independent of the local name.

Attribute uses   The use attribute within an attribute declaration controls the occurrence of the attribute. It can have one of three values: required, prohibited, or optional:/

```
<attribute name="begin" type="xsd:date" use="required"/>
```

TIP   For a review of schema structure and function, including an XML document and sample schemas, see "Using W3C XML Schema" by Eric van der Vlist at www.xml.com/pub/a/2000/11/29/schemas/part1.html.

Understanding Schema for Datatype Definitions

Schema for Datatype Definitions, the schema document in Appendix A of XML Schema Part 2: Datatypes, is an XML document that extends the capabilities of XML in defining datatypes. The schema defines 44 datatypes, called built-in datatypes, and provides a format for user-derived datatypes from any of these 44.

TIP   Schema for Datatype Definitions is available at www.w3.org/TR/xmlschema-2/#schema.

Datatypes are covered in detail in Chapter 7. In this section, we briefly review the basic datatypes and their important features.

Datatypes in XML Schema are specified by a name and a target namespace. They are constructed by using a simple type definition and facets. The facets are classified into two groups: fundamental facets and constraining facets.

The fundamental facets define the datatypes. There are five fundamental facets:

bounded

cardinality

equal

numeric

ordered

There are constraining facets that limit the range of possible values of a datatype:

enumeration

fractionDigits

length

maxExclusive

maxInclusive

maxLength

minExclusive

minInclusive

minLength

pattern

```
totalDigits

whiteSpace
```

For additional information on facets in XML datatypes, see Chapter 7.

Datatypes can be divided into two major groups:

- Primitive datatypes, which are not derived from any other datatypes.
- Derived datatypes, which are derived from other datatypes.

The primitive datatypes are all built-in datatypes, but derived datatypes can include both built-in and user-derived types.

The 19 primitive datatypes defined in the Schema for Datatype Definitions include many familiar datatypes from programming languages, but the definitions are not necessarily exactly the same as in any particular programming language.

The following are the built-in primitive datatypes:

string	boolean
decimal	float
double	duration
dateTime	time
date	gYearMonth
gYear	gMonthDay
gDay	gMonth
hexBinary	base64Binary
anyURI	QName
NOTATION	

The 25 built-in derived datatypes are derived from the primitive datatypes and from other built-in derived datatypes using simple type definitions and one of three methods: restriction, list, or union. Schema designers can use these same datatypes and methods to derive new datatypes.

The built-in derived datatypes are listed here:

normalizedString	token
language	NMTOKEN
NMTOKENS	Name

NCName	ID
IDREF	IDREFS
ENTITY	ENTITIES
integer	nonPositiveInteger
negativeInteger	long
int	short
byte	nonNegativeInteger
unsignedLong	unsignedInt
unsignedShort	unsignedByte
positiveInteger	

See Chapter 7 for definitions and examples of these 44 built-in datatypes.

Examining Other Standard XML Schemas

In addition to the W3C Schema Recommendation and the two schemas included in this recommendation (Schema for Structures and Schema for Datatype Definitions), there are other W3C recommendations and working drafts that include schema documents and many more are in development.

The following are some of the current W3C schema documents:

• Resource Description Framework (RDF) Schema Specification 1.0 is a Candidate Recommendation as of March 2000. The specification can be viewed at www.w3.org/TR/rdf-schema. RDF is a framework for processing metadata and enabling applications to exchange machine-understandable information on the Web. For more information on RDF, see Chapter 13.

• Modularization of XHTML in XML Schema is a Working Draft as of March 2001. A second Working Draft is in process and is expected to be available soon. The current Working Draft is available at www.w3.org/TR/xhtml-m12n-schema. Modularization of XHTML in XML Schema is discussed in more detail in the next section.

• Synchronized Multimedia Integration Language (SMIL) 2.0 is a Recommendation as of August 2001. The SMIL specification is modular and includes schema documents for the SMIL modules. The SMIL specification is available at www.w3.org/TR/smil20. The SMIL schemas are discussed in more detail later in this chapter.

Modularization of XHTML in XML Schema

XHTML 1.1–Module-based XHTML was advanced to a W3C Recommendation on May 31, 2001. XHTML 1.1 is XHTML 1.0 Strict reformulated as modules. Because it's based on XHTML 1.0 Strict, XHTML 1.1 does not support deprecated elements and attributes. The modules included in XHTML 1.1 are shown in Table 10.1.

TABLE 10.1: XHTML 1.1 Modules

Module Name	Description
Base Module	Base URI element and attribute
Bi-directional Text Module	Bi-directional rules element
Client-side Image Map Module	Client-side image map elements
Edit Module	Editing-related markup elements and attributes
Forms Module	Form elements and attributes
Hypertext Module	The `a` element and its attributes
Image Module	The `img` element and attributes
Intrinsic Events Module	Event elements and attributes
Link Module	The `link` element and attributes
List Module	List elements
Metainformation Module	The `meta` element and attributes
Object Module	`object` and `param` elements and attributes
Presentation Module	Simple presentation elements and attributes
Scripting Module	Script elements and attributes
Server-side Image Map Module	Elements for image selection and transmitting coordinates
Structure Module	Basic structural elements of XHTML
Stylesheet Module	The `style` element and attributes
Table Module	Table elements and attributes
Text Module	Basic text elements and attributes

TIP For more information on XHTML 1.1–Module-Based XHTML, see the Recommendation at www.w3.org/TR/xhtml11 and Modularization of XHTML at www.w3.org/TR/xhtml-modularization.

Modularization of XHTML in XML Schema is a separate document that consists of a complete group of XML Schema modules corresponding to the XHTML 1.1 modules. It was released as a W3C Working Draft on March 22, 2001. It consists of two main parts: a set of schema modules for the modules in XHTML 1.1 and a set of modularization conventions that defines how the modules work with each other and how they can be modified to extend XHTML.

The Modularized XHTML Schema uses three types of files:

Hub document   This is the base document; it consists of annotations and modules and corresponds to the DTD "driver" file in the Modularization of XHTML Recommendation. The user can comment out any modules that are not used.

Module container files   These include modules and containers organized according to the module's function. The hub document is a module container, and there are 10 other module container files.

Element modules   The element modules include definitions for elements, attributes, and content models.

Each schema module includes several components, although not all components are required for each module. The components are shown in Table 10.2. Components 1 and 2 plus either component 3 or some combination of components 4 through 7 are required for each module.

TABLE 10.2: Components of Schema Modules

Number	Name	Description
1	Schema element	`<xsd:schema>`...`</xsd:schema>`
2	Annotation block	Documentation section
3	Module elements	Statements, import statements, or other modules
4	Content model groups	`.content`, `.class`, or `.mix` groups
5	Attributes and attribute groups	`.attrib` or `.attlist`
6	Element type definitions	`complexType` definitions
7	Element definitions	Individual element definitions

The XHTML Schema modules include modules corresponding to the XHTML 1.1 modules as well as modules defining the basic document framework. The XHTML Schema modules also currently include modules no longer supported in XHTML, although it's expected that these modules will not be included in the future drafts. For example, the applet module, the style attribute module, and the name identification module are all deprecated in XHTML 1.1.

The group of modules that must be included in any schema document that uses the XHTML namespace is shown in Table 10.3.

TABLE 10.3: Required Schema Modules for XHTML Schema

Number	Schema Name	Description
1	xhtml-notations-1.xsd	SGML notations
2	xhtml-datatypes-1.xsd	Common datatypes
3	xhtml-events-1.xsd	Common event attributes
4	xhtml-attribs-1.xsd	Common attribute groups
5	xhtml11-model-1.xsd	Common content model groups
6	xhtml-charent-1.xsd	Character entities
7	xhtml-text-1.xsd	Text elements
8	xhtml-blkphras-1.xsd	Block element definitions
9	xhtml-blkstruct-1.xsd	Block structural element definitions
10	xhtml-inlphras-1.xsd	Inline element definitions
11	xhtml-inlstruct-1.xsd	Inline structural element definitions
12	xhtml-hypertext-1.xsd	a element definition
13	xhtml-list-1.xsd	List element definitions
14	xhtml-ruby-1.xsd	Ruby annotations
15	xhtml-struct-1.xsd	Basic structural element definitions

The numbers in the left column are for clarification only. They are not part of the specification itself.

These schemas are grouped into module containers. Schemas 1 through 6 are included in xhtml-framework-1.xsd, schemas 7 and 12 through 15 are included in xhtml-core-1.xsd, and schemas 8 through 11 are included in xhtml-text-1.xsd (schema 7).

The hypertext schema module (xhtml-hypertext-1.xsd) is one example of the XHTML schema modules. Note how its components follow the structure shown in Table 10.2.

The following is a breakdown of the hypertext schema:

1. The schema begins with an XML declaration and a schema element declaration. The names of elements in the modules are unqualified (elementFormDefault="unqualified"); therefore, it's not necessary to use a namespace prefix for XHTML elements.

```
<?xml version="1.0" encoding="UTF-8"?>
<xsd:schema xmlns:xsd="http://www.w3.org/2000/10/XMLSchema"
    targetNamespace="http://www.w3.org/1999/xhtml"
    xmlns:xsi="http://www.w3.org/2000/10/XMLSchema
    -instance"
xsi:schemaLocation="http://www.w3.org/2000/10/XMLSchema
    http://www.w3.org/2000/10/XMLSchema.xsd"
    elementFormDefault="unqualified"
    version="1.1">
```

2. The next section is the annotation block with the documentation for this schema module. It includes the formal public identifier as well as the author, version, and date and a brief explanation of the function of the module.

```
<xsd:annotation>
   <xsd:documentation>
/**
* This is the XML Schema Hypertext module for XHTML
*   This is a REQUIRED module.
*   Please use this formal public identifier to identify it:
*           "-//W3C//ELEMENTS XHTML Hypertext 1.0//EN"
*/
   </xsd:documentation>
   <xsd:documentation>
/**
* Versioning block
* Author: Daniel Austin
* $RCSfile: schema_module_defs.html,v $
* $Revision: 1.1 $
* $Date: 2001/03/22 02:11:41 $
* $Author: shane $
* (remove the NO below to see the full revision log)
* Log: $NOLog: $
*/
   </xsd:documentation>
   <xsd:documentation>
/**
* Hypertext
*        a
*     This module declares the anchor ('a') element type,
*     which defines the source of a hypertext link. The
*     destination (or link 'target') is identified via
*     its 'id' attribute rather than the 'name' attribute
*     as was used in HTML.
*/
   </xsd:documentation>
<xsd:documentation source="xhtml-copyright-1.txt"/>
</xsd:annotation>
```

3. The next section defines an attribute group named a.attlist. This group includes all the attributes that can be used with the a element. This attribute group references another attribute group named Common.attrib, which is a part of another required schema module, xhtml-attribs-1.xsd.

```
<!-- a -->
<xsd:attributeGroup name="a.attlist">
  <xsd:attributeGroup ref="Common.attrib"/>
```

4. All of the attribute names and types are then defined. The types are part of another required schema module, xhtml-datatypes-1.xsd. In the datatypes schema module, these types are derived from XML Schema datatypes.

```
<xsd:attribute name="href" type="URI"/>
<xsd:attribute name="charset" type="Charset"/>
<xsd:attribute name="type" type="ContentType"/>
<xsd:attribute name="hreflang" type="LanguageCode"/>
<xsd:attribute name="rel" type="LinkTypes"/>
<xsd:attribute name="rev" type="LinkTypes"/>
<xsd:attribute name="accesskey" type="Character"/>
<xsd:attribute name="tabindex" type="Number"/>
```

5. A wildcard, anyAttribute, is used with a namespace value of ##other. This provides for validation of any attributes that have a namespace other than the specified one (http://www.w3.org/1999/xhtml) or that do not have a namespace (unqualified).

```
<xsd:anyAttribute namespace="##other"/>
</xsd:attributeGroup>
```

6. A complex type named a.type is defined. It has mixed content (mixed="true") that includes a reference to a content model group named InlNoAnchor.mix (which is a part of another required schema module, xhtml11-model-1.xsd) and a reference to the a.attlist attribute group defined earlier in this schema module.

```
<xsd:complexType name="a.type" mixed="true">
    <xsd:group ref="InlNoAnchor.mix"/>
    <xsd:attributeGroup ref="a.attlist"/>
</xsd:complexType>
```

7. The a element is declared, with a type of a.type, as defined in the complex type definition in the preceding step.

```
<xsd:element name="a" type="a.type"/>
</xsd:schema>
```

The complete code for the hypertext schema is shown is Listing 10.1.

Listing 10.1 **The Hypertext Module Schema**

```
<?xml version="1.0" encoding="UTF-8"?>
<xsd:schema xmlns:xsd="http://www.w3.org/2001/XMLSchema"
    targetNamespace="http://www.w3.org/1999/xhtml"
    xmlns:xsi=
    "http://www.w3.org/2001/XMLSchema-instance"
    xsi:schemaLocation=
    "http://www.w3.org/2001/XMLSchema
      http://www.w3.org/2001/XMLSchema.xsd"
    elementFormDefault="unqualified"
    version="1.1">
```

```
<xsd:annotation>
   <xsd:documentation>
/**
* This is the XML Schema Hypertext module for XHTML
*  This is a REQUIRED module.
*  Please use this formal public identifier to identify it:
*          "-//W3C//ELEMENTS XHTML Hypertext 1.0//EN"
*/
   </xsd:documentation>
   <xsd:documentation>
/**
* Versioning block
* Author: Daniel Austin
* $RCSfile: schema_module_defs.html,v $
* $Revision: 1.1 $
* $Date: 2001/03/22 02:11:41 $
* $Author: shane $
* (remove the NO below to see the full revision log)
* Log: $NOLog: $
*/
   </xsd:documentation>
   <xsd:documentation>
/**
* Hypertext
*         a
*     This module declares the anchor ('a') element type, which
*     defines the source of a hypertext link. The destination
*     (or link 'target') is identified via its 'id' attribute
*     rather than the 'name' attribute as was used in HTML.
*
*/
   </xsd:documentation>
   <xsd:documentation source="xhtml-copyright-1.txt"/>
/**
*   This is XHTML, a reformulation of HTML as a modular XML
*   application.
*     The Extensible HyperText Markup Language (XHTML)
*     Copyright 1998-2000 World Wide Web Consortium
*     (Massachusetts Institute of Technology, Institut National
*      de Recherche en Informatique et en Automatique,
*      Keio University).
*      All Rights Reserved.
*
*     Permission to use, copy, modify and distribute the XHTML
*     DTD and its accompanying documentation for any purpose
*     and without fee is hereby granted in perpetuity,
*     provided that the above copyright notice and this
*     paragraph appear in all copies.  The copyright holders
*     make no representation about the suitability of the DTD
*     for any purpose.
*     It is provided "as is" without expressed or
```

```
*      implied warranty.
*/
    </xsd:documentation>
  </xsd:annotation>
  <!-- a -->
    <xsd:attributeGroup name="a.attlist">
      <xsd:attributeGroup ref="Common.attrib"/>
      <xsd:attribute name="href" type="URI"/>
      <xsd:attribute name="charset" type="Charset"/>
      <xsd:attribute name="type" type="ContentType"/>
      <xsd:attribute name="hreflang" type="LanguageCode"/>
      <xsd:attribute name="rel" type="LinkTypes"/>
      <xsd:attribute name="rev" type="LinkTypes"/>
      <xsd:attribute name="accesskey" type="Character"/>
      <xsd:attribute name="tabindex" type="Number"/>
      <xsd:anyAttribute namespace="##other"/>
    </xsd:attributeGroup>
    <xsd:complexType name="a.type" mixed="true">
      <xsd:group ref="InlNoAnchor.mix"/>
      <xsd:attributeGroup ref="a.attlist"/>
    </xsd:complexType>
    <xsd:element name="a" type="a.type"/>
</xsd:schema>
```

Synchronized Multimedia Integration Language (SMIL) Schema

SMIL is a markup language designed specifically for multimedia. SMIL 2.0 was advanced to Recommendation status by the W3C in August 2001 and includes DTDs as well as schemas for the SMIL modules.

SMIL synchronizes multimedia files (audio, video, animation) to play in the order and time sequence you specify and to act as a single stream during download and playback.

The SMIL specification is modular and includes 10 major modules, which are further subdivided into many other modules. Table 10.4 shows the 10 major SMIL 2.0 modules.

TABLE 10.4: SMIL Modules

Name	Description
Animation	Animation on a timeline, animation on a motion path, and uneven spacing of points in time
Content Control	Controls to adjust content depending on user system
Layout	Visual positioning and volume control
Linking	Navigation through a multimedia presentation
Media Objects	The seven media types recognized by SMIL

Continued on next page

TABLE 10.4 CONTINUED: SMIL Modules

Name	Description
Metainformation	Meta element and metadata element
Structure	Basic SMIL structural elements
Timing and Synchronization	Controls to coordinate and synchronize playback
Time Manipulations	Acceleration, deceleration, and reverse playback
Transition Effects	Fades and wipes

The SMIL specification includes a Language profile that includes all the core SMIL modules and defines how they work together. It's designed for direct playback of SMIL files on the Web. SMIL is scalable, and other profiles can be defined by extending the SMIL Basic profile. SMIL Basic includes the following 6 of the 10 SMIL modules:

- Content Control

- Layout

- Linking

- Media Objects

- Structure

- Timing and Synchronization

SMIL Basic is designed for devices such as mobile phones and portable CD players. New profiles for other types of devices can be created by adding other SMIL modules to the SMIL Basic configuration.

The SMIL 2.0 BasicLayout module is one of the modules contained within the SMIL Layout module. This module includes the `layout` element and a child element of `layout`, the `root-layout` element, that sets the total size of the playback area. The multimedia clips play in specified regions of the root layout. The `region` element, another child of the `layout` element, includes a size and a position relative to the root layout and an `id` attribute. The BasicLayout schema is one example of the SMIL module schemas. Here's a breakdown of the BasicLayout schema:

1. The schema begins with a `schema` element declaration. Note that the elements are qualified (`elementFormDefault="qualified"`). The target namespace is the BasicLayout schema. The public URI for this schema is `http://www.w3.org/2001/SMIL20/PR/smil20-BasicLayout.xsd`.

   ```
   <schema xmlns="http://www.w3.org/2001/XMLSchema"
       xmlns:smil20="http://www.w3.org/2001/SMIL20/PR/"
   ```

```
xmlns:smil20lang="http://www.w3.org/2001/SMIL20/PR/
  Language"
xmlns:BasicLayout=
  "http://www.w3.org/2001/SMIL20/PR/BasicLayout"
targetNamespace="http://www.w3.org/2001/SMIL20/PR/
  BasicLayout"
elementFormDefault="qualified">
```

2. An `import` element is used to import the SMIL namespace so that these elements can be validated in an instance document.

```
<!-- import the definitions in the smil20 namespace -->
<import namespace="http://www.w3.org/2001/SMIL20/PR/"
  schemaLocation="smil20.xsd"/>
```

3. The `layout`, `root-layout`, and `region` elements are declared. The type values include a `smil20lang` prefix to indicate their associated namespace.

```
<!-- declare global elements in this module -->
<element name="layout" type="smil20lang:layoutType"
  substitutionGroup="smil20lang:layout"/>
<element name="root-layout" type="smil20lang:
  root-layoutType"
  substitutionGroup="smil20lang:root-layout"/>
<element name="region" type="smil20lang:regionType"
  substitutionGroup="smil20lang:region"/>
```

4. The `region` attribute is declared.

```
<!-- declare global attributes in this module -->
<attribute name="region" type="string"/>
</schema>
```

The complete code for the BasicLayout schema is shown in Listing 10.2.

Listing 10.2   The SMIL 2.0 BasicLayout Schema

```
<!--
XML Schema for the SMIL 2.0 modules
This is SMIL 2.0
Copyright 1998-2000 W3C (MIT, INRIA, Keio), All Rights Reserved
Public URI: http://www.w3.org/2001/SMIL20/PR/
  smil20-BasicLayout.xsd
Author: Aaron Michael Cohen (Intel)
Revision: 2001/05/18
Schema for the BasicLayout module namespace,
-->
<schema xmlns="http://www.w3.org/2001/XMLSchema"
  xmlns:smil20="http://www.w3.org/2001/SMIL20/PR/"
  xmlns:smil20lang=
    "http://www.w3.org/2001/SMIL20/PR/Language"
```

```
      xmlns:BasicLayout=
        "http://www.w3.org/2001/SMIL20/PR/BasicLayout"
      targetNamespace="http://www.w3.org/2001/SMIL20/PR/
        BasicLayout"
      elementFormDefault="qualified">
  <!-- these URL's will have to be expanded to their full
      and proper locations -->
  <!-- import the definitions in the smil20 namespace -->
  <import namespace="http://www.w3.org/2001/SMIL20/PR/"
      schemaLocation="smil20.xsd"/>
  <!-- declare global elements in this module -->
  <element name="layout" type="smil20lang:layoutType"
      substitutionGroup="smil20lang:layout"/>
  <element name="root-layout" type="smil20lang:root-layoutType"
      substitutionGroup="smil20lang:root-layout"/>
  <element name="region" type="smil20lang:regionType"
      substitutionGroup="smil20lang:region"/>
  <!-- declare global attributes in this module -->
  <attribute name="region" type="string"/>
  </schema>
```

Exploring Interesting Non-Standard XML Schema

Many interesting public schemas are also available and can be found in schema registries and repositories as well as on other Web sites. Another resource for finding public schemas is the W3C XML Schema page at www.w3.org/XML/Schema. This page includes links to XML tools, resources, schemas, and specifications.

It's important to check the copyright information and terms of use if you're considering using a public schema document to make sure that your use conforms to any specified restrictions.

XML Schema for ISBN

XML Schema for ISBN was written by Roger Costello and Roger Sperberg. An ISBN (International Standard Book Number) consists of 10 characters. These 10 characters are divided into four parts:

- A group/country identifier
- A publisher identifier
- A title identifier
- A check digit

These four parts are usually separated by spaces or hyphens. The position of the spaces or hyphens varies depending on the number of characters in the group/country identifier (first space or hyphen) and the publisher identifier (second space or hyphen). The last space or hyphen is always between the 9th and 10th characters because it precedes the check digit (10th character).

This schema presents a simple type definition for ISBN and then restricts this definition by using a pattern facet corresponding to the group/country identifier. Type definitions are derived for the range of group/country identifiers. Full documentation is included within the schema. You can find a link to this schema on the OASIS XML Schema page (`www.oasis-open.org/cover/schemas.html#OtherSchemaReferences`).

Listing 10.3 shows the restriction definitions for ISBNs whose country identifier is 80 (Czechoslovakia).

Listing 10.3   The Restriction Definitions for Czechoslovakian ISBNs

```
<xsd:pattern value="80-\d([0-9]|-){6}\d-[0-9x]">
<xsd:annotation>
   <xsd:documentation>group/country ID = 80
   (hyphen after the 2nd digit) Country =
   Czech Republic and Slovakia check digit is 0-9 or
   'x'
   </xsd:documentation>
</xsd:annotation>
</xsd:pattern>
<xsd:pattern value="80\s\d([0-9]|\s){6}\d\s[0-9x]">
<xsd:annotation>
   <xsd:documentation>group/country ID = 80 (space after the
   2nd digit) Country = Czech Republic and Slovakia check
   digit is 0-9 or 'x'
   </xsd:documentation>
</xsd:annotation>
</xsd:pattern>
```

Because the check digit is calculated using a formula based on the values of the other nine characters, it's not possible to calculate the check digit directly using XML. In this case, an XSLT document is used for this calculation.

The schema with the simple type definition (another schema in which it's used), a sample instance document, and an XSLT file are also available at `www.xfront.com/isbn.html`.

Log Markup Language Schema

The Log Markup Language (LOGML) is an XML application designed to describe server access log files. The authors are John Punin, Mukkai Krishnamoorthy, and Gerard Uffelman of the Rensselaer Polytechnic Institute.

The data in server access logs is extremely useful to Web site owners because it can provide information about which pages in a site are accessed, at what times, for how long, and so on. LOGML uses the Extensible Graph Markup and Modeling Language (XGMML) to create graphs to annotate the information from the server access logs. Generally, access logs include information from a single 24-hour period. Using LOGML, you can combine these logs to create reports for longer periods of time.

> **TIP**   More information on XGMML (and another interesting schema) is available at `www.cs.rpi` `.edu/~puninj/XGMML/draft-xgmml.html`.

LOGML files can also be used in HTML files by using XSLT, can be combined with Scalable Vector Graphics (SVG) to create graphs of the information, and can be used with RDF to produce metainformation about Web servers.

A LOGML file typically has three sections:

- A graph of user visits showing the pages visited
- Additional information on hosts, user agents, and keywords
- A report of user sessions, including total time on the Web site

LOGML includes seven datatypes (`boolean`, `number`, `NMToken`, `ID`, `string`, `URI`, and `date`) and several elements and attributes, including elements for all the data categories found in server access log files. These data categories include host, domain, directory, user agent, referrer, Hypertext Transfer Protocol (HTTP) code, HTTP method, HTTP version, and user session.

The following markup shows the user session section of the LOGML schema.

1. The element `userSessions` is declared.

```
<!-- XML schema for LOGML 1.0 -->
<!-- Authors: John Punin, Mukkai Krishnamoorthy,
    and Gerard Uffelman -->
<!-- Computer Science Department -->
<!-- Rensselaer Polytechnic Institute -->
<!-- logml.xsd,v 1.0 06/29/2001 -->
<xsd:element name="userSessions">
```

2. This is followed by a complex type definition, including a sequence that includes one element, the `userSession` element. (A sequence can include one or more items.)

```
<xsd:complexType>
   <xsd:sequence>
   <xsd:element ref="userSession" minOccurs="1"
     maxOccurs="unbounded"/>
   </xsd:sequence>
```

3. An attribute group is referenced (`count-att`). The `count-att` group includes the `count` attribute, which is a number type.

```
   <xsd:attributeGroup ref="count-att"/>
```

4. Two attributes, `max_edges` and `min_edges`, are declared.

```
   <xsd:attribute name="max_edges" type="number.type"/>
   <xsd:attribute name="min_edges" type="number.type"/>
</xsd:complexType>
</xsd:element>
```

5. A second element, `userSession`, is declared, followed by a complex type definition. This includes a sequence, an attribute group, and attribute declarations.

```
   <xsd:element name="userSession">
<xsd:complexType>
   <xsd:sequence>
   <xsd:element ref="path" minOccurs="1" maxOccurs="1"/>
   </xsd:sequence>
   <xsd:attributeGroup ref="lml-global-atts"/>
   <xsd:attribute name="ureferer" type="uri.type"/>
   <xsd:attribute name="entry_page" type="uri.type"/>
   <xsd:attribute name="start_time" type="date.type"/>
   <xsd:attribute name="access_count" type="number.type"/>
</xsd:complexType>
</xsd:element>
```

6. A third element, path, is declared, followed by a complex type definition.

```
   <xsd:element name="path">
<xsd:complexType>
   <xsd:sequence>
   <xsd:element ref="uedge" minOccurs="1"
     maxOccurs="unbounded"/>
   </xsd:sequence>
   <xsd:attributeGroup ref="count-att"/>
</xsd:complexType>
</xsd:element>
```

7. The final element in the user session section, uedge, is declared, followed by a complex type definition.

```
<xsd:element name="uedge">
<xsd:complexType>
    <xsd:attributeGroup ref="edge-atts"/>
    <xsd:attribute name="utime" type="date.type"/>
</xsd:complexType>
</xsd:element>
```

TIP   The Log Markup Language 1.0 Specification, including DTD, schema, and references, is available at www.xml.org/xml/schema/64399227/draft-logml.html.

Public schemas offer XML authors and schema designers the opportunity to use and study many different types of schema documents. Schema registries, repositories, the W3C schema page, and the multitude of Web sites featuring schemas are the best resources for information and links to public schemas.

Summary

Schema for Schemas and Schema for Datatype Definitions are the two most important XML Schemas. They delineate the actual structure of XML Schema components and datatypes. The XML Schema Recommendations (Part 1: Structures and Part 2: Datatypes) consist mainly of text that explains the content of these two schemas.

A study of these two schemas provides a foundation for understanding the underlying structure and function of XML Schema. The reader is encouraged to browse these two documents on the W3C Web site.

The Modularization of XHTML Recommendation, the SMIL Recommendation, and the RDF Candidate Recommendation all include XML Schemas. Since XML Schema advanced to a W3C Recommendation in May 2001, it's expected that other XML/XHTML W3C documents will eventually include XML Schemas. XML Schemas are not the only XML documents that can be used to validate XML instance documents—DTDs and alternate schema languages can also be used for validation—but XML Schemas are XML documents (unlike DTDs) that offer strong datatype support, including 44 built-in datatypes and the option of creating user-derived datatypes from these 44 types. For more information on alternative schema languages, see Chapter 12, and for more information on DTDs, see Chapters 2, 4, and 9.

Other public XML Schemas are also available, including the ISBN Schema and the Log Markup Language Schema discussed in this chapter. The Usage section of the W3C Schema page at www.w3.org/XML/Schema is a very good resource for the latest XML Schemas, including both W3C documents and other public documents.

CHAPTER 11

Using Appropriate Metadata

- Understanding the limitations of DTDs

- Understanding the limitations of schemas

- Discovering the best uses for DTDs

- Discovering the best uses for schemas

- Examining case studies and scenarios

C hoosing the appropriate metadata scenario is essential to the efficiency and continued viability of one's XML projects. Metadata defines the appropriate content of an XML document as well as its physical layout and logical structure. There will be times when a DTD will best suit the needs of the document, and there will be other occasions when XML Schema is more appropriate. The key is knowing which is best for the task at hand and which of the two choices is the wisest.

This chapter explores the metadata requirements that should be addressed to assure the greatest success. The advantages and limitations of both DTD and XML Schema are explored along with case examples and scenarios.

Limitations of DTDs

There are inherent weaknesses and limitations, as well as strengths, to all types of markup, whether it's the Standard Generalized Markup Language (SGML), the Hypertext Markup Language (HTML), or the Extensible Markup Language (XML). It's important to be able to accentuate the strengths of a metadata document and downplay the limitations. Before you can do this with confidence, you should have a good grasp of those strengths and weaknesses.

The Document Type Definition (DTD) was the original tool to define and provide the necessary structure and definitions needed for XML. DTDs have *not* outlived their usefulness and will in all likelihood continue to be a viable solution for the near future. However, they have some limitations that prevent them from being the end-all answer to XML data definition. Although these limitations do not immediately reject the DTD as a metadata definition, it's sometimes worthwhile to consider them when determining the worthiness of a metadata choice.

This section addresses limitations inherent to DTDs and provides workarounds and suggestions for maintaining XML integrity. The list of limitations is not extensive, but they need to be addressed. Keep in mind that the DTD is a carryover from SGML (which is the language XML was derived from), but because XML is more Web-centric, ongoing document evolution has revealed some weaknesses.

The key limitations of DTDs are as follows:

- DTDs are not well-formed XML.
- XML and DTDs use different syntax.
- A separate parser and application programming interface (API) is needed for DTDs and the XML itself.
- There's limited support for defining new datatypes in DTDs.

- Mixed content is cumbersome.

- DTDs have limited content modeling capabilities.

- There's a lack of support in DTDs for effectively using namespaces.

- It's difficult to express certain types of structures of the document with DTDs.

Not Well-Formed XML

The first consideration is that DTDs are not well-formed XML. Because DTDs are not written in XML, they cannot be validated as such. This limitation is a result of the heritage of SGML and the compactness of the DTD syntax and language. Because DTDs are not constructed of XML, they're not extensible like XML. Therefore, limitations that might be introduced in the DTD document remain limitations. Usually, a DTD is either too restrictive or too liberal and wide-ranging, with no mechanism to modify it short of a rewrite.

Different Syntax

Because XML Schema and DTDs use a different syntax (schemas are XML; DTDs aren't), it can be cumbersome for developers to create both comfortably. The inability to use the same language to describe the data that is used for the data proper is a growing weakness of the DTD. As XML evolves, it only makes sense that the describing documents evolve along with it. The DTD is a cul-de-sac, in that there's nowhere else to go. This is not a concern for stable markup languages such as SGML, but it's a definite weakness when DTDs are used with XML. It has been said that if XML is so capable of data description, it should be able to describe itself. DTDs will never be able to meet that lofty goal because they remain mired in their primordial roots.

Separate Parsers and APIs

The fact that the DTD and XML syntax is so different typically prevents you from using one parser/validator to handle all documents. A separate parser and API is usually needed for each. Therefore, software requirements can become bloated. Even though human readability of both the DTD and XML is still maintained, machine readability efficiency is reduced. As XML continues to expand and newer uses are found in all industries, this limitation of DTDs will become greater.

TIP Note that some parsers, such as Xerces, Oracle, and MSXML, essentially have two parsers built into them: one to validate (parse DTD or schema rules) and one to check for well-formedness.

Limited Support for Defining New Datatypes

There's limited support for defining new datatypes in DTDs. In fact, there's a noticeable lack of datatyping at all in DTDs, particularly in the element content. Mixed content will continue to be a problem in the DTD definition. There's no easy way to state that PCDATA should contain only alphabetic characters. As XML grows in complexity and importance, this limitation will become more unwieldy. The following is a quote from the W3C that describes some of the new datatype features:

> *New complex types are defined using the* complexType *element and such definitions typically contain a set of element declarations, element references, and attribute declarations. The declarations are not themselves types, but rather an association between a name and the constraints, which govern the appearance of that name in documents, governed by the associated schema. Elements are declared using the* element *element, and attributes are declared using the* attribute *element.*

Mixed Content Is Cumbersome

Unfortunately, DTDs cannot easily specify that an element can contain either text or text followed by a few list items, for example. In addition, they can't specify that an element should contain only numeric content, a natural number, or a floating-point number. DTD structure is rigid and fairly narrow, and although it might be possible to kludge together an entry that will allow such a scenario, it's simply easier to use a different tool for the job: XML Schema.

Again, this was not much of a problem with the legacy of SGML, or with humans reading the data, but software suffers tremendously in this regard and needs strong datatyping to perform efficiently. With the newest tools, the DTD is seen as lacking in specificity as well as robustness.

The fact that the DTD is a very simple document can be an asset to simple XML applications. Unfortunately, its simplicity soon begins to limit the types of XML applications that can rely on the DTD to provide the flexibility that the real world often requires. A simple but all too common example would be defining an address. The DTD to define an address might look like this:

```
<!ELEMENT address (name,street,city,state,zipcode)>
<!ELEMENT name (#PCDATA)>
<!ELEMENT street (#PCDATA)>
<!ELEMENT city (#PCDATA)>
<!ELEMENT state (#PCDATA)>
<!ELEMENT zipcode (#PCDATA)>
```

It defines the following XML document:

```
<?xml version="1.0" encoding="UTF-8"?>
<!DOCTYPE address SYSTEM "address.dtd">
<address>
    <name>Joe Jones</name>
    <street>123 School Street</street>
    <city>Ontario</city>
    <state>California</state>
    <zipcode>91762</zipcode>
</address>
```

This looks simple enough, and in the textbook sense, it's just fine. But with DTDs, you can't specify the following, for example:

- Two lines for the street element
- Five digits for the zip code
- A two-letter state abbreviation

DTDs simply lack the precision needed for tasks like this. DTDs are excellent for defining simple data, elements, and attributes, but the more narrowly defined needs of real-world applications cannot be met with a simple DTD. More precision is always needed, and the DTD cannot keep up with this requirement. This limitation will only become more obvious with time, and as the software evolves and grows in complexity, so must its defining documents.

Limited Content Model Capabilities

DTDs have limited content model capabilities. Although DTDs allow you to define element hierarchy, it's difficult to construct complex element content models. For example, you can't require exactly 15 occurrences of a given element type. The DTD does not lend itself well to data abstraction because of its inherent weaknesses in defining element content and lack of precision. To conceptually migrate from abstract to physical is beyond the basic capabilities of the DTD. Again, it could possibly be accomplished by some very creative programming, but the results would most likely be confusing and unsatisfactory.

Structures of the Document

A number of limitations arise as increasingly complex DTDs are created, such as it's difficult to express certain types of structures of the document. For example, you cannot mix datatypes in a DTD. If this is important for the success of the document project, a workaround must be created or a different method of document declaration is required. Because one of the central tenets of XML is simplicity (along with extensibility), it seems counterproductive to create overly complex documents if better methods are available.

Lack of Support for Effectively Using Namespaces

Another shortcoming is the lack of support in DTDs for effectively using namespaces. Namespaces are an important aspect of the XML vocabulary, and namespace validation is vital for correct application and location of the document within the namespace. DTDs are not intended to contain namespace Uniform Resource Identifiers (URIs); they rely on the namespace prefix. If a DTD contains a namespace declaration, it must be a prefixed name. If the prefix changes in the document but not in the DTD, the document becomes invalid.

Breaking a single DTD into smaller, modular DTDs is a shortcoming that can loom large for larger-scale applications. DTDs lack much in the way of extensibility and aren't intended to scale well. Because DTDs are not XML (nor can they be treated as such), there's none of the modularity or extensibility of XML that would encourage structurally elegant designs. As software programs grow in length and complexity, DTDs become increasingly more difficult to follow and understand. Although entity references are intended to provide some modularity (albeit on a limited scale), there's no substitute for truly modular design and reusable components. Again, it doesn't take long for a DTD to cross over from manageable to incomprehensible.

Limitations of XML Schema

Despite the overall enthusiasm that has been generated for XML Schema, it does have some limitations. This list is not so much a list of schema limitations as it is a list of the advantages to still employing DTDs. Each point will be examined and the relative weakness of XML Schema will be discussed.

The following are limitations of XML Schema:

- XML Schema doesn't provide for compact document rules.
- XML Schema doesn't allow you to specialize via parameter entities.
- XML Schema is too complicated if your document is made up primarily of text strings.
- There currently aren't that many tools that provide extensive support for XML Schemas.

Compactness of the Document Rules

XML Schema, because of its XML derivation, can tend to be a little wordy at times. Although this is a definite plus for describing complex or compound datatypes, it may be overkill for a document made up of simple text strings or other straightforward content types.

Look at the XML Schema element definition for an element made up of two strings (string_a and string_b):

```
<xsd:element name="string1">
   <xsd:complexType>
     <xsd:element ref="string_a"/>
     <xsd:element ref="string_b"/>
   </xsd:complexType>
</xsd:element>
```

This describes an element named string1 that requires two child elements, string_a and string_b, neither of which have any options available.

Here's the same declaration in DTD form:

```
<!ELEMENT string1 (string_a,string_b) >
```

As you can see in this example, the DTD is much more compact. This carries even further as we provide qualifiers and options.

To illustrate how DTDs may be better in situations in which compactness of the document rules is important, Table 11.1 shows a series of XML Schema declarations and their DTD equivalents.

The first example shows that the declaration for an alternate content is very compact. It becomes more obvious with additional qualifiers, such as multiple occurrences of content. Keep in mind, however, that these examples are based on simple text strings, an inherent limitation to DTDs but *not* to XML Schema.

TABLE 11.1: XML Schema and Its DTD Equivalent

XML Schema	DTD Equivalent

`<xsd:element name="string1">`
` <xsd:complexType>`
`  <xsd:choice>`
`   <xsd:element ref="string_a"/>`
`   <xsd:element ref="string_b"/>`
`  </xsd:choice>`
` </xsd:complexType>`
`</xsd:element>`
	`<!ELEMENT string1 (string_a |`
	`string_b) >`

Continued on next page

TABLE 11.1 CONTINUED: XML Schema and Its DTD Equivalent

XML Schema	DTD Equivalent

``xml
<xsd:element name="string1">
 <xsd:complexType>
  <xsd:choice>
   <xsd:element ref="string_a"/>
   <xsd:sequence>
   <xsd:element ref="string_b"/>
   <xsd:element ref="string_c"/>
   </xsd:sequence>
  </xsd:choice>
 </xsd:complexType>
</xsd:element>
``
	``
	<!ELEMENT string1
	(string_a|(string_b,
	string_c)) >
	``

``xml
<xsd:element name="string1">
 <xsd:complexType>
  <xsd:element ref="string_a" minOccurs="0"/>
  <xsd:element ref="string_b"
  maxOccurs="unbounded"/>
  <xsd:element ref="string_c"
  minOccurs="0" maxOccurs="unbounded"/>
 </xsd:complexType>
</xsd:element>
``
	``
	<!ELEMENT string1
	(string_a?,string_b+,
	string_c*) >
	``

``xml
<xsd:element name="string1">
 <xsd:complexType>
  <xsd:attribute name="string_a"
  type="xsd:
  string" use="required"/>
 </xsd:complexType>
</xsd:element>
``
	``
	<!ATTLIST string1 string_a
	CDATA #REQUIRED>
	``

``xml
<xsd:element name="string1">
 <xsd:complexType>
  <xsd:attribute name="string_a" type="
  xsd:string" use="optional"/>
 </xsd:complexType>
</xsd:element>
``
	``
	<!ATTLIST string1 string_a
	CDATA #IMPLIED>
	``

Continued on next page

TABLE 11.1 CONTINUED: XML Schema and Its DTD Equivalent

XML Schema	DTD Equivalent

```<xsd:elementname="string1">```
``` <xsd:complexType>```
``` <xsd:attribute name="string_a" use="required">```
``` <xsd:simpleType base="xsd:string">```
``` <xsd:enumeration value="string_x"/>```
``` <xsd:enumeration value="string_y"/>```
``` <xsd:enumeration value="string_z"/>```
``` </xsd:simpleType>```
``` </xsd:attribute>```
``` </xsd:complexType>```
```</xsd:element>```
	```<!ATTLIST string1 string_a```
	```(string_x|string_y|string_z)```
	```#REQUIRED;>```

```<xsd:elementname="string1">```
``` <xsd:complexType>```
``` <xsd:attribute name="string_a"```
``` type="xsd:string" use="fixed"```
``` value="string_x"/>```
``` </xsd:complexType>```
```</xsd:element>```
	```<!ATTLIST string1 string_a```
	```CDATA #FIXED "string_x">```

It's obvious in each of these examples that the XML Schema (although very XML-ish) is not nearly as compact or simple as the DTD declaration stating the same thing. This is one of the drawbacks of schemas. However, you can provide many more details using XML Schema.

Parameter Entities

Parameter entity declaration is a definite strength of the DTD. It's not as easy to add parametric references to XML Schema. However, if the use of the DTD is limiting to the document(s) as a whole, XML Schema may be the better choice.

XML Schema lacks support for these DTD features:

- CDATA sections
- Comments
- Processing instructions (supported through NOTATION)
- Entity references
- Character reference

The lack of these features severely limits the users' ability to augment and append the schema to include specialized entities and parametric references.

Note that *general entities* can be used to provide some of the more unusual uses of parameter entities. XML Schema 1.0 does not attempt to systematically reconstruct all possible uses of parameter entities.

Although XML Schema (version 1.0) lacks support for some features of the DTD, it does support these features:

- The separation of `element` and `complexType`
- Attribute groups
- Named model groups
- Type extension and restriction mechanisms
- The `import` and `include` elements for composing schemas

Text Strings

The DTD is tough to beat for simple (at least in terms of noncomplex datatypes) XML documents. XML Schema, although entirely adequate for just about any purpose in XML, may be overkill for defining simple XML documents. Look again at Table 11.1 and see if the simpler format will serve your purpose. Not using XML Schema is by no means primitive, especially if a DTD is the better tool for the job. After all, the lever was invented several millennia ago, but it's still the most effective tool for prying things apart.

You can use both XML Schema and DTDs to define text strings, but the concern is in creating an overly complex definition document that is not only more difficult to read by humans, but also has a greater potential for bugs because of its complexity. XML Schema is a more complicated document modeling language. If you're only working with text strings, DTDs are better suited to handle this task.

The simplest tool is (more often than not) the preferable tool, as long as it doesn't leave you painted into a corner by being *too* simple.

If you can view the entire scope of the document, the choice of metadata model becomes easier.

Available Tools

If the software tools that you have to work with lend themselves more favorably to DTDs than to XML Schema, and if there's no other compelling reason to avoid DTDs, perhaps

DTDs would still be the best choice. Because the DTD has been the de facto standard for document definition since the 1980s (SGML), many DTD tools already exist. It would be wise to survey what may already be in place as far as project resources (or if need be, future requirements).

XML Spy from Altova (www.altova.com) and Turbo XML from TIBCO (www.tibco.com/products/extensibility/solutions/turbo_xml.html) are XML-related DTD editors that are widely used in the industry. XML Spy has many advanced features in addition to DTD editing, such as conversion to XML Schema. Other editors include Cooktop (www.xmleverywhere.com/cooktop) and ezDTD (www.garshol.priv.no/download/xmltools/prod/ezDTD.html), both of which are freeware. For more free tools see Free XML Tools and Software at www.garshol.priv.no/download/xmltools.

In addition to editors, some popular DTD parsers and interpreters are DTDParse, a Perl module developed by Norman Walsh (http://sourceforge.net/projects/dtdparse), and two Java-based parsers, both named DTD Parser. You can find Ron Bourret's version of DTD Parser at www.rpbourret.com/schemas and one developed by Mark Wutka at www.wutka.com/dtdparser.html. There may be more available by the time this book goes to press, so take another look at the Free XML Tools and Software at www.garshol.priv.no/download/xmltools. Also check out XMLSOFTWARE at www.xmlsoftware.com.

Another software tool for DTD validation is Saxon by Michael Kay (available at http://saxon.sourceforge.net). Saxon comes integrated with tools for the Extensible Stylesheet Language Transformations (XSLT) and is very worthy of your attention.

TIP   Saxon is a Java framework for processing XML documents optimized for XML-to-XML/SGML/HTML conversions. Essentially, it's an XSLT engine (1.0 recommendation) that can also be used as a Java development framework. The XSLT implementation is fast and fully conformant and provides many useful extensions. Through its API, Java and XSLT code can be combined. Saxon is built on top of Simple API for XML (SAX) 2.0 and Document Object Model (DOM) 1.0 and should work with any compliant implementation of these. It also supports the XSLT part of Java API for XML Processing (JAXP).

Best Uses and Advantages for DTDs

The DTD may be best suited for documents intended for a limited range of applicability. For defining XHTML (or HTML), the DTD is well suited because it's usually a read-once, write-often scenario without a great deal of dynamic input from the document authors. The DTD serves its purpose of validation very well and supplies the common denominator needed for those types of files. In the case of XHTML, it's more important for the wide audience (and myriad of user agents) the markup is intended to satisfy that the DTD is stable.

For localized uses, for example, within a small industry or specialty application, a simple DTD can meet the requirements with a small amount of extra parsing and validation. If the XML document is being transformed for viewing on the Web, the DTD might be the best choice.

The DTD will, in all likelihood, remain with us for a long time because it's central to SGML, and therefore XML and XHTML, and it's still a reasonable tool for the job it's intended to do.

A DTD might be the best choice if the document contains primarily these three types of content:

- Text strings
- Mixed content, consisting of text strings and child elements
- A simple set of child elements

These are important because XML Schema does not support PCDATA, CDATA, or entities as well as the DTD does, and if the XML is composed of mainly these types of data, the DTD is the best choice. Also, the DTD is able to take advantage of the SGML-derived `ignore` and `include` directives, which offer modularity to the DTD.

Many users find the DTD simpler to read and understand, and this can be an advantage for simple, text-driven documents that have user-included definitions, entities, and character references.

Documents that are meant to be validated using XML 1.0 or that must support XHTML or SGML integration would also benefit from the DTD scenario.

Best Uses and Advantages of XML Schema

XML Schema offers a number of advantages over the DTD:

- It's written in XML.
- It offers stronger datatyping.
- It offers an extensive (and extensible) class and type system.
- It can be extended per XML rules.
- It supports XML namespaces.
- It supports mixed content modeling.

These advantages explain what some of the best uses for XML Schema are, and we cover these items in more detail in the following sections.

Written in XML

Schemas are written in XML, whereas DTDs are not; therefore, because the language and syntax are the same for both, the XML Schema and XML document can use the same validation and parsing applications. This alone can help prevent the insidious software bloat that comes with machine-processing intelligent, precision documents through a variety of software. As far as the human readable/writeable angle of XML, it's a pleasure (and relief) to not have to learn yet another syntax and markup just to define the markup itself. With XML Schema, because the XML is the same for everything, a developer can get up to speed quite rapidly, using the same editors and tools for all the documents—metadata included. In addition, software vendors are encouraged to create and market (or otherwise distribute) editors and applications that can serve double duty for the XML and the defining document. It would be nice to be able to learn one tool and to effectively and efficiently define, create, and edit all the documents in an XML project using that one tool. A lot of headway has already been made in this regard, with more on the horizon.

The same applies to parsers and processors: one tool for both jobs (parsing the schema and the XML document) can only encourage a greater acceptance of XML throughout the Web and the industry.

Offers Stronger Datatyping

XML Schema (because of its derivation from XML) offers stronger datatyping. Though many feel that datatyping in XML is weak compared to C++ or other programming languages, it's still better than in DTDs in this regard. This is crucial for applications that have specific requirements for what the elements (and attributes) should contain. For instance, with the address example used earlier, it makes sense to require just two uppercase letters for the `state` element and five (or nine) digits for the `zipcode` element. XML Schema offers one of the only ways to accomplish these simple datatype requirements for XML documents.

Any application of XML that cannot allow confusion between datatypes should (or must) use schemas for the defining metadata. There's no compelling reason to consider DTDs in these instances, and if they are used, datatype checking routines are necessary. It's simpler to start with the correct metadata and allow the XML Schema to declare datatypes than it is to try to foresee all the instances of mistakes that can be made in the data itself.

Offers an Extensive Class and Type System

XML Schema offers an extensive (and extensible) class and type system, which allows (and encourages) reusing markup constructs instead of parameter entities. Inheritance can be facilitated through classes, and classes may be created by the guidelines presented for extensibility.

TIP   The W3C XML Schema Recommendations offer the templates and models to create simple or complex types that can be contained in sharable and accessible libraries or used as building blocks for creating new schema.

Can Be Extended per XML Rules

Code (and type) reusability can become a powerful rapid-development tool, in conjunction with a programming language such as Java, to allow quick deployment of XML Schema through reusable datatype constructs and classes as extensions to both XML and Java.

There are three accepted ways to extend an XML Schema:

- Use another schema language to supplement XML Schema.
- Declare additional extensions through XSLT or another XML transformation.
- Write more API code.

Of these three, the two most popular methods are the first and second, because writing API code is more complicated and should be done by application programmers.

You can embed another schema language, such as RELAX, Schematron, or TREX, within the original schema language (such as XML Schema) to contain all of the constraints in one schema document. In addition, most schema languages have a common ancestry (XML) and therefore share many qualities. The downside is that, because multiple schema languages are required (if you embed multiple schema languages), another vocabulary must be learned and expressed. Also, the language, and therefore the schema, may become obsolete, requiring a full rewrite.

Writing additional API code also weighs in with pluses and minuses. The greatest drawback is the specificity of code to platform and application. With the exception of Java, most programming languages are not as portable as one would like, so any API modifications must be viewed with the entire scope of the project (and the lifetime of the application) in mind. The advantage of extending APIs is that the languages used are very powerful and can accomplish just about anything that is required.

For most purposes, the advantages of using style sheets in XSLT and XPath are that the languages are members of the XML family and there's a reasonable amount of programming tools available to work with. Another advantage to this method is that the documents can be self checking (as well as cross-checked) and parsed with the same processor as the final XML file. Also, the evolution of these languages will keep pace with XML Schema because they are all cut from the same cloth, so to speak. XPath in particular is a powerful and expressive language that is assured long-term support and growth. The only drawback is the need for an extra style sheet document, but that seems like a small price to pay.

Support for XML Namespaces

The support for XML namespaces allows documents from different namespaces (and sources) to be validated and combined for sharing constructs and classes, assuring the avoidance of namespace collisions and conflicts.

DTD has no mechanism for namespaces. If you want to use namespaces within a DTD vocabulary, the namespace would have to be treated like any other attribute. If that namespace uses namespace prefixes, those prefixes would have to be defined as a part of the element type or attribute name because DTDs don't recognize prefixes (or colons) as significant. XML Schema on the other hand, does support XML namespaces. In the root element of your schema document (`schema`), you can define the target namespace for your vocabulary. The following is a quote from the W3C regarding schemas and namespaces (you can find the quote at `www.w3.org/TR/2000/WD-xmlschema-0-20000407/#NS`):

> *A schema can be viewed as a collection (vocabulary) of type definitions and element declarations whose names belong to a particular namespace called a target namespace. The target namespace enables us to distinguish between definitions and declarations from different vocabularies. For example, target namespaces would enable us to distinguish between the declaration for* `element` *in the XML Schema language vocabulary, and a declaration for* `element` *in a hypothetical chemistry language vocabulary. The former is part of the* `http://www.w3.org/1999/` `XMLSchema` *target namespace, and the latter is part of another target namespace.*

Mixed Content Modeling

Along with the strong datatyping mentioned earlier, XML Schema excels at mixed content modeling where DTDs fail. XML Schema can easily define the type and occurrence behavior of data within the document. This allows you to use the XML syntax to create a richer data set and a much less convoluted document definition.

XML Schema, because it's written in XML, is in every sense of the word the metadata for XML. Although DTD does what it says it will in defining a document, XML Schema goes several steps further in that it grows and evolves along with the document it's defining (as well as adapts to new and subtle changes within the document's demands for definition).

Usage Examples

One of the best ways to compare the relative merits of the two metadata models is through simple case studies and the scenarios developed to meet the desired goals of the XML project.

In each of the following examples, we'll describe the situation and current (and perhaps future) needs that the metadata must meet and compare the advantages and disadvantages of the DTD and the XML schema.

These are examples based loosely on reality and are intended to demonstrate the relative points being made. One could, in all likelihood, refine them and apply them to real-world situations.

Example 1

In this example, we'll examine a simple physician's patient mailing/billing address scheme. We need to store and retrieve the following data:

- Patient name (alphanumeric)
- Mailing street address (alphanumeric)
- Mailing city (alphanumeric)
- Mailing state (two-letter abbreviation)
- Mailing zip code (numeric)
- Billing street address (alphanumeric)
- Billing city (alphanumeric)
- Billing state (two-letter abbreviation)
- Billing zip code (numeric)

This looks pretty straightforward, and it's certainly within the scope of a DTD *if* the XML author is willing to sacrifice a few features and not be able to specify data constraints.

These are the fields that present a problem:

- Mailing state (two-letter abbreviation)
- Mailing zip code (numeric)
- Billing state (two-letter abbreviation)
- Billing zip code (numeric)

As discussed earlier in the chapter, DTDs are not suited to qualifying either datatype or data length. There's no easy or convenient way to declare a two-letter abbreviation or a five-digit numeric in the DTD.

A typical DTD for this, the zip code in this example, might be as follows:

```
<!ELEMENT MailingZipCode (#PCDATA)>
```

Unfortunately, this declaration doesn't specify that five would be an appropriate choice for the number of digits. This example allows just about anything. (The same concept applies to the state entries, too.)

Here is how an XML Schema declaration would typically read:

```
<xsd:simpleType name="MailingZipCode">
   <xsd:restriction base="xsd:string">
      <xsd:pattern value="[0-9]{7}"/>
   </xsd:restriction>
</xsd:simpleType>
```

Optionally, the line `xsd:pattern value="[0-9]{7}"` could be added within the `xsd:pattern value="[0-9]{7}+[0-9]{4}"` element to insist that the full zip code (Zip+4) be used.

The W3C Recommendation states that "a canonical *lexical representation* is a set of literals from among the valid set of literals for a datatype such that there is a one-to-one mapping between literals in the canonical *lexical representation* and values in the value space."

Along the same line of thinking, in the preceding example, what if there was need for *two* street address entries? Again, there's no convenient way of declaring this in DTD, but XML Schema will allow it:

```
<xsd:element type="MailingStreetAddress"
   minOccur="1" maxOccur="2"/>
```

This markup allows a second (but not a third) mailing street address entry. If need be, `MailingStreetAddress` could be broken down further in the XML Schema to specify the actual address number (number or alphanumeric) and street name.

One of the key points here is the need to look over the landscape of the data and get a good sense of the type, frequency, and desired constraints to datatype before committing to a metadata scenario.

Example 2

In this example, we'll look at a patient record at a physician's office. You could use the basic address scenario from the preceding section, adding such things as a patient ID number, insurance provider number, and insurance group number.

DTDs would not handle this new data (patient ID numbers, insurance provider number, and insurance group number) well. As a matter of fact, all you could do is require it to be an ID or character string. Other than that, you don't have much control. However, using XML

Schema, you can derive new datatypes and, therefore, specify the number and type of characters that the element is intended to contain. This becomes increasingly important when addressing the patient prescription elements and dosages.

In this type of XML document, there's a great possibility that data may be accessed by different departments, such as billing, laboratory, pharmacy, and so on. Each element needs to be able to store *exactly* the data needed and in the correct manner.

Often, a database will be used to store data for accounting, but the data should be embedded into the XML as needed, so some scheme for calling the Structured Query Language (SQL) or other database language needs to be included.

Each of these potential datatype requirements can be declared in XML Schema as integers or Booleans (whether certain tests have been conducted) as well as terminology and specialized markup. Even though the datatyping in XML Schema is not as strong as it is in other languages, it still goes a long way to ensure data integrity.

You might include the following in a list of potential elements:

- Patient vital data
  - Patient date of birth (date)
  - Patient age (integer)
  - Patient sex (M/F)
  - Patient height (integer cm, for centimeter, or mixed feet/inches)
  - Patient weight (integer kg, for kilogram, or integer pounds)
  - Patient blood pressure (mixed integer)
  - Patient pulse (integer)
  - Patient respiration (integer)
- Patient allergies
  - Penicillin (Boolean)
  - Sulfa drugs (Boolean)
  - Seasonal (Boolean)
- Patient chronic conditions/medical history (encrypted?)
  - Dx (mixed content: date and text)
  - Rx (mixed content: date and text)
  - Follow up DX (mixed content: date and text)
- Patient prescription record/history (encrypted?)
  - Rx (mixed content: date prescribed, dosage, and text)

Looking over this list of potential elements, the datatypes they require, and the units that may need specifying, it should be obvious that XML Schema is the only answer. Imagine how difficult it would have been (and less than ideal) to declare all these with the limitations of DTD.

The data may need encryption, and although this is possible in DTDs, it's far easier to accomplish using XML Schema.

Example 3

The previous two examples should clarify the distinct advantages of XML Schema over DTDs. With the first example, a patient's address information is defined with contingencies for billing and mutiline street addresses. The second example added specialized number formats that could be used to define patient and insurance numbers.

Next, we examined the patient vital records used by the medical personnel in the physician's office. In this example, we look at a record for billing and accounting in the office.

Again, as was noted and shown in the previous sections, although the DTD is perfectly capable of defining the overall data structure, it falls short of assuring that the data is of the proper type and in many cases the right length. This is very important when the billing department gets a turn with the data.

As most of us have found out, it doesn't take much in the way of a typo to open up all sorts of avenues to confusion. By creating a strict format and content model for insurance policy number and provider code, the potential for mistakes is reduced at least as far as the datatyping is concerned.

To create billing record, the following would be good choices:

- Patient ID number (alphanumeric, required)
- Date of visit (date, required)
- Visit code (alphanumeric, required, industry standard format?)
- Insurance provider code (alphanumeric, required, industry standard format?)
- Policy number (alphanumeric)
- Co-payment (Boolean)
- Co-payment amount (currency)
- Method of payment (text)
- Balance (currency)
- Date of insurance provider billing (date)
- Amount of insurance billing (currency)

As was true with the previous examples, XML Schema can place constraints on the datatype well above and beyond the generic #PCDATA of the DTD. Because the data in this example may be output to a spreadsheet or database, data consistency is crucial so applications don't choke or protest on mismatched data elements.

The billing department XML Schema would be the most likely to interface to a database, and support for such has been built into the XML Schema plans. Currently supported are mechanisms for Java Database Connectivity (JDBC), Online Analytical Processing (OLAP), Open Database Connectivity (ODBC), and others. The fact that XML is evolving will only broaden support for interfacing to a database and provide greater support across the board.

Example 4

One more example that the physician office XML needs to incorporate, as a spin-off of the patient record, would be the actual medical history.

This offers some very interesting possibilities. First, this type of record would be easiest to define in a DTD because it's mainly text (or simple mixed content such as date attributes and the like)—not that you should switch gears between DTD and XML Schema, just that of all the scenarios presented so far, this is the only one that might benefit from using a DTD.

Looking at the needs of this portion of the XML, and laying out the requirements, a list will start to form:

- Medical history: Patient
  - Condition (text, date)
  - Treatment (text, date)
  - Prescriptions (text, date)
  - Responded to treatment (Boolean)
  - Follow-up (text, date)
- Medical history: Family
  - Condition (text, date)
  - Treatment (text, date)
  - Prescriptions (text, date)
  - Responded to treatment (Boolean)
  - Relationship (text, date)

This data can be encrypted for the protection of the patient's privacy using any of the methods described in "XML Encryption Syntax and Processing" found at www.w3.org/TR/xmlenc-core/. Because other departments in the office (billing and so on) have little use for the data in these sections, it presents no problems to them if this data is encrypted. If another physician would need access to the data, a public key could be provided and the rest of the records (billing, vital statistics, and so on) could be ignored. In other words, the data would be filtered for the user.

As stated, the medical history vocabulary could be defined with a DTD, but with so many more tools and possibilities available in XML Schema, it makes the most sense to define the XML with the XML Schema metadata. You also have the option of mixing both approaches: using XML Schema and DTDs. Many developers advocate against this approach. By mixing document modeling languages, you require the use of multiple tools and require developers' skill sets to include both languages.

Example 5

By now, one might suspect that the DTD is useless. One area of XML where the DTD continues to thrive is electronic publishing. Because the DTD is a descendent of SGML (and more so than XML Schema in many ways), the DTD has maintained a strong foothold in the document publication and markup fields. This is different from pure data sharing, as in the physician example, or Electronic Data Interchange (EDI) for banking. When a government agency has two decades of documents marked up in SGML, you can bet that the DTD is still the metadata of choice.

Along this line of thinking, recall that the DTD excels at defining text markup in an efficient and compact manner. Because a DTD can be converted to XML Schema, there's little chance of total obsolescence. DTDs also allow an easier method of user-defined entities and provide other tools for text handling, so it would seem that the DTD has a long (if narrow) future.

If one is considering a move from DTD to XML Schema, keep in mind that XML Schema (as of this writing) does *not* support these DTD declarations:

- CDATA sections
- Comments
- Character reference
- XML headers
- Parameter ENTITY declarations
- General ENTITY declarations
- Multiple ATTLIST declarations

However, XML Schema *does* translate these declarations, as shown in Table 11.2:

TABLE 11.2: DTD-to-Schema Translations

DTD	Schema Equivalent
#PCDATA	Supported as a particle of `simple datatype`
ATTLIST	`attribute` declarations are grouped into `attributeGroup` declarations
CDATA attribute	A simple datatype string
NOTATION attribute	Supported as a simple datatype
ANY	any
EMPTY	Uses the `nillable` attribute for elements
?	As `maxOccurs` and `minOccurs` attributes
+	As `maxOccurs` and `minOccurs` attributes
*	As `maxOccurs` and `minOccurs` attributes

Summary

Metadata defines the appropriate content of an XML document as well as the physical layout and logical structure of the document. Choosing an appropriate metadata model is crucial to the efficiency and continued viability of an XML document project or application. In this chapter, we explored both metadata types, DTD and XML Schema, and we examined the advantages and disadvantages of each type closely.

There are many historical and practical limitations of each metadata scheme and tools to determine the appropriateness of each. Special attention should be paid to element definitions and datatypes.

Datatype and scope are determining factors in a metadata decision. Of special note is the fact that schema is written in XML and is machine-readable. We provided real-world examples of uses of each method; you can, for example, use XML Schema for medical records and office practices. In Chapter 12, we'll discuss other schema languages available to you.

CHAPTER 12

Other Schema Languages

- Examining RELAX

- Understanding TREX

- Understanding RELAX NG

- Examining Schematron

- Examining Microsoft's schema initiatives

- Comparing alternate schema languages

everal schema languages exist in addition to the W3C XML Schema. These alternate schema languages were developed because the W3C XML Schema Recommendation was not yet available (released in May 2001) and because many schema developers felt that there was a need for simpler schema languages that could also validate XML documents. Other schema languages will continue to have a part in XML development because they are easy to use for schema design and validation and they provide an extension of the current capabilities of the W3C XML Schema.

Alternative schema languages include the REgular LAnguage description for XML (RELAX), Tree Regular Expressions for XML (TREX), RELAX NG (a combination of RELAX and TREX that stands for REgular LAnguage for XML Next Generation), and Schematron. RELAX NG was released in June 2001 and replaces both RELAX and TREX. It includes features of both RELAX and TREX, so we will review the features of both languages and then their incorporation into one language, RELAX NG. The beta version of Schematron 1.5 (released in January 2001) will also be discussed in detail, as well as Microsoft's schema initiatives.

RELAX

RELAX is a schema language that was developed at the Information Technology Research and Standardization Centre (INSTAC) in Japan by Makoto Murata. RELAX was approved as an ISO/IEC standard (DTR 22250-1) in May 2001.

Like other schema languages, including the W3C XML Schema, RELAX uses XML document syntax to describe XML document structures and supports validation of these documents. A document written in RELAX is called a RELAX *grammar*. XML documents can be validated against a RELAX grammar. Several RELAX validators are available, including versions for C++, Java, and Visual Basic. Links to these validators are available on the RELAX home page at `www.xml.gr.jp/relax`. Tools for using RELAX and other schema languages are discussed in Chapter 14.

RELAX includes most features of the W3C XML Schema Recommendation; however, some features (default values, entities, and notations) were deliberately excluded so existing XML processors could be used.

Listing 12.1 shows a simple XML document named `contact.xml`.

Listing 12.1   *contact.xml*

```
<?xml version="1.0">
<!DOCTYPE contact SYSTEM "contact.dtd">
<contact>
```

```
        <first_name>Joe</first_name>
        <last_name>Smith</last_name>
        <street_address>611 Ridgewood Drive</street_address>
        <city>Denver</city>
        <state>Colorado</state>
        <zipcode>80210</zipcode>
        <phone>
          <phone_work>303-4667339</phone_work>
          <phone_home>303-9842361</phone_home>
          <fax>303-4667357</fax>
        </phone>
        <email>JSmith@earthlink.net</email>
        <contact_date>2001-09-14</contact_date>
    </contact>
```

This XML file was originally validated against the Document Type Definition (DTD) named contact.dtd, shown in Listing 12.2. The DOCTYPE declaration in line 2 of Listing 12.1 (<!DOCTYPE contact SYSTEM "contact.dtd">) is specifically meant to validate this XML document against the file named contact.dtd. Line 2 should be removed if contact.xml is validated against a schema document, whether the schema is a W3C XML Schema or an alternative schema language.

Listing 12.2 *contact.dtd*

```
<?xml version="1.0" encoding="UTF-8"?>
<!--This document is designed as a format for using contact
    data-->
<!ELEMENT contact (first_name, last_name, street_address,
    city, state,zipcode,phone,email,contact_date)>
<!ELEMENT first_name (#PCDATA)>
<!ELEMENT last_name (#PCDATA)>
<!ELEMENT street_address (#PCDATA)>
<!ELEMENT city (#PCDATA)>
<!ELEMENT state (#PCDATA)>
<!ELEMENT zipcode (#PCDATA)>
<!ELEMENT phone (phone_work,phone_home*,fax*)>
<!ELEMENT phone_work (#PCDATA)>
<!ELEMENT phone_home (#PCDATA)>
<!ELEMENT fax (#PCDATA)>
<!ELEMENT email (#PCDATA)>
<!ELEMENT contact_date (#PCDATA)>
```

Here is how a RELAX grammar to validate `contact.xml` is created:

1. We start with a `module` element because this is the element used to contain a RELAX grammar.

```
<module
    moduleVersion="1.2"
    relaxCoreVersion="1.0"
    xmlns="http://www.xml.gr.jp/xmlns/relaxCore">
<!--RELAX document-->
</module>
```

TIP   The RELAX namespace is `http://www.xml.gr.jp/xmlns/relaxCore` and it's used in all RELAX grammars and in the corresponding XML documents.

2. We follow the `module` element with the `interface` element, which specifies the root element of the document to be validated. In this case, the root element is `contact`.

```
<interface>
    <export label="contact"/>
</interface>
```

3. For every element in `contact.xml`, there's a corresponding element rule. The element rule shows any subelements of the element rule and also includes the attribute `role`, whose value describes the content of the element rule. There's also a corresponding `tag` that accompanies the element rule. The value of the `name` attribute in the `tag` element matches the value of `role` in the element rule.

```
<elementRule role="contact">
    <sequence>
      <ref label="first_name"/>
      <ref label="last_name"/>
      <ref label="street_address"/>
      <ref label="city"/>
      <ref label="state"/>
      <ref label="zipcode"/>
      <ref label="phone"/>
      <ref label="email"/>
      <ref label="contact_date"/>
    </sequence>
</elementRule>
<tag name="contact"/>
```

4. A series of references using the `label` attribute of the element definitions is given within the sequence. We follow it with the element rules and tags for these elements. Note that we use a `type` attribute in `elementRule`. The values for `type` can be any W3C XML

Schema built-in datatype, as defined in Part 2 of the W3C XML Schema Recommendation (www.w3.org/TR/xmlschema-2). User-defined datatypes, however, are not allowed in RELAX.

```
<elementRule role="first_name" type="string"/>
<tag name="first_name"/>
<elementRule role="last_name" type="string"/>
<tag name="last_name"/>
<elementRule role="street_address" type="string"/>
<tag name="street_address"/>
<elementRule role="city" type="string"/>
<tag name="city"/>
<elementRule role="state" type="string"/>
<tag name="state"/>
<elementRule role="zipcode" type="string"/>
<tag name="zipcode"/>
```

5. The phone element has subelements, so another sequence is necessary.

```
<elementRule role="phone">
   <sequence>
     <ref label="phone_work"/>
     <ref label="phone_home"/>
     <ref label="fax"/>
   </sequence>
</elementRule>
<tag name="phone"/>
```

6. The elements phone_home and fax can occur zero or more times. To specify these occurrence constraints, we use the occurs attribute. The occurs attribute can be used with sequence, choice, or ref element. There are three possible values for occurs:

- * means the element occurs zero or more times.

- + means the element occurs one or more times.

- ? means the element occurs zero or one time.

```
<elementRule role="phone">
   <sequence>
     <ref label="phone_work"/>
     <ref label="phone_home" occurs="*"/>
     <ref label="fax" occurs="*"/>
   </sequence>
</elementRule>
<tag name="phone"/>
```

7. These element references with occurrence constraints are followed by the element rules and tags for the elements referred to in the sequence.

```
<elementRule role="phone_work" type="string"/>
<tag name="phone_work"/>
<elementRule role="phone_home" type="string"/>
<tag name="phone_home"/>
<elementRule role="fax" type="string"/>
<tag name="fax"/>
```

8. Then, we list the rest of the element rules. We specify the contact_date element as a date type. The format for the date type in the instance document is *CCYY-MM-DD*, with an optional time-zone specification.

```
<elementRule role="email" type="string"/>
<tag name="email"/>
<elementRule role="contact_date" type="date"/>
<tag name="contact_date"/>
```

9. Constraints can be specified on datatypes in RELAX. In this case, we specify constraints for zipcode, phone_work, phone_home, fax, and email elements. (These new element rules replace those defined earlier.)

```
<elementRule role="zipcode" type="string"/>
   <pattern value="\d{5}(-\d{4})?"/>
<tag name="zipcode"/>
<elementRule role="phone_work" type="string"/>
   <pattern value="\d{3}-\d{7}"/>
<tag name="phone_work"/>
<elementRule role="phone_home" type="string"/>
   <pattern value="\d{3}-\d{7}"/>
<tag name="phone_home"/>
<elementRule role="fax" type="string"/>
   <pattern value="\d{3}-\d{7}"/>
<tag name="fax"/>
<elementRule role="email" type="string"/>
   <pattern value=".+@.+"/>
<tag name="email"/>
```

RELAX Datatypes

RELAX also includes two datatypes specific to RELAX: none and emptyString.

The none datatype is an empty datatype that is used to prohibit attributes. In the following example, the element referenced by the tag (name="zipcode") cannot have attributes:

```
<!--RELAX grammar-->
<tag name="zipcode">
```

Continued on next page

```
        <attribute type="none"/>
    </tag>
```

The emptyString datatype allows only an empty string, as in this example:

```
<!--RELAX grammar-->
<elementRule role="emp" type="emptyString"/>
<!--instance document-->
<emp></emp>
```

The pattern constraint on the string type is exactly the same for phone_work, phone_home, and fax. Unlike W3C XML Schema, RELAX does not allow us to write a single definition (a user-defined type) and reuse it. In this case, RELAX does, however, offer reuse of attribute definitions and of subelements. Attribute pools for reusing attribute definitions and hedge rules for reusing subelements are shown later in this section.

The complete markup for contact.rlx, the RELAX module corresponding to contact.xml, is shown in Listing 12.3.

Listing 12.3   *contact.rlx*, RELAX grammar for *contact.xml*

```
<?xml version="1.0" encoding="UTF-8"?>
<module
    moduleVersion="1.2"
    relaxCoreVersion="1.0"
    xmlns="http://www.xml.gr.jp/xmlns/relaxCore">
<interface>
    <export label="contact"/>
</interface>
<elementRule role="contact">
    <sequence>
      <ref label="first_name"/>
      <ref label="last_name"/>
      <ref label="street_address"/>
      <ref label="city"/>
      <ref label="state"/>
      <ref label="zipcode"/>
      <ref label="phone"/>
      <ref label="email"/>
      <ref label="contact_date"/>
    </sequence>
</elementRule>
<tag name="contact"/>
<elementRule role="first_name" type="string"/>
<tag name="first_name"/>
<elementRule role="last_name" type="string"/>
```

```
<tag name="last_name"/>
<elementRule role="street_address" type="string"/>
<tag name="street_address"/>
<elementRule role="city" type="string"/>
<tag name="city"/>
<elementRule role="state" type="string"/>
<tag name="state"/>
<elementRule role="zipcode" type="string"/>
    <pattern value=="\d{5}(-\d{4})?"/>
<tag name="zipcode"/>
<elementRule role="phone">
    <sequence>
      <ref label="phone_work"/>
      <ref label="phone_home" occurs="*"/>
      <ref label="fax" occurs="*"/>
    </sequence>
</elementRule>
<tag name="phone"/>

<elementRule role="phone_work" type="string"/>
    <pattern value="\d{3}-\d{7}"/>
<tag name="phone_work"/>
<elementRule role="phone_home" type="string"/>
    <pattern value="\d{3}-\d{7}"/>
<tag name="phone_home"/>
<elementRule role="fax" type="string"/>
    <pattern value="\d{3}-\d{7}"/>
<tag name="fax"/>
<elementRule role="email" type="string"/>
    <pattern value=".+@.+"/>
<tag name="email"/>
<elementRule role="contact_date" type="date"/>
<tag name="contact_date"/>
</module>
```

RELAX grammars offer several other features, including empty elements, mixed content, multiple subelements, attributes, and enumerations.

The type attribute is not used with empty elements. Empty elements must be directly specified as empty to contain no content:

```
<elementRule role="hr">
    <empty/>
</elementRule>
<tag name="hr"/>
```

The markup in the following example is valid and can use the type attribute, even though no content is specified because the element has not been specified as empty:

```
<elementRule role="email" type="string"/>
```

Mixed content, or text that is not placed directly between an element's opening and closing tags, can be declared with the mixed element:

```
<!--RELAX grammar-->
<elementRule role="license">
    <mixed>
      <choice occurs="+">
        <ref label="name"/>
        <ref label="bdate"/>
      </choice>
    </mixed>
</elementRule>
<!--instance document-->
His driver's license said
<license>
<name>Joe Smith</name>, born on
<bdate>1988-01-25</bdate>
</license>
```

A single subelement is declared with a reference in the element rule of the parent element:

```
<!--RELAX grammar-->
<elementRule role="name">
    <ref label="first"/>
</elementRule>
<tag name="name"/>
<elementRule role="first" type="string"/>
<tag name="first"/>
<!--instance document-->
<name>
<first>Wally</first>
</name>
```

Multiple subelements can be specified using `sequence` or `choice`. If the subelements should appear in a particular order, `sequence` is used:

```
<!--RELAX grammar-->
<elementRule role="shopping">
    <sequence>
      <ref label="apples"/>
      <ref label="oranges"/>
    </sequence>
</elementRule>
```

If the subelements can appear in any order, `choice` is used. In the following example, the choice can occur zero or more times:

```
<!--RELAX grammar-->
<elementRule role="shopping">
    <choice occurs="*">
```

```
         <ref label="apples"/>
         <ref label="oranges"/>
      </choice>
   </elementRule>
```

Attributes can be specified after the `tag` element, and constraints may be added after the attribute declaration, as shown in the following example:

```
<!--RELAX grammar-->
<elementRule role="shopping">
   <choice occurs="*">
      <ref label="apples"/>
      <ref label="oranges"/>
   </choice>
</elementRule>
<tag name="shopping">
<attribute name="quantity" required="true" type="integer"/>
<attribute name="cost" type="decimal"/>
   <fractionDigits value="2"/>
<attribute name="purchasedate" type="date"/>
</tag>
```

An attribute pool can also be created so that a set of attributes may be reused:

```
<!--RELAX grammar-->
<attPool role="shop">
<attribute name="fruits" type="string">
   <enumeration value="apples"/>
   <enumeration value="oranges"/>
   <enumeration value="bananas"/>
</attribute>
</attPool>
...
<tag name="Mondayshop">
   <ref role="shop"/>
</tag>
<tag name="Fridayshop">
   <ref role="shop"/>
</tag>
```

An enumeration is used to list all the possible values for the `shop` role. Other attributes not included in the attribute pool may also be specified within the `tag` element, as in this example:

```
<!--RELAX grammar-->
<tag name="Fridayshop">
<ref role="shop"/>
<attribute name="vegetable" type="string">
   <maxLength value="10"/>
</attribute>
</tag>
```

RELAX also includes a component called a hedge rule, which enables the reuse of sub-elements. In the following example, the phone sequence (marked by the sequence element) is labeled phone.elements and can be reused:

```
<!--RELAX grammar-->
<hedgeRule label="phone.elements">
  <sequence>
    <ref label="phone_work"/>
    <ref label="phone_home"/>
    <ref label="fax"/>
  </sequence>
</hedgeRule>
...
<elementRule role="phone">
  <hedgeRef label="phone.elements" occurs="+"/>
</elementRule>
<elementRule role="communication">
  <hedgeRef label="phone.elements" occurs="+"/>
</elementRule>
```

For further information on RELAX, see the following:

- J. David Eisenberg's tutorial "Validating XML with RELAX" at `http://catcode.com/relax_tut/index.html`

- J. David Eisenberg's article "Learning to RELAX" at `www.xml.com/pub/a/2000/10/16/relax/index.html`

- The RELAX home page at `www.xml.gr.jp/relax`

- The RELAX FAQ at `www.xml.gr.jp/relax/faq-e.html`

- The tutorial "HOW TO RELAX" at `www.xml.gr.jp/relax/html4/howToRELAX_full_en.html`

- A DTD-to-RELAX converter at `www.horobi.com/Projects/RELAX/Archive/DTD2RELAX.html`

TREX

TREX is a schema language developed by James Clark. A TREX document is an XML document that specifies a pattern for other XML documents and supports validation of documents that match the pattern. A Java implementation to validate TREX is available at `www.thaiopensource.com/trex/jtrex.html`. Tools for using TREX and other schema languages are discussed in Chapter 14.

First, we'll create a TREX document to validate `contact.xml` (shown in Listing 12.1), and then we'll review some of the other features of the TREX schema language.

Here's how to create a TREX schema to validate `conntact.xml`:

1. We start with a `grammar` element. This element encloses the TREX pattern.

   ```
   <grammar>
   ```

2. This is followed by a `start` element. The `start` element describes the TREX pattern.

   ```
   <grammar>
       <start>
   ```

   A `grammar` element has a single `start` element and zero or more `define` elements. (The `define` element is discussed later in this section.) The `grammar` and `start` elements are only required for creating TREX modules with definitions. If the schema is very simple and does not include any `define` elements, a module is not necessary and the `grammar` and `start` elements can be excluded. The XML document, `contact.xml`, is simple but does include one `define` element. We will create a TREX module for validating it to illustrate the necessary steps.

3. Next the elements `contact`, `first_name`, `last_name`, `street_address`, `city`, `state`, and `zipcode` are declared.

   ```
   <grammar>
       <start>
         <element name="contact">
           <element name="first_name"/>
           <element name="last_name"/>
           <element name="street_address"/>
           <element name="city"/>
           <element name="state"/>
           <element name="zipcode"/>
         </element>
       </start>
   </grammar>
   ```

Note that no datatypes or other information are included with our element definitions so far.

TREX has three elements that are used to specify the number of occurrences of an element. If an element is not enclosed within one of these three, it means it's a required element that can only occur once. The following table shows these three TREX elements.

Element	Occurrence	DTD equivalent
optional	zero or one	?
zeroOrMore	zero or more	*
oneOrMore	one or more	+

4. The next element is phone, which includes three subelements. The subelements phone_home and fax can occur zero or more times, so we will enclose them in a zeroOr-More element.

```
<element name="phone>
   <element name="phone_work"/>
     <zeroOrMore>
       <element name="phone_home"/>
       <element name="fax"/>
     </zeroOrMore>
</element>
```

5. We use the define element to create a named element group (phone_group) that can be referenced using the ref element. We can specify that the subelements phone_home and fax occur zero or more times by using the markup from Step 4 within this TREX define element.

```
<element name="phone>
     <ref name="phone_group"/>
   </element>
</start>
   <define name="phone_group">
     <element name="phone_work"/>
       <zeroOrMore>
         <element name="phone_home"/>
         <element name="fax"/>
       </zeroOrMore>
   </define>
</grammar>
```

Note that the start element is closed before the define element is declared and that the grammar element is closed at the end of the document.

6. Next, we declare the email and contact_date elements.

```
<element name="phone">
     <ref name="phone_group"/>
   </element>
   <element name="email"/>
   <element name="contact_date"/>
</start>
   <define name="phone_group">
   ...
```

7. TREX does not include any of its own built-in datatypes, but it has the capability of being combined with a datatyping vocabulary such as Part 2 of the W3C XML Schema Recommendation. The specific datatyping vocabulary you can use in a TREX document, however, depends on the implementation you're using.

The `data` element is used to add datatypes to the TREX elements previously declared. The `ns` attribute can be used to specify the namespace of the datatype. If an element pattern does not include an `ns` attribute, the `ns` attribute of the nearest ancestor that has an `ns` attribute is used. Because the `contact` element is the ancestor of all of the other elements in our XML document, we specify an `ns` attribute as part of the `contact` element declaration.

```
<element name="contact"
    xmlns:xsd="http://www.w3.org/2001/XMLSchema">
    <element name="first_name">
      <data type="xsd:string"/>
    </element>
    <element name="last_name">
      <data type="xsd:string"/>
    </element>
    <element name="street_address">
      <data type="xsd:string"/>
    </element>
    <element name="city">
      <data type="xsd:string"/>
    </element>
    <element name="state">
      <data type="xsd:string"/>
    </element>
</element>
```

The only datatype declared so far is `xsd:string`. A `string` type could also be specified using the `anyString` pattern, as shown in the following markup.

```
<element name="contact">
    <element name="first_name">
      <anyString/>
    </element>
    <element name="last_name">
      <anyString/>
    </element>
    <element name="street_address">
      <anyString/>
    </element>
    <element name="city">
      <anyString/>
    </element>
    <element name="state">
      <anyString/>
    </element>
</element>
```

8. The elements in Step 7 are straightforward `string` datatypes without any restrictions. However, the next element, `zipcode`, can use a datatype derived from `string`. TREX allows this through the use of anonymous datatypes. These datatypes must be represented by an XML element in a different namespace. The element must also include a `trex:role="datatype"` attribute to signify that this is an anonymous datatype. For the element `zipcode`, our element definition includes a `trex` prefix, the `trex:role="datatype"` attribute, and the TREX and the W3C XML Schema namespaces.

```
<element name="zipcode"
    xmlns="http://www.thaiopensource.com/trex"
    xmlns:xsd="http://www.w3.org/2001/XMLSchema"
    xmlns:trex="http://www.thaiopensource.com.trex">
    <xsd:restriction base="xsd:string"
        trex:role="datatype">
      <xsd:pattern value="\d{5}(-\d{4})?"/>
    </xsd:restriction>
</element>
```

9. Next, we define the datatypes for `email` and `contact_date`. The `email` element requires another anonymous datatype and `string` pattern. The `contact_date` element uses a date type.

```
<element name="email"
    xmlns="http://www.thaiopensource.com/trex"
    xmlns:xsd="http://www.w3.org/2001/XMLSchema"
    xmlns:trex="http://www.thaiopensource.com.trex">
    <xsd:restriction base="xsd:string" trex:role="datatype">
      <xsd:pattern value=".+@.+"/>
    </xsd:restriction>
</element>
<element name="contact_date">
    <data type="xsd:date"/>
</element>
```

10. Next we define datatypes for `phone_work`, `phone_home`, and `fax`. Unlike with W3C XML Schema, only anonymous datatypes can be used for derived datatypes, so a derived datatype definition cannot be reused. Even though these three elements (`phone_work`, `phone_home`, and `fax`) each use the same datatype definition, it must be defined for each.

```
<element name="phone">
    <ref name="phone_group"/>
</element>
</start>
<define name="phone_group">
    <element name="phone_work"
      xmlns="http://www.thaiopensource.com/trex"
```

```
                    xmlns:xsd="http://www.w3.org/2001/XMLSchema"
                    xmlns:trex="http://www.thaiopensource.com.trex">
                     <xsd:restriction base="xsd:string"
                        trex:role="datatype">
                       <xsd:pattern value="\d{3}-\d{7}"/>
                     </xsd:restriction>
                  </element>
                   <zeroOrMore>
                   <element name="phone_home"
                    xmlns="http://www.thaiopensource.com/trex"
                    xmlns:xsd="http://www.w3.org/2001/XMLSchema"
                    xmlns:trex="http://www.thaiopensource.com.trex">
                     <xsd:restriction base="xsd:string"
                       trex:role="datatype">
                        <xsd:pattern value="\d{3}-\d{7}"/>
                     </xsd:restriction>
                  </element>
                   <element name="fax"
                    xmlns="http://www.thaiopensource.com/trex"
                    xmlns:xsd="http://www.w3.org/2001/XMLSchema"
                    xmlns:trex="http://www.thaiopensource.com.trex">
                     <xsd:restriction base="xsd:string"
                        trex:role="datatype">
                       <xsd:pattern value="\d{3}-\d{7}"/>
                     </xsd:restriction>
                  </element>
                   </zeroOrMore>
              </define>
           </grammar>
```

The complete markup for the TREX document, contact.trex, is shown in Listing 12.4.

Listing 12.4   *contact.trex*, a TREX schema for *contact.xml*

```
<grammar>
   <start>
     <element name="contact"
       xmlns:xsd="http://www.w3.org/2001/XMLSchema">
       <element name="first_name">
         <data type="xsd:string"/>
       </element>
       <element name="last_name">
         <data type="xsd:string"/>
       </element>
       <element name="street_address">
         <data type="xsd:string"/>
       </element>
```

```
      <element name="city">
        <data type="xsd:string"/>
      </element>
      <element name="state">
        <data type="xsd:string"/>
      </element>
      <element name="zipcode"
        xmlns="http://www.thaiopensource.com/trex"
        xmlns:xsd="http://www.w3.org/2001/XMLSchema"
        xmlns:trex="http://www.thaiopensource.com.trex">
        <xsd:restriction base="xsd:string"
           trex:role="datatype">
          <xsd:pattern value="\d{5}(-\d{4})?"/>
        </xsd:restriction>
      </element>
      <element name="phone>
        <ref name="phone_group"/>
      </element>
      <element name="email"
        xmlns="http://www.thaiopensource.com/trex"
        xmlns:xsd="http://www.w3.org/2001/XMLSchema"
        xmlns:trex="http://www.thaiopensource.com.trex">
        <xsd:restriction base="xsd:string"
           trex:role="datatype">
          <xsd:pattern value=".+@.+"/>
        </xsd:restriction>
      </element>
      <element name="contact_date">
        <data type="xsd:date"/>
      </element>
    </element>
  </start>
  <define name="phone_group">
    <element name="phone_work"
    xmlns="http://www.thaiopensource.com/trex"
    xmlns:xsd="http://www.w3.org/2001/XMLSchema"
    xmlns:trex="http://www.thaiopensource.com.trex">
      <xsd:restriction base="xsd:string" trex:role="datatype">
        <xsd:pattern value="\d{3}-\d{7}"/>
      </xsd:restriction>
    </element>
      <zeroOrMore>
      <element name="phone_home"
        xmlns="http://www.thaiopensource.com/trex"
        xmlns:xsd="http://www.w3.org/2001/XMLSchema"
        xmlns:trex="http://www.thaiopensource.com.trex">
      <xsd:restriction base="xsd:string" trex:role="datatype">
        <xsd:pattern value="\d{3}-\d{7}"/>
      </xsd:restriction>
      </element>
      <element name="fax"
```

```
            xmlns="http://www.thaiopensource.com/trex"
            xmlns:xsd="http://www.w3.org/2001/XMLSchema"
            xmlns:trex="http://www.thaiopensource.com.trex">
            <xsd:restriction base="xsd:string" trex:role="datatype">
            <xsd:pattern value="\d{3}-\d{7}"/>
            </xsd:restriction>
            </element>
            </zeroOrMore>
        </define>
    </grammar>
```

TREX offers several other features, including attributes, choice, and interleaving. A TREX attribute pattern is similar to a TREX element pattern. For example, our instance document includes an element car with the attributes model and year as follows:

```
<element name="car">
  <attribute name="model">
    <anyString/>
  </attribute>
  <attribute name="year">
    <anyString/>
  </attribute>
</element>
```

An attribute element by itself is a required attribute. Attribute occurrence can also be specified with one of the three occurrence elements shown in Step 3 earlier in this section (optional, zeroOrMore, or oneOrMore).

The anyString pattern matches any string, including the empty string, and can be used with elements as well as attributes. Rather than specifying anyString as shown previously, a more precise datatype could be used for the year, as in this example:

```
<element name="car"
    xmlns:xsd="http://www.w3.org/2001/XMLSchema">
    <attribute name="model">
      <anyString/>
    </attribute>
    <attribute name="year">
      <data type="xsd:gYear"/>
    </attribute>
</element>
```

TIP   The anyString pattern matches any string, but TREX also includes a string pattern that matches a specific string. The string pattern normalizes the white space in both the pattern string and the string being matched. This can be modified by using a whiteSpace attribute on the string element with the value equal to preserve.

The define element can be used to create a reusable set of attributes in the same way it's used to create a set of reusable subelements. In this example, a set of attributes named car-info is created:

```
<element name="car">
   <ref name="carinfo"/>
</element>
...
<define name="carinfo"
   xmlns:xsd="http://www.w3.org/2001/XMLSchema">
   <oneOrMore>
     <attribute name="model">
       <anyString/>
     </attribute>
     <attribute name="year">
       <data type="xsd:gYear"/>
     </attribute>
   </oneOrMore>
</define>
```

We can also use a choice element to have the option to reuse some subelements in a subelements group. For example, suppose our instance document includes the following markup:

```
<book>
   <chapter>
     <title>Schema Structures and Components</title>
     <author>Chelsea Valentine</author>
     <date>2001</date>
   </chapter>
   <chapter>
     <title>Schema Datatypes</title>
     <author>Lucinda Dykes</author>
     <pages>48</pages>
   </chapter>
</book>
```

We can write a TREX schema to validate the preceding markup as follows:

```
<element name="book"
   xmlns:xsd="http://www.w3.org/2001/XMLSchema">
   <oneOrMore>
     <element name="chapter">
       <element name="title">
         <data type="xsd:string"/>
       </element>
       <element name="author">
         <data type="xsd:string"/>
```

```
      </element>
        <choice>
          <element name="pages">
            <data type="xsd:nonNegativeInteger"/>
          </element>
          <element name="date">
            <data type="xsd:gYear"/>
          </element>
        </choice>
      </element>
    </oneOrMore>
  </element>
```

TREX also includes a unique feature called interleaving. The `interleave` pattern allows child elements to occur in any order. If we wanted the subelements of `chapter` in the previous instance document to appear in any order, we could specify this as follows:

```
<element name="book"
    xmlns:xsd="http://www.w3.org/2001/XMLSchema">
    <oneOrMore>
      <element name="chapter">
        <interleave>
          <element name="title">
            <data type="xsd:string"/>
          </element>
          <element name="author">
            <data type="xsd:string"/>
          </element>
            <choice>
              <element name="pages">
                <data type="xsd:nonNegativeInteger"/>
              </element>
              <element name="date">
                <data type="xsd:gYear"/>
              </element>
            </choice>
        </interleave>
      </element>
    </oneOrMore>
  </element>
```

For more information on TREX, see the following:

- J. David Eisenberg's article "TREX Basics" at www.xml.com/pub/a/2001/04/11/trex.html

- The TREX home page at www.thaiopensource.com/trex

- The TREX specification at www.thaiopensource.com/trex/spec.html

- James Clark's extensive TREX tutorial at www.thaiopensource.com/trex/tutorial.html

RELAX NG

RELAX NG is a schema language based on RELAX and TREX. A RELAX NG schema defines a pattern for an XML document. RELAX NG is still in development by the OASIS RELAX NG technical committee. A specification for RELAX NG version 0.9 was released on August 11, 2001 and can be viewed at www.oasis-open.org/committees/relax-ng/spec-20010811.html. A Java implementation to validate RELAX NG is available at www.thaiopensource.com/relaxng/jing.html. Tools for using RELAX NG and other schema languages are discussed in Chapter 14.

The OASIS RELAX NG technical committee describes RELAX NG in the following quote from the RELAX NG home page (www.oasis-open.org/committees/relax-ng/index.shtml):

> *The key features of RELAX NG are that it is simple, easy to learn, uses XML syntax, does not change the information set of an XML document, supports XML namespaces, treats attributes uniformly with elements so far as possible, has unrestricted support for unordered content, has unrestricted support for mixed content, has a solid theoretical basis, and can partner with a separate datatyping language.*

First, we'll create a RELAX NG schema for contact.xml (Listing 12.1) and then review some additional features of RELAX NG:

1. We start with a grammar element, followed by a start element. As in TREX, these elements are not required for simple RELAX NG schemas.

```
<grammar>
   <start>
```

2. Next, we declare the elements contact, first_name, last_name, street_address, city, state, and zipcode.

```
<grammar>
   <start>
     <element name="contact">
       <element name="first_name"/>
       <element name="last_name"/>
       <element name="street_address"/>
       <element name="city"/>
       <element name="state"/>
       <element name="zipcode"/>
     </element>
   </start>
</grammar>
```

3. We add a namespace declaration to the contact element definition, using the default namespace for RELAX NG, http://relaxng.org/ns/structures/0.9.

```
<element name="contact"
   xmlns="http://relaxng.org/ns/structures/0.9">
```

A namespace prefix can also be used, such as in this line.

```
xmlns:rng="http://relaxng.org/ns/structures/0.9"
```

4. Next, we define the phone element using element definitions and occurrence elements. RELAX NG includes the three occurrence elements of TREX, as previously shown in Step 3 of the TREX section.

```
<element name="phone>
   <element name="phone_work"/>
   <zeroOrMore>
   <element name="phone_home"/>
   <element name="fax"/>
   </zeroOrMore>
</element>
```

As in TREX, we can also name a pattern using a define element. The following example is an alternative pattern for the phone element.

```
<element name="phone>
   <ref name="phone_group"/>
</element>
</start>
   <define name="phone_group">
   <element name="phone_work"/>
      <zeroOrMore>
      <element name="phone_home"/>
      <element name="fax"/>
      </zeroOrMore>
   </define>
</grammar>
```

5. We declare the elements email and contact_date.

```
<element name="phone>
   <ref name="phone_group"/>
</element>
<element name="email"/>
<element name="contact_date"/>
</start>
   <define name="phone_group">
```

Like RELAX and TREX, RELAX NG does not include any built-in datatypes of its own, but it has the capability of being combined with a datatyping vocabulary such as Part 2 of the W3C XML Schema Recommendation. As with TREX, the specific datatyping vocabulary you can use in a RELAX NG document, however, depends on the implementation you're using. Datatypes are specified by using a `data` pattern with a `datatypeLibrary` attribute value of the datatype library being used, as well as by using a `type` attribute value of the specific datatype from this library. For example, the `first_name` element can be specified with a datatype.

```
<element name="first_name">
    <data type="string"
    datatypeLibrary=
    "http://www.w3.org/2001/XMLSchema-datatypes"/>
</element>
```

It's very cumbersome to specify the `datatypeLibrary` attribute for every element, particularly if each element is referencing the same datatype library. RELAX NG allows this attribute to be inherited, so a `data` element will use the value from the closest ancestor that specifies a datatype library value. It's generally easiest to specify this attribute on the root element of the schema, which in this case is the `contact` element.

```
<element name="contact"
xmlns="http://relaxng.org/ns/structures/0.9"
datatypeLibrary=
"http://www.w3.org/2001/XMLSchema-datatypes">
```

6. The data element is used to add datatypes to the RELAX NG elements previously declared.

```
<element name="contact"
xmlns="http://relaxng.org/ns/structures/0.9"
datatypeLibrary=
"http://www.w3.org/2001/XMLSchema-datatypes">
  <element name="first_name">
    <data type="string"/>
  </element>
  <element name="last_name">
    <data type="string"/>
  </element>
  <element name="street_address">
    <data type="string"/>
  </element>
  <element name="city">
    <data type="string"/>
  </element>
  <element name="state">
    <data type="string"/>
  </element>
</element>
```

For string datatypes without constraining parameters, the text pattern can be used in place of the data pattern:

```
<element name="state">
   <text/>
</element>
```

7. The elements we've defined so far have the string datatype, a simple built-in datatype from W3C XML Schema Part 2: Datatypes. Datatypes in RELAX NG can also include parameters to constrain the base datatype. These are defined using a param element with a name attribute with the value of the constraining parameter. The constraining parameters that can be used depend on the datatype library. Our next element, zipcode, has a datatype using a pattern constraint on the string datatype.

```
<element name="zipcode">
   <data type="string">
     <param name="pattern">\d{5}(-\d{4})?</param>
   </data>
</element>
```

8. Next, we define datatypes for email and contact_date.

```
<element name="email">
   <data type="string">
     <param name="pattern">.+@.+</param>
   </data>
</element>
<element name="contact_date">
   <data type="date"/>
</element>
```

9. We define datatypes for phone_work, phone_home, and fax. Although RELAX NG allows constraints on datatypes, it currently does not support user-defined datatypes, so it's not possible to reuse a set of constraints except by restating them. These three elements have the same derived datatype, but it must be stated for each one.

```
<element name="phone_work">
   <data type="string">
     <param name="pattern">\d{3}-\d{7}</param>
   </data>
</element>
<element name="phone_home">
   <data type="string">
     <param name="pattern">\d{3}-\d{7}</param>
   </data>
</element>
<element name="fax">
```

```
      <data type="string">
        <param name="pattern">\d{3}-\d{7}</param>
      </data>
    </element>
```

The complete markup for the RELAX NG schema contact.rng is shown in Listing 12.5.

Listing 12.5   *contact.rng*, **a RELAX NG schema for** *contact.xml*

```xml
<grammar>
  <start>
    <element name="contact"
    xmlns="http://relaxng.org/ns/structures/0.9"
    datatypeLibrary=
    "http://www.w3.org/2001/XMLSchema-datatypes">
      <element name="first_name">
        <data type="string"/>
      </element>
      <element name="last_name">
        <data type="string"/>
      </element>
      <element name="street_address">
        <data type="string"/>
      </element>
      <element name="city">
        <data type="string"/>
      </element>
      <element name="state">
        <data type="string"/>
      </element>
      <element name="zipcode">
        <data type="string">
          <param name="pattern">\d{5}(-\d{4})?</param>
        </data>
      </element>
      <element name="phone>
        <ref name="phone_group"/>
      </element>
      <element name="email">
        <data type="string">
          <param name="pattern">.+@.+</param>
        </data>
      </element>
      <element name="contact_date">
        <data type="date"/>
      </element>
    </element>
  </start>
  <define name="phone_group">
    <element name="phone_work">
      <data type="string">
```

```
              <param name="pattern">\d{3}-\d{7}</param>
            </data>
          </element>
          <zeroOrMore>
            <element name="phone_home">
              <data type="string">
                <param name="pattern">\d{3}-\d{7}</param>
              </data>
            </element>
            <element name="fax">
              <data type="string">
                <param name="pattern">\d{3}-\d{7}</param>
              </data>
            </element>
          </zeroOrMore>
        </define>
      </grammar>
```

RELAX NG supports several other features, including choice, attributes, enumerations, lists, and interleaving. A `choice` pattern can be used for a choice of subelements or attributes. If a choice option includes more than one subelement, the subelements can be joined in a group. For example, we can modify the instance document from the section "TREX" to the following form:

```
<book>
    <chapter>
      <title>Schema Structures and Components</title>
    </chapter>
    <chapter>
      <date>2001</date>
      <pages>48</pages>
    </chapter>
</book>
```

We can then create a RELAX NG schema using `choice` and `group` to describe the pattern of this document:

```
<element name="book">
    xmlns="http://relaxng.org/ns/structures/0.9"
    datatypeLibrary=
      "http://www.w3.org/2001/XMLSchema-datatypes">
    <oneOrMore>
      <element name="chapter">
        <choice>
          <element name="title">
            <data type="string"/>
          </element>
          <group>
```

```
          <element name="pages">
            <data type="nonNegativeInteger"/>
          </element>
          <element name="date">
            <data type="gYear"/>
          </element>
        </group>
      </choice>
    </element>
  </oneOrMore>
</element>
```

Attribute patterns in RELAX NG have the same structure as element patterns. The order of attributes is not significant. Attribute elements that occur without a modifying element to define occurrence are required attributes. The group and choice patterns can be used with attributes in the same way they're used with elements.

The text pattern is the default for attributes and does not have to be specified. The text pattern is also the default for empty attributes:

```
<attribute name="fruit">
  <text/>
</attribute>
```

An empty attribute could also be specified in shorter form as follows:

```
<attribute name="fruit"/>
```

Empty elements, however, must be specified as empty:

```
<element name="shopping">
  <empty/>
</element>
```

A value pattern can be used with a choice pattern to specify an enumerated list of values for an element or an attribute, as in this example:

```
<element name="car">
  <attribute name="model">
    <choice>
      <value type="string">Ford</value>
      <value type="string">Chevrolet</value>
    </choice>
  </attribute>
</element>
```

TIP If there's no ancestor with a `datatypeLibrary` attribute, the default datatype library is the RELAX NG datatype library. It includes two types: `string` and `token`. The `string` type is string data without white space normalization (removing leading and trailing white space characters and collapsing sequences of white spaces to a single white space). The `token` type is string data after white space normalization.

The list pattern matches a white-space-separated list of tokens. A list can be specified with a specific number of items, or an occurrence element can be used. For example, the following specifies a list of two years:

```
<element name="leapyears">
    <list>
      <data type="gYear"/>
      <data type="gYear"/>
    </list>
</element>
```

This specifies a list of one or more years:

```
<element name="leapyears">
   <oneOrMore>
      <list>
       <data type="gYear"/>
      </list>
   </oneOrMore>
</element>
```

RELAX NG also includes the `interleave` pattern of TREX. An `interleave` pattern can be used to allow child elements to occur in any order instead of being restricted to occur in the order they are specified in the schema. For example, an `interleave` pattern has been added to this simple schema to allow the `customer` element to contain the `name`, `city`, and `date` elements in any order:

```
<element name="sale">
   <oneOrMore>
     <element name="customer">
       <interleave>
         <element name="name">
           <data type="string"/>
         </element>
         <element name="city">
           <data type="string"/>
         </element>
         <element name="date">
           <date type="date"/>
         </element>
```

```
        </interleave>
      </element>
    </oneOrMore>
  </element>
```

RELAX NG supports modularity in several ways. It includes an `externalRef` pattern to access a pattern in a separate external file, the `define` pattern to create named patterns that can be referenced from within the same schema, a `combine` attribute to join multiple definitions with the same name, and an `include` element to merge grammars from more than one RELAX NG schema. Definitions can be replaced using a combination of `include` and `define`. For more details on using the modularity features of RELAX NG, see the RELAX NG specification at `www.oasis-open.org/committees/relax-ng/spec-20010811.html` and the RELAX NG Tutorial at `www.oasis-open.org/committees/relax-ng/tutorial-20010810.html`.

Appendix B of the RELAX NG Tutorial includes a comparison with RELAX and examples of using RELAX NG to create functionality equivalent to the hedge rules and attribute pools of RELAX.

On August 17, 2001, James Clark released an experimental Non-XML Syntax for RELAX NG. This is not a part of RELAX NG and does not originate from the OASIS Technical Committee. A document describing this syntax can be viewed at `www.thaiopensource.com/relaxng/nonxml/syntax.html`.

A Working Draft of RELAX NG DTD Compatibility Annotations was released on September 3, 2001. It defines annotations in RELAX NG that can be used to support some of the features of XML 1.0 DTDs, which are not directly supported in RELAX NG.

For more information on RELAX NG, see the following:

- The latest news on RELAX NG, available in RELAX NG—The XML Cover Pages by Robin Cover at `http://xml.coverpages.org/relax-ng.html`

- The RELAX NG page at `www.thaiopensource.com/relaxng`

- The OASIS Technical Committee RELAX NG page at `www.oasis-open.org/committees/relax-ng`

- The RELAX NG DTD Compatibility Annotations, currently a Working Draft, at `www.oasis-open.org/committees/relax-ng/annotate-20010810.html`

- Guidelines for using W3C XML Schema datatypes with RELAX NG at `www.oasis-open.org/committees/relax-ng/xsd-20010907.html`

Schematron

Schematron, developed by Rick Jelliffe, is a structural-based schema language rather than a grammar-based schema language such as W3C XML Schema, RELAX, TREX, and RELAX NG. Schematron is based on patterns that contain rules that enforce logical constraints. In other words, it doesn't validate elements and attributes; instead, it validates patterns of relationship between items. Rick Jelliffe describes the underlying premise of schema construction using Schematron in the following quote from an interview with Simon St.Laurent (www.xmlhack.com/read.php?item=121):

> *The purpose of a schema is to make various assertions that should constrain a document; to report on the presence or absence of patterns. So the result of validation may be a complex set of values. Various backends should make use of that set of information, each in their way.*

Schematron uses XPath and the Extensible Stylesheet Language Transformations (XSLT) to create a style sheet that is then run against the instance document you want to validate. The focus is on validation and on providing useful error messages to assist the validation process. Error messages are output as the user's choice of text, XML, or HTML. Error messages are presented all at once rather than being debugged in branch order as in grammar-based schema languages. Finding an error in the beginning of the instance document code does not prevent you from finding out at the same time about errors occurring later in the code. Schematron also provides information about the node location of the error, so error information is much more specific and useful.

To use Schematron for validation, some knowledge of XPath, XSLT, and DTDs is necessary, as well as an XSLT processor (Saxon or MSXML3). The Resource Directory (RDDL) for Schematron 1.5 at www.ascc.net/xml/schematron offers links and downloads for Schematron resources.

A Schematron document is an XML document that consists of a `schema` element, a namespace, and one or more patterns. The patterns consist of rules, which contain logical constraints on schema components. The rules contain XSLT/XPath expressions, which are expressions used to test logical assertions about the relationships between items in the instance document. These assertions are tested in the validation process, and the user receives output about invalid assertions in the form of error messages. For example, an assertion can be made that one element is a child of another element, and this assertion can be tested against an instance document.

Constraints are grouped to form `rules`. A rule contains a `context` attribute whose value identifies the object (XPath node) to which the constraint(s) is applied. A `rule` element can contain an `assert` and/or a `report` element. Both `assert` and `report` elements contain a `test` attribute, which is an XSLT/XPath expression that is evaluated and returns a Boolean value: `true` or `false`. (The `assert` and `report` elements are similar to XSLT `xsl:if` elements, which also use a `test` attribute.) An `assert` element triggers a message if the test expression evaluates to false, and a `report` element triggers a message if the test expression evaluates to true. A `report` element is used to report qualities of an instance. An `assert` element is used to find errors, as in the following example:

```
<!-- Schematron schema -->
<rule context="lecture">
   <assert test="@price">
      <name/> must include a price
   </assert>
</rule>
<!-- instance document -->
<lecture price="10">Introduction</lecture>
```

In the example, the context is `lecture`, and the `assert` element is evaluating whether a `price` attribute is present. If it is, no message is generated. If it's not present—in other words, if the test assertion is false—the `assert` statement returns a value of false, which triggers an error message using the value of the `context` attribute in place of `<name/>`:

```
lecture must include a price
```

The `name` element is optional. The preceding example could also be written as follows:

```
<rule context="lecture">
   <assert test="@price">
      lecture must include a price
   </assert>
</rule>
```

The `name` element is useful when the `context` attribute includes more than one node, as in this example:

```
<rule context="book|CD|video">
   <assert test="parent::salesitem">
      <name/> must be contained within a salesitem element
   </assert>
</rule>
```

As in the preceding example, the `name` element is used for substituting a name into the output stream. In this case, each of the `context` attribute values will be tested against the assertion.

The `name` element returns the tag name of the corresponding node in the error message and helps to identify the location of the error in the instance document. A `name` element can include an optional `path` attribute in which an additional XSLT/XPath expression can be specified—this allows a different node to be tested than the one specified in the `context` attribute.

Here's how to create a Schematron schema to validate `contact.xml`:

1. We start with an XML declaration, followed by a `schema` element that includes the Schematron namespace and a schema name, which is designated by the `name` attribute.

```
<?xml version ="1.0"?>
<schema xmlns="http://www.ascc.net/xml/schematron"
    name="contact">
```

2. A `pattern` element with the `name` attribute with the value of `Document Structure`, the first pattern in this schema, is added.

```
<pattern name="Document Structure">
```

3. Next, we add a `rule` element for the basic document structure, with a `context` value `/` (the whole document).

```
<rule context="/">
```

4. Then we add an `assert` element to test that the `schema` element contains a `contact` element. A message will be output by the validator if this test returns false.

```
<assert test="//contact">A Schematron schema
    should have a contact element.</assert>
```

5. A `report` element to test that the `contact` element is the root element for the document is added. A message will be output by the validator if this test returns true.

```
<report test="//contact">A contact element is
    the root element for this document.</report>
```

A `report` element is not really necessary in this case, but it's included to illustrate the report format. The `report test` is exactly the same as the preceding `assert test`— because it returns true in both cases (`assert test` and `report test`), a message will be generated by the `report` element but not by the `assert` element.

6. Next, we add an `assert` element to test that the `contact` element contains a `first_name` element.

```
<assert test="//contact/first_name">
    A Schematron schema should have first_name
    element inside the schema element.
</assert>
```

7. We add `assert` elements for each child element of the `contact` element, including the phone element but not the child elements of the phone element. The form is the same as in the preceding markup.

```
<assert test="//contact/last_name">A Schematron schema
should have last_name element inside the schema element.
</assert>
<assert test="//contact/street_address">A Schematron
```

```
schema should have street_address element inside the schema
element.</assert>
<assert test="//contact/city">A Schematron schema should
have city element inside the schema element.</assert>
<assert test="//contact/state">A Schematron schema should
have state element inside the schema element.</assert>
<assert test="//contact/zipcode">A Schematron schema should
have zipcode element inside the schema element.</assert>
<assert test="//contact/phone">A Schematron schema should
have phone element inside the schema element.</assert>
<assert test="//contact/email">A Schematron schema should
have email element inside the schema element.</assert>
<assert test="//contact/contact_date">A Schematron
schema should have contact_date element inside the schema
element.</assert>
```

8. A report element to test that there's only one contact element in the instance document is added.

```
<report test="count(//contact)>1">There should only be
    one contact per document.</report>
```

9. We then add `report` elements for each child element of the contact element, including the phone element but not the child elements of the phone element. The form is the same as in the preceding markup.

```
<assert test="//contact/first_name">A Schematron schema
    should have first_name element inside the contact
    element.</assert>
<report test="count(//contact/first_name)>1">There
    should only be one first_name per document.</report>
    ...
<assert test="//contact/contact_date">A Schematron schema
    should have contact_date element inside the contact
    element.</assert>
<report test="count(//contact/contact_date)>1">There
    should only be one contact_date per document.</report>
```

10. Now, we close the `rule` and the `pattern` elements and add a new `pattern` element with the name `Contact Elements`.

```
    </rule>
</pattern>
<pattern name="Contact Elements">
```

11. In this pattern, we're testing parent-child relationships. For each of the elements already included in the Document Structure pattern, we add a rule element followed by an assert element that tests whether the node specified in the context attribute occurs only within the contact element.

```
<rule context="first_name">
  <assert test="parent::contact">The element
   <name/> should only appear inside the contact
   element.</assert>
</rule>
…
<rule context="contact_date">
  <assert test="parent::contact">The element <name/>
    should only appear inside the contact element.
  </assert>
</rule>
```

Note that, although similar to the assert test in the preceding pattern, this assert test is testing a different logical constraint—is this element contained *only* in the contact element and nowhere else? In other words, is this element a child of contact and not a child of any other element?

12. Now we add a report element that tests whether the node specified in the context attribute contains any child elements. In this case, report test is not the same as assert test. The report test is whether the first_name element has any child elements.

```
<rule context="first_name">
  <assert test="parent::contact">The element <name/>
    should only appear inside the contact element.
  </assert>
  <report test="child::*">A <name/> element cannot
    contain sub-elements, remove any additional
    markup.</report>
</rule>
…
<rule context="contact_date">
  <assert test="parent::contact">The element <name/>
    should only appear inside the contact element.
  </assert>
  <report test="child::*">A <name/> element cannot
    contain sub-elements, remove any additional
    markup.</report>
</rule>
</pattern>
```

13. We add a new pattern element with the name Phone Elements.

```
<pattern name="Phone Elements">
```

14. Then we add a `rule` element and an `assert` element. The `assert` element tests whether the phone element contains a `phone_work` element.

```
<rule context="phone">
  <assert test="phone_work">A phone element should
    contain phone_work elements.</assert>
```

15. A report element is added. The `report` element uses a `count` function to test if there are zero phone_home elements.

```
<report test="count(phone_home)=0">0 phones -
  There can be zero (or more) phone_home
  elements per phone element.</report>
```

16. Next, we add two more `report` elements. The first one tests if there is one `phone_home` element and the second one tests if there are two `phone_home` elements.

```
<report test="count(phone_home)=1">1 or more
  phones - There can be zero (or more) phone_home
  elements per phone element.</report>
<report test="count(phone_home)=2">2 or more
  phones - There can be (or more) phone_home
  elements per phone element.</report>
```

The `report` element will generate a message that tells the user how many phone_home elements are present in the instance document.

17. The preceding two steps for the `fax` element are repeated.

```
<report test="count(fax)=0">0 phones - There can
  be zero (or more) fax elements per phone
  element.</report>
<report test="count(fax)=1">1 or more phones -
  There can be zero (or more) fax elements per
  phone element.</report>
<report test="count(fax)=2">2 or more phones -
  There can be zero (or more) fax elements per
  phone element.</report>
</rule>
```

The `report` element will generate a message that tells the user how many fax elements are present in the instance document.

18. Finally, we close the `pattern` and `schema` elements.

```
  </pattern>
</schema>
```

The complete markup for `contact_schematron.sch` is shown in Listing 12.6. Documentation and formatting elements have been added.

Listing 12.6 *contact_schematron.sch*, a Schematron Schema for *contact.xml*

```xml
<?xml version="1.0"?>
<schema xmlns="http://www.ascc.net/xml/schematron"
    name="contact">
    <title>schema for contact.xml</title>
    <p>This schema document validates the contact document
      model.</p>
    <p>This schema document was created on October 1, 2001</p>
    <pattern name="Document Structure">
      <p>These rules provide the basic document structure.</p>
      <rule context="/">
        <assert test="//contact">A Schematron schema should
          have a contact element.</assert>
        <report test="//contact">A contact element is the root
          element for this document.</report>
        <report test="count(//contact)>1">There should only be
           one contact per document.</report>
        <assert test="//contact/first_name">A Schematron schema
          should have first_name element inside the contact
          element.</assert>
        <report test="count(//contact/first_name)>1">There
          should only be one first_name per document.</report>
        <assert test="//contact/last_name">A Schematron schema
          should have last_name element inside the schema
          element.</assert>
        <report test="count(//contact/last_name)>1">There
          should only be one last_name per document.</report>
        <assert test="//contact/street_address">A Schematron
          schema should have street_address element inside the
          contact element.</assert>
         <report test="count(//contact/street_address)>1">There
          should only be one street_address per document.
         </report>
        <assert test="//contact/city">A Schematron schema should
          have city element inside the contact element.</assert>
        <report test="count(//contact/city)>1">There should only
          be one city per document.</report>
        <assert test="//contact/state">A Schematron schema
          should have state element inside the contact
          element.</assert>
        <report test="count(//contact/state)>1">There should
          only be one state per document.</report>
        <assert test="//contact/zipcode">A Schematron schema
          should have zipcode element inside the contact
          element.</assert>
        <report test="count(//contact/zipcode)>1">There should
          only be one zipcode per document.</report>
        <assert test="//contact/phone">A Schematron schema
          should have phone element inside the contact
```

```
      element.</assert>
    <report test="count(//contact/phone)>1">There should
      only be one phone per document.</report>
    <assert test="//contact/email">A Schematron schema
      should have email element inside the contact
      element.</assert>
    <report test="count(//contact/email)>1">There should
      only be one email per document.</report>
    <assert test="//contact/contact_date">A Schematron
      schema should have contact_date element inside the
      contact element.</assert>
    <report test="count(//contact/contact_date)>1">There
      should only be one contact_date per document.</report>
  </rule>
</pattern>
<pattern name="Contact Elements">
  <p>These rules define the parent/child relationship for
    each element that is an allowable child of the contact
    element. They require that the defined element cannot
    occur anywhere else in the document, except as a child
    of the contact element.
  </p>
  <rule context="first_name">
    <assert test="parent::contact">The element <name/>
      should only appear inside the contact element.
    </assert>
    <report test="child::*">A <name/> element cannot
      contain sub-elements, remove any additional markup.
    </report>
  </rule>
  <rule context="last_name">
    <assert test="parent::contact">The element <name/>
      should only appear inside the contact element.
    </assert>
    <report test="child::*">A <name/> element cannot
      contain sub-elements, remove any additional markup.
    </report>
  </rule>
  <rule context="street_address">
    <assert test="parent::contact">The element <name/>
      should only appear inside the contact element.
    </assert>
    <report test="child::*">A <name/> element cannot
      contain sub-elements, remove any additional markup.
    </report>
  </rule>
  <rule context="city">
    <assert test="parent::contact">The element <name/>
      should only appear inside the contact element.
    </assert>
    <report test="child::*">A <name/> element cannot contain
```

```
        sub-elements, remove any additional markup.</report>
      </rule>
      <rule context="state">
        <assert test="parent::contact">The element <name/>
          should only appear inside the contact element.
        </assert>
        <report test="child::*">A <name/> element cannot
          contain sub-elements, remove any additional markup.
        </report>
      </rule>
      <rule context="zipcode">
        <assert test="parent::contact">The element <name/>
          should only appear inside the contact element.
        </assert>
        <report test="child::*">A <name/> element cannot
          contain sub-elements, remove any additional markup.
        </report>
      </rule>
      <rule context="email">
        <assert test="parent::contact">The element <name/>
          should only appear inside the contact element.
        </assert>
        <report test="child::*">A <name/> element cannot
          contain sub-elements, remove any additional markup.
        </report>
      </rule>
      <rule context="contact_date">
        <assert test="parent::contact">The element <name/>
          should only appear inside the contact element.
        </assert>
        <report test="child::*">A <name/> element cannot
          contain sub-elements, remove any additional markup.
        </report>
      </rule>
    </pattern>
    <pattern name="Phone Elements">
      <p>Defines the content model for the phone element</p>
      <rule context="phone">
        <assert test="phone_work">A phone element should contain
          phone_work elements.</assert>
        <report test="count(phone_home)=0">0 phones - There can
          be zero (or more) phone_home elements per phone
          element.</report>
        <report test="count(phone_home)=1">1 or more phones -
          There can be zero (or more) phone_home elements per
          phone element.</report>
        <report test="count(phone_home)=2">2 or more phones -
          There can be zero (or more) phone_home elements per
          phone element.</report>
        <report test="count(fax)=0">0 phones - There can be zero
          (or more) fax elements per phone element.</report>
```

```
      <report test="count(fax)=1">1 or more phones - There
         can be zero (or more) fax elements per phone
         element.</report>
      <report test="count(fax)=2">2 or more phones - There
         can be zero (or more) fax elements per phone
         element.</report>
   </rule>
   <rule context="phone_work">
      <assert test="parent::phone">The element <name/> should
         only appear inside the phone element.</assert>
   </rule>
   <rule context="phone_home">
      <assert test="parent::phone">The element <name/> should
         only appear inside the phone element.</assert>
   </rule>
   <rule context="fax">
      <assert test="parent::phone">The element <name/> should
         only appear inside the phone element.</assert>
   </rule>
   </pattern>
</schema>
```

How to Validate an XML Document Using Schematron

To validate your XML document using Schematron, you need the following items:

Instant Saxon   Saxon is an XSLT processor that you can use to compile the schema and apply the schema to the XML document. You can download Instant Saxon at `http://users.iclway.co.uk/mhkay/saxon`.

`schematron-basic.xsl`   Download this file at `www.ascc.net/xml/schematron/1.5/basic1-5/schematron-basic.xsl`.

`skeleton1-5.xsl`   Download this file at `www.ascc.net/xml/schematron/1.5/skeleton1-5.xsl`.

Schematron schema document   You'll need to create this file, or you can use Listing 12.6 as a tester.

XML document   You'll need to create this file. You can use Listing 12.1 as a tester. Listing 12.1 will validate without any errors; therefore, if you want to see what your schema can really do, modify the XML document accordingly.

Continued on next page

(Remove line 2 of the code in Listing 12.1 before testing:

```
<!DOCTYPE contact SYSTEM "contact.dtd">
```
This line of code is designed for validating contact.xml against contact.dtd.)

Follow these instructions to validate your XML document:

1. From the command prompt on your PC, navigate to the folder containing Saxon. The following command navigates to the InstantSaxon folder on the C drive: **C:\ cd InstantSaxon**

2. Compile the schema into a runtime validator. To do this, enter the following command at the prompt: **C:\InstantSaxon>saxon contact_schematron.sch schematron-basic.xsl > file.xsl**. The resulting XSLT document (file.xsl) is the file used to validate your document. You can name this file anything you want.

3. Finally, you have to apply the validator against the schema. The XSLT document generated in the preceding step (file.xsl) will be applied to the XML document. In our example, we apply file.xsl to contact.xml (Listing 12.1). To do this enter, the following command at the prompt: **C:\InstantSaxon>saxon contact.xml file.xsl**.

If errors exist, error messages will be displayed in the command prompt window. Any true report statements will also be displayed. If no error messages appear, your sample XML document validated correctly.

Note that if the documents do not reside in the same folder as saxon.exe, you'll need to use paths to address them.

The graphic below shows the command window for validation of contact.xml. All three of the statements are report statements. There are no error messages.

Continued on next page

If `contact.xml` is modified so the phone_home element is not contained within the phone element, validating this document will produce error messages as shown here.

Both the `report` and `assert` elements can include a `diagnostics` attribute, which is a method of adding instance data to the content of the error report that is generated. These can refer to an `id` attribute in the item being tested and provide a way to, for example, find out the actual content of an erroneous value in the instance document being validated, as shown here:

```
<rule context="Delivery">
   <assert test="/shipping/@rate"='5'" diagnostics="a1">
     A shipping element must include a rate attribute with a value of 5.
   </assert>
...
<diagnostics>
   <diagnostic id="a1">
     The shipping rate is <value-of select="/shipping/@rate"/>
   </diagnostic>
</diagnostics>
```

Schematron also includes `phase` and `active` elements, which allow subsets of constraints to be applied at different phases of a document life cycle. A `phase` element comes before the `pattern` element in a Schematron schema and includes an `id` attribute and one or more `active` elements. The `active` element has a `pattern` attribute that references the `id` attribute of the `pattern` element:

```
<schema xmlns="http://www.ascc.net/xml/schematron"
   name="book" defaultPhase="firstdraft">
   <phase id="outline">
     <active pattern="intro"/>
     <active pattern="ch1"/>
   </phase>
```

```
    <phase id="firstdraft">
      <active pattern="ch2"/>
    </phase>
    <pattern name="Introduction" id="intro">
    …
    </pattern>
    <pattern name="Chapter 1" id="ch1">
    …
    </pattern>
    <pattern name="Chapter 2" id="ch2">
    …
    </pattern>
  </schema>
```

Constraints are applied selectively according to the phase of the document life cycle. The default phase is specified by the `defaultPhase` attribute in the `schema` element. Schematron is the only schema language that supports dynamic content.

Schematron rules can be extended by using an `extends` element. The `extends` element has a `rule` attribute that references the `id` of a `rule` element. When you're using an `extends` element, the `rule` element that it references has an `id` attribute in place of a `context` attribute and also has an `abstract` attribute with a value of `true`. The content of the referenced `rule` element is applied in the context of the `rule` element that contains the `extends` element. In the following example, the `international` rule is referenced by the `USSales` rule and applied in that context:

```
<pattern name="sales">
    <rule abstract="true" id="international">
    <assert test="...">
    <name/>…
    </assert>
    </rule>
…
    <rule context="USSales">
    <extends rule="international"/>
    <assert test="…">
```

Schematron is the only schema language that supports co-constraints. For example, if the sum of the child elements of the `account` element must equal 100, this can be expressed in Schematron as follows:

```
<rule context="account">
    <assert test="sum(*)=100">
      The sum of the child elements of account must
      equal 100.
    </assert>
</rule>
```

Schematron also supports co-constraints through support of conditional definitions for elements and attributes. In the following rule, the element `apple` is not required to have any attributes; however, if it does have attributes, it must have both the `color` and `size` attributes:

```
<rule context="apple">
    <assert test="not(@color) or (@color and @size)">
      The apple element must not have a color attribute
      without a size attribute.
    </assert>
    <assert test="not(@size) or (@color and @size)">
      The apple element must not have a size attribute
      without a color attribute.
    </assert>
</rule>
```

Schematron supports choice among attributes. In this way, multiple attributes can be associated with an element but the element is constrained to one attribute at a time:

```
<rule context="apple">
    <assert test="@color or @size">
      The apple element must contain a color or a size
      attribute.
    </assert>
    <assert test="count(attribute::*)=1">
      The apple element can only contain one attribute.
    </assert>
</rule>
```

Schematron supports four content models: empty, text, element, and mixed. These content models can be specified by the following XPath expressions:

- Empty = `not(*)`
- Text = `string-length(text())>0`
- Element = `count(element::*)=count(*)`
- Mixed = content is mixed by default

After the Schematron schema is created, a Schematron XSLT style sheet is used to transform the schema document to a validating style sheet that can be applied to XML instance documents. There are several types of Schematron XSLT style sheets available on the Schematron site at `www.ascc.net/xml/schematron/1.5`:

- Schematron-basic generates a style sheet that returns the text output of the assert and report statements.
- Schematron-message generates a style sheet that can handle `xml:message` elements and send them to standard output.

- Schematron-report generates a style sheet that can produce an HTML-formatted message using frames, with links to error messages organized by patterns.

- Schematron-xml generates a style sheet that can produce an XML-formatted message.

Schematron has elements and attributes for documenting schemas and for formatting error messages. These documentation features are designed for printing schemas or displaying them in hypertext documents and include the following:

p **element**   A formatting element that can contain other formatting elements (dir, emph, and/or span) and can include id, icon, and class attributes

dir   A formatting element to designate the direction of text flow (right-to-left or left-to-right)

emph   A formatting element used to emphasize text

span   A formatting element used to apply a class attribute to an inline selection of text

Schematron constraints can also be embedded within a W3C XML Schema document. The Schematron namespace is included in the XML Schema document, and an appinfo element is used to contain a Schematron constraint, as shown in this example:

```
<xsd:schema xmlns:xsd="http://www.w3.org/2001/XMLSchema"
   xmlns:sch="http://www.ascc.net/xml/schematron">
<xsd:annotation>
   <xsd:documentation xml:lang="en">
     Version 3.7
   </xsd:documentation>
   <xsd:appinfo>
     <sch:pattern name="sales">
       <rule context="NMTax">
         <assert test="/order/shipTo/@state='NM'">
           <name/> is charged only for sales within the state
         </assert>
       </rule>
     </sch:pattern>
   </xsd:appinfo>
<xsd:annotation>
```

For more information on Schematron, see the following:

- The Schematron home page at www.ascc.net/xml/resource/schematron/schematron.html

- A short Schematron tutorial available at www.zvon.org/HTMLonly/SchematronTutorial/General/contents.html

- The Schematron 1.5 specification at www.ascc.net/xml/schematron/1.5/

- "Schematron: validating XML using XSLT," an extensive tutorial by Leigh Dodds, available at `www.ldodds.com/papers/schematron_xsltuk.html`

- The sample Schematron schema (an example of a complete schema document) for the Web Accessibility Initiative (WAI) Guidelines and a corresponding test XML file on the Schematron-Basic page at `www.ascc.net/xml/schematron/1.5/basic1-5/schematron-basic.html`

- "Validating XML with Schematron," an article by Chimezie Ogbuji, at `www.xml.com/lpt/a/2000/11/22/schematron.html`

- "Extending XML Schemas" on the XML Schemas Best Practices pages by Roger Costello at `www.xfront.com/ExtendingSchemas.html`

Microsoft's Schema Initiatives

Microsoft's schema initiatives include the BizTalk Framework and the XML-Data Reduced (XDR) schema language. The BizTalk Framework is a framework for implementing XML schema and XML elements for messages between applications. BizTalk Framework schemas are documents and messages in XML. Schemas available for public use are available on the BizTalk site at `www.biztalk.org`. Free registration is required in order to access the schema library and other resources on the BizTalk site. At the time this book was written, the schema repository included only three W3C XML Schemas and 455 XDR schemas. There's no access to a central list of schemas in the repository; therefore, each schema must be searched for and accessed by industry and subcategories within each industry.

XDR schemas were developed prior to the W3C XML Schema Recommendation and have a very similar structure to XML Schema. Schema use in the Microsoft XML Parser (MSXML) is based on XDR. The XDR schema language is based on the W3C XML-Data Note from January 1998 (`www.w3.org/TR/1998/NOTE-XML-data`) and the Document Content Description (DCD) for XML (`www.w3.org/TR/NOTE-dcd`). XDR does not support inheritance or other features of object-oriented design. XDR schemas can be validated using MSXML, which is available at `http://msdn.microsoft.com/downloads/default.asp?URL=/code/sample.asp?url=/msdn-files/027/001/677/msdncompositedoc.xml`.

An XDR schema to validate `contact.xml` is created as follows:

1. We start with an XML declaration, followed by a `Schema` element that includes the namespace for XDR schema.

```
<?xml version="1.0"?>
<Schema xmlns="urn:schemas-microsoft-com:xml-data">
```

We can also include a name attribute in the Schema element.

```
<Schema name="contact"
    xmlns="urn:schemas-microsoft-com:xml-data">
```

2. Next, we define the elements contact, first_name, last_name, street_address, city, state, zipcode, phone_work, phone_home, fax, email and contact_date. XDR uses ElementType to define elements.

```
<ElementType name="contact"/>
<ElementType name="first_name"/>
<ElementType name="last_name"/>
<ElementType name="street_address"/>
<ElementType name="city"/>
<ElementType name="state"/>
<ElementType name="zipcode"/>
<ElementType name="phone_work"/>
<ElementType name="phone_home"/>
<ElementType name="fax"/>
<ElementType name="email"/>
<ElementType name="contact_date"/>
```

XDR elements can include an optional content attribute, which specifies the content model of that element. There are four possible values for the content attribute:

- textOnly contains text and nothing else; it cannot contain child elements.

- eltOnly contains elements only; these child elements must occur in the order specified in the schema.

- mixed contains a mixture of text and elements; this is the default value for the content attribute.

- empty cannot contain text or child elements but can have attributes.

3. A content attribute with the value textOnly is added to the content, first_name, last_name, street_address, city, state, zipcode, phone_work, phone_home, fax, and email elements.

```
<ElementType name="contact" content="textOnly"/>
<ElementType name="first_name" content="textOnly"/>
<ElementType name="last_name" content="textOnly"/>
<ElementType name="street_address" content="textOnly"/>
<ElementType name="city" content="textOnly"/>
<ElementType name="state" content="textOnly"/>
<ElementType name="zipcode" content="textOnly"/>
<ElementType name="phone_work" content="textOnly"/>
<ElementType name="phone_home" content="textOnly"/>
<ElementType name="fax" content="textOnly"/>
```

```
<ElementType name="email" content="textOnly"/>
```

XDR has an order attribute, which specifies how sequences of elements can appear in the instance document. Values for order include the following:

- seq specifies that child elements must appear in the same order they're specified in the schema.

- one specifies that only one of the child elements can appear.

- many specifies that child elements can appear in any order and any number of times.

4. We add the phone element with an order attribute with the value seq and a content attribute with the value eltOnly. Then we reference the child elements already defined (phone_work, phone_home, fax) with an element element and a type attribute. The type attribute references the name value in previously defined element definitions.

```
<ElementType name="phone" order="seq" content="eltOnly">
    <element type="phone_work"/>
    <element type="phone_home"/>
    <element type="fax"/>
</ElementType>
```

The occurrence of a child element can be constrained by using the minOccurs and max-Occurs attributes:

- minOccurs specifies the minimum number of times a child element can occur. Valid values are 0 or 1, and the default value is 1.

- maxOccurs specifies the maximum number of times a child element can occur. Valid values are 1 and * (as many times as necessary or not at all). The default value is 1 except when the content attribute is specified as mixed—in this case, the default is *.

5. The phone_home and fax elements are optional and can occur zero, one, or more times. We specify a minOccurs value of 0 and maxOccurs value of * for these two elements.

```
<ElementType name="phone" order="seq" content="eltOnly">
    <element type="phone_work"/>
    <element type="phone_home" minOccurs="0" maxOccurs="*"/>
    <element type="fax" minOccurs="0" maxOccurs="*"/>
</ElementType>
```

XDR supports a range of datatypes, as show in the following list:

id	idref
idrefs	nmtoken
nmtokens	enumeration
string	number

```
int                    fixed.14.4

boolean                dateTime

dateTime.tz            date

time                   time.tz

i1                     i2

i4                     i8

r8,float               r4

uuld                   uri

bin.hex                bin.base64

char
```

These datatypes are very similar to those used in XML Schema. Enumeration is also used in XML Schema, although not as a datatype. Datatypes in XDR that are not included in XML Schema are `fixed.14.4` (a number with no more than 14 digits to the left of the decimal point and no more than 4 digits to the right of the decimal point), the subtypes of integer (`i1`, `i2`, `i4`, `i8`. `ui1`, `ui2`, `ui4`, `ui8`), `uulf` (hexadecimal digits representing octets), and `char` (specifies a number corresponding to Unicode representation of the character).

XML Schema, however, includes additional built-in datatypes as well as support for user-defined datatypes. Any of the datatypes included in XDR but not included as built-in types in XML Schema could be defined in a user-defined type in XML Schema. XDR schemas do not include support for user-derived datatypes. See Chapter 7 for further information on XML Schema datatypes.

6. The XDR datatype namespace is added to the `Schema` element. This allows the inclusion of XDR datatypes in element definitions.

```
<Schema name="contact"
xmlns="urn:schemas-microsoft-com:xml-data"
xmlns:dt="urn:schemas-microsoft-com:datatypes">
```

7. We add a datatype to the `contact_date` element. The datatype must include the `dt` prefix because it's part of the XDR datatype namespace. The XDR `date` datatype has the same format as the XML Schema date datatype (ISO 8601: *CCYY-MM-DD*).

```
<ElementType name="contact_date" dt:type="date"/>
```

If `ElementType` contains a datatype, the `content` type is assumed to be `textOnly` and does not need to be specified.

Note that the only element that was able to use a datatype in this schema was the contact_date element. Although the other elements could have been specified as `string` datatypes, there's no clear advantage to doing so in this case if the datatype cannot be further constrained—by adding a pattern constraint to a string, for example.

XDR schema includes `maxLength` and `minLength` attributes that can be used to constrain the length of a `string`, `number`, `bin.hex`, or `bin.base64` datatype. Both `maxLength` and `minLength` are inclusive values. For `string` and `number` datatypes, these length attributes specify the number of characters. For `bin.hex` and `bin.base64` datatypes, these length attributes specify the number of bytes.

Listing 12.7 shows the complete markup for `contact.xdr`.

Listing 12.7   *contact.xdr*

```
<?xml version ="1.0"?>
<Schema name="contact"
    xmlns="urn:schemas-microsoft-com:xml-data"
    xmlns:dt="urn:schemas-microsoft-com:datatypes">
<ElementType name="contact" content="textOnly">
<ElementType name="first_name" content="textOnly"/>
<ElementType name="last_name" content="textOnly"/>
<ElementType name="street_address" content="textOnly"/>
<ElementType name="city" content="textOnly"/>
<ElementType name="state" content="textOnly"/>
<ElementType name="zipcode" content="textOnly"/>
<ElementType name="phone_work" content="textOnly"/>
<ElementType name="phone_home" content="textOnly"/>
<ElementType name="fax" content="textOnly"/>
<ElementType name="email" content="textOnly"/>
<ElementType name="contact_date" dt:type="date"/>
<ElementType name="phone" order="seq" content="eltOnly">
    <element type="phone_work"/>
    <element type="phone_home" minOccurs="0" maxOccurs="*"/>
    <element type="fax" minOccurs="0" maxOccurs="*"/>
</ElementType>
</ElementType>
</Schema>
```

XDR also includes a `model` attribute that can be used to define the content model of an element as either `open` or `closed`. If the content model is defined as `open`, an instance document can include additional child elements and attributes from other namespaces. If the content model is defined as `closed`, all information must follow the rules in the XDR schema and additional namespaces may not be imported. The default value for `model` is `open`. For additional information on XDR's open content model, see "Content Model" at `http://msdn.microsoft.com/library/en-us/xmlsdk30/htm/xmconcontentmodel.asp` and "Extensibility" at `http://msdn.microsoft.com/library/en-us/xmlsdk30/htm/xmconextensibility.asp`.

A `group` element can be used to specify constraints on a subset of child elements and can include `order`, `minOccurs`, and `maxOccurs` attributes. For example, the `phone` element in `contact.xdr` could use a `group` element to create a subset that included a choice of `phone_work` or `phone_home`:

```
<ElementType name="phone">
    <element type="phone_work"/>
    <group order="one">
      <element type="phone_home"/>
      <element type="fax"/>
    </group>
</ElementType>
```

An `AttributeType` element specifies an attribute type that can include a data `type` attribute and a `required` attribute. The `attribute` element is used in `ElementType` and references a defined `AttributeType` name. An attribute can appear only once per element:

```
<ElementType name="online_sales"/>
    <AttributeType name="item" dt:type="int" required="yes"/>
    <attribute type="item"/>
</ElementType>
```

The `enumeration` datatype can be used in an `AttributeType` element (but not in an `ElementType` element) to define a set of string values, as in the following example:

```
<AttributeType name="item" dt:type="enumeration"
    dt:values="local US intl"/>
```

`AttributeType` and `attribute` can also include default values:

```
<AttributeType name="item" default="book"/>
...<AttributeType name="cd" dt:type="int"/>
<attribute type="cd" default="100"/>
```

TIP   A group of annotations to XDR schema are available through Microsoft SQL Server 2000. These annotations can be used to specify XML-to-relational-database mapping, including mapping elements and attributes to tables and columns in a specific database. More details on these SQL annotations are available at `http://msdn.microsoft.com/library/en-us/xmlsql/ac_mschema_78q1.asp`.

For more information on XDR and Microsoft's BizTalk Framework, see the following:

- "BizTalk Framework Overview" at `www.biztalk.org/home/framework.asp`
- BizTalk Schema Repository at `www.biztalk.org/library/search_objects.asp` (Note that you must become a registered user to assess this material. Go to `www.biztalk.org/home/newuser.asp` to register.)

- "Introduction to XDR Schemas" in the Microsoft.com library at `http://msdn.microsoft` `.com/library/en-us/xmlsdk30/htm/xmconintroductiontoschemas.asp`

- "XDR Schema" in the Microsoft.com library at `http://msdn.microsoft.com/library/` `default.asp?url=/library/en-us/comsrv2k/htm/cs_rp_xmlrefcatalog_ffdb.asp`

Comparison of Alternate Schema Languages

The schema language that you choose to use to validate XML documents depends on the particular features of your instance document. Each language has pluses and minuses, defined for the most part by the needs of the individual user. A general review of the major advantages and disadvantages of alternate schema languages is presented in the following section, followed by a detailed comparison of the features of XML Schema and the five alternate schema languages discussed previously in this chapter.

Advantages and Disadvantages of Alternate Schema Languages

This section highlights the advantages and disadvantages of the schema languages covered in this chapter, as shown in Table 12.1.

TABLE 12.1: Advantages and Disadvantages of Alternate Schema Languages

Schema Language	Advantages	Disadvantages
RELAX	Simple to learn and use	No default values, entities, or notations
	Can use XML Schema built-in datatypes Modularization	No user-defined datatypes
TREX	Simple to learn and use	No default values, entities, or notations
	Can use XML Schema datatypes if supported by implementation	No built-in datatypes (datatype support depends on implementation)
	define element allows reuse of elements and attributes	No reuse of user-defined datatypes
RELAX NG	Simple to learn and use	No user-defined datatypes
	Combines best features of RELAX and TREX	Only two built-in datatypes; other datatype support depends on implementation
	Can use XML Schema datatypes if supported by implementation	
	Datatype namespaces can be inherited; less tedious than using datatypes in TREX	
	Supports modularity	
	Compatibility Annotations (Working Draft) and Non-XML Syntax (experimental) support some DTD features not supported by current version of W3C XML Schema	

Continued on next page

TABLE 12.1 CONTINUED: Advantages and Disadvantages of Alternate Schema Languages

Schema Language	Advantages	Disadvantages
Schematron	Supports constraints not possible in other schema languages, including XML Schema	Requires at least some knowledge of XPath and XSLT
	Useful error messages in choice of output format (text, XML, HTML)	No built-in-datatypes
	Error messages presented all at once for quicker debugging	Can't use XML Schema datatypes
Microsoft XDR	Simple to learn and use	Can't use XML Schema datatypes
	Extensive built-in datatypes (though not as extensive as XML Schema)	Poor support of constraints

Comparison of XML Schema and Alternate Schema Languages

Dongwon Lee and Wesley Chu compared the features of six schema languages—DTD, XML Schema, XDR, Schema for Object-Oriented XML (SOX), Schematron, and Document Structure Description (DSD)—in their August 2000 article "Comparative Analysis of Six XML Schema Languages" (www.cobase.cs.ucla.edu/tech-docs/dongwon/ucla-200008 .html). Their article includes additional information about features and languages not included in the comparison that follows, but it does not include information about RELAX, TREX, or RELAX NG.

The following tables and discussion include detailed information about the features supported by XML Schema and by the five alternate schema languages reviewed in this chapter.

In the following tables, support for features is classified as follows:

- Y = full support
- N = no support
- P = partial support

If a language has equivalent features, it's considered to have full or partial support of a specified feature.

Table 12.2 shows the general structure features and that all six languages use XML syntax and support the use of namespaces.

TABLE 12.2: General Structure

General Structure	RELAX	TREX	RELAX NG	Schematron	XDR	XML Schema
Uses XML syntax	Y	Y	Y	Y	Y	Y
Supports namespaces	Y	Y	Y	Y	Y	Y
Includes and/or imports namespaces	Y	Y	Y	N	N	Y

XML Schema supports default values for simple type elements but is the only schema language to support default values for elements. Most element features are supported by all six languages, as shown in Table 12.3.

RELAX supports reuse of elements through hedge rules and also supports context-sensitive element content.

Most schema languages support minimum and maximum occurrence constraints, although RELAX, TREX, and RELAX NG use DTD equivalent forms of constraints, such as zero or more, one or more, or zero or one.

Only Schematron and XDR support an open concept model. In an open concept model, additional elements and attributes can be added within an element without being declared.

Schematron is the only language that allows conditional definitions of elements, such as "element A" can be present only if "element B" is also present.

TABLE 12.3: Elements

Elements	RELAX	TREX	RELAX NG	Schematron	XDR	XML Schema
Default values	N	N	N	N	N	Y
Content model						
1) Empty	Y	Y	Y	Y	Y	Y
2) Text	Y	Y	Y	Y	Y	Y
3) Element	Y	Y	Y	Y	Y	Y
4) Mixed	Y	Y	Y	Y	Y	Y
5) Context-sensitive	Y	N	Y	N	N	Y
6) Open	N	N	N	Y	Y	N
Ordered sequence	Y	Y	Y	Y	Y	Y

Continued on next page

TABLE 12.3: Elements

Elements	RELAX	TREX	RELAX NG	Schematron	XDR	XML Schema
Unordered sequence	Y	Y	Y	Y	Y	Y
Choice among elements	Y	Y	Y	Y	Y	Y
Min and max occurrence constraints	P	P	P	Y	Y	Y
Conditional definition	N	N	N	Y	N	N

XDR and XML Schema support default values for attributes. RELAX NG supports default values through the RELAX NG DTD Compatibility Annotations (www.oasis-open.org/committees/relax-ng/annotate-20010810.html). All six languages support optional and required attributes, and all offer at least partial support for constraining attribute values. Only Schematron fully supports conditional attribute definitions. All of this is outlined in Table 12.4.

TABLE 12.4: Attributes

Attributes	RELAX	TREX	RELAX NG	Schematron	XDR	XML Schema
Default values	N	N	N	N	Y	Y
Choice among attributes	N	Y	Y	Y	N	N
Optional attributes	Y	Y	Y	Y	Y	Y
Constrain attribute values	P	P	P	Y	P	Y
Conditional definition	N	N	N	Y	N	N

Only XML Schema provides support of inheritance via restriction and extension of a base type, as shown in Table 12.5. This is similar to the use of inheritance in object-oriented programming languages.

TABLE 12.5: Inheritance

Inheritance	RELAX	TREX	RELAX NG	Schematron	XDR	XML Schema
Restriction of base type	N	N	N	N	N	Y
Extension of base type	N	N	N	N	N	Y

A nonattribute is an element or a composite of an element and an attribute. RELAX NG supports ID and IDREF through RELAX NG DTD Compatibility Annotations, but otherwise RELAX, TREX, and RELAX NG do not support the use of a unique ID or keys, as shown in Table 12.6.

A key is both unique and not null. A foreign key includes a referencing attribute (IDREF or keyref) and an object being referenced.

TABLE 12.6: ID and Key

ID or Key	RELAX	TREX	RELAX NG	Schematron	XDR	XML Schema
Unique attribute	N	N	N	Y	Y	Y
Unique nonattribute	N	N	N	Y	P	Y
Key for attribute	N	N	N	Y	N	Y
Key for nonattribute	N	N	N	Y	N	Y
Foreign key for attribute	N	N	N	Y	P	Y
Foreign key for nonattribute	N	N	N	N	N	Y

XML Schema is the only language that supports user-defined datatypes, and it also includes the largest number (44) of built-in datatypes.

XDR is notable for its absence of support for constraints on datatype values. Table 12.7 shows the various languages and which types of datatypes they support.

TABLE 12.7: Datatypes

Datatypes	RELAX	TREX	RELAX NG	Schematron	XDR	XML Schema
Built-in	2	0	2	0	33	44
User-defined	N	N	N	N	N	Y
Constraints on datatype values	Y	Y	Y	Y	N	Y

There are many features to consider when choosing an XML Schema language. As stated by James Clark, the developer of TREX and one of the developers of RELAX NG, in an interview in *Dr. Dobbs Journal* ("A Triumph of Simplicity: James Clark on Markup Languages and XML" by Eugene Kim, *Dr. Dobbs Journal*, July 2001, pp. 56–60):

> *"The field of application of XML has become so broad, so diverse, that it's basically impossible to come up with one schema language that will suit everybody."*

For further comparisons and discussions of schema languages, see the following resources:

- "Schemarama" by Leigh Dodds at www.xml.com/pub/a/2001/02/07/schemarama.html

- "Daring to Do Less with XML" by Michael Champion at www.xml.com/pub/a/2001/05/02/champion.html

- "Time for Consolidation" by Leigh Dodds at www.xml.com/pub/a/2001/06/06/deviant.html

Summary

Alternate schema languages have played a role in XML and schema development long before the W3C XML Schema Recommendation was released and will continue to do so in the future development of XML.

It's becoming clear that no one schema language can address all the features of any possible instance documents. Each language has a particular set of features that are the most useful for a specific set of instance documents.

Schema languages can be subdivided into grammar-based and rules-based languages. Most schema languages are grammar based. Schematron is the major rules-based schema language. Both types of schema languages have advantages and disadvantages depending on the basic needs of the schema user. Grammar-based schemas, in general, offer the most support for datatypes, whereas rules-based schemas offer the most support for expressing constraints and conditions.

The W3C XML Schema has the strongest support for datatypes. Many other schema languages reference the W3C XML Schema datatypes, however, and are much simpler and easier to use than W3C XML Schema. No other schema language so far offers the features of user-derived datatypes that are available in XML Schema.

Schematron offers a way to test logical assertions regarding document structure that are not possible to test with any other schema language so far. Schematron supports any logical assertions that can be described using XPath, including conditional assertions. A Schematron schema can be embedded in an XML Schema document so features of both schema languages can be used to validate an instance document.

RELAX NG supports most features of XML Schema and adds additional features that are not supported in XML Schema. The RELAX NG DTD Compatibility Annotations offer support for attribute default values, ID/IDREF/IDREFS, and documentation. RELAX NG is a simple and elegant schema language, and features continue to be added.

Schema development is definitely a work in progress and will continue to evolve along with the rest of the XML family of languages and applications.

CHAPTER 13

Schema-Based Initiatives

- Understanding WSDL

- Examining RDF

- Exploring XGMML

- Exploring schema alternatives for XML vocabularies

I n addition to the W3C XML Schema Recommendation and the alternate schema languages discussed in Chapter 12, there are several schema-based initiatives that address the issues of using metadata and providing vocabularies (schemas) for information interchange.

The major schema-based initiatives are Web Services Description Language (WSDL), Resource Description Framework (RDF), and Extensible Graph Markup and Modeling Language (XGMML). Other alternatives for XML vocabularies include Document Schema Definition Language (DSDL), Examplotron, Hook, and Document Structure Description (DSD).

WSDL

A *Web service* is a set of functions grouped into a unit that can be published to a network for use by other programs. Web services expand the concept of sharing information on the Web into sharing services on the Web. Web services are the components used to create open distributed systems and allow sharing of digital services. Some examples of reusable components are shipping information, currency conversion, language translation, and user authentication functions.

The Web services platform includes WSDL, XML, Simple Object Access Protocol (SOAP), Hypertext Transfer Protocol (HTTP), and Universal Description, Discovery and Integration (UDDI) services. The focus in this section is on the *Web Services Description Language (WSDL)*, but it also includes a discussion of the role of each of these other platforms in Web services implementation. The Web services platform technologies, including WSDL, are still in development.

WSDL provides a method to describe the basic form of Web service requests with different network protocols and message formats. WSDL 1.1 is a W3C note as of March 2001 (www.w3.org/TR/wsdl). WSDL defines a *service* as a collection of ports. A *port* is specified by associating a network address with a binding. A *binding* is a protocol and a data format specification for a specific port type. Bindings are reusable.

WSDL is an XML format that is extensible to any network protocol or message format. The W3C note describes bindings with HTTP GET/POST, SOAP 1.1, and MIME, but WSDL is not limited to these bindings.

The basic form of a WSDL document includes two parts, a set of abstract definitions and a set of concrete descriptions.

In his article "Web Services Description Language (WSDL) Explained" at http://msdn .microsoft.com/library/en-us/dnwebsrv/html/wsdlexplained.asp?frame=true, Carlos Tapang makes this statement:

> *The abstract sections define SOAP messages in a platform- and language-independent manner; they do not contain any machine- nor language-specific elements....Site-specific matters such as serialization are then relegated to the bottom sections, which contain concrete descriptions.*

The following are the abstract definitions found in WSDL documents:

Types   Datatype definitions using a type system such as XML Schema datatypes (but not limited to this type system):

```
<types>
  <schema
  targetNamespace="http://example.com/euro.xsd"
  xmlns="http://www.w3.org/2001/XMLSchema">
    <element name="currency">
      <complexType>
        <all>
          <element name="exchange" type="float"/>
        </all>
      </complexType>
    </element>
  </schema>
</types>
```

Message   Abstract definitions of the data:

```
<message name="GetExchangeRateInput">
  <part name="body" element="exchange"/>
</message>
```

Operation   Abstract description of an action of a specific service:

```
<operation name="GetExchangeRate">
  <input message="GetExchangeRateInput"/>
  <output message="GetExchangeRateOutput"/>
</operation>
```

Port type   Abstract set of operations of a specific service:

```
<portType name="ExchangeRatePortType">
...
</portType>
```

The following are the concrete descriptions found in WSDL documents:

Binding   Protocol and data format specification for a specific port type:

```
<binding name="ExchangeRateSoapBinding"
    type="ExchangeRatePortType">
    <soap:binding style="document"
```

```
          transport="http://schemas.xmlsoap.org/soap/http"/>
    <operation name="GetExchangeRate">
      <soap:operation soapAction="http://example.com/GetExchangeRate"/>
      <input>
        <soap:body use="literal"/>
      </input>
      <output>
        <soap:body use="literal"/>
      </output>
    </operation>
  </binding>
```

Port   A binding associated with a network address:

```
<port name="ExchangeRatePort" binding="ExchangeRateSoapBinding">
  <soap:address location="http://example.com/exchangerate"/>
</port>
```

Service   Port address of the binding:

```
<service name="ExchangeRateService">
  <port name="ExchangeRatePort"
    binding="ExchangeRateSoapBinding">
    <soap:address
      location="http://example.com/exchangerate"/>
  </port>
</service>
```

Table 13.1 details the components of a WSDL document.

TABLE 13.1: Components of a WSDL document

Element	Occurrence
definitions	One (root element)
import	Zero or unlimited
types	Zero or one
message	Zero or unlimited
portType	Zero or unlimited
binding	Zero or unlimited
service	Zero or unlimited

These components must appear in a specific order: import, types, message, portType, binding, and service. Any of the abstract sections (types, message, and portType) may be in a separate file and imported into the WSDL document.

The following example shows the WSDL definition of a Web service providing auction bid information. The service consists of one operation: `GetLastBid`. The request takes an item offered in an online auction (`currentItem`, a string type) and returns the value of the last bid on this item (`level`, a float type). Here's how a WSDL document for the online auction bid service is created:

1. We start with an XML declaration.

```
<?xml version="1.0"?>
```

2. Next, we add a `definitions` element with a `name` attribute and a `target namespace` attribute.

```
<definitions name="AuctionBid"
    target namespace="http://example.com/auctionbid.wsdl">
```

A WSDL document is a set of definitions. The root element is the `definitions` element.

3. Additional namespaces are added to the root element. The default namespace is the WSDL framework namespace.

```
<definitions name="AuctionBid"
    target namespace="http://example.com/auctionbid.wsdl"
    xmlns:auc="http://example.com/auctionbid.xsd"
    xmlns:tns="http://example.com/auctionbid.wsdl"
    xmlns:soap="http://schemas.xmlsoap.org/wsdl/soap/"
    xmlns="http://schemas.xmlsoap.org/wsdl/">
```

4. Next, we add a `types` element with the child element `schema`. We include namespace definitions in the `schema` element.

```
<types>
    <schema
        targetNamespace="http://example.com/auctionbid.xsd"
        xmlns="http://www.w3.org/2001/XMLSchema">
    </schema>
    </types>
```

Although any prefix other than `xml` can be used for a namespace, a set of standard namespace prefixes and URIs are generally used in XSDL documents. Table 13.2 shows prefixes and URIs commonly used in WSDL.

TABLE 13.2: WSDL Namespaces

Prefix	Namespace	Description
wsdl	http://schemas.xmlsoap.org/wsdl/	WSDL framework
soap	http://schemas.xmlsoap.org/wsdl/soap/	WSDL SOAP binding
http	http://schemas.xmlsoap.org/wsdl/http/	WSDL HTTP GET/POST binding
mime	http://schemas.xmlsoap.org/wsdl/mime/	WSDL MIME binding
soapenc	http://schemas.xmlsoap.org/soap/encoding/	SOAP encoding
soapenv	http://schemas.xmlsoap.org/soap/envelope	SOAP envelope
xsi	http://www.w3.org/2001/XMLSchema-instance	XSD instance
xsd	http://www.w3.org/2001/XMLSchema	XSD schema
tns	Varies	Current document (by convention)

Importing Namespaces in WSDL

An import element can be used to import a namespace in WSDL. The namespace is associated with the document using the location attribute in the import element:

```
<definitions>
    <import namespace="http://www.lanw.com/namespaces/pub.wsdl"
    location="http://www.lanw.com/namespaces/pub/wsdl.xsd"/>
</definitions>
```

The types element contains datatype definitions for the exchanged messages. The W3C XML Schema datatypes system is the preferred type system for WSDL documents, but WSDL does allow other type systems to be added via extensibility elements. We can omit the types element if there are no datatypes to declare.

5. We add element definitions from the target namespace. These definitions are contained within the schema element.

```
<types>
    <schema
    targetNamespace="http://example.com/auctionbid.xsd"
    xmlns="http://www.w3.org/2001/XMLSchema">
        <element name="bidRequest">
          <complexType>
            <all>
              <element name="currentItem" type="string"/>
            </all>
```

```
        </complexType>
      </element>
      <element name="bid">
        <complexType>
          <all>
            <element name="level" type="float"/>
          </all>
        </complexType>
      </element>
    </schema>
  </types>
```

6. Next, we add a message element that contains a part element. Then we add a name attribute to the message element and to the part element. The message name value must be unique for message elements in the document, and the part name value must be unique for part elements in a message element. Multiple part elements can be included in a message element.

```
<message name="GetLastBidInput">
  <part name="body"/>
</message>
```

7. An element attribute is added to the part element.

```
<message name="GetLastBidInput">
  <part name="body" element="auc:bidRequest"/>
</message>
```

The element attribute refers to an XSD element. A type attribute can also be included and refers to an XSD simpleType or complexType. A binding may reference the part name in order to specify binding information about the part.

8. We add a second message element and part element.

```
<message name="GetLastBidOutput">
  <part name="body" element="auc:bid"/>
</message>
```

9. We include a portType element containing an operation element. Then we add a name attribute to the portType element. This name must be unique for portType elements in the document. We add a name attribute to the operation element.

```
<portType name="AuctionBidPortType">
  <operation name="GetLastBid">
  </operation>
</portType>
```

WSDL supports four types of operations:

- One-way, which receives a message

- Request-response, which receives a message and sends a message
- Solicit-response, which sends a message and receives a message
- Notification, which sends a message

10. An `input` element and an `output` element for a request-response operation are added. An optional `fault` element can be included in a request-response operation and is used to specify the message format for any error messages (other than those specific to the protocol).

```
<portType name="AuctionBidPortType">
   <operation name="GetLastBid">
     <input message="tns:GetLastBidInput"/>
     <output message="tns:GetLastBidOutput"/>
   </operation>
</portType>
```

11. We add a `binding` element to define a message format for the operation and for messages defined by the `portType` element. There can be an unlimited number of bindings for a given `port type`. Then we add a `type` attribute to the binding element that references the `portType` that it binds. A binding must specify only one protocol.

```
<binding name="AuctionBidSoapBinding"
       type="tns:AuctionBidPortType">
</binding>
```

12. In this case, we're using a SOAP binding. (SOAP is discussed in the next section of this chapter.) We add an `operation` element and `input` and `output` elements within the binding element.

```
<binding name="AuctionBidSoapBinding"
       type="tns:AuctionBidPortType">
     <soap:binding style="document"
     transport="http://schemas.xmlsoap.org/soap/http"/>
     <operation name="GetLastBid">
       <soap:operation
         soapAction="http://example.com/GetLastBid"/>
       <input>
         <soap:body use="literal"/>
       </input>
       <output>
         <soap:body use="literal"/>
       </output>
     </operation>
</binding>
```

WSDL includes a binding for SOAP, as well as HTTP GET/POST and MIME. SOAP, HTTP, and MIME bindings in WSDL are discussed later in this chapter.

13. A service element with a name attribute is added. We include a port element within the service element. The port element contains an address element with a location attribute. The service element can also include an optional documentation element.

```
<service name="AuctionBidService">
   <port name="AuctionBidPort"
      binding="tns:AuctionBidBinding">
      <soap:address
         location="http://example.com/auctionbid"/>
   </port>
</service>
```

The complete markup is shown in Listing 13.1.

Listing 13.1   *auctionbid.wsdl*

```
<?xml version="1.0"?>
<definitions name="AuctionBid"
    target namespace="http://example.com/auctionbid.wsdl"
    xmlns:auc="http://example.com/auctionbid.xsd"
    xmlns:tns="http://example.com/auctionbid.wsdl"
    xmlns:soap="http://schemas.xmlsoap.org/wsdl/soap/"
    xmlns="http://schemas.xmlsoap.org/wsdl/">
<types>
   <schema
      targetNamespace="http://example.com/auctionbid.xsd"
      xmlns="http://www.w3.org/2001/XMLSchema">
      <element name="bidRequest">
        <complexType>
          <all>
            <element name="currentItem" type="string"/>
          </all>
        </complexType>
      </element>
      <element name="bid">
        <complexType>
          <all>
            <element name="level" type="float"/>
          </all>
        </complexType>
      </element>
   </schema>
</types>
<message name="GetLastBidInput">
   <part name="body" element="auc:bidRequest"/>
</message>
<message name="GetLastBidOutput">
   <part name="body" element="auc:bid"/>
</message>
<portType name="AuctionBidPortType">
```

```
      <operation name="GetLastBid">
        <input message="tns:GetLastBidInput"/>
        <output message="tns:GetLastBidOutput"/>
      </operation>
  </portType>
  <binding name="AuctionBidSoapBinding"
      type="tns:AuctionBidPortType">
      <soap:binding style="document"
        transport="http://schemas.xmlsoap.org/soap/http"/>
      <operation name="GetLastBid">
        <soap:operation soapAction="http://example.com/GetLastBid"/>
        <input>
          <soap:body use="literal"/>
        </input>
        <output>
          <soap:body use="literal"/>
        </output>
      </operation>
  </binding>
  <service name="AuctionBidService">
      <port name="AuctionBidPort"
        binding="tns:AuctionBidSoapBinding">
        <soap:address
          location="http://example.com/auctionbid"/>
      </port>
  </service>
  </definitions>
```

For more information on WSDL and on Web services, see the following resources:

- W3C WSDL 1.1 Note at `www.w3.org/TR/wsdl`

- "Web Services Description Language (WSDL) Explained" by Carlos Tapang at `http://msdn.microsoft.com/library/en-us/dnwebsrv/html/wsdlexplained.asp`

- "A Web Services Primer" by Venu Vasudevan at `www.xml.com/pub/a/2001/04/04/webservices/index.html`

- IBM's Web Services Toolkit at `www.alphaworks.ibm.com/tech/webservicestoolkit`

- Chapter 21, "Introducing SOAP and XML Protocols," *Mastering XML, Premium Edition* by Chuck White, Liam Quin, and Linda Burman (Sybex, 2001)

SOAP

Simple Object Access Protocol (SOAP) is a protocol that specifies a method that uses XML to perform *remote procedure calls (RPCs)* with transport protocols, such as HTTP, as the underlying protocols. The development of SOAP has been anything but straightforward. SOAP was originally developed by Microsoft, DevelopMentor, and UserLand. Further development of

SOAP didn't take place until the development of the W3C XML Schema and the strong typing system of W3C XML Schema datatypes. SOAP is now a part of the XML Protocol Working Group (www.w3.org/2000/xp). SOAP 1.2—written by DevelopMentor, Sun, Canon, and Microsoft—was released as a W3C Working Draft on October 2, 2001. The Working Draft consists of two parts: Part 1: Messaging Framework (www.w3.org/TR/soap12-part1) and Part 2: Adjuncts (www.w3c.org/TR/2001/WD-soap12-part2-20011002).

As defined in the W3C Working Draft, SOAP 1.2 consist of four basic parts:

- An *envelope* that describes what is in a message and how to process it. All SOAP messages are encoded in XML.

- A set of encoding rules for application-defined datatypes.

- A convention for remote procedure calls and responses.

- A binding convention for exchanging messages through the use of an underlying protocol.

WSDL includes a binding for SOAP 1.1 that can include the following protocol-specific specifications:

soap:binding The soap:binding element indicates that a binding is bound to the SOAP protocol, and this element must be used when specifying SOAP bindings. The value of the style attribute is the default for the operation. The value is assumed to be document if it's omitted. The transport attribute indicates to which transport of SOAP the binding corresponds. Here's an example:

```
<soap:binding style="document"
    transport="http://schemas.xmlsoap.org/soap/http"/>
    <operation name="GetLastBid">
    ...
    </operation>
```

soap:address The soap:address element indicates an address for a SOAP endpoint and specifies a port address, as in this example:

```
<soap:address location="http://example.com/auctionbid"/>
```

soap:operation The soap:operation element is an optional specification of the URI for the SOAPAction HTTP header. It can include a style attribute that specifies whether the message is RPC oriented (contains parameters and return values) or document oriented (contains documents). If the style attribute is omitted, document is the assumed value. The soapAction attribute specifies a value for the SOAPAction header for an operation. This value is required for the HTTP protocol binding of SOAP, but it must *not* be specified for other SOAP protocol bindings:

```
<soap:operation
    soapAction="http://example.com/GetLastBid"/>
```

`soap:header`   The `soap:header` element indicates header definitions. The `message` attribute and the `part` attribute reference the specific message part that defines the header type. The style is assumed to be `document` because headers do not contain parameters:

```
<soap:header message="GetLastBidInput" part="body"
    use="encoded"
    encodingStyle="http://schemas.xmlsoap.org/soap/http"
    namespace="http://example.com/auctionbid"/>
```

For more details on using SOAP in WSDL, see the W3C WSDL 1.1 Note (`www.w3.org/TR/wsdl`).

For other information on SOAP, see the following resources:

- The SOAP 1.2 Working Draft at `www.w3.org/TR/2001/WD-soap12-20010709`

- The XML Protocol Working Group at `www.w3.org/2000/xp`

- SOAP FAQ at `www.develop.com/soap/soapfaq.htm`

- "A Brief History of SOAP" by Don Box at `www.xml.com/pub/a/2001/04/04/soap.html`

- Chapter 21, "Introducing SOAP and XML Protocols," *Mastering XML, Premium Edition* by Chuck White, Liam Quin, and Linda Burman (Sybex, 2001)

HTTP

The *Hypertext Transfer Protocol (HTTP)* is protocol for transferring information between browsers and Web servers. When a client connects to a computer and makes a request for a Web page, HTTP transactions occur. Multiple HTTP transactions are required for viewing a single Web page. The current version of HTTP is 1.1 (`ftp://ftp.isi.edu/in-notes/rfc2616.txt`), which is supported by almost all Web servers and Web browsers.

WSDL includes a binding for HTTP 1.1 that can include the following protocol-specific specifications:

- *Specification that a binding uses the HTTP protocol.* This example uses HTTP `GET` as the value for the `verb` attribute:

```
<binding name="xy" type="AuctionBidPortType">
    <http:binding verb="GET"/>
    <operation name="GetLastBid">
      <http:operation location="GetLastBid/A(part1)B(part2)"/>
        ...
    </operation>
</binding>
```

HTTP `POST` can also be used, as in the following example:

```
<binding name="xz" type="AuctionBidPortType">
    <http:binding verb="POST"/>
```

```
<operation name="GetLastBid">
  <http:operation location="GetLastBid"/>
    ...
</operation>
</binding>
```

- *Specification of a port address.* The `location` attribute within the `http:address` element specifies a base URI for the port:

```
<port...>
  <http:address location="http://example.com/"/>
</port>
```

- *Specification of a relative address for each operation.* The `location` attribute within the `http:operation` element specifies a relative URI for the `operation` element. This is combined with the URI from the `http:address` element to produce the full URI for the HTTP request:

```
<binding name="xz" type="AuctionBidPortType">
  <http:binding verb="POST"/>
  <operation name="GetLastBid">
    <http:operation location="GetLastBid"/>

      ...
  </operation>
</binding>
...
<port...>
<http:address location="http://example.com/"/>
</port>
```

For more information on using HTTP in WSDL, see the W3C WSDL 1.1 Note (www.w3.org/TR/wsdl).

Here are some resources for other information on HTTP:

- Current version of HTTP/1.1 at ftp://ftp.isi.edu/in-notes/rfc2616.txt

- "HTTP/1.1 Explained" by Luke Knowland at
  http://hotwired.lycos.com/webmonkey/geektalk/97/12/index4a.html?tw=backend

- "HTTP Headers Revealed!" by Dr. Richard Blaylock at
  http://hotwired.lycos.com/webmonkey/99/36/index3a.html?tw=backend

MIME

Multipurpose Internet Mail Extensions (MIME) is a standard developed to extend the capabilities of e-mail by allowing e-mail to include types of data other than just plain text.

MIME binding can be used in WSDL, but only some MIME formats are specified at the time of this writing. Any MIME type can be used; however, using a `mime:content` element, as shown in the fourth item in the following list, is the most effective.

WSDL defines MIME bindings for these MIME types:

- *Specification for `multipartRelated` MIME type.* In this example, the response (output) includes multiple parts encoded in the MIME format multipart/related. The `part` attribute specifies the name of the message part. The `type` attribute specifies the MIME type string:

```
<output>
    <mime:multipartRelated>
        <mime:part>
          <soap:body parts="body" use="literal"/>
        </mime:part>
        <mime:part>
          <mime:content part="intro" type="text/html"/>
        </mime:part>
        <mime:part>
          <mime:content part="graphic" type="image/jpeg"/>
        </mime:part>
    </mime:multipartRelated>
</output>
```

- *Specification for `text/xml` MIME type.* In this expanded example, a SOAP request has been sent via the SOAP HTTP 1.1 binding and the response includes multiple parts in a MIME multipart/related format. The `soap:body` element in this example has been used as a MIME element, which indicates that the content type is `text/xml`:

```
<binding name="AuctionBidSoapBinding"
     type="tns:AuctionBidPortType">
<soap:binding style="document"
     transport="http://schemas.xmlsoap.org/soap/http"/>
<operation name="GetLastBid">
    <soap:operation
       soapAction="http://example.com/GetLastBid"/>
    <input>
      <soap:body use="literal"/>
    </input>
    <output>
      <mime:multipartRelated>
        <mime:part>
          <soap:body parts="body" use="literal"/>
        </mime:part>
        <mime:part>
          <mime:content part="header" type="image/gif"/>
```

```
        </mime:part>
        <mime:part>
          <mime:content part="main" type="text/html"/>
        </mime:part>
      </mime:multipartRelated>
    </output>
  </operation>
</binding>
```

The `text/xml` MIME format can also be specified directly. For example, if the return format is XML but the schema is not known beforehand, a generic `mime` element is used to specify `text/xml`:

```
<mime:content type="text/xml"/>
```

To specify XML that is not in a SOAP envelope and has a known schema, the `mime:mimeXML` element can be used. The `part` attribute refers to a named message part that specifies the schema of the root XML element:

```
<mime:mimeXML part="schema"/>
```

- *Specification for `application/x-www-form-urlencoded` MIME type.* The `enctype` attribute of a `form` element specifies the content type used to encode the form data to be sent to the server. The default content type is `application/x-www-urlencoded`:

```
<mime:content part="form1"
      type="application/x-www-urlencoded"/>
```

- *Specification for other MIME types (by specifying the MIME type string).* Either of these two lines of markup can be used to specify all MIME types:

```
<mime:content/>
<mime:content type="*/*"/>
```

Or any MIME type can be specified with a `mime:content` element:

```
<mime:content part="body" type="video/mpeg"/>
```

Here are some resources for more information on MIME:

- The MIME Information Page at `http://hunnysoft.com/mime`

- MIME Media types at `ftp.isi.edu/in-notes/iana/assignments/media-types/media-types` (specifies MIME media types in categories: text, multipart, message, application, image, audio, video, and model)

- MIME content types at `www.utoronto.ca/webdocs/HTMLdocs/Book/Book-3ed/appb/mimetype.html`

- RFC 2045 MIME Part One: Format of Internet Message Bodies at `www.ietf.org/rfc/rfc2045.txt`

- RFC 2046 MIME Part Two: Media Types at `www.ietf.org/rfc/rfc2046.txt`

UDDI

Universal Description, Discovery and Integration Service (UDDI) is a mechanism for dynamically finding Web services. A UDDI interface is used to connect to services provided by external partners. A UDDI registry provides a place for businesses to publish services as well as a place for clients to obtain services.

UDDI is built upon SOAP. It's cross-platform and cross-industry. There are three types of information available in a UDDI registry:

White pages   Contact and general business information (services, categories, URLs)

Yellow pages   Information about Web services a business provides and how an application finds a particular service

Green pages   Technical details and binding information

UDDI, like all Web services technologies, is still in development, but over 200 companies have joined the UDDI registry at `www.uddi.org`.

For more information on UDDI, see the following resources:

- "About UDDI" at `www.uddi.org/about.html`
- "Why UDDI Will Succeed, Quietly: Two Factors Push Web Services Forward" at `www.stencilgroup.com/ideas_scope_200104uddi.html`
- Chapter 27, "Microsoft .NET and XML," *Mastering XML, Premium Edition* by Chuck White, Liam Quin, and Linda Burman (Sybex, 2001)

RDF

Resource Description Framework (RDF) became a W3C Recommendation in February 1999. RDF is a system for describing and interchanging metadata about resources on the Web. As discussed in Chapter 1, metadata is a special kind of data that describes and models other data. RDF includes both a model for metadata and a syntax that enables the interchange of metadata on the Web in machine-understandable form.

There's currently very little metadata available on the Web. The main way to access information is through search engines. Search engine strategy continues to be very crude because of the lack of metadata. For example, to search for a list of publications on the Web by a specific author, you could search on the author's name and hope that the query would find Web documents that included the author's name in the title, keywords, or text content of the page. It's not currently possible to search based on a category of metadata, such as a list of all authors of Web documents.

The W3C RDF Recommendation (`www.w3.org/TR/REC-rdf-syntax`), Resource Description Framework (RDF) Model and Syntax Specification, outlines the three basic object types of RDF:

Resource   A resource is any component that has a Uniform Resource Identifier (URI). Uniform Resource Locators (URLs) are subsets of URIs. For example, `http://www.lanw.com` is a URL and therefore also a URI. A resource can be a Web site, a Web page, a specific element on a Web page, or an object not necessarily accessible on the Web, such as a book.

Property   A property in RDF is a resource. A property has a specific meaning, a set of permitted values, and relationships with other properties. A property can also have its own properties and be used like any other resource. Because a property is a resource, it can be described with RDF. Properties are objects in RDF and are not attributes of a class.

Statement   An RDF statement includes a specific resource, a named property, and a value of the property for that resource. An RDF statement consists of three parts: a resource (*subject*), property (*predicate*), and value (*object*). RDF statements are also called *triples* because they consist of three parts.

Figure 13.1 is a graph representation of an RDF statement, also known as a *node and arcs diagram*. The graph representation of RDF statements is presented in the RDF Model and Syntax Specification. In this example, the subject is the resource `http://www.lanw.com/training/Schematron/`, the predicate is `written by`, and the object is `mailto:chelsea@lanw.com`. The two nodes are the subject and the object, and the arc that connects the two nodes is the predicate. In this example, the object is a string, `mailto:chelsea@lanw.com`, called a *literal*. The object and the predicate can also be resources.

FIGURE 13.1:

A node and arcs diagram

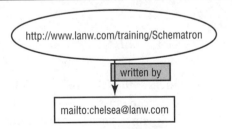

As shown in Figure 13.2, all three components of an RDF statement can be resources. RDF statements can also be combined into one diagram, as shown in Figure 13.3.

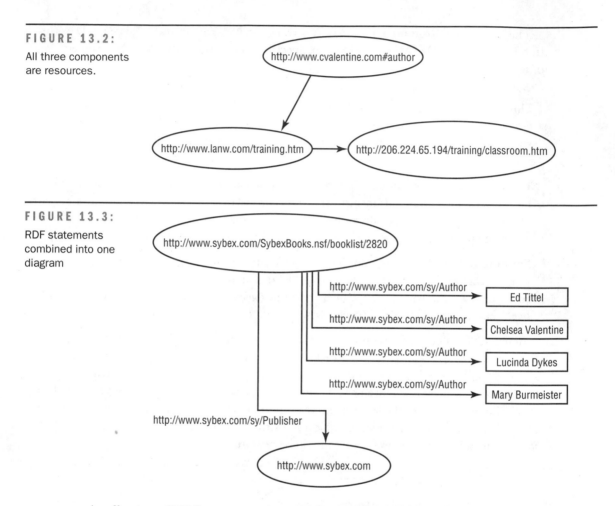

FIGURE 13.2:

All three components are resources.

FIGURE 13.3:

RDF statements combined into one diagram

A collection of RDF statements is an RDF *model*. A model is a directed graph of RDF statements that describes Web-based resources. These graphs are the abstract model of RDF.

The vocabulary (schema) of RDF resources is the RDF Schema. The RDF Schema Specification 1.0 has been a W3C Candidate Recommendation since March 2000 and is available at `www.w3.org/TR/rdf-schema`. The RDF Schema Specification outlines a method of defining the vocabulary needed to describe resources and their relationships.

An RDF document is a list of descriptions. These descriptions are associated with a resource and include a set of properties. In XML, RDF metadata is contained in an element named `rdf:RDF`. This element contains a sequence of XML elements that defines the properties of the resource, for example:

```
<rdf:RDF>
<rdf:Description>
...
</rdf:Description>
</rdf:RDF>
```

The `rdf:Description` element can include either one or zero of the following two attributes, or it can be anonymous:

- about defines any resource and is either an absolute or relative URL:

```
<rdf:Description about="http://www.lanw.com/training/">
```

- ID defines a resource using a fragment identifier (a resource may not be defined more than once):

```
<rdf:Description ID="fg24">
```

- `rdf:Description` without an `about` or `ID` attribute is considered an anonymous resource.

The `rdf:Description` element contains a sequence of XML elements, which describe the properties of the resource. The URI associated with the property is the expanded name of the element. If the element is empty, it must have an `rdf:resource` attribute whose value is a URI.

There are two RDF namespaces:

- `http://www.w3.org/1999/02/22-rdf-syntax-ns#`, prefix `rdf`, for RDF syntax components

- `http://www.w3.org/2000/01/rdf-schema#`, prefix `rdfs`, for RDF schema components

The following code presents the information in Figure 13.1 in XML/RDF format:

```
<rdf:RDF
    xmlns:rdf="http://www.w3.org/1999/02/22-rdf-ns#"
    xmlns:rdfs="http://www.w3.org/2000/01/rdf-schema#"
    xmlns:cv="http://www.cvalentine.com">
    <rdf:Description about="http://www.lanw.com/training.htm">
      <cv:author>
        <rdf:Description about="mailto:chelsea@lanw.com"/>
      </cv:author>
    </rdf:Description>
</rdf:RDF>
```

RDF Schema defines an `rdfs:Container` element that can group subclasses of sets of resources. An `rdfs:Container` element contains sets of resources. There are three subclasses of `rdfs:Container`:

`rdf:Bag`   An unordered set of resources; duplicate values are permitted.

`rdf:Seq`   An ordered set of resources; duplicate values are permitted.

`rdf:Alt`   A list of resources or literals that are alternatives for a value of a property. It can be used to list alternate URIs, alternate languages, or any alternative value for a single resource.

The RDF statements in Figure 13.3 can be shown in XML/RDF format as follows:

```
<rdf:RDF
   xmlns:rdf="http://www.w3.org/1999/02/22-rdf-ns#"
   xmlns:rdfs="http://www.w3.org/2000/01/rdf-schema#"
   xmlns:sy="http://www.sybex.com">
   <rdf:Description about=
   "http:// www.sybex.com/SybexBooks.nsf/booklist/2820">
     <sy:Publisher>
       <rdf:Description about="http://www.sybex.com"/>
     </sy:Publisher>
     <sy:Author>
       <rdf:Seq ID="MasteringXHTMLAuthors"
           rdf:_1="Ed Tittel"
           rdf:_2="Chelsea Valentine"
           rdf:_3="Lucinda Dykes"
           rdf:_4="Mary Burmeister"/>
     </sy:Author>
   </rdf:Description>
</rdf:RDF>
```

The RDF Schema Specification also addresses several specific areas where resource metadata can be used to address specific problems, including these:

PICS   Platform for Internet Content Selection (PICS) is a method of associating metadata (PICS *labels*) with Internet content. For more information on PICS, see the PICS specification at www.w3.org/PICS.

RDF supports PICS labels but does not specifically support direct mapping from PICS to RDF. A PICS mapping with XML and RDF is described in PICS Rating Vocabularies in XML/RDF, a W3C note dated March 2000 and available at www.w3.org/TR/2000/NOTE-rdf-pics-20000327.

Web page description   RDF schema provides a machine-understandable system to describe Web pages and supports vocabularies such as the Dublin Core. See "The Dublin Core" later in this chapter for more details on this set of Web metadata.

Web site mapping and navigation   A site map is a guide to the resource content of a Web site. Site navigation is a set of paths through these resources. RDF Schema allows you to describe site mapping and navigation via a hierarchical classification scheme that defines the relationships of named structures in the Web site.

Platform for Privacy Preferences Project   The W3C Platform for Privacy Preferences Project (P3P) vocabulary can be described in RDF. The P3P specifies metadata regarding a site's data collection practices, the role of personal preferences in this data collection, and the method for interchange of this data. For more information on P3P, see `www.w3.org/P3P`.

For more details on RDF, see these resources:

- The W3C RDF Model and Syntax Specification at `www.w3.org/TR/1999/REC-rdf-syntax-19990222`
- The W3C RDF Schema Specification 1.0 at `www.w3.org/TR/rdf-schema`
- The RDF tutorial by Pierre-Antoine Champin at `www710.univ-lyon1.fr/~champin/rdf-tutorial`
- "What Is RDF?" by Tim Bray at `www.xml.com/pub/a/2001/01/24/rdf.html`
- "An Introduction to RDF" by Uche Ogbuji at `www-106.ibm.com/developerworks/library/w-rdf`
- Chapter 20, "Understanding RDF," *Mastering XML*, *Premium Edition* by Chuck White, Liam Quin, and Linda Burman (Sybex, 2001)

The Dublin Core

To use metadata effectively for information search and retrieval on the Web, three components are needed: a vocabulary (schema), a grammar (the Dublin Core), and a framework (RDF).

The Dublin Core Metadata Element Set is a semantic building block for Web metadata. It consists of 15 elements, which are broad categories for creating descriptions of resources:

Title   The name of the resource

Author or Creator   The person or organization responsible for the resource content

Subject and Keywords   The topic of the resource

Description   The textual description of the resource content

Publisher   The entity responsible for making the resource available

Other Contributor   A person or organization other than the author or creator who has made significant intellectual contributions to the content of the resource

Date   The date the resource became available, given in the form *YYYY* or *YYYY-MM-DD*

Resource Type   The category of the resource

Format   The characteristics of the resource that are used to decide which software and/or hardware are needed to use the resource

Resource Identifier   A unique identifier of the resource, such as a URL or an ISBN

Source   A resource from which the present resource is derived

Language   The language of the resource content

Relation   An identifier of an additional resource and its relationship to the present resource

Coverage   The spatial and/or temporal characteristics of the resource content

Rights Management   The rights management for the resource

The W3C suggests that Web developers begin to annotate existing Web data with RDF by embedding descriptions in the headers of Web documents and encourages Web developers to use the Dublin Core specification for metadata.

For example, embedding the XML/RDF metadata from Figure 13.1 into an HTML document looks something like this:

```
<html>
<head>
    <rdf:RDF
      xmlns:rdf="http://www.w3.org/1999/02/22-rdf-ns#"
      xmlns:rdfs="http://www.w3.org/2000/01/rdf-schema#"
      xmlns:cv="http://www.cvalentine.com">
    <rdf:Description about=
      "http://www.lanw.com/training.htm">
      <cv:author>
        <rdf:Description about="mailto:chelsea@lanw.com"/>
      </cv:author>
    </rdf:Description>
    </rdf:RDF>
</head>
<body>
<p>This document includes RDF metadata.</p>
</body>
</html>
```

Although the RDF metadata in the preceding example does not use the Dublin Core specification for metadata, it could be reformulated to do so.

Other metadata elements may be needed in addition to the Dublin Core to fully describe particular resources, but the elements of the Dublin Core can be used as the basic building blocks. RDF provides a means of combining the Dublin Core with additional vocabularies.

For additional information on the Dublin Core, see the following resources:

- The Dublin Core Metadata Element Set, Version 1.0: Reference Description at `http://dublincore.org/documents/1998/09/dces/#`
- The Dublin Core Metadata Initiative home page at `http://dublincore.org`
- "An Introduction to Dublin Core" by Stuart Weibel and Eric Miller at `www.xml.com/pub/a/2000/10/25/dublincore/index.html`
- Chapter 23, "Introducing the Dublin Core," *Mastering XML, Premium Edition* by Chuck White, Liam Quin, and Linda Burman (Sybex, 2001)

The Semantic Web

The Semantic Web is a vision of Tim Berners-Lee and the W3C for automating data and information processing on the Web by adding semantic meaning through the use of metadata. If data included not only content, but also machine-readable information on the meaning and context, it could be used in a much different way than is currently possible.

The two key technologies for developing the Semantic Web are XML and RDF. XML provides the means to add arbitrary structure to documents through user-defined elements. RDF provides the means to express meaning. An RDF document makes assertions that certain objects (resources) have properties with specific values. Because these resources are defined using a URI, they're specific and unique.

The Semantic Web requires one other component to ensure that different identifiers referencing the same concept—for example, phone numbers—have a way to discover their common meaning. This third component is ontology. In Web terms, an *ontology* is a document that defines the relationships among terms. A Web ontology includes a taxonomy, which defines objects and their relationships to each other, and a set of inference rules. For example, in the case of phone numbers, a specific value for area code infers a particular value for city, even though city is not a direct part of the area code data. Ontologies and metadata could improve Web searches by allowing precise searches rather than general and often useless searches using keywords.

The key that ties all of this together is software that can collect Web data and semantic information from many sources, process this information, and exchange it with other programs. The Semantic Web provides the basic foundation and framework to make this type of technology possible, but at the time of this writing, it remains a vision that has a long way to go before it can be implemented. The development and use of RDF will be a major contributor to the possibility of realizing this vision.

Here are some sources for more information on the Semantic Web:

- "The Semantic Web," an article by Tim Berners-Lee, James Hendler, and Ora Lassila, available online at `www.sciam.com/2001/0501issue/0501berners-lee.html` and available in print in the May 2001 issue of *Scientific American*

- The W3C Semantic Web Activity page at `www.w3.org/2001/sw`

- Chapter 25, "Additional XML Vocabularies," *Mastering XML, Premium Edition* by Chuck White, Liam Quin, and Linda Burman (Sybex, 2001)

XGMML

Graph Markup Language (GML), first described in 1996, is a standard for describing graphs and exchanging graphs between different programs. Extensible Graph Markup and Modeling Language (XGMML) is an XML application based on GML. XGMML was developed in the computer science department at Rensselaer Polytechnic Institute.

A GML description of a graph is a set of key-value pairs. A key is a string identifier, such as `graph`, `node`, or `edge`. A value is a number, a string, or a list of key-value pairs. The following rule from the XGMML 1.0 Draft Specification (`www.cs.rpi.edu/~puninj/XGMML/draft-xgmml.html#Intro`) is used to convert GML to XGMML:

> *A GML key is a name of an XGMML element if its value is a list of key-value pairs. A GML key is the name of an XGMML attribute if its value is a number or string.*

XGMML uses all the elements of GML as well as additional elements specific to XGMML. XSL can be used with XGMML to translate graphs to different formats.

A graph, G, can be described as a set of nodes, V, and a set of edges, E:

G = (V,E)

Each edge is either an ordered (*directed*) or an unordered (*undirected*) set of nodes. Graphs can also be described in data object terms: the elements are nodes and the edges are data objects. A Web site can be described as a set of pages (nodes) and hyperlinks (edges), creating a graph representation of site structure. XGMML documents can be used in this way to specify structural information about a Web site.

An XGMML document describes a graph. The following example shows an XGMML document for a graph with four nodes and two edges:

```
<?xml version="1.0"?>
<!DOCTYPE graph PUBLIC
    "-//Lucinda Dykes//graph description//EN"
    "http://www.lucinda.ws/XGMML/xgmml.dtd">
<graph directed="1" id="12">
<node id="1" label="Node 1"/>
<node id="2" label="Node 2"/>
<node id="3" label="Node 3"/>
<node id="4" label="Node 4"/>
<edge source="1" target="2" label="Edge 1"/>
<edge source="3" target="4" label="Edge 2"/>
</graph>
```

The root element is graph, which contains node and edge elements. Additional meta information about node and edge elements can be included by using an att element.

XGMML documents can be validated against the XGMML DTD (www.cs.rpi.edu/~puninj/XGMML/draft-xgmml.html#XGMML-DTD) or the XGMML Schema (www.cs.rpi.edu/~puninj/XGMML/draft-xgmml.html#XGMML-Schema).

XGMML can be included in other XML documents by using the following XGMML namespace and prefix:

```
xmlns:xgmml="http://www.cs.rpi.edu/XGMML"
```

All XGMML elements can contain the following global attributes:

id   Unique numerical identification within one XGMML document

name   String to identify an element

label   Text representation of an element

labelanchor   Position of the label relative to the graphic representation of an element

---

TIP   XGMML classifies attributes as safe or unsafe, based on GML's safe and unsafe key names. An unsafe key name is a name that is discarded by an application program when changes are made to a graph. These key names start with an uppercase letter.

A graph element can also include the following attributes:

directed   Boolean; graph is directed if value is 1 (true).

vendor   Application that created the file; unsafe.

scale   Scales the size of the display; unsafe.

`rootnode`   Identifies the root node of a graph; unsafe.

`layout`   The layout that can be applied to display a graph; unsafe.

`graphic`   Boolean; if value is 1 (true), the XGMML file includes a graphical representation of the graph.

In addition, a `graph` element can include XML attributes (`xmlns`, `xml:lang`, and `xml:space`) as well as XLink attributes.

A `node` element specifies the properties of a node object. A `node` element can contain a `graphics` element (graphical representation) and an `att` element (meta information about the node).

A `node` element can contain global attributes, XLink attributes, and the following two attributes:

`edgeanchor`   Positions the edges related to the node

`weight`   Value of the node weight; used in weight graphs

For each `edge` element, at least two `node` elements must be included in the `graph` element. An edge is between a source node and a target node. An `edge` element can contain a `graphics` element and an `att` element.

An `edge` element can contain global attributes, XLink attributes, and the following three attributes:

`source`   ID of the source node of the edge

`target`   ID of the target node of the edge

`weight`   Value of the edge weight

The `att` element can include global attributes and three other attributes to describe metadata:

`name`   Name of the meta information

`value`   Value of the meta information

`object`   Object type of the meta information; default type is `string`

A `graph` element can be contained in an `att` element. When it is, the resulting graph is a subgraph of the main graph.

A `graphics` element can contain a `line`, `center`, or `att` element. The `line` element is used to represent an edge. It contains two or more `point` elements. The `point` elements include `x`, `y`, and `z` attributes with numeric values. A `center` element is a `point` element with `x`, `y`, and `z` attributes that represent the central point of a graphical representation.

A `graphics` element can also include an extensive set of attributes to specify the exact graphical representation. These attributes are described in the XGMML 1.0 Draft Specification.

XGMML includes several datatypes, as shown in Table 13.3.

TABLE 13.3 : XGMML Datatypes

Name	Description
Boolean	True (1) or false (0) values.
number	Integer or real values.
string	XML Literals, but without any quoted characters.
URI	Strings in URI format.
anchor	Enumerated type for relative position, with direction values: `c` (center), `n` (north), `ne` (northeast), `e` (east), `se` (southeast), `s` (south), `sw` (southwest), `w` (west), and `nw` (northwest).
type-graphics	Enumerated type; value depends on the application reading the XGMML document.
line	Enumerated type; values include `Arrow` (arrow position), `Capstyle` (end of a line), `Joinstyle` (line joints), and `Arcstyle` (style of an arc).
text	Includes two types, `justify` (text justification) and `font` (name of font family for text display).
color	String that defines the color to be used by a graphic object.
angle	String that defines the angle used by an arc.
object	GML values of an object: `list`, `string`, `real`, or `integer`

Example XGMML files, including an example of a simple Web site structure graph, are part of the XGMML 1.0 Draft Specification. Additional XGMML examples can be downloaded at `www.cs.rpi.edu/~puninj/XGMML/XGMML_EXP`.

For further information on XGMML, see the following:

- The XGMML 1.0 Draft Specification at `www.cs.rpi.edu/~puninj/XGMML/draft-xgmml.html`
- The XGMML home page at `www.cs.rpi.edu/~puninj/XGMML`
- Graphical representation of several Web sites and one book can be viewed at the Graph Gallery at `www.cs.rpi.edu/~puninj/XGMML/GALLERY`

Schema Alternatives for XML Vocabularies

Several schema alternatives for XML vocabularies have been developed. The XML Cover Pages XML Schemas page at `www.oasis-open.org/cover/schemas.html` includes an extensive list of schema languages as well as links to news items and further information about each of these schema languages. This page also includes links to further resources and tools for schema languages.

In this section, we will briefly review four schema alternatives:

- Examplotron
- Document Structure Description (DSD)
- Hook
- Document Schema Definition Language (DSDL)

Examplotron

Examplotron, edited by Eric van der Vlist of Dyomedea, is designed to use instance documents as a simple schema language. Version 0.4 (`http://examplotron.org/0/4`) was released in March 2001 but is not yet complete.

Examplotron documents can be used as a validation language. XSLT is used to transform Examplotron documents into XSLT style sheets that can validate documents with the same structure.

The following example shows a very simple Examplotron document:

```
<?xml version="1.0" encoding="UTF-8"?>
<contact>
    <name>Ralph Jones</name>
    <phone source="work">505 867-4598</phone>
</contact>
```

This schema will validate all documents that have the same structure—three elements (`contact`, `name`, `phone`) and one attribute (`source`)—and no namespace. The Examplotron compiler, `compile.xsl`, transforms the Examplotron document into a style sheet that can be used to validate other documents. The Examplotron compiler must be run using the XSLT processor, Saxon (`http://saxon.sourceforge.net`). Error messages will be generated for any components that do not validate with the XSLT style sheet.

Examplotron is similar to Schematron (see Chapter 12 for more information on Schematron). Like Schematron, Examplotron uses XSL to compile and run a validator. There is not, however, a separate Examplotron schema document.

Examplotron includes an `occurs` attribute to control occurrences of schema items. The `occurs` attribute can have one of the following three values:

- *   Zero or more occurrences
- +   One or more occurrences

. Exactly one occurrence

? Zero or one occurrence

In the following example, an `occurs` attribute has been added to the `phone` element:

```
<?xml version="1.0" encoding="UTF-8"?>
<contact xmlns:ex="http://examplotron.org/0/">
    <name>Ralph Jones</name>
    <phone source="work" ex:occurs="*">505 867-4598</phone>
</contact>
```

Examplotron includes an `assert` attribute that can be used to define assertions as XPath expressions:

```
<?xml version="1.0" encoding="UTF-8"?>
<total xmlns:ex="http://examplotron.org/0/"
    ex:assert="sum(subtotal)=99">
<!-- The sum of the values of the "subtotal" element needs
    to be equal to 99 -->
    <subtotal eg:occurs="+">99</subtotal>
</total>
```

Examplotron also includes an `import` element that provides for consolidating the patterns found in different Examplotron documents. The `import` element is specified as an XLink:

```
<?xml version="1.0" encoding="UTF-8"?>
<contact xmlns:ex="http://examplotron.org/0/"
    xmlns:xlink="http://www.w3.org/1999/xlink">
<ex:import xlink:href="examplotron_a.xml"/>
    <name>Ralph Jones</name>
    <name>Joe Smith</name>
    <phone source="work" ex:occurs="*">505 867-4598</phone>
</contact>
```

In this example, the Examplotron document `examplotron_a.xml` (which specifies two name elements) is imported into the current Examplotron document.

Examplotron provides a very intuitive and easy method to write simple schemas. It is still being developed The draft specification includes a "To Do" list with proposed items to be included in future, more-complete versions of this language.

For more information on Examplotron, see these resources:

- The XSLT compiler for Examplotron at `http://examplotron.org/0/4/compile.xsl`

- The W3C XML Schema for Examplotron at `http://examplotron.org/0/4/examplotron.xsd`

DSD

Document Structure Description (DSD) is an XML Schema language developed by AT&T Lab Research and BRICS, University of Aarhus, Denmark. DSD is designed to provide stronger document descriptions than currently possible with DTDs or the current W3C XML Schema Recommendation and to further XML technologies such as Cascading Style Sheets (CSS) and XSL Transformations (XSLT).

A DSD document defines a grammar for a set of XML documents, documentation for the set, and a CSS-like notation for specifying the default parts of documents.

Five major goals for DSD are outlined in the DSD 1.0 specification:

- Describe content and attributes that are dependent on context.
- Define CSS-like rules for default attribute values and default content.
- Complement XSLT.
- Allow descriptions of what references may point to.
- Allow redefinitions of syntactic classes.

The following example shows a simple DSD schema that contains a single element:

```
<DSD IDRef="contact" DSDVersion="1.0">
   <Title>Contact_DSD</Title>
   <ElementDef ID="contact">
     <StringType/>
   </ElementDef>
   <Default>
     <Context><Element Name="contact"/></Context>
     <DefaultContent>
       Contact list
     </DefaultContent>
   </Default>
</DSD>
```

In this example, the DSD root element contains an IDRef attribute that refers to the element and a DSDVersion attribute. The default value defined for the content inside the contact element is Contact list.

A default associates a set of default elements and attributes with a Boolean expression. A default value is applied to an attribute or element if it contains a default attribute or element with the same name or its Boolean expression is true or omitted.

Defaults can also be specified in the instance document. The namespace DSD must be declared with the value http://www.brics.dk/DSD.

DSD provides a set of rules for determining the hierarchy of defaults:

- A default specified in an instance document has the highest priority.

- The specificity of defaults in a document is determined by the specificity of the Boolean expressions. If the Boolean expression is omitted, the default has the minimum specificity.

- A default (*a*) in an instance document has higher specificity than another default (*b*) in an instance document if the element containing *a* is a descendant of the element containing *b*.

The following example shows a fragment of a DSD document that specifies defaults:

```
<DSD:Default>
    <Context><Element Name="contact"/></Context>
    <DefaultAttribute Name="work_phone" Value="8008880202"/>
</DSD:Default>
<DSD:Default>
    <Context>
      <Element Name="contact">
        <Attribute Name="home_phone" Value="5059882792"/>
        <Attribute Name="work_phone" Value="8008880202"/>
      </Element>
    </Context>
    <DefaultAttribute Name="fax" Value="8008880203"/>
</DSD:Default>
```

In this example, the DSD processor augments all attributes contained in the contact element with the default attribute (Name="fax" Value="8008880203").

A DSD element description (Element) includes an element name and a constraint. An element definition (ElementDef) associates an element description with an element ID. An element description with an IDRef attribute is called *indirect*, and an element description with a name attribute is called *direct*. In the following example, the element definition includes an optional class attribute and two kinds of content (phone_home and fax):

```
<ElementDef ID="contact">
    <AttributeDecl Name="class" Optional="yes"/>
    <OneOrMore>
      <Element IDRef="phone_work"/>
    </OneOrMore>
    <Element Name="option1" Defaultable="yes">
      <Content IDRef="phone_home"/>
    </Element>
    <Element Name="option2" Defaultable="yes">
      <Content IDRef="fax"/>
    </Element>
</ElementDef>
```

A constraint definition associates an ID with a particular constraint. A constraint expression is a sequence of constraint terms, as in the following example:

```
<DSD IDRef="contact1" DSDVersion="1.0">
  <Title>Phones</Title>
  ...
  <ElementDef ID="contact">
    <Constraint IDRef="contact_constraint"/>
  </ElementDef>
  <ConstraintDef ID="contact_constraint">
    <AttributeDecl Name="class" Optional="yes"/>
    <OneOrMore>
      <Element IDRef="option_element"/>
    </OneOrMore>
    <Element Name="option1" Defaultable="yes">
      <Content IDRef="phone_work"/>
    </Element>
    <Element Name="option2" Defaultable="yes">
      <Content IDRef="phone_home"/>
    </Element>
  </ConstraintDef>
  ...
</DSD>
```

An attribute description (`Attribute`) consists of a name and a string type. An attribute declaration (`AttributeDecl`) is a name and a type. The following example shows two attribute descriptions:

```
<DSD:Default>
  <Context>
    <Element Name="contact">
      <Attribute Name="home_phone" Value="5059882792"/>
      <Attribute Name="work_phone" Value="8008880202"/>
    </Element>
  </Context>
  <DefaultAttribute Name="fax" Value="8008880203"/>
</DSD:Default>
```

This example shows an attribute declaration:

```
<AttributeDecl Name="class" Optional="yes"/>
```

A content description specifies a set of elements with a content expression. There are several available content expressions, most of which (with the exception of `If-Then` and `If-Else` conditional expressions) are similar to expressions in other schema languages:

```
Sequence
```

```
Optional
```

```
ZeroOrMore

OneOrMore

Union

AnyElement

Empty

If-Then

If-Else
```

The following example shows the use of a content expression Sequence:

```
<DSD IDRef="contact" DSDVersion="1.0">
    <Title>Price tables</Title>
    <ElementDef ID="contact">
      <OneOrMore>
        <Sequence>
          <Element Name="name"/>
          <StringType IDRef="Name"/>
          <Element Name="phone"/>
          <StringType IDRef="PhoneNumber"/>
          <Element Name="fax"/>
          <StringType IDRef="FaxNumber"/>
        </Sequence>
      </OneOrMore>
    </ElementDef>
    ...
</DSD>
```

For more information on DSD, see these resources:

- The DSD 1.0 Specification at `www.brics.dk/DSD/dsddoc.html`

- The DSD home page at `www.brics.dk/DSD/`

- "The DSD Schema Language" at `www.brics.dk/DSD/papers.html`

Hook

Hook 0.2, authored by Rick Jelliffe, also the author of Schematron, is subtitled "A One-Element Language for Validation of XML Documents based on Partial Order." The description and specification for this minimalist schema language is available at `www.ascc.net/xml/hook`.

A Hook schema is an element that contains a list of element names. This list presents a specific ordering of the element names, and validation consists of checking conformity to the specified ordering.

The Hook language includes these attributes:

`targetNamespace`   Specifies the namespace to be validated

`friendly`   Indicates that elements from other namespaces are permitted (`true` or `false` values)

`short`   Indicates whether all the elements in the namespace have been mentioned (`true` or `false` values)

`top`   Indicates whether the first element in the schema must be the local namespace root element (`true` or `false` values)

Hook also includes an `order` element. The `order` element specifies the order of the schema elements. Elements grouped in square brackets are in the same level or order. A period on an element specifies that an element may not include subelements. A semicolon on a group of elements specifies that an element cannot be contained by elements in the group, although an element can be followed by elements from the group.

Several examples of Hook schemas are included in the description of Hook. The simplest of these examples is the following, which shows how ordering works in Hook:

```
<hook:order>A B. C</hook:order>
```

In this example, the following is true:

- The A element can contain the B and/or C elements.

- The A element can be followed by the B and/or C elements.

- The B element cannot contain the A and/or the C elements.

For more information on Hook, see the Resource Directory (RDDL) for Hook 0.2 at `www.ascc.net/xml/hook/`.

DSDL

Document Schema Definition Language (DSDL) was approved in June 2001 as an ISO Work Item (ISO JTC1/SC34/WG1). It's based on extensions to RELAX NG (see Chapter 12 for more information on RELAX NG).

SGML DTDs support formal modeling of document structures but do not allow details of datatypes to be specified in an XML-compatible way. W3C XML Schema Part 2: Datatypes allows datatypes to be used to validate SGML elements and attributes but does not allow the relationships between the values of different element content and attributes to be validated.

DSDL is designed to integrate descriptions of document structures, datatypes, and data relationship constraints that can be applied to data represented using SGML and its derivatives, including XML. It's hoped that this will make it possible to automate processing of structured information for business uses.

A further draft of DSDL is expected in December 2001.

Here's where you can get more information on DSDL:

- The XML Cover Pages XML Schemas page at `www.oasis-open.org/cover/schemas.html#dsdl` for a description of DSDL

- "Proposal for a New Work Item," the DSDL submission to the IOC, at `www.y12.doe.gov/sgml/sc34/document/0223.doc` (automatically opens or downloads a Word document, depending on the browser you're using)

Summary

A multitude of schema-based initiatives is currently under development. These initiatives cover a wide range of solutions to XML document validation and focus on different aspects of validation. Many of these schema initiatives have the underlying aim of making machine-understandable content available for automatic data processing on the Web.

WSDL is a part of the Web services platform and is specifically designed to define a basic structure for Web service requests with different network protocols and message formats. However, WSDL is only a part of the Web services platform, which also includes several supporting technologies such as SOAP, HTTP, MIME, and UDDI.

RDF is designed for describing and exchanging metadata about Web resources. RDF is one of the technologies essential to the Semantic Web. RDF also could provide a means for Web searches based on metadata—this, however, would require that Web pages routinely include metadata elements like the Dublin Core elements.

XGMML describes graphs and defines a format for exchanging graphs. XGMML is also well suited as a language to describe the basic graph structure of a Web site.

Examplotron and Hook, like many of the alternative schema languages described in Chapter 12, are designed with the aim of simplifying schema design and structure.

DSDL and DSD focus on document structure, although DSDL also includes specifications for datatypes and data relationships.

There's a wide range to choose from, but the usefulness of these schema initiatives is context specific and depends almost entirely on the particular needs of the user.

CHAPTER 14

Schema and Related Tools

- Examining XML Schema validators

- Surveying available W3C-compliant tools

- Surveying available tools for alternate schema languages

- Evaluating other tools and resources for schema development

The basic purpose of XML Schema and alternate schema languages is to enable XML users to assess the validity of XML documents. Schemas enable machine validation of the structure of XML documents. Validating an instance document involves using the constraints defined in a schema document to check the structure and hierarchy of the elements and attributes in an instance document as well as to check the structure of the content contained in the elements and attributes.

Validating parsers, schema validity testers, and other tools are available for validating XML documents against DTDs, XML Schema, and alternate schema languages, although most of these tools are still in development. In addition to validators, conversion tools are available to convert DTDs to schemas and to convert from one schema language to another. Commercial integrated development environment (IDE) packages for editing and validating XML instance documents, DTDs, and schemas are also available.

XML Schema Validators

The W3C XML Schema Recommendation is defined in terms of an abstract data model known as the XML Information Set (www.w3.org/TR/xml-infoset), also called the XML Infoset. The XML Infoset, a W3C Recommendation as of October 2001, specifies a set of definitions of the information in well-formed XML documents. The information set is made up of information items, which are abstract representations of document items. The information set includes 11 items:

- Document information item
- Element information items
- Attribute information items
- Processing instruction information items
- Unexpanded entity reference information items
- Character information items
- Comment information items
- Document type declaration information item
- Unparsed entity information items
- Notation information items
- Namespace information items

The document information item (which corresponds to the root element of the document) and the document type declaration information item are unique in the document. All other information items are matched one to one with the corresponding items in the document.

If the information items in an instance document follow the constraints specified in the corresponding information items in a schema, the document has *local-schema validity*. Parent-child relationships are also checked, and the validity of a parent element is checked against the validity of child information items. If an instance document has local-schema validity and parent-child validity, the instance document is valid. Validators are designed to test both of these conditions.

The W3C maintains a list of tools with links to current validators for XML Schema and to other schema tools on the W3C XML Schema page at www.w3.org/XML/Schema#Tools. This list is updated frequently and is a very useful source of current information.

Several XML Schema validating parsers and schema validity testers are available, as shown in Table 14.1. They are discussed in further detail in the following sections.

TIP The validating parsers require the use of a programming language.

TABLE 14.1: XML Schema Validators

Item	Type	Language(s)
XSV	Validity tester	Python
IBM XML Schema Quality Checker	Validity tester	Java
MSXML	Validating parser	C++, JavaScript, Visual Basic, VBScript
Xerces-C	Validating parser	C++, COM, Perl
Xerces-J	Validating parser	Java

XSV

The XML Schema Validator (XSV) was designed by Henry S. Thompson and Richard Tobin at the University of Edinburgh. Documents can be validated through an online form (www.w3.org/2001/03/webdata/xsv), or the validator can be downloaded (ftp://ftp .cogsci.ed.ac.uk/pub/XSV/XSV12.EXE) and installed on the user's computer.

The online form is similar in format to the W3C HTML and XHTML validators. A schema file can be uploaded from the user's computer and validated, or both a schema file and an instance document can be validated if they are available on the Web. Schema files and instance documents can be validated on the user's computer if the user downloads and installs the validator.

A validation report is generated that includes the following information:

- Target, which is the path and filename of the tested file.

- docElt, which is the URI for the schema being validated (or validated against).

- Validation type, which is either strict or lax; if the validation is lax, the file is well formed but has not been validated.

- Validity of the validating schema document.

- Validity of the instance document.

- instanceAssessed, which is either `true` (an instance document was tested) or `false` (a schema file was tested, not an instance document).

- List of schema resources. `Attempt to import succeeded` means the validator has found and loaded the correct schema document.

- A list of schema-validity problems found in the target (schema or instance document). If there are any problems, line numbers and specific errors are listed.

The default output format of the validation report is text/xml with an XSLT style sheet, but additional options for output include HTML or plain text.

The online version of XSV is shown in Figure 14.1. The XML Schema document corresponding to the instance document `contact.xml` (Listing 12.1 in Chapter 12) is `contact.xsd` (Listing 7.1 in Chapter 7).

FIGURE 14.1:

The W3C Validator for XML Schema online

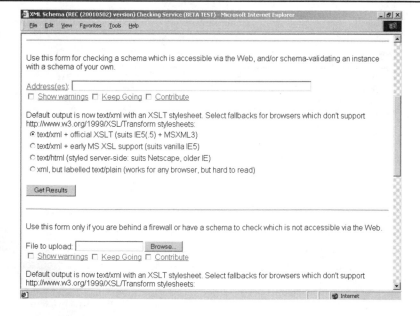

The validation results from uploading `contact.xsd` online via the XSV Web page are shown in Figure 14.2. They are as follows:

- The target file is `contact.xsd`.

- The URI is `http://www.w3.org/2001/XMLSchema`.

- The target file is valid.

- The validator was able to find and load the schema documents `http://www.w3.org/2001/XMLSchema` and `http://www.w3.org/XML/1998/namespace`.

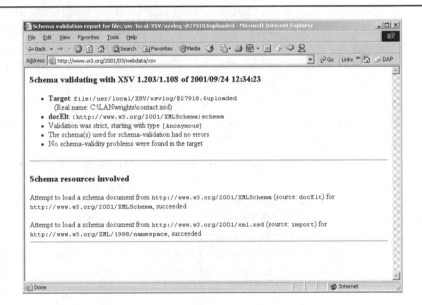

An extensive information page, including details on the schema features covered by XSV and known bugs in XSV, can be viewed at `www.ltg.ed.ac.uk/~ht/xsv-status.html`.

IBM XML Schema Quality Checker

The IBM XML Schema Quality Checker is designed to test whether schema components conform to the W3C XML Schema Recommendation. It's available for download at `www.alphaworks.ibm.com/tech/xmlsqc`.

This schema validity tester does not have the ability to test an instance document against a schema—a validating parser is needed for that. It can test the validity of a single schema document or test multiple schemas referenced from a schema document via `import` or `include`. It can also run in batch mode to test multiple schema documents at one time.

It runs on all Java platforms and requires Java 2 Runtime Environment version 1.3.1, also called JRE 1.3.1., which can be downloaded at `http://java.sun.com/j2se/1.3/jre`.

A report is generated with specific error messages if the schema is not completely valid, and possible solutions may be included with the error message.

For more information on the IBM XML Schema Quality Checker, see the FAQ at `www.alphaworks.ibm.com/tech/xmlsqc`.

Microsoft's XML Parser

The Microsoft XML Core Services 4 release to manufacturing (RTM), previously called Microsoft XML Parser (MSXML) 4, was released in October 2001. This version offers extended support for the W3C XML Schema Recommendation as well as DTDs and XML-Data Reduced (XDR) schemas. (See Chapter 12 for more details on the XDR schema language.)

XML Core Services RTM is limited to the Windows platform. XML Core Services RTM 4 offers validation of XML Schema based on Simple API for XML (SAX) when you use the SAX parser and also supports validation based on the Document Object Model (DOM) with the `schemaLocation` attribute.

XML Core Services RTM requires the use of either C++, JavaScript, VBScript, or VisualBasic.

MSXML 2.5 shipped with Windows 2000, and MSXML 3 was released in November 2000. Because the MSXML parser is installed by default in "side-by-side" mode, previous versions are not replaced when a newer version is installed. Previous versions also supported a "replace" mode, but this feature has been removed from the latest version. MSXML 3 is still available for download at `http://msdn.microsoft.com/downloads/default.asp?URL=/code/sample.asp?url=/msdn-files/027/001/596/msdncompositedoc.xml`.

Xerces

The Apache Software Foundation produces two XML validating parsers, one using C++ (Xerces C++) and one using Java (Xerces2 Java Parser). These parsers were developed by the Apache Software Foundation in cooperation with IBM.

At the time of writing, the latest version of Xerces-C++ is version 1.5.2, which can be downloaded at `http://xml.apache.org/dist/xerces-c`. Xerces-C++ offers limited support of the specifications of the W3C XML Schema Recommendation. It does not support nine of the built-in datatypes, identity constraints, or constraints on particle derivation. More details about the XML Schema support in Xerces-C++ are available at `http://xml.apache.org/xerces-c/schema.html`.

Xerces2 Java Parser version 2, the latest version of the Xerces parser using Java, is available in beta release and can be downloaded at `http://xml.apache.org/xerces2-j/index.html`. Xerces2 Java Parser offers much more extensive support for the W3C Schema Recommendation than Xerces-C++ does. The XML Schema validation engine was resigned for Xerces2 Java Parser version 2, which is the first version of Xerces-J to support validating XML instance documents against XML Schema documents.

Xerces2 Java Parser no longer supports using the `xsi:noNamespaceSchemaLocation` or `xsi:schemaLocation` attribute in the root element of the document, although this may change in future releases. The current beta release has the capability of validating schemas directly. For more information on turning on the validation features in Xerces2 Java Parser, see `http://xml.apache.org/xerces2-j/faq-general.html#faq-1` and `http://xml.apache.org/xerces2-j/faq-pcfp.html`.

For more information on Xerces-C++, see the FAQ page at `http://xml.apache.org/xerces-c/faqs.html`. For more information on Xerces2 Java Parser, see the FAQ page at `http://xml.apache.org/xerces2-j/faqs.html`.

TIP   The W3C XML Schema Test Collection was publicly released by the W3C in September 2001 and can be downloaded at `www.w3.org/2001/05/xmlschema-test-collection/results-master.html`. The test collection work is designed to coordinate test collections for XML Schema processors. The home page for the W3C XML Schema Test Collection can be viewed at `www.w3.org/2001/05/xmlschema-test-collection`.

Survey of Available W3C-Compliant Tools

In addition to schema validity testers and validating parsers, a schema conversion tool, an XML datatypes library, and two commercial IDEs for XML Schema documents and other XML documents are currently available.

dtd2xs

The dtd2xs tool translates DTDs into XML Schema documents. It's available as a Java class, a Java application, and a Web tool. The latest version, Version 1.52 at the time of this writing, can be downloaded at `http://puvogel.informatik.med.uni-giessen.de/dtd2xs/download`.

An additional tool, xsbrowser, can be used to view a DTD or XML Schema document (which is documented in human-readable language) using a Web browser. You can download xsbrowser from `http://puvogel.informatik.med.uni-giessen.de/xsbrowser/download`.

The viewer does not have to understand DTD or XML Schema syntax to use the tool. The only requirement is a Web browser with support for JavaScript, Java applets, and CSS1. The browser does not have to support XML.

Both XML IDEs (XML Spy and Turbo XML) offer built-in DTD-to-schema conversion.

For additional information on DTD-to-XML-Schema conversion with the dtd2xs tool, see the following articles:

- "From DTDs to XML Schemas" at www.webreference.com/xml/column34
- "Converting DTDs to XML Schemas" at www.webreference.com/xml/column35

XML Datatypes Library

Sun's XML Datatypes Library can be used from any Java application that incorporates the XML Schema Part 2: Datatypes Recommendation. It's used to validate strings that contain datatypes and to convert strings into Java objects.

A trial version of the Sun XML Datatypes Library can be downloaded at www.sun.com/software/xml/developers/xsdlib/download.html. The Datatypes Library, however, is based on the XML Schema Part 2: Datatypes Proposed Recommendation and not on the final May 2001 recommendation.

For more information on the Sun XML Datatypes library, see the following resources:

- XML Datatypes README file at www.sun.com/software/xml/developers/xsdlib/README.html
- "Sun's Java Technology Implementation of XML Schema Part 2" at www.sun.com/software/xml/developers/xsdlib

XML Spy 4.1

XML Spy Suite 4.1 by Altova includes three programs:

- XML Spy IDE
- XML Spy Document Editor
- XSLT Designer

Each program is available separately or as part of XML Spy Suite. They can be downloaded for a free 30-day trial at www.xmlspy.com/download.html.

XML Spy Suite 4.1 supports the W3C XML Schema Recommendation and includes the following capabilities:

- Writing schema documents using a GUI editor or a text editor

- Checking for well-formed documents
- Testing schema validity
- Generating schema documentation
- Creating XML instance documents based on the schema
- Validating instance documents against schema
- Using an XSLT editor to generate HTML documents from the XML instance document
- Importing and exporting from databases
- Generating a schema from a database table
- Converting documents using a document-conversion tool

XML Schema documents can be created in XML Spy via the graphical interface or the text editor. Schemas can be tested to see if they are well formed by clicking a button, and well-formed documents can be tested for validity by clicking another button.

XML Spy can automatically create extensive schema documentation in either HTML or Microsoft Word format. To create schema documentation, choose Generate Documentation from the Schema Design menu. A new window appears where you choose the output format and the information to include in the documentation. Figure 14.3 shows an excerpt from the XML Spy documentation in Word format for contact.xsd (Listing 7.1 in Chapter 7).

The documentation includes the schema location, the target namespace, and a list of all the elements, simple types, complex types, and attributes used in the schema. It also displays diagrams of each element, attribute, simple type, and complex type plus documentation of the namespace, type, schema source code, datatype facets, and/or child elements. A diagram of a simple or complex type also indicates which elements use that type.

XML instance documents can be created using the graphical interface or the text editor. An instance document can then be tested to see if it's well formed, and then it can be validated against a schema or DTD.

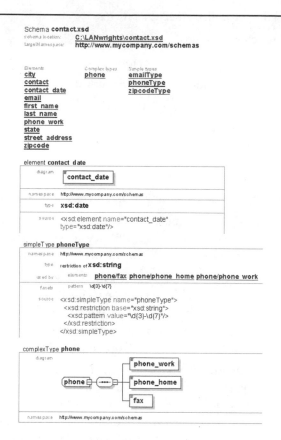

FIGURE 14.3:

Excerpt from XML Spy 4.1 schema documentation for `contact.xsd`

An example of XML Spy conversion from a DTD to an XML Schema document is shown in Chapter 9. When you convert from a DTD to an XML Schema document, you have the opportunity to create more specific datatypes; for example, you can go from a `string` datatype to a pattern restriction derived from a `string` datatype. Any converter will create a general schema document from a DTD, but some specific datatypes need to be hand-coded (even with XML Spy).

XSLT Designer, one of the components of XML Spy Suite, is a GUI approach to creating XSLT style sheets. After designating a schema and an instance document, you can drag and drop elements into the main design window and add presentational markup. Once the design is in place, XSLT Designer can automatically generate a corresponding XSLT style sheet.

Listing 14.1 shows the markup for a very simple XML Schema document, `commerce.xsd`. This schema defines three elements: `commerce`, `bank`, and `city`.

Listing 14.1   *commerce.xsd*

```
<?xml version="1.0" encoding="UTF-8"?>
<xsd:schema targetNamespace="http://www.mycompany.com/schemas"
  xmlns="http://www.mycompany.com/schemas"
  xmlns:xsd="http://www.w3.org/2001/XMLSchema"
  elementFormDefault="qualified">
  <xsd:element name="commerce">
    <xsd:annotation>
      <xsd:documentation>Bank Data</xsd:documentation>
    </xsd:annotation>
    <xsd:complexType>
      <xsd:sequence>
        <xsd:element name="bank">
          <xsd:complexType>
            <xsd:complexContent>
              <xsd:extension base="xsd:anyType">
                <xsd:attribute name="branch" type="xsd:ID"/>
              </xsd:extension>
            </xsd:complexContent>
          </xsd:complexType>
        </xsd:element>
        <xsd:element name="city">
          <xsd:complexType>
            <xsd:complexContent>
              <xsd:extension base="xsd:anyType">
                <xsd:attribute name="branch_division"
                  type="xsd:IDREFS"/>
              </xsd:extension>
            </xsd:complexContent>
          </xsd:complexType>
        </xsd:element>
      </xsd:sequence>
    </xsd:complexType>
  </xsd:element>
</xsd:schema>
```

Listing 14.2 shows an instance document, commerce.xml, that can be validated against commerce.xsd.

Listing 14.2   *commerce.xml*

```
<?xml version="1.0" encoding="UTF-8"?>
<commerce xmlns="http://www.mycompany.com/schemas"
    xmlns:xsi="http://www.w3.org/2001/XMLSchema-instance"
    xsi:schemaLocation="http://www.mycompany.com/schemas
    commerce.xsd">
    <bank branch="145">Northern </bank>
    <city branch_division="A5">Portland</city>
</commerce>
```

XSLT Designer was used to create the XSLT style sheet, `commerce.xslt`, that specifies the styles to be applied to the instance document, `commerce.xml`. The markup for `commerce.xslt` is shown in Listing 14.3.

Listing 14.3   *commerce.xslt*

```
<?xml version="1.0" encoding="UTF-8"?>
<xsl:stylesheet version="1.0"
    xmlns:xsl="http://www.w3.org/1999/XSL/Transform"
    xmlns:xsd="http://www.w3.org/2001/XMLSchema"
    xmlns="http://www.mycompany.com/schemas">
    <xsl:template match="/">
      <html>
      <head>
      </head>
      <body>
        <xsl:apply-templates/>
      </body>
      </html>
    </xsl:template>
    <xsl:template match="bank">
      <span style="font-family:Arial; font-size:medium">
        <xsl:apply-templates/>
      </span>
    </xsl:template>
    <xsl:template match="city">
      <span style="font-family:Arial; font-size:medium">
        <xsl:apply-templates/>
      </span>
    </xsl:template>
</xsl:stylesheet>
```

This simple style sheet applies the Arial font family in medium size to the indicated elements (`bank` and `city`) for display as HTML.

To create a project and generate an HTML file, follow these steps:

1. Once the style sheet is created, open a new project window by selecting Project ➤ New Project.

2. Specify the schema and the instance files by choosing Project ➤ Add Files to Project.

3. Set the properties of the project: Choose the schema file for validation, choose the XSLT file for XSL transformation of XML files, and choose a destination folder and file extension for the output file (HTML file). Then select Project ➤ Project Properties.

4. With the instance document open in the main window, generate the HTML file by choosing XSL ➤ XSL Transformation.

The HTML file will then appear in the main window. This file can also be previewed in the XSLT Designer main window in IE Preview mode, as shown in Figure 14.4.

FIGURE 14.4:

HTML file created from the XSLT file `contact.xslt`

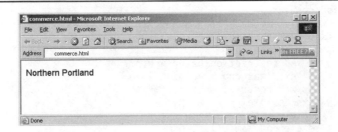

XML Spy also includes options for importing and exporting from databases. A simple database table can be created in Microsoft Access from the elements in contact.xml (Listing 12.1 in Chapter 12). This database can then be imported to XML Spy and converted to an XML file (choose Convert ➤ Import Database Data). The XML file produced by importing the database contact.mdb is named contact_db.xml and is shown in Listing 14.4.

Listing 14.4 *contact_db.xml*

```
<Import>
   <Row>
      <ID>1</ID>
      <first_name>Joe</first_name>
      <last_name>Smith</last_name>
      <address>611 Ridgewood Dr</address>
      <city>Denver</city>
      <state>CO</state>
      <zipcode>80210</zipcode>
      <phone_work>303-4667339</phone_work>
      <phone_home>303-9842361</phone_home>
      <fax>303-4667357</fax>
      <contact_date>2001-09-23</contact_date>
   </Row>
</Import>
```

The reverse can also be done. Information from XML files can be exported to an existing database (Convert ➤ Export to Text Files/Database). XML Schema documents can also be created from existing database files. For example, the database contact.mdb can be converted into an XML Schema document (Convert ➤ Create Database Schema). The schema document that is created from contact.mdb is shown in Listing 14.5.

Listing 14.5   *contact_db.xsd*

```xml
<?xml version="1.0" encoding="UTF-8"?>
<xsd:schema xmlns:xsd="http://www.w3.org/2001/XMLSchema">
  <xsd:element name="Contact">
    <xsd:complexType>
      <xsd:sequence>
        <xsd:element name="ID" type="xsd:integer"/>
        <xsd:element name="first_name">
          <xsd:simpleType>
            <xsd:restriction base="xsd:string">
              <xsd:maxLength value="50"/>
            </xsd:restriction>
          </xsd:simpleType>
        </xsd:element>
        <xsd:element name="last_name">
          <xsd:simpleType>
            <xsd:restriction base="xsd:string">
              <xsd:maxLength value="50"/>
            </xsd:restriction>
          </xsd:simpleType>
        </xsd:element>
        <xsd:element name="address">
          <xsd:simpleType>
            <xsd:restriction base="xsd:string">
              <xsd:maxLength value="50"/>
            </xsd:restriction>
          </xsd:simpleType>
        </xsd:element>
        <xsd:element name="city">
          <xsd:simpleType>
            <xsd:restriction base="xsd:string">
              <xsd:maxLength value="50"/>
            </xsd:restriction>
          </xsd:simpleType>
        </xsd:element>
        <xsd:element name="state">
          <xsd:simpleType>
            <xsd:restriction base="xsd:string">
              <xsd:maxLength value="50"/>
            </xsd:restriction>
          </xsd:simpleType>
        </xsd:element>
        <xsd:element name="zipcode">
          <xsd:simpleType>
            <xsd:restriction base="xsd:string">
              <xsd:maxLength value="50"/>
            </xsd:restriction>
          </xsd:simpleType>
        </xsd:element>
```

```
          <xsd:element name="phone_work">
            <xsd:simpleType>
              <xsd:restriction base="xsd:string">
                <xsd:maxLength value="50"/>
              </xsd:restriction>
            </xsd:simpleType>
          </xsd:element>
          <xsd:element name="phone_home">
            <xsd:simpleType>
              <xsd:restriction base="xsd:string">
                <xsd:maxLength value="50"/>
              </xsd:restriction>
            </xsd:simpleType>
          </xsd:element>
          <xsd:element name="fax">
            <xsd:simpleType>
              <xsd:restriction base="xsd:string">
                <xsd:maxLength value="50"/>
              </xsd:restriction>
            </xsd:simpleType>
          </xsd:element>
          <xsd:element name="contact_date">
            <xsd:simpleType>
              <xsd:restriction base="xsd:string"/>
            </xsd:simpleType>
          </xsd:element>
        </xsd:sequence>
      </xsd:complexType>
    </xsd:element>
</xsd:schema>
```

As with converting DTDs to schemas, the resulting schema document is general. Because the basic structure is already in place, however, this document can be easily "cleaned up" to create more specific datatypes as needed and to change or remove the maxLength restrictions that correspond to the field length value in the database.

With a few minor modifications (adding a processing instruction, adding a root element with a namespace, and removing the import and row elements), the XML file created by importing a table from a database validates against the contact_db.xsd XML Schema file. The new instance document, contact_db_1.xml, is show in Listing 14.6.

Listing 14.6   *contact_db_1.xml*

```xml
<?xml version="1.0" encoding="UTF-8"?>
<Contact xmlns:xsi="http://www.w3.org/2001/XMLSchema-instance"
    xsi:noNamespaceSchemaLocation="C:\contact_db.xsd">
    <ID>1</ID>
    <first_name>Joe</first_name>
```

```
    <last_name>Smith</last_name>
    <address>611 Ridgewood Dr</address>
    <city>Denver</city>
    <state>CO</state>
    <zipcode>80210</zipcode>
    <phone_work>303-4667339</phone_work>
    <phone_home>303-9842361</phone_home>
    <fax>303-4667357</fax>
    <contact_date>2001-09-23</contact_date>
</Contact>
```

XML Spy includes a document conversion tool that is accessed through the DTD/Schema menu. Choose Convert DTD/Schema from this menu and then choose one of the following conversion formats:

- DTD
- DCD Schema
- XML-Data Schema
- BizTalk Schema
- W3C Schema

In addition to these five formats, additional formats are available for creating new documents in XML Spy, as shown in Table 14.2. From the File menu, choose New, and then choose a document format.

TABLE 14.2: Document Formats in XML Spy

file extension	document type
.asp	Active Server Page
.cml	Chemical Markup Language
.ent	External Entity
.htm/.html	HTML document
.math	Mathematical Markup Language
.mml	Mathematical Markup Language
.mtx	MetaStream XML
.rdf	Resource Description Framework
.smil	SMIL
.svg	SVG
.txt	Text
.vml	VoiceXML
.wml	Wireless Markup Language

Continued on next page

TABLE 14.2 CONTINUED: Document Formats in XML Spy

file extension	document type
.xhtml	XHTML
.xsl	XSL style sheet
.xslt	XSLT

The XML Spy Suite includes an extensive Help menu as well as four tutorials:

- Intro to XML
- XML Editing and Validation
- Schema/DTD Editing and Validation
- XSL Editing and Transformation

More information on XML Spy is available at www.xmlspy.com.

Turbo XML 2.2.1

Turbo XML by Tibco Extensibility is a combination of three separate programs:

- XML Authority
- XML Instance
- XML Console

These three programs come packaged together as Turbo XML and are not available separately. A 30-day free trial of Turbo XML can be downloaded at www.tibco.com/products/extensibility/solutions/turbo_xml.html.

Turbo XML supports the W3C XML Schema Recommendations. It includes the following capabilities:

- Writing schema documents using a GUI editor or a text editor
- Checking for well-formed documents
- Testing schema validity
- Generating schema documentation
- Creating XML instance documents based on the schema
- Validating instance documents against schemas
- Transforming documents with XSLT
- Performing batch transformation with XSLT

- Importing and exporting from databases

- Generating a DTD from a database table

- Performing batch validation and conversion

- Converting documents

Turbo XML and XML Spy have similar capabilities, although there are some notable differences in schema documentation, XSLT support, database import, support for batch processing, and file conversion options.

Schema documentation can be created automatically. With a schema document open, choose SchemaDoc from the Tools menu. An HTML document is generated that shows schema components, processing instructions, and number of elements, attributes, and datatypes. An element list and attribute list are presented in diagrams along with documentation that includes a description, attributes, uses, content, type, and source code. The attribute list also includes a list of the elements that use each attribute. The type includes a hyperlink to the appropriate section of the Schema Recommendation. Complex type diagrams are also included. The complex type diagram from the Turbo XML documentation of contact.xsd is shown in Figure 14.5. Unlike XML Spy, Turbo XML does not offer the option of also creating the documentation in Microsoft Word format.

FIGURE 14.5:

Complex Type diagram
from Turbo XML
documentation of
`contact.xsd`

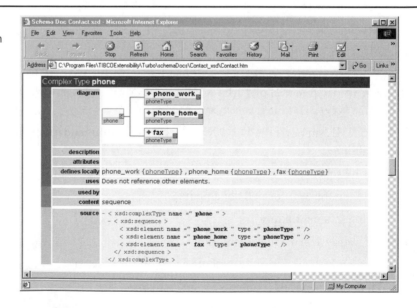

Although Turbo XML includes processing for XSLT, this is only available with a preexisting style sheet. Turbo XML does not include an XSLT editor to generate style sheets. It does support batch transformation of XML files based on a given style sheet and can also do batch validation and conversion.

Turbo XML imports and exports from databases. From the File menu, chose Import ➤ ODBC Table. Next, you're asked to specify the source of the database table. Turbo XML creates a DTD based on the database table. There is no option to create a schema from a database file.

Turbo XML also includes a document conversion tool that can be accessed in two different ways:

- From the File menu, choose Save As. The following document formats are some that are available:
  - DTD
  - W3C Schema
  - XDR schema
  - Biz Talk schema
  - SOX (V2; Schema for Object-oriented XML)
  - OneSoft schema (extended form of XML Data)
  - Oracle iFS schema
  - TAM schema (another form of XML Data schema)
  - MetaSchema (associates additional information with a schema)
- From the File menu, choose Export. The following additional document formats are available, as well as all the choices from the Save As menu:
  - SGML DTD
  - DCD schema
  - DDML (Document Definition Markup Language) schema
  - RELAX schema

When Export is used, the file is converted to the chosen format but the original file is left open and unchanged.

TIP   Several different choices are available in Turbo XML for saving and converting Microsoft schemas: XDR, BizTalk, OneSoft, and TAM. However, when a simple XML Schema document (`contact.xsd`) was converted in Turbo XML to each of these formats (`.xdr`, `.biz`, `.osc`, and `.tam`), the resulting schema documents were identical except for the file extension. All of these formats are based on XML-Data (`www.w3.org/TR/1998/NOTE-XML-data`). For more information on Microsoft's schema initiatives, see Chapter 12.

Turbo XML does not have a formal tutorial, but the Quick Tour and Getting Started choices from the Help menu are basically tutorial files. There's also an extensive Help menu.

More information on Turbo XML is available at `www.tibco.com/products/extensibility/index.html`.

Turbo XML and XML Spy are similar, but they have enough differences that it warrants a close comparison to see which features are important to you if you're considering an XML editing tool. Neither editor is perfect, and as with HTML editors, the final output often requires some modification. Both are easy to use and do not require a large investment of time before they can be used to create and validate DTDs, schemas, and XML instance documents.

Survey of Available Tools for Alternate Schema Languages

In addition to tools for creating, validating, and converting XML Schema documents, several tools are available for alternate schema languages. We'll review the available tools for the following schema languages:

- RELAX
- TREX
- RELAX NG
- Schematron
- XDR

For more information on alternate schema languages and sample schema documents, see Chapter 12.

RELAX

A RELAX schema is called a RELAX grammar. A conversion tool and several validators are available for RELAX.

RELAX grammars can be generated from DTDs with a conversion tool called DTD2RELAX that can be downloaded at `www.horobi.com/Projects/RELAX/Archive/ DTD2RELAX.html`. It's very easy to use and is available in both a GUI version and a command-line version.

Choose the DTD file to be converted, and then choose either UTF-8 or UTF-16 encoding for the output. The RELAX grammar will be saved in the same folder as the original DTD.

XML documents can be validated against a RELAX grammar using a RELAX validator or using Turbo XML. RELAX validators are available in Java, C++, Visual Basic, and XSLT.

You can download a validator (also called a *verifier*) for RELAX from the following pages:

- Java verifier at `http://groups.yahoo.com/group/reldeve/files/Verifier%20for%20Java`

- C++ verifier at `www.egroups.com/files/reldeve/relaxInCpp.zip`

- Visual Basic verifier at `www.geocities.co.jp/SiliconValley-Bay/4639/vbrelaxen.htm`

- XSLT verifier at `www.geocities.co.jp/SiliconValley-Bay/4639/intro.htm`

TREX

A TREX schema specifies a pattern for an XML document and supports validation of documents that match the pattern. A style sheet for converting RELAX schema to TREX schema and a Java validator are available.

An XSLT style sheet for converting a RELAX grammar to a TREX schema is available at `www.thaiopensource.com/trex/from-relax.xsl`. Save this XSL file and then use Saxon or Instant Saxon from a command prompt to convert the RELAX document to a TREX document.

In this example, the RELAX document is `contact.rlx`. To convert this document, you'd type the following, for example:

```
C:\cd InstantSaxon
saxon contact.rlx from-relax.xsl
```

A complete TREX schema is displayed in the command window after the conversion.

For more information on which processors can be used with this style sheet, see the TREX home page at `www.thaiopensource.com/trex`.

A Java implementation to validate TREX is available at `www.thaiopensource.com/trex/ jtrex.html`. There are two versions available for download, a JAR file for use with parsers that implement SAX and a Win32 executable file.

To use the Win32 file to validate an instance document, run the TREX validator from the command window by typing the following, for example:

```
C:\ cd TREX
trex contact_relax.trex contact_tr.xml
```

In this example, the TREX schema is `contact_relax.trex` and the instance document is `contact_tr.xml`. The validator will generate a list of errors or, if the file validates, a message like this:

```
C:\ cd TREX
trex contact_relax.trex contact_tr.xml
Elapsed time 219 milliseconds
```

For more information on using the TREX validator, see the download page at `www.thaiopensource.com/trex/jtrex.html`.

RELAX NG

RELAX NG is a schema language based on RELAX and TREX. A conversion tool, a style sheet for converting RELAX schema to RELAX NG schema, and several validators are available.

DTDinst is a conversion tool for converting DTDs to XML instance format; it's also capable of converting DTDs to RELAX NG format. DTDinst allows you to handle parameter entities and convert them into higher-level semantic constructs. DTDinst is available for download as a JAR file at `www.thaiopensource.com/dtdinst`. A Java runtime environment must be installed on your system for you to use DTDinst.

An XSLT style sheet for converting a RELAX grammar to a RELAX NG schema is available at `www.thaiopensource.com/relaxng/from-relax.xsl`. Save this XSL file, and then use Saxon or Instant Saxon by typing the following, for example, at the command prompt to convert the RELAX document to a RELAX NG document:

```
C:\cd InstantSaxon
saxon contact.rlx from-relax-ng.xsl
```

In this example, the RELAX document is contact.rlx, and the XSLT style sheet has been renamed `from-relax-ng.xsl`. A complete RELAX NG schema is displayed in the command window after the conversion.

A Java implementation to validate RELAX NG is available at `www.thaiopensource.com/relaxng/jing.html`. There are two versions available for download, a JAR file for use with parsers that implement SAX and a Win32 executable file.

To use the Win32 file to validate an instance document, use the Jing validator from the command window by typing the following, for example:

```
C:\cd jing
jing contact.rng contact_ng.xml
```

In this example, the RELAX NG document is `contact.rng` and the instance document is `contact_ng.xml`. For more information on using the Jing validator, see the download page.

A Visual Basic validator is also available for RELAX NG and can be downloaded at `www.geocities.co.jp/SiliconValley-Bay/4639/vbrelaxng/vbrelaxng.html`.

The Sun Multi-Schema XML Validator can be used to validate RELAX NG schemas as well as RELAX, TREX, DTDs, and a subset of XML Schema Part 1. It's a Java technology and is accessed via a command prompt. The Sun validator can be downloaded at `www.sun.com/software/xml/developers/multischema`. Registration is required but the download is free.

The RELAX NG Project at Source Forge is a space for test cases and other software related to RELAX NG. It can be viewed at `http://sourceforge.net/projects/relaxng`.

Schematron

Schematron is a structural-based schema language rather than a grammar-based schema language such as W3C XML Schema, RELAX, TREX, or RELAX NG. It validates patterns of relationship between items. Schematron schema can be validated using Saxon or Instant Saxon and Schematron XSL files. The Schematron XSL files can be downloaded at `www.ascc.net/xml/schematron`. Complete instructions for validating Schematron files using Saxon or Instant Saxon are shown in the Schematron section of Chapter 12.

Schematron schema can also be validated using the Topologi Schematron Validator. It's available for free download at `www.topologi.com/default.htm`. The latest version, released on October 25, 2001, uses the Microsoft XML Core Services 4 RTM.

XDR

XML-Data Reduced (XDR) schema language is a part of Microsoft's BizTalk Framework. An XSLT style sheet, a browser tool, and a validator are available for XDR schema.

The XDR-XSD Converter is an XSLT style sheet for converting XDR schema to XML Schema documents. However, the XML Schema documents are based on the October 2000 Candidate Recommendation. As with other converters, additional modifications will be needed in the resulting file. The style sheet can be downloaded at `http://msdn.microsoft.com/downloads/default.asp?URL=/code/sample.asp?url=/msdn-files/027/001/539/msdncompositedoc.xml`.

A tool is available for Internet Explorer that offers the options of validating XML and viewing XSL output when viewing an XML file in Internet Explorer. This tool enables both of these options to be accessible if you right-click on the document in the Internet Explorer browser. This tool can be downloaded at `http://msdn.microsoft.com/downloads/default .asp?URL=/code/sample.asp?url=/MSDN-FILES/027/000/543/msdncompositedoc.xml`.

XDR Schema can be validated using the Microsoft XML Core Services 4 RTM, as discussed earlier in this chapter in the section "XML Schema Validators." MSXML 3 does not support XML Schema, but Microsoft XML Core Services 4 RTM offers almost total support.

Other Tools and Resources for Schema Development

The W3C XML Schema page at `www.w3.org/XML/Schema` is frequently updated and includes a list of the latest tools for XML Schema, including validating parsers, conversion tools, and an assortment of other XML Schema tools.

Robin Cover's XML Schema page is an excellent resource for the latest news and tools for XML Schema and alternate schema languages. The main page can be viewed at `www .oasis-open.org/cover/schemas.html`. The schema section of the site includes subsections on the following:

- XML Schema
- XDR
- DCD
- SOX
- DDML
- Schematron
- Datatypes for DTDs
- DSD
- RELAX
- TREX
- Schematron
- RELAX NG
- Examplotron
- Hook
- DSDL

Additional schema processors and tools are available on the XMLSOFTWARE site at www.xmlsoftware.com/T988979103.851.

The IBM developerWorks site includes an extensive collection of articles on XML. A recent series of articles focuses on XML tools for developers and includes XML tools for C/C++, Java, Perl, and PHP Hypertext Processor (PHP). IBM's developerWorks site can be viewed at www-106.ibm.com/developerworks. For the series of articles on XML tools, see the following:

- "C/C++ Developers: Fill Your XML Toolbox" at www-106.ibm.com/developerworks/xml/library/x-ctlbx.html

- "Java Developers: Fill Your XML Toolbox" at www-106.ibm.com/developerworks/xml/library/java-xml-toolkit/index.html

- "Perl Developers: Fill Your XML Toolbox" at www-106.ibm.com/developerworks/xml/library/perl-xml-toolkit/index.html

- "PHP Developers: Fill Your XML Toolbox" at www-106.ibm.com/developerworks/xml/library/php-xml-toolkit.html

Summary

Schema development is still rapidly changing. Both the XML Schema language and the alternate schema languages are in development, as well as the corresponding validators and tools.

XML Schema has the largest group of tools of any of the schema languages, including at least five validating parsers. XML Schema's strong support for datatypes and for user-derived datatypes is not currently matched by any other schema language, so it would be expected to continue in the forefront of schema development. Other languages (notably RELAX NG and Schematron), however, offer capabilities not available in the current W3C XML Schema Recommendation. Relax NG supports most features of XML Schema and adds additional features that are not supported in XML Schema. Schematron is the only schema language so far that supports co-constraints. The conditional assertions available in Schematron are not possible in XML Schema, but they can be embedded in an XML Schema document to combine the capabilities of both languages.

The two XML IDEs, XML Spy and Turbo XML, offer many tools in one package for editing instance documents, editing schemas, validating instance documents, and converting schemas and DTDs from one schema language to another. They're both easy to learn and easy to use. Both support the W3C XML Schema Recommendation and include support for other schema languages.

Validation is a critical step in using XML documents, and several options are available for validating XML instance documents against a schema document. The route you chose to take to validate XML documents depends on the schema language you use for validation and the tools available for that language.

APPENDIX A

Important Specifications and Standards

There are many standards that will help you in your experiences with XML Schema and schemas in general. This appendix gathers references to a plethora of those standards for you.

W3C

The W3C site is your be-all and end-all site for information regarding XML, XML Schema, and other related information. The following are some URLs from the site that you may find helpful:

Extensible Markup Language (XML) 1.0 (Second Edition)
www.w3.org/TR/REC-xml

Modularization of XHTML in XML Schema (Working Draft)
www.w3.org/TR/xhtml-m12n-schema

Namespaces
www.w3.org/TR/REC-xml-names

Resource Description Framework (RDF) Schema Specification 1.0 (Candidate Recommendation)
www.w3.org/TR/2000/CR-rdf-schema-20000327

The Extensible Stylesheet Language (XSL)
www.w3.org/Style/XSL

W3C Scalable Vector Graphics (SVG)
www.w3.org/Graphics/SVG/Overview.htm8

W3C XML Pointer, XML Base and XML Linking
www.w3.org/XML/Linking

XForms—The Next Generation of Web Forms
www.w3.org/MarkUp/Forms

XHTML 1.1—Module-based XHTML
www.w3.org/TR/xhtml11

XHTML Basic
www.w3.org/TR/xhtml-basic

XHTML 1.0: The Extensible HyperText Markup Language
www.w3.org/TR/xhtml1

XML Base
www.w3.org/TR/xmlbase

XML Linking Language (XLink) Version 1.0
www.w3.org/TR/xlink

XML Path Language (XPath) Version 1.0
www.w3.org/TR/xpath

XML Pointer Language (XPointer) Version 1.0
www.w3.org/TR/xptr

XML Schema Part 0: Primer
www.w3.org/TR/xmlschema-0

XML Schema Part 1: Structures
www.w3.org/TR/xmlschema-1

XML Schema Part 2: Datatypes
www.w3.org/TR/xmlschema-2

XML Schema
www.w3.org/XML/Schema

XSL Transformations (XSLT) Version 1.0
www.w3.org/TR/xslt

ISO

The International Organization for Standardization (ISO) is home of many standards, including ones related to XML. On the ISO Web site (www.iso.org), enter the site, click the Standards search link, and search for the ISO number to access these standards:

- ISO 8879:1986: Standard Generalized Markup Language (SGML)
- ISO 8859: ISO-Latin-X standards
- ISO 646: ISO 7-bit coded character set for information interchange

- ISO 8601: Representations of dates and times
- ISO 8601 Draft Revision: Representations of dates and times, draft revision, 2000

IETF

The Internet Engineering Task Force (IETF) also includes some helpful standards:

IANA-LANGCODES
IANA (Internet Assigned Numbers Authority) Registry of Language Tags
`www.isi.edu/in-notes/iana/assignments/languages`

IETF RFC 2141
RFC 2141: URN Syntax
`www.ietf.org/rfc/rfc2141.txt`

IETF RFC 2279
RFC 2279: UTF-8, a transformation format of ISO 10646
`www.ietf.org/rfc/rfc2279.txt`

IETF RFC 2376
RFC 2376: XML Media Types
`www.ietf.org/rfc/rfc2376.txt`

IETF RFC 2396
RFC 2396: Uniform Resource Identifiers (URI): Generic Syntax
`www.ietf.org/rfc/rfc2396.txt`

IETF RFC 2732
RFC 2732: Format for Literal IPv6 Addresses in URLs
`www.ietf.org/rfc/rfc2732.txt`

Schema Alternatives

The following are references to alternative schema language standards:

Schematron
`www.ascc.net/xml/resource/schematron/schematron.html`

REgular LAnguage Descriptions for XML Next Generation (RELAX NG)
www.oasis-open.org/committees/relax-ng/index.shtml

Examplotron
www.examplotron.org

DTD for XML Schema: Structures

The DTD for XML Schema: Structures is provided in this appendix. Note that there is *no* implication here that the schema element must be the root element of a document.

Although this DTD is nonnormative, any XML document that does not validate against it is most likely not a valid schema document. The only exceptions would be documents with multiple namespace prefixes for the XML Schema namespace itself. Accordingly, the following are sensible development strategies that users are encouraged to adopt until XML Schema-based authoring tools and validators are more widely available:

- Authoring XML Schema documents using this DTD and DTD-based authoring tools

- Specifying this DTD as the DOCTYPE of documents intended to be XML Schema documents and validating those documents with a validating XML parser

This document is reproduced from the W3C site at www.w3.org/TR/1999/ WD-xmlschema-1-19991217/structures.html.

Listing B:1	DTD for XML Schema: Structures

Copyright ©1999 W3C® (MIT, INRIA, Keio), All Rights Reserved. W3C liability, trademark, document use and software licensing rules apply.

```
<!-- DTD for XML Schemas: Part 1: Structures
     Public Identifier: "-//W3C//DTD XMLSCHEMA 200102//EN"
   Official Location: http://www.w3.org/2001/XMLSchema.dtd -->
<!-- Id: XMLSchema.dtd,v 1.30 2001/03/16 15:23:02 ht Exp  -->
<!-- With the exception of cases with multiple namespace
     prefixes for the XML Schema namespace, any XML document
     which is not valid per this DTD given redefinitions in its
     internal subset of the 'p' and 's' parameter entities below
     appropriate to its namespace declaration of the XML Schema
     namespace is almost certainly not a valid schema. -->

<!-- The simpleType element and its constituent parts are
     defined in XML Schema: Part 2: Datatypes -->
<!ENTITY % xs-datatypes PUBLIC 'datatypes' 'datatypes.dtd' >

<!-- the following can be overriden in the internal subset of
     a schema document to establish a different namespace
     prefix -->
<!ENTITY % p 'xs:'>

<!-- if %p is defined (e.g. as foo:) then you must also define
     %s as the suffix for the appropriate namespace declaration
     (e.g. :foo) -->
<!ENTITY % s ':xs'>

<!ENTITY % nds 'xmlns%s;'>

<!-- Define all the element names, with optional prefix -->
<!ENTITY % schema "%p;schema">
```

```
<!ENTITY % complexType "%p;complexType">
<!ENTITY % complexContent "%p;complexContent">
<!ENTITY % simpleContent "%p;simpleContent">
<!ENTITY % extension "%p;extension">
<!ENTITY % element "%p;element">
<!ENTITY % unique "%p;unique">
<!ENTITY % key "%p;key">
<!ENTITY % keyref "%p;keyref">
<!ENTITY % selector "%p;selector">
<!ENTITY % field "%p;field">
<!ENTITY % group "%p;group">
<!ENTITY % all "%p;all">
<!ENTITY % choice "%p;choice">
<!ENTITY % sequence "%p;sequence">
<!ENTITY % any "%p;any">
<!ENTITY % anyAttribute "%p;anyAttribute">
<!ENTITY % attribute "%p;attribute">
<!ENTITY % attributeGroup "%p;attributeGroup">
<!ENTITY % include "%p;include">
<!ENTITY % import "%p;import">
<!ENTITY % redefine "%p;redefine">
<!ENTITY % notation "%p;notation">

<!-- annotation elements -->
<!ENTITY % annotation "%p;annotation">
<!ENTITY % appinfo "%p;appinfo">
<!ENTITY % documentation "%p;documentation">

<!-- Customization entities for the ATTLIST of each element
     type. Define one of these if your schema takes advantage
     of the anyAttribute='##other' in the schema for
     schemas -->

<!ENTITY % schemaAttrs ''>
<!ENTITY % complexTypeAttrs ''>
<!ENTITY % complexContentAttrs ''>
<!ENTITY % simpleContentAttrs ''>
<!ENTITY % extensionAttrs ''>
<!ENTITY % elementAttrs ''>
<!ENTITY % groupAttrs ''>
<!ENTITY % allAttrs ''>
<!ENTITY % choiceAttrs ''>
<!ENTITY % sequenceAttrs ''>
<!ENTITY % anyAttrs ''>
<!ENTITY % anyAttributeAttrs ''>
<!ENTITY % attributeAttrs ''>
<!ENTITY % attributeGroupAttrs ''>
<!ENTITY % uniqueAttrs ''>
<!ENTITY % keyAttrs ''>
<!ENTITY % keyrefAttrs ''>
<!ENTITY % selectorAttrs ''>
<!ENTITY % fieldAttrs ''>
<!ENTITY % includeAttrs ''>
```

```
<!ENTITY % importAttrs ''>
<!ENTITY % redefineAttrs ''>
<!ENTITY % notationAttrs ''>
<!ENTITY % annotationAttrs ''>
<!ENTITY % appinfoAttrs ''>
<!ENTITY % documentationAttrs ''>

<!ENTITY % complexDerivationSet "CDATA">
<!-- #all or space-separated list drawn from
     derivationChoice -->

<!ENTITY % blockSet "CDATA">
<!-- #all or space-separated list drawn from derivationChoice
     + 'substitution' -->

<!ENTITY % mgs '%all; | %choice; | %sequence;'>
<!ENTITY % cs '%choice; | %sequence;'>
<!ENTITY % formValues '(qualified|unqualified)'>


<!ENTITY % attrDecls    '((%attribute;| %attributeGroup;)*,(%anyAttribute;)?)'>

<!ENTITY % particleAndAttrs '((%mgs; | %group;)?,
   %attrDecls;)'>

<!-- This is used in part2 -->
<!ENTITY % restriction1 '((%mgs; | %group;)?)'>

%xs-datatypes;

<!-- the duplication below is to produce an unambiguous
     content model which allows annotation everywhere -->
<!ELEMENT %schema; ((%include; | %import; | %redefine; | %annotation;)*,
                   ((%simpleType; | %complexType;
                    | %element; | %attribute;
                    | %attributeGroup; | %group;
                    | %notation; ),
                   (%annotation;)*)* )>

<!ATTLIST %schema;
   targetNamespace        %URIref;              #IMPLIED
   version                CDATA                 #IMPLIED
   %nds;                  %URIref;              #FIXED
      'http://www.w3.org/2001/XMLSchema'
   xmlns                  CDATA                 #IMPLIED
   finalDefault           %complexDerivationSet; ''
   blockDefault           %blockSet;             ''
   id                     ID                    #IMPLIED
   elementFormDefault     %formValues;          'unqualified'
   attributeFormDefault   %formValues;          'unqualified'
   xml:lang               CDATA                 #IMPLIED
   %schemaAttrs;>
```

```
<!-- Note the xmlns declaration is NOT in the Schema for
     Schemas,because at the Infoset level where schemas
     operate, xmlns(:prefix) is NOT an attribute! -->

<!-- The declaration of xmlns is a convenience for schema
     authors -->

<!-- The id attribute here and below is for use in external
     references from non-schemas using simple fragment
     identifiers. It is NOT used for schema-to-schema
     reference, internal or external. -->

<!-- a type is a named content type specification which
     allows attribute declarations-->
<!-- -->

<!ELEMENT %complexType; ((%annotation;)?,
                         (%simpleContent;|%complexContent;|
                          %particleAndAttrs;))>

<!ATTLIST %complexType;
          name %NCName; #IMPLIED
          id   ID #IMPLIED
          abstract %boolean; #IMPLIED
          final %complexDerivationSet; #IMPLIED
          block %complexDerivationSet; #IMPLIED
          mixed (true|false)'false'
          %complexTypeAttrs;
>

<!-- particleAndAttrs is shorthand for a root type -->

<!-- mixed is disallowed if simpleContent, overriden if
     complexContent has one too. -->

<!-- If anyAttribute appears in one or more referenced
     attributeGroups and/or explicitly, the intersection of
     the permissions is used -->

<!ELEMENT %complexContent; (%restriction;|%extension;)>
<!ATTLIST %complexContent;
          mixed (true|false) #IMPLIED
          id    ID            #IMPLIED
          %complexContentAttrs;>

<!-- restriction should use the branch defined above, not
     the simple one from part2; extension should use the full
     model  -->

<!ELEMENT %simpleContent; (%restriction;|%extension;)>
<!ATTLIST %simpleContent;
```

```
              id     ID              #IMPLIED
         %simpleContentAttrs;>

<!-- restriction should use the simple branch from part2,
     not the one defined above; extension should have no
     particle -->

<!ELEMENT %extension; (%particleAndAttrs;)>
<!ATTLIST %extension;
          base  %QName;       #REQUIRED
          id    ID            #IMPLIED
          %extensionAttrs;>

<!-- an element is declared by either: a name and a type
     (either nested or referenced via the type attribute)
     or a ref to an existing element declaration -->

<!ELEMENT %element; ((%annotation;)?, (%complexType;| %simpleType;)?,
   (%unique; | %key; | %keyref;)*)>
<!-- simpleType or complexType only if no type|ref attribute -->
<!-- ref not allowed at top level -->
<!ATTLIST %element;
             name %NCName;            #IMPLIED
             id    ID                 #IMPLIED
             ref  %QName;             #IMPLIED
             type %QName;             #IMPLIED
             minOccurs  %nonNegativeInteger; #IMPLIED
             maxOccurs  CDATA             #IMPLIED
             nillable   %boolean;         #IMPLIED
             substitutionGroup  %QName;   #IMPLIED
             abstract   %boolean;         #IMPLIED
             final      %complexDerivationSet; #IMPLIED
             block      %blockSet;        #IMPLIED
             default    CDATA             #IMPLIED
             fixed      CDATA             #IMPLIED
             form       %formValues;      #IMPLIED
             %elementAttrs;
>

<!-- type and ref are mutually exclusive.
     name and ref are mutually exclusive, one is required -->
<!-- In the absence of type AND ref, type defaults to type of
     substitutionGroup, if any, else the ur-type, i.e.
     unconstrained -->
<!-- default and fixed are mutually exclusive -->

<!ELEMENT %group; ((%annotation;)?,(%mgs;)?)>
<!ATTLIST %group;
          name         %NCName;                #IMPLIED
          ref          %QName;                 #IMPLIED
          minOccurs    %nonNegativeInteger;    #IMPLIED
```

```
         maxOccurs    CDATA                  #IMPLIED
         id           ID                     #IMPLIED
         %groupAttrs;
>

<!ELEMENT %all; ((%annotation;)?, (%element;)*)>
<!ATTLIST %all;
         minOccurs    (1)                    #IMPLIED
         maxOccurs    (1)                    #IMPLIED
         id           ID                     #IMPLIED
         %allAttrs;>

<!ELEMENT %choice; ((%annotation;)?,
   (%element;| %group;| %cs; | %any;)*)>
<!ATTLIST %choice;
         minOccurs    %nonNegativeInteger;   #IMPLIED
         maxOccurs    CDATA                  #IMPLIED
         id           ID                     #IMPLIED
         %choiceAttrs;
>

<!ELEMENT %sequence; ((%annotation;)?,
   (%element;| %group;| %cs; | %any;)*)>
<!ATTLIST %sequence;
         minOccurs    %nonNegativeInteger;   #IMPLIED
         maxOccurs    CDATA                  #IMPLIED
         id           ID                     #IMPLIED
         %sequenceAttrs;
>

<!-- an anonymous grouping in a model, or a top-level named
     group definition, or a reference to same -->

<!-- Note that if order is 'all', group is not allowed inside.
     If order is 'all' THIS group must be alone (or referenced
     alone) at the top level of a content model
-->
<!-- If order is 'all', minOccurs==maxOccurs==1 on element/any
     inside -->
<!-- Should allow minOccurs=0 inside order='all' . . . -->

<!ELEMENT %any; (%annotation;)?>
<!ATTLIST %any;
            namespace       CDATA                  '##any'
            processContents (skip|lax|strict)      'strict'
            minOccurs       %nonNegativeInteger;   '1'
            maxOccurs       CDATA                  '1'
            id              ID                     #IMPLIED
            %anyAttrs;>

<!-- namespace is interpreted as follows:
        ##any  - - any non-conflicting WFXML at all
```

```
      ##other  - - any non-conflicting WFXML from namespace
      other than targetNamespace

      ##local  - - any unqualified non-conflicting
       WFXML/attribute one or - - any non-conflicting
       WFXML from more URI the listed namespaces references

      ##targetNamespace ##local may appear in the above list,
        with the obvious meaning -->

<!ELEMENT %anyAttribute; (%annotation;)?>
<!ATTLIST %anyAttribute;
          namespace        CDATA              '##any'
          processContents (skip|lax|strict)  'strict'
          id               ID                 #IMPLIED
          %anyAttributeAttrs;
>

<!-- namespace is interpreted as for 'any' above -->
<!-- simpleType only if no type|ref attribute -->
<!-- ref not allowed at top level, name if at top level -->

<!ELEMENT %attribute; ((%annotation;)?, (%simpleType;)?)>
<!ATTLIST %attribute;
          name     %NCName;      #IMPLIED
          id       ID            #IMPLIED
          ref      %QName;       #IMPLIED
          type     %QName;       #IMPLIED
          use      (prohibited|optional|required) #IMPLIED
          default  CDATA         #IMPLIED
          fixed    CDATA         #IMPLIED
          form     %formValues;  #IMPLIED
          %attributeAttrs;>
<!-- type and ref are mutually exclusive.
     name and ref are mutually exclusive, one is required
-->
<!-- default for use is optional when nested, none
     otherwise -->
<!-- default and fixed are mutually exclusive -->
<!-- type attr and simpleType content are mutually
     exclusive -->

<!-- an attributeGroup is a named collection of attribute
     decls, or a reference there to -->

<!ELEMENT %attributeGroup; ((%annotation;)?,
                   (%attribute; | %attributeGroup;)*,
                   (%anyAttribute;)?) >
<!ATTLIST %attributeGroup;
               name     %NCName;    #IMPLIED
               id       ID          #IMPLIED
               ref      %QName;     #IMPLIED
          %attributeGroupAttrs;>
```

```
<!-- ref if no content, no name.  ref if not top level -->

<!-- better reference mechanisms -->
<!ELEMENT %unique; ((%annotation;)?, %selector;, (%field;)+)>
<!ATTLIST %unique;
          name   %NCName;       #REQUIRED
          id     ID             #IMPLIED
          %uniqueAttrs;
>

<!ELEMENT %key;  ((%annotation;)?, %selector;, (%field;)+)>
<!ATTLIST %key;
          name   %NCName;       #REQUIRED
          id     ID             #IMPLIED
          %keyAttrs;
>

<!ELEMENT %keyref; ((%annotation;)?, %selector;, (%field;)+)>
<!ATTLIST %keyref;
          name    %NCName;       #REQUIRED
          refer   %QName;        #REQUIRED
          id      ID             #IMPLIED
          %keyrefAttrs;
>

<!ELEMENT %selector; ((%annotation;)?)>
<!ATTLIST %selector;
          xpath %XPathExpr; #REQUIRED
          id    ID          #IMPLIED
          %selectorAttrs;
>
<!ELEMENT %field; ((%annotation;)?)>
<!ATTLIST %field;
          xpath %XPathExpr; #REQUIRED
          id    ID          #IMPLIED
          %fieldAttrs;
>

<!-- Schema combination mechanisms -->
<!ELEMENT %include; (%annotation;)?>
<!ATTLIST %include;
          schemaLocation %URIref; #REQUIRED
          id             ID       #IMPLIED
          %includeAttrs;
>

<!ELEMENT %import; (%annotation;)?>
<!ATTLIST %import;
          namespace       %URIref; #IMPLIED
          schemaLocation %URIref; #IMPLIED
          id              ID       #IMPLIED
```

```
            %importAttrs;
>

<!ELEMENT %redefine; (%annotation; | %simpleType; |
    %complexType; | %attributeGroup; | %group;)*>
<!ATTLIST %redefine;
          schemaLocation %URIref; #REQUIRED
          id              ID       #IMPLIED
          %redefineAttrs;
>

<!ELEMENT %notation; (%annotation;)?>
<!ATTLIST %notation;
          name        %NCName;    #REQUIRED
          id          ID          #IMPLIED
          public      CDATA       #REQUIRED
          system      %URIref;    #IMPLIED
          %notationAttrs;
>

<!-- Annotation is either application information or
     documentation -->
<!-- By having these here they are available for datatypes as
     well as all the structures elements -->

<!ELEMENT %annotation; (%appinfo; | %documentation;)*>
<!ATTLIST %annotation; %annotationAttrs;>

<!-- User must define annotation elements in internal subset
     for this to work -->
<!ELEMENT %appinfo; ANY>   <!-- too restrictive -->
<!ATTLIST %appinfo;
          source    %URIref;     #IMPLIED
          id        ID           #IMPLIED
          %appinfoAttrs;
>
<!ELEMENT %documentation; ANY>   <!-- too restrictive -->
<!ATTLIST %documentation;
          source    %URIref;   #IMPLIED
          id        ID         #IMPLIED
          xml:lang  CDATA      #IMPLIED
          %documentationAttrs;>

<!NOTATION XMLSchemaStructures PUBLIC
       'structures' http://www.w3.org/2001/XMLSchema.xsd' >
<!NOTATION XML PUBLIC
       'REC-xml-1998-0210'
       'http://www.w3.org/TR/1998/REC-xml-19980210' >
```

APPENDIX C

XML Schema Components and Datatypes

This appendix provides you with a guide to the XML Schema language. The following are defined:

XML Schema elements   An alphabetical listing of all elements (and their attributes)

XML Schema facets   An alphabetical listing of all facets (and their attributes)

XML Schema datatypes   An alphabetical listing of all built-in datatypes

XML Schema Elements

This section includes all the XML Schema elements defined by XML Schema Part 1: Structures. For each element, you'll find the following:

- Description
- Attributes
- Context (content model and allowable parent[s])
- Example

  The Structures recommendation can be found at `www.w3.org/TR/xmlschema-1`.

all

The `all` element defines an unordered group of elements. It's a child of a `complexType` or `group` element and may include `element` or `annotation` elements.

Attributes

Attribute Name	Value Space	Default Value	Required	Description
id	ID			Defines a unique identifier for the element.
maxOccurs	1	1		Defines the maximum number of times the model group can occur.
minOccurs	0 | 1	1		Defines the minimum number of times the model group can occur.

Context

Content Model: `(annotation?, element*)`

Allowable Parents: `complexType, group`

Example

```
<xsd:element name="publications">
  <xsd:complexType>
    <xsd:sequence>
      <xsd:element name="book" minOccurs="0"
        maxOccurs="unbounded">
        <xsd:complexType>
          <xsd:all>
            <xsd:element name="title" type="xsd:string"/>
            <xsd:element name="author" type="xsd:string"/>
          </xsd:all>
        </xsd:complexType>
      </xsd:element>
    </xsd:sequence>
  </xsd:complexType>
</xsd:element>
```

annotation

The annotation element is the container element for comment-related elements, such as appInfo and documentation. The appInfo element defines information intended for an application, whereas the documentation element defines information for human consumption. You can use the annotation element to add comments to your schema document. Annotations can be defined at the top level, under the schema element, as well as within almost every other schema component. Although XML Schema defines these constructions, the specification does not define how this information should be interpreted.

Attributes

Attribute Name	Value Space	Default Value	Required	Description
id	ID			Defines a unique identifier for the element.

Context

Content Model:	(appinfo | documentation)*
Allowable Parents:	all, any, anyAttribute, attribute, attributeGroup, choice, complexContent, complexType, element, enumeration, extension, field, group, import, include, key, keyref, length, list, maxExclusive, maxInclusive, maxLength, minExclusive, minInclusive, minLength, notation, pattern, restriction, schema, selector, sequence, simpleContent, simpleType, union, unique

Example

```
<xsd:element name="book">
  <xsd:annotation>
    <xsd:documentation>
       The content models for child elements are defined
       using named complex types
    </xsd:documentation>
  </xsd:annotation>
  <xsd:complexType>
    <xsd:sequence>
      <xsd:element name="title" type="titleType"/>
      <xsd:element name="description" type="descType"/>
    </xsd:sequence>
  </xsd:complexType>
</xsd:element>
```

any

The any element is a wildcard used as a placeholder for other elements in a content model. The content defined may be validated against any namespace. Using the namespace attribute, you can define the target namespace for the content. This is helpful when you need to include elements for another language within your document model.

Attributes

Attribute Name	Value Space	Default Value	Required	Description
id	*ID*			Defines a unique identifier for the element.
maxOccurs	*nonNegative Integer* | unbounded	1		Defines the maximum number of times the model group can occur.
minOccurs	*nonNegative Integer*	1		Defines the minimum number of times the model group can occur.

namespace	(##any | ##other) | List of (*anyURI* | (##target- Namespace | ##local))	##any	##any: content may belong to any namespace. ##other: content may belong to any namespace other than the target namespace. ##tar- getNamespace: element belongs to the target name- space. ##local: element doesn't belong to any namespace. Otherwise, you can include the URI of a namespace.
processContents	lax | skip | strict	strict	strict: validation is required, and a declaration must be found. skip: no validation necessary; the element must simply be well formed. lax: element is validated if possible.

Context

Content Model: (annotation?)

Allowable Parents: choice, sequence

Example

```
<xsd:element name="pubs">
   <xsd:complexType>
     <xsd:sequence>
       <xsd:any namespace="http://www.namespace.com"
          minOccurs="0" maxOccurs="unbounded"
          processContents="lax"/>
     </xsd:sequence>
   </xsd:complexType>
</xsd:element>
```

anyAttribute

The anyAttribute element is a wildcard used as a placeholder for other attributes in a content model. The content defined may be validated against any namespace. Using the namespace attribute, you can define the target namespace for the content. This is helpful when
you need to include attributes for another language within your document model.

Attributes

Attribute Name	Value Space	Default Value	Required	Description
id	*ID*			Defines a unique identifier for the element.
maxOccurs	*nonNegative-Integer* | unbounded	1		Defines the maximum number of times the model group can occur.
minOccurs	*nonNegative-Integer*	1		Defines the minimum number of times the model group can occur.
namespace	(##any | ##other) | List of (*anyURI* | (##target-Namespace | ##local))	##any		##any: content may belong to any namespace. ##other: content may belong to any namespace other than the target namespace. ##target-Namespace: content belongs to the target namespace. ##local: content doesn't belong to any namespace. Otherwise, you can include the URI of a namespace.
processContents	lax | skip | strict	strict		strict: validation is required, and a declaration must be found. skip: no validation necessary; the content must simply be well formed. lax: content is validated if possible.

Context

Content Model: (annotation?)

Allowable Parents: attributeGroup, complexType, extension

Example

```
<xsd:element name="pubs">
  <xsd:complexType>
    <xsd:sequence>
      <xsd:any namespace="http://www.namespace.com"
        minOccurs="0" maxOccurs="unbounded"
        processContents="lax"/>
    </xsd:sequence>
      <xsd:anyAttribute
        namespace="http://www.namespace.com"/>
  </xsd:complexType>
</xsd:element>
```

appInfo

The appInfo element defines information intended for the processing application. This defined information does not affect schema validation.

Attributes

Attribute Name	Value Space	Default Value	Required	Description
source	*anyURI*			Defines the URI location that contains additional appInfo information.

Context

Content Model:	{any}
Allowable Parent:	annotation

Example

```
<xsd:annotation>
  <xsd:appInfo>
    <!-- instruction for processor go here. Content
      may include non schema elements -->
  </xsd:appInfo>
</xsd:annotation>
```

attribute

An attribute declaration (specified by the attribute element) defines the attribute name, occurrence information, and (optionally) a default value. Attribute declarations are commonly defined as an attributeGroup or as a part of a complexType. Declarations may include or reference simpleType definitions that derive a new datatype.

Attributes

Attribute Name	Value Space	Default Value	Required	Description
default	*string*			Defines a default value that is used if attribute is omitted from the document instance.
fixed	*string*			Defines a fixed value for the attribute.
form	qualified | unqualified			qualified: attribute must be namespace qualified. unqualified: attribute is not namespace qualified.
id	*ID*			Defines a unique identifier for the element.
name	*NCName*			Defines the name for the attribute.
ref	*QName*			References a predefined attribute.
type	*QName*			Identifies a named datatype.
use	optional | prohibited | required	optional		optional: attribute is not required to occur. prohibited: attribute cannot be used. required: attribute is required to occur.

Context

Content Model: (annotation? , (simpleType?))

Allowable Parents: attributeGroup, complexType, extension, schema

Example

```
<xsd:element name="img" minOccurs="1" maxOccurs="unbounded">
   <xsd:complexType>
     <xsd:attribute name="href" type="uriReference"
       use="required"/>
   </xsd:complexType>
</xsd:element>
```

attributeGroup

The `attributeGroup` element defines a group of attributes. An attribute group definition is an association between a name and a set of attribute declarations, enabling reuse of the same set in several complex type definitions.

Attributes

Attribute Name	Value Space	Default Value	Required	Description
id	ID			Defines a unique identifier for the element.
name	NCName			Defines the name for the attribute group.
ref	QName			References other named attribute groups.

Context

Content Model: (annotation?, ((attribute | attributeGroup)*, anyAttribute?))

Allowable Parents: attributeGroup, complexType, extension, redefine, schema

Example

```
<xsd:attributeGroup name="commonAttributes">
   <xsd:attribute name="title" type="xsd:string"/>
   <xsd:attribute name="id" type="xsd:ID"/>
   <xsd:attribute name="style" type="xsd:string"/>
</xsd:attributeGroup>
```

choice

The `choice` element is a compositor that, when used, allows for a choice in a content model. It allows the author to choose from one of the contained element declarations.

Attributes

Attribute Name	Value Space	Default Value	Required	Description
id	ID			Defines a unique identifier for the element.

maxOccurs	*nonNegative-Integer* | unbounded	1		Defines the maximum number of times the model group can occur.
minOccurs	*nonNegative-Integer*	1		Defines the minimum number of times the model group can occur.

Context

Content Model: `(annotation?, (element | group | choice | sequence | any)*)`

Allowable Parents: `choice, complexType, group, sequence`

Example

```
<xsd:element name="genre">
  <xsd:complexType>
    <xsd:choice>
      <xsd:element name="rock" type="xsd:string" minOccurs="1"
        maxOccurs="1"/>
      <xsd:element name="classical" type="xsd:string" minOccurs="1"
        maxOccurs="1"/>
      <xsd:element name="blues" type="xsd:string" minOccurs="1"
        maxOccurs="1"/>
    </xsd:choice>
  </xsd:complexType>
</xsd:element>
```

complexContent

The `complexContent` element allows authors to extend or restrict a content model. This element is used when authors want to derive new content using extension or restriction methods.

Attributes

Attribute Name	Value Space	Default Value	Required	Description
id	*ID*			Defines a unique identifier for the element.
mixed	*Boolean*			If true, content specified is mixed.

Context

Content Model: `(annotation?, (restriction | extension))`

Allowable Parent: `complexType`

Example

```
<xsd:complexType name="workWeekType">
  <xsd:complexContent>
    <xsd:restriction base="weekType">
      <xsd:element name="Monday" type="xsd:string"/>
      <xsd:element name="Tuesday" type="xsd:string"/>
      <xsd:element name="Wednesday" type="xsd:string"/>
      <xsd:element name="Thursday" type="xsd:string"/>
      <xsd:element name="Friday" type="xsd:string"/>
    </xsd:restriction>
  </xsd:complexContent>
</xsd:complexType>
```

complexType

The complexType element is used to define complex content models. An element is considered a complex type if it contains attributes or child elements. A complex type element can be defined locally (nested within other element declarations) or globally as a named type.

Attributes

Attribute Name	Value Space	Default Value	Required	Description
abstract	*Boolean*	false		When abstract is set equal to true, the complexType element cannot be used to validate an element. To use the complexType element, you would have to derive a type.
block	#all | List of (extension | restriction)			#all: prevents the use of any types derived from the current type in the instance document. Otherwise, the author can block the derivation using either extension or restriction.
final	#all | List of (extension | restriction)			Restricts the derivation of a new type. Functions similarly to the block attribute.

id	ID		Defines a unique identifier for the element.
mixed	Boolean	false	If true, content specified is mixed.
name	NCName		Defines a name for the complexType element.

Context

Content Model: (annotation? , (simpleContent | complexContent | ((group | all | choice |sequence)? , ((attribute | attributeGroup)* , anyAttribute?))))

Allowable Parents: element, redefine, schema

Example

```
<xsd:complexType name="bookType">
  <xsd:sequence>
    <xsd:element name="title" type="xsd:string"/>
    <xsd:element name="author" type="xsd:string"/>
    <xsd:element name="description" type="xsd:string"/>
  </xsd:sequence>
</xsd:complexType>
```

documentation

Similar to an XML comment, the documentation element provides information intended for human consumption.

Attributes

Attribute Name	Value Space	Default Value	Required	Description
source	anyURI			Defines the URI location that contains additional documentation.
xml:lang	language			Defines the language, identified using an RFC 3066 code (i.e., en for English).

Context

Content Model: {any}

Allowable Parent: annotation

Example

```
<xsd:element name="book">
   <xsd:annotation>
     <xsd:documentation>
       The content models for child elements are defined using
          named complex types.
     </xsd:documentation>
   </xsd:annotation>
   <xsd:complexType>
     <xsd:sequence>
       <xsd:element name="title" type="titleType"/>
       <xsd:element name="description" type="descType"/>
     </xsd:sequence>
   </xsd:complexType>
</xsd:element>
```

element

The element element is used for element declarations, which define element names, types, and optionally, a default value and identity constraints. Element declarations can be defined globally and then referenced within a content model, or they can be defined locally within other content models.

Attributes

Attribute Name	Value Space	Default Value	Required	Description
abstract	*Boolean*	false		When abstract is set equal to true, the element can only appear in content models when substitution is allowed.
block	#all | List of (extension | restriction | substitution)			#all: prevents the use of any types derived from the current type in the instance document. Otherwise, the author can block the derivation using either extension or restriction.
default	*string*			Defines a default value that is used if element is omitted

			from the document instance.
final	#all | List of (extension | restriction)		Restricts the derivation of a new type. Functions similarly to the block attribute.
fixed	*string*		Defines a fixed value for the element.
form	qualified | unqualified		qualified: element must be namespace qualified. unqualified: element is not namespace qualified.
id	*ID*		Defines a unique identifier for the element.
maxOccurs	*nonNegative-Integer* | unbounded	1	Defines the maximum number of times the element can occur.
minOccurs	*nonNegative-Integer*	1	Defines the minimum number of times the element can occur.
name	*NCName*		Defines a name for the element.
nillable	*Boolean*	false	If true, the element may have a nil value defined in the instance document.
ref	*QName*		References another element declaration.
substitution-Group	*QName*		If used, the element is a member of the defined substitution group.
type	*QName*		Defines a named datatype.

Context
Content Model: (annotation? , ((simpleType | complexType)? , (key | keyref | unique)*))

Allowable Parents: `all`, `choice`, `schema`, `sequence`

Example

```
<xsd:element name="book">
   <xsd:complexType>
     <xsd:sequence>
       <xsd:element name="title" type="xsd:string"/>
       <xsd:element name="author" type="xsd:string"/>
       <xsd:element name="description" type="xsd:string"/>
     </xsd:sequence>
   </xsd:complexType>
</xsd:element>
```

extension

A type of derivation, the `extension` element allows you to extend a content model. Using this element, you can add an element and/or elements to an existing content model.

Attributes

Attribute Name	Value Space	Default Value	Required	Description
base	*QName*		Yes	Defines the base datatype that is to be extended.
id	*ID*			Defines a unique identifier for the element.

Context

Content Model: `(annotation?, ((attribute | attributeGroup)*, anyAttribute?))`

Allowable Parents: `simpleContent`, `complexContent`

Example

```
<xsd:complexType name="newBookType">
   <xsd:complexContent>
     <xsd:extension base="bookType">
       <xsd:sequence>
         <xsd:element name="description" type="xsd:string"/>
         <xsd:element name="isbn" type="xsd:string"/>
       </xsd:sequence>
     </xsd:extension>
   </xsd:complexContent>
</xsd:complexType>
```

field

The field and selector elements work together as children of a key, keyRef, or unique element. The field element is used to identify the attribute or element field relative to each selected element that has to be unique within the scope of the set of selected elements. The field element uses an xpath attribute that contains an XPath expression to identify a node set.

Attributes

Attribute Name	Value Space	Default Value	Required	Description
id	ID			Defines a unique identifier for the element.
xpath	A subset of an XPath expression		Yes	Defines the node set to which uniqueness is to be applied.

Context

Content Model: (annotation?)

Allowable Parents: simpleContent, complexContent

Example

```
<xsd:key name="bookKey">
    <xsd:selector xpath="publications/book"/>
    <xsd:field xpath="@id"/>
</xsd:key>

<xsd:keyref name="bookRef" refer="bookKey">
    <xsd:selector xpath="publications/review"/>
    <xsd:field xpath="book/@bookRef"/>
</xsd:keyref>
```

group

The group element allows the author to group element declarations. You cannot use this element to group attribute declarations. The group element must be a global definition (as a child of the schema element).

Attributes

Attribute Name	Value Space	Default Value	Required	Description
name	*NCName*			Defines a name for the element group.

Context

Content Model: (annotation?, (all | choice | sequence))

Allowable Parents: choice, complexType, schema, sequence

Example

```
<xsd:group base="bookType">
  <xsd:sequence>
    <xsd:element name="description" type="xsd:string"/>
    <xsd:element name="isbn" type="xsd:string"/>
  </xsd:sequence>
</xsd:group>
```

import

The import element is used to import a schema document from a namespace other than the target namespace.

Attributes

Attribute Name	Value Space	Default Value	Required	Description
id	*ID*			Defines a unique identifier for the element.
schema-Location	*anyURI*		Yes	Defines the location of the schema document.
namespace	*anyURI*			Defines a target namespace for the imported data.

Context

Content Model: (annotation?)

Allowable Parent: schema

Example

```xsd
<xsd:schema
    xmlns:xsd="http://www.w3.org/2001/XMLSchema"
    elementFormDefault="qualified"
    targetNamespace="http://www.lanw.com/namespaces/pub"
    xmlns="http://www.lanw.com/namespaces/pub">

    <xsd:import schemaLocation="http://www.lanw.com/books.xsd"
        namespace="http://www.lanw.com/namespaces/books"/>
</xsd:schema>
```

include

The include element is used to include a schema from the same target namespace.

Attributes

Attribute Name	Value Space	Default Value	Required	Description
id	ID			Defines a unique identifier for the element.
schema-Location	anyURI		Yes	Defines the location of the schema document.

Context

Content Model:	(annotation?)
Allowable Parent:	schema

Example

```xsd
<xsd:schema
    xmlns:xsd="http://www.w3.org/2001/XMLSchema"
    elementFormDefault="qualified"
    targetNamespace="http://www.lanw.com/namespaces/pub"
    xmlns="http://www.lanw.com/namespaces/pub">

    <xsd:include schemaLocation="http://www.lanw.com/books.xsd"/>
</xsd:schema>
```

key

Using the key and keyref elements, you can define relationships between elements. These elements can also take advantage of XPath, thereby allowing you to specify the scope of a uniqueness constraint. The key element functions much like the `unique` element. The `keyref` element is used to reference the key.

Attributes

Attribute Name	Value Space	Default Value	Required	Description
id	*ID*			Defines a unique identifier for the element.
name	*NCName*		Yes	Defines a name for the key.

Context

Content Model: (annotation?, (selector, field+))

Allowable Parent: element

Example

```
<xsd:key name="bookKey">
   <xsd:selector xpath="publications/book"/>
   <xsd:field xpath="@id"/>
</xsd:key>

<xsd:keyref name="bookRef" refer="bookKey">
   <xsd:selector xpath="publications/review"/>
   <xsd:field xpath="book/@bookRef"/>
</xsd:keyref>
```

keyref

Using the key and `keyref` elements, you can define relationships between elements. These elements can also take advantage of XPath, thereby allowing you to specify the scope of a uniqueness constraint. The key element functions much like the `unique` element. The `keyref` element is used to reference the key.

Attributes

Attribute Name	Value Space	Default Value	Required	Description
id	*ID*			Defines a unique identifier for the element.
name	*NCName*		Yes	Defines a name for the key reference.
refer	*QName*		Yes	References a key.

Context

Content Model: `(annotation?, (selector, field+))`

Allowable Parent: `element`

Example

```
<xsd:key name="bookKey">
   <xsd:selector xpath="publications/book"/>
   <xsd:field xpath="@id"/>
</xsd:key>

<xsd:keyref name="bookRef" refer="bookKey">
   <xsd:selector xpath="publications/review"/>
   <xsd:field xpath="book/@bookRef"/>
</xsd:keyref>
```

list

The `list` element creates a datatype that consists of a white-space-separated list of values. The `list` element uses `itemType` to define the base type that is to be used for the list.

Attributes

Attribute Name	Value Space	Default Value	Required	Description
id	ID			Defines a unique identifier for the element.
itemType	QName			Defines the base datatype for the list.

Context

Content Model: `(annotation?, simpleType?)`

Allowable Parent: `simpleType`

Example

```
<xsd:simpleType name="isbnType">
   <xsd:restriction base="xsd:string">
     <xsd:pattern value="[0-9]{10}"/>
   </xsd:restriction>
</xsd:simpleType>

<xsd:simpleType name="isbnTypeList">
   <xsd:list itemType="isbnType"/>
</xsd:simpleType>
```

notation

The notation element is used to declare links to external non-XML data and then associate an external application to handle the non-XML data. XML Schema notations are similar to XML DTD notations.

Attributes

Attribute Name	Value Space	Default Value	Required	Description
id	ID			Defines a unique identifier for the element.
name	NCName		Yes	Identifies the name of the associated NOTATION datatype.
public	anyURI		Yes	Defines a public identifier.
system	anyURI			Defines a system identifier, normally pointing to a processing application.

Context

Content Model: (annotation?)

Allowable Parent: schema

Example

```
<xsd:notation name="jpeg"
    public="image/jpeg" system="viewer.exe"/>

<xsd:element name="picture">
    <xsd:complexType>
      <xsd:simpleContent>
        <xsd:extension base="xsd:hexBinary">
          <xsd:attribute name="pictype">
            <xsd:simpleType>
              <xsd:restriction base="xsd:NOTATION">
                <xsd:enumeration value="jpeg"/>
                <xsd:enumeration value="gif"/>
              </xsd:restriction>
            </xsd:simpleType>
          </xsd:attribute>
        </xsd:extension>
      </xsd:simpleContent>
    </xsd:complexType>
</xsd:element>
```

restriction

The `restriction` element creates a datatype that is a subset of an existing type. You can apply a restriction using facets that limit properties of a datatype. For example, you can use the `maxLength` or `minLength` facets to define the maximum and minimum number of characters allowed for a given datatype. Each datatype has a specifically defined list of allowable facets.

Attributes

Attribute Name	Value Space	Default Value	Required	Description
base	QName			Defines the base datatype.
id	ID			Defines a unique identifier for the element.

Context

Content Model: `(annotation?, (simpleType?, (minExclusive | minInclusive | maxExclusive | maxInclusive | totalDigits | fractionDigits | length | minLength | maxLength | enumeration | whiteSpace | pattern)*))`

Allowable Parent: `simpleType`

Example

```
<xsd:simpleType name="isbnType">
   <xsd:restriction base="xsd:string">
     <xsd:pattern value="[0-9]{10}"/>
   </xsd:restriction>
</xsd:simpleType>
```

schema

The `schema` element is the document (or root) element of a W3C XML Schema document. This element must be the outermost element.

Attributes

Attribute Name	Value Space	Default Value	Required	Description
attribute-FormDefault	qualified | unqualified	unqualified		Defines whether attributes are considered by default to be qualified (in a namespace).

blockDefault	#all	List of (extension | restriction | substitution)		If #all, blocks all derivations of datatypes using substitution groups from being used in the schema. Otherwise, you can specify the type of derivation that is to be blocked.
element-FormDefault	qualified | unqualified	unqualified	Defines whether elements are considered by default to be qualified (in a namespace).
finalDefault	#all | List of (extension | restriction)		Blocks all derivations. Similar to blockDefault.
id	*ID*		Defines a unique identifier for the element.
targetNamespace	*anyURI*		Defines the namespace for the instance documents.
version	*token*		Defines the version of the schema.
xml:lang	*language*		Defines the language of the document using an RFC 3066 code (i.e., en for English).

Context

Content Model: ((include | import | redefine | annotation)*, (((simpleType | complexType | group | attributeGroup) | element | attribute | notation), annotation*)*)

Allowable Parent: N/A

Example

```
<xsd:schema
    xmlns:xsd="http://www.w3.org/2001/XMLSchema"
    elementFormDefault="qualified"
    targetNamespace="http://www.lanw.com/namespaces/pub"
    xmlns="http://www.lanw.com/namespaces/pub">

<xsd:element name="publications">
    <xsd:complexType>
      <xsd:sequence>
        <xsd:element name="book" maxOccurs="unbounded">
          <xsd:complexType>
            <xsd:sequence>
              <xsd:element name="title" type="xsd:string"/>
              <xsd:element name="author" type="xsd:string"/>
              <xsd:element name="description" type="xsd:string"/>
            </xsd:sequence>
          </xsd:complexType>
        </xsd:element>
      </xsd:sequence>
    </xsd:complexType>
</xsd:element>
</xsd:schema>
```

selector

The `field` and `selector` elements work together as children of a `key`, `keyRef`, or `unique` element. The `selector` element is used to identify the attribute or element that is to be unique. The `selector` element uses an `xpath` attribute that contains an XPath expression to identify the element or attribute.

Attributes

Attribute Name	Value Space	Default Value	Required	Description
id	ID			Defines a unique identifier for the element.
xpath	A subset of XPath expression		Yes	Defines the element or attribute to be selected within the defined field.

Context

Content Model: (annotation?)

Allowable Parents: key, keyref, unique

Example

```
<xsd:key name="bookKey">
    <xsd:selector xpath="publications/book"/>
    <xsd:field xpath="@id"/>
</xsd:key>

<xsd:keyref name="bookRef" refer="bookKey">
    <xsd:selector xpath="publications/review"/>
    <xsd:field xpath="book/@bookRef"/>
</xsd:keyref>
```

sequence

The sequence element is a compositor that, when used, requires a sequence to be used for a content model. The sequence element defines an ordered group of elements. It's similar to the comma (,) connector used in XML DTDs.

Attributes

Attribute Name	Value Space	Default Value	Required	Description
id	*ID*			Defines a unique identifier for the element.
maxOccurs	*nonNegative-Integer* | unbounded	1		Defines the maximum number of times the model group can occur.
minOccurs	*nonNegative-Integer*	1		Defines the minimum number of times the model group can occur.

Context

Content Model: (annotation?, (element | group | choice | sequence | any)*)

Allowable Parents: complexType, group, sequence

Example

```
<xsd:element name="publications">
  <xsd:complexType>
    <xsd:sequence>
      <xsd:element name="book" maxOccurs="unbounded">
        <xsd:complexType>
          <xsd:sequence>
            <xsd:element name="title" type="xsd:string"/>
            <xsd:element name="author" type="xsd:string"/>
            <xsd:element name="description" type="xsd:string"/>
          </xsd:sequence>
        </xsd:complexType>
      </xsd:element>
    </xsd:sequence>
  </xsd:complexType>
</xsd:element>
```

simpleContent

The simpleContent element defines a simple content definition for an element. It's common practice to extend or restrict elements using this element.

Attributes

Attribute Name	Value Space	Default Value	Required	Description
id	ID			Defines a unique identifier for the element.

Context

Content Model: (annotation?, (element | group | choice | sequence | any)*)

Allowable Parent: complexType

Example

```
<xsd:element name="book">
  <xsd:complexType>
    <xsd:simpleContent>
      <xsd:extension base="xsd:string">
        <xsd:attribute ref="editor"/>
      </xsd:extension>
    </xsd:simpleContent>
  </xsd:complexType>
</xsd:element>
```

simpleType

The simpleType element is used to define all attributes and elements that contain only text and do not have attributes associated with them. When defining simple types, you can use XML Schema datatypes to restrict the text contained by the element or attribute.

Attributes

Attribute Name	Value Space	Default Value	Required	Description
final	#all | (list | union | restriction)			Defines how datatypes may be derived from the simple type.
id	ID			Defines a unique identifier for the element.
name	NCName			Defines a name for the simple type.

Context

Content Model: (annotation?, (restriction | list | union))

Allowable Parents: attribute, element, list, restriction, schema, union

Example

```
<xsd:simpleType name="isbnType">
  <xsd:restriction base="xsd:string">
    <xsd:pattern value="[0-9]{10}"/>
  </xsd:restriction>
</xsd:simpleType>
```

union

The union element creates a datatype that is derived from multiple datatypes. It uses an attribute to define all base types participating in the union.

Attributes

Attribute Name	Value Space	Default Value	Required	Description
id	ID			Defines a unique identifier for the element.
memberTypes	List of QName			Defines the base types that will participate in the union.

Context

Content Model: (annotation?, (simpleType*))

Allowable Parent: simpleType

Example

```
<xsd:simpleType name="exampleTypeUnion">
   <xsd:union memberTypes="oneType twoType"/>
</xsd:simpleType>
```

unique

The unique element is used to specify that any attribute or element value must be unique within a defined scope. The unique element may contain a selector or field element.

Attributes

Attribute Name	Value Space	Default Value	Required	Description
id	ID			Defines a unique identifier for the element.
name	NCName		Yes	Defines the name of the identity constraint.

Context

Content Model: (annotation? , (selector , field+))

Allowable Parent: element

Example

```
<xsd:unique name="bookID">
   <xsd:selector xpath="publications/book"/>
   <xsd:field xpath="@id"/>
</xsd:unique>
```

XML Schema Constraining Facets

There are 12 possible constraining facets:

```
enumeration

fractionDigits

length

maxExclusive

maxInclusive

maxLength

minExclusive

minInclusive

minLength

pattern

totalDigits

whiteSpace
```

They are defined in the following sections (in alphabetical order).

enumeration

The `enumeration` element constrains the value of the datatype to a defined set of values. For example, a simple type definition can define a named datatype (`dayType`) that allows for one of the seven days of the week as its value.

Attributes

Attribute Name	Value Space	Default Value	Required	Description
id	*ID*			Defines a unique identifier for the type.
value	*anySimpleType*			Defines one of the values for the enumerated list. Each value is defined with its own element.

Context

Content Model: (annotation?)

Allowable Parent: restriction

Example

```
<xsd:simpleType name="dayType">
   <xsd:restriction base="xsd:string">
     <xsd:enumeration value="Monday"/>
     <xsd:enumeration value="Tuesday"/>
     <xsd:enumeration value="Wednesday"/>
     <xsd:enumeration value="Thursday"/>
     <xsd:enumeration value="Friday"/>
     <xsd:enumeration value="Saturday"/>
     <xsd:enumeration value="Sunday"/>
   </xsd:restriction>
</xsd:simpleType>
```

fractionDigits

The fractionDigits element defines the maximum number of digits allowable for the fractional part of a datatype derived from a decimal datatype.

Attributes

Attribute Name	Value Space	Default Value	Required	Description
id	*ID*			Defines a unique identifier for the type.
fixed	*Boolean*	false		If true, derived types cannot alter values defined by this type.
value	*nonNegative-Integer*			Defines the maximum number of digits in the fraction portion of the number.

Context

Content Model: (annotation?)

Allowable Parent: restriction

Example

```xml
<xsd:simpleType name="numericType">
   <xsd:restriction base="xsd:decimal">
     <xsd:totalDigits value="10"/>
     <xsd:fractionDigits value="3"/>
   </xsd:restriction>
</xsd:simpleType>
```

length

The `length` element is a nonnegative integer that defines the number of units of length, which vary depending on the datatype. For example, for a `string` datatype, the units of length are measured in characters, whereas for a `hexBinary` datatype, units are measured in octets (8 bits) of binary data.

Attributes

Attribute Name	Value Space	Default Value	Required	Description
id	*ID*			Defines a unique identifier for the type.
fixed	*Boolean*	false		If true, derived types cannot alter values defined by this type.
value	*nonNegativeInteger*			Defines the allowable length for the type.

Context

Content Model: (annotation?)

Allowable Parent: restriction

Example

```xml
<xsd:simpleType name="isbnType">
   <xsd:restriction base="xsd:string">
     <xsd:length value="10" fixed="true"/>
   </xsd:restriction>
</xsd:simpleType>
```

maxExclusive

The maxExclusive element defines the exclusive upper bound for a datatype with the ordered property. Because it's exclusive, the defined value may *not* be included within the value space. For example, you can define an upper bound of 100 for an integer datatype; in this case, the datatype may accept any integer less than 100.

Attributes

Attribute Name	Value Space	Default Value	Required	Description
id	*ID*			Defines a unique identifier for the type.
fixed	*Boolean*	false		If true, derived types cannot alter values defined by this type.
value	*anySimpleType*			Defines the upper limit for a datatype. The value defined is one higher than the allowable type.

Context

Content Model: (annotation?)

Allowable Parent: restriction

Example

```
<xsd:simpleType name="upperType">
  <xsd:restriction base="xsd:integer">
    <xsd:maxExclusive value="101"/>
  </xsd:restriction>
</xsd:simpleType>
```

maxInclusive

The maxInclusive element defines the inclusive upper bound for a datatype with the ordered property. Because it's inclusive, the defined value may be included within the value space. For example, you can define an upper bound of 100 for an integer datatype; in this case, the datatype may accept any integer less than or equal to 100.

Attributes

Attribute Name	Value Space	Default Value	Required	Description
id	*ID*			Defines a unique identifier for the type.
fixed	*Boolean*	false		If true, derived types cannot alter values defined by this type.
value	*anySimpleType*			Defines the upper limit for a datatype. The allowable type may be less than or equal to the defined value.

Context

Content Model: (annotation?)

Allowable Parent: restriction

Example

```
<xsd:simpleType name="editionType">
  <xsd:restriction base="xsd:nonNegativeInteger">
    <xsd:minInclusive value="1"/>
    <xsd:maxInclusive value="10"/>
  </xsd:restriction>
</xsd:simpleType>
```

maxLength

The maxLength element specifies a nonnegative integer that defines the maximum number of units of length. The units of length vary depending on the datatype.

Attributes

Attribute Name	Value Space	Default Value	Required	Description
id	*ID*			Defines a unique identifier for the type.

fixed	*Boolean*	false		If true, derived types cannot alter values defined by this type.
value	*nonNegative-Integer*			Defines the maximum length for the type.

Context

Content Model: (annotation?)

Allowable Parent: restriction

Example

```
<xsd:element name="myString">
  <xsd:simpleType>
    <xsd:restriction base="xsd:normalizedString">
      <xsd:maxLength value="10"/>
    </xsd:restriction>
  </xsd:simpleType>
</xsd:element>
```

minExclusive

The minExclusive element defines the exclusive lower bound for a datatype with the ordered property. Because it's exclusive, the defined value may *not* be included within the value space. For example, you can define a lower bound of 10 for an integer datatype; in this case, the datatype may accept any integer greater than 10.

Attributes

Attribute Name	Value Space	Default Value	Required	Description
id	*ID*			Defines a unique identifier for the type.
fixed	*Boolean*	false		If true, derived types cannot alter values defined by this type.
value	*anySimpleType*			Defines the lower limit for a datatype. The defined value is one lower than the allowable type.

Context

Content Model: `(annotation?)`

Allowable Parent: `restriction`

Example

```
<xsd:simpleType name="lowerType">
   <xsd:restriction base="xsd:integer">
     <xsd:minExclusive value="99"/>
   </xsd:restriction>
</xsd:simpleType>
```

minInclusive

The `minInclusive` element defines the inclusive lower bound for a datatype with the ordered property. Because it's inclusive, the defined value may be included within the value space. For example, you can define a lower bound of 10 for an integer datatype; in this case, the datatype may accept any integer greater than or equal to 10.

Attributes

Attribute Name	Value Space	Default Value	Required	Description
`id`	*ID*			Defines a unique identifier for the type.
`fixed`	*Boolean*	`false`		If `true`, derived types cannot alter values defined by this type.
`value`	*anySimpleType*			Defines the lower limit for a datatype. The allowable type may be greater or equal to the defined value.

Context

Content Model: `(annotation?)`

Allowable Parent: `restriction`

Example
```
<xsd:simpleType name="editionType">
  <xsd:restriction base="xsd:nonNegativeInteger">
    <xsd:minInclusive value="1"/>
    <xsd:maxInclusive value="10"/>
  </xsd:restriction>
</xsd:simpleType>
```

minLength

The minLength element specifies a nonnegative integer that defines the minimum number of units of length. The units of length vary depending on the datatype.

Attributes

Attribute Name	Value Space	Default Value	Required	Description
id	*ID*			Defines a unique identifier for the type.
fixed	*Boolean*	false		If true, derived types cannot alter values defined by this type.
value	*nonNegative-Integer*			Defines the minimum length of the type.

Context

Content Model: (annotation?)

Allowable Parent: restriction

Example
```
<xsd:simpleType name="productCodeType">
  <xsd:restriction base="xsd:string">
    <xsd:minLength value="5"/>
  </xsd:restriction>
</xsd:simpleType>
```

pattern

The pattern element constrains the lexical space to literals that must match a defined pattern. The value must be a regular expression (defined in Chapter 7). For example, you can define a pattern for ISBNs. If you use the `pattern` facet, the value could be defined as follows: `<xsd:pattern value="[0-9]{10}"/>`.

Attributes

Attribute Name	Value Space	Default Value	Required	Description
id	*ID*			Defines a unique identifier for the element.
value	*anySimpleType*			Value may be any regular expression.

Context

Content Model: `(annotation?)`

Allowable Parent: `restriction`

Example

```
<xsd:simpleType name="isbnType">
   <xsd:restriction base="xsd:string">
     <xsd:pattern value="[0-9]{10}"/>
   </xsd:restriction>
</xsd:simpleType>
```

totalDigits

The `totalDigits` element defines the maximum number of digits allowable for a datatype derived from a `decimal` datatype.

Attributes

Attribute Name	Value Space	Default Value	Required	Description
id	*ID*			Defines a unique identifier for the type.
fixed	*Boolean*	false		If `true`, derived types cannot alter values defined by this type.
value	*positiveInteger*			Defines the maximum number of digits for the number type.

Context

Content Model: `(annotation?)`

Allowable Parent: `restriction`

Example

```
<xsd:element name="money">
  <xsd:simpleType>
    <xsd:restriction base="xsd:decimal">
      <xsd:totalDigits value="4"/>
      <xsd:fractionDigits value="2"/>
    </xsd:restriction>
  </xsd:simpleType>
</xsd:element>
```

whiteSpace

The `whiteSpace` element and its `value` attribute specify how white space (tabs, line feeds, carriage returns, and spaces) is processed. The `whiteSpace` facet's `value` attribute can accept only one of three values: `preserve`, `replace`, or `collapse`.

Attributes

Attribute Name	Value Space	Default Value	Required	Description
`id`	*ID*			Defines a unique identifier for the type.
`fixed`	*Boolean*	`false`		If `true`, derived types cannot specify a `whiteSpace` value (`collapse`, `preserve`, or `replace`) different than the one specified by this type.
`value`	`collapse | preserve | replace`			`collapse`: any series of white space characters are collapsed into a single space. `preserve`: all white space is preserved. `replace`: all white space characters are replaced with single spaces.

Context

Content Model: `(annotation?)`

Allowable Parent: `restriction`

Example

```
<xsd:simpleType name="token">
   <xsd:restriction base="xsd:normalizedString">
     <xsd:whiteSpace value="collapse"/>
   </xsd:restriction>
</xsd:simpleType>
```

Built-In Datatypes

The following sections identify the datatype name, allowable facets, and an example for each built-in datatype.

Primitive Built-In Datatypes

These are the primitive built-in datatypes. The fundamental facets are described in *name:value* form.

anyURI

Fundamental Facets

bounded:false

cardinality:countably infinite

numeric:false

ordered:false

Constraining Facets

length

minLength

maxLength

pattern

enumeration

whiteSpace

Example

```
<!-- schema -->
<xsd:element name="address">
   <xsd:simpleType>
      <xsd:restriction base="xsd:anyURI">
         <xsd:enumeration value=
            "http://www.w3.org/TR/2000/PR-xlink-20001220/"/>
         <xsd:enumeration value=
            "http://www.w3.org/TR/xmlschema-2/"/>
      </xsd:restriction>
   </xsd:simpleType>
</xsd:element>
<!-- instance document -->
<address>http://www.w3.org/TR/xmlschema-2/</address>
```

base64Binary

Fundamental Facets

bounded:false

cardinality:countably infinite

numeric:false

ordered:false

Constraining Facets

length

minLength

maxLength

pattern

enumeration

whiteSpace

Example

```
<!-- schema -->
<xsd:element name="binaryto64" type="xsd:base64Binary"/>
<!-- instance document -->
<binaryto64>AC2xaQ</binaryto64>
```

boolean

Fundamental Facets
```
bounded:false

cardinality:finite

numeric:false

ordered:false
```

Constraining Facets
```
pattern

whiteSpace
```

Example
```
<!-- schema -->
<xsd:element name="choose" default="true" type="xsd:boolean"/>
<!-- instance document, using default value -->
<choose/>
<!-- instance document, not using default value -->
<choose>false</choose>
```

date

Fundamental Facets
```
bounded:false

cardinality:countably infinite

numeric:false

ordered:partial
```

Constraining Facets
```
pattern

enumeration

whiteSpace

maxInclusive

maxExclusive

minInclusive

minExclusive
```

Example

```
<!-- schema -->
<xsd:element name="anniversary" type="xsd:date"/>
<!-- instance document -->
<anniversary>1960-07-15</anniversary>
```

dateTime

Fundamental Facets

bounded:false

cardinality:countably infinite

numeric:false

ordered:partial

Constraining Facets

pattern

enumeration

whiteSpace

maxInclusive

maxExclusive

minInclusive

minExclusive

Example

```
<!-- schema -->
<xsd:element name="time_of_birth">
   <xsd:simpleType>
      <xsd:restriction base="xsd:dateTime">
        <xsd:enumeration value="1950-06-25T04:15:00"/>
        <xsd:enumeration value="1988-12-14T21:30:05"/>
      </xsd:restriction>
   </xsd:simpleType>
</xsd:element>
<!-- instance document -->
<time_of_birth>1950-06-25T04:15:00</time_of_birth>
```

decimal

Fundamental Facets

bounded:false

cardinality:countably infinite

enumeric:true

ordered:total

Constraining Facets

totalDigits

fractionDigits

pattern

whiteSpace

enumeration

maxInclusive

maxExclusive

minInclusive

Example

```
<!-- schema -->
<xsd:element name="money">
   <xsd:simpleType>
     <xsd:restriction base="xsd:decimal">
       <xsd:totalDigits value="4"/>
       <xsd:fractionDigits value="2"/>
     </xsd:restriction>
   </xsd:simpleType>
</xsd:element>
<!-- instance document -->
<money>14.98</money>
```

double

Fundamental Facets

bounded:true

cardinality:finite

numeric:true

ordered:total

Constraining Facets

pattern

enumeration

whiteSpace

maxInclusive

maxExclusive

minInclusive

minExclusive

Example

```
<!-- schema -->
<xsd:element name="myDouble" type="xsd:double"/>
<!-- instance document -->
<myDouble>-133.459e-12</myDouble>
```

duration

Fundamental Facets

bounded:false

cardinality:countably infinite

numeric:false

ordered:partial

Constraining Facets

pattern

enumeration

whiteSpace

maxInclusive

maxExclusive

minInclusive

minExclusive

Example

```
<!-- schema -->
<xsd:element name="vacation">
   <xsd:simpleType>
     <xsd:restriction base="xsd:duration">
       <xsd:pattern value="P\d+D\d+H\d+M\d+S"/>
     </xsd:restriction>
   </xsd:simpleType>
</xsd:element>
```

```
<!-- instance document -->
<vacation>P10D2H30M45S</vacation>
```

float
Fundamental Facets
bounded:true

cardinality:finite

numeric:true

ordered:total

Constraining Facets
pattern

enumeration

whiteSpace

maxInclusive

maxExclusive

minInclusive

minExclusive

Example
```
<!-- schema -->
<xsd:element name="charge">
   <xsd:simpleType>
      <xsd:restriction base="xsd:float">
        <xsd:minExclusive value="1.00"/>
        <xsd:maxExclusive value="100.00"/>
      </xsd:restriction>
   </xsd:simpleType>
</xsd:element>
<!-- instance document -->
<charge>19.99</charge>
```

gDay
Fundamental Facets
bounded:false

cardinality:countably infinite
```
```

```
numeric:false
```

```
ordered:partial
```

Constraining Facets

```
pattern
```

```
enumeration
```

```
whiteSpace
```

```
maxInclusive
```

```
maxExclusive
```

```
minInclusive
```

```
minExclusive
```

Example

```
<!-- schema -->
<xsd:element name="checkpoint" type="xsd:gDay"/>
<!-- instance document -->
<checkpoint>---15</checkpoint>
```

gMonth

Fundamental Facets

```
bounded:false
```

```
cardinality:countably infinite
```

```
numeric:false
```

```
ordered:partial
```

Constraining Facets

```
pattern
```

```
enumeration
```

```
whiteSpace
```

```
maxInclusive
```

```
maxExclusive
```

```
minInclusive
```

```
minExclusive
```

Example
```
<!-- schema -->
<xsd:element name="school_starts" type="xsd:gMonth"/>
<!-- instance document -->
<school_starts>--09--</school_starts>
```

gMonthDay

Fundamental Facets

bounded:false

cardinality:countably infinite

numeric:false

ordered:partial

Constraining Facets

pattern

enumeration

whiteSpace

maxInclusive

maxExclusive

minInclusive

minExclusive

Example
```
<!-- schema -->
<xsd:element name="birthday" type="xsd:gMonthDay"/>
<!-- instance document -->
<birthday>--10-25</birthday>
```

gYear

Fundamental Facets

bounded:false

cardinality:countably infinite

numeric:false

ordered:partial

Constraining Facets

```
pattern

enumeration

whiteSpace

maxInclusive

maxExclusive

minInclusive

minExclusive
```

Example

```
<!-- schema -->
<xsd:element name="interval">
   <xsd:simpleType>
     <xsd:restriction base="xsd:gYear">
       <xsd:minInclusive value="1776"/>
       <xsd:maxInclusive value="1976"/>
     </xsd:restriction>
   </xsd:simpleType>
</xsd:element>
<!-- instance document -->
<interval>1842</interval>
```

gYearMonth

Fundamental Facets

```
bounded:false

cardinality:countably infinite

numeric:false

ordered:partial
```

Constraining Facets

```
pattern

enumeration

whiteSpace

maxInclusive

maxExclusive
```

```
minInclusive

minExclusive
```

Example
```
<!-- schema -->
<xsd:element name="graduation" type="xsd:gYearMonth"/>
<!-- instance document -->
<graduation>1996-05Z</graduation>
```

hexBinary

Fundamental Facets
```
bounded:false

cardinality:countably infinite

numeric:false

ordered:false
```

Constraining Facets
```
length

minLength

maxLength

pattern

enumeration

whiteSpace
```

Example
```
<!-- schema -->
<xsd:element name="hex1" type="xsd:hexBinary"/>
<!-- instance document -->
<hex1>FFCC9E</hex1>
```

NOTATION

Fundamental Facets
```
bounded:false

cardinality:countably infinite

numeric:false

ordered:false
```

Constraining Facets

```
length

minLength

maxLength

pattern

enumeration

whiteSpace
```

Example

```
<!-- schema -->
<xsd:notation name="swf" public="image/swf"
    system="SWF_viewer.exe"/>
<xsd:element name="myAnimation">
   <xsd:complexType>
     <xsd:complexContent>
       <xsd:extension base="xsd:anyType">
         <xsd:attribute name="note" type="notationType"/>
       </xsd:extension>
     </xsd:complexContent>
   </xsd:complexType>
</xsd:element>
<xsd:simpleType name="notationType">
   <xsd:restriction base="xsd:NOTATION">
     <xsd:enumeration value="swf"/>
     <xsd:enumeration value="fla"/>
   </xsd:restriction>
</xsd:simpleType>
<!-- instance document -->
<myAnimation note="swf">Schema Lesson</myAnimation>
```

QName

Fundamental Facets

```
bounded:false

cardinality:countably infinite

numeric:false

ordered:false
```

Constraining Facets

```
length
```

minLength

maxLength

pattern

enumeration

whiteSpace

Example
```
<!-- instance document -->
<xmlns:rr="http://railroads.com/schema">
<!-- the track_number element's namespace is
    http://railroads.com/schema -->
<rr:track_number>15546</rr:track_number>
```

string

Fundamental Facets
```
bounded:false

cardinality:finite

numeric:false

ordered:false
```

Constraining Facets
```
length

minLength

maxLength

pattern

enumeration

whiteSpace
```

Example
```
<!-- schema -->
<xsd:element name="myString" type="xsd:string"/>
<!-- instance document -->
<myString>This is a simple string literal</myString>
```

time

Fundamental Facets

bounded:false

cardinality:countably infinite

numeric:false

ordered:partial

Constraining Facets

pattern

enumeration

whiteSpace

maxInclusive

maxExclusive

minInclusive

minExclusive

Example

```
<!-- schema -->
<xsd:element name="meeting" type="xsd:time"/>
<!-- instance document -->
<meeting>10:30:00Z</meeting>
```

Derived Built-In Datatypes

The following are the derived built-in datatypes.

byte

Constraining Facets

totalDigits

fractionDigits

pattern

whiteSpace

enumeration

maxInclusive

```
    maxExclusive

    minInclusive

    minExclusive
```

Example

```
<xsd:complexType name="myBytes">
   <xsd:choice>
     <xsd:element name="byte1" type="xsd:byte"/>
     <xsd:element name="byte2" type="xsd:byte"/>
     <xsd:element name="byte3" type="xsd:byte"/>
   </xsd:choice>
</xsd:complexType>
<!-- instance document -->
<byte2>55</byte2>
```

ENTITIES

Constraining Facets

```
    length

    minLength

    maxLength

    enumeration

    whiteSpace
```

Example

```
<!-- schema -->
<xsd:notation name="jpg" public="image/jpg" system="JPG_viewer.exe"/>
<xsd:notation name="gif" public="image/gif" system="GIF_viewer.exe"/>
<xsd:notation name="png" public="image/png" system="PNG_viewer.exe"/>
<xsd:complexType name="entityref">
   <xsd:sequence>
     <xsd:element name="gallery">
       <xsd:complexType>
         <xsd:complexContent>
           <xsd:extension base="xsd:anyType">
             <xsd:attribute name="images" type="imageTypes"/>
           </xsd:extension>
         </xsd:complexContent>
       </xsd:complexType>
     </xsd:element>
   </xsd:sequence>
</xsd:complexType>
```

```
<xsd:element name="gallery">
  <xsd:complexType>
    <xsd:complexContent>
      <xsd:extension base="xsd:anyType">
        <xsd:attribute name="images" type="imageTypes"/>
      </xsd:extension>
    </xsd:complexContent>
  </xsd:complexType>
</xsd:element>
<xsd:simpleType name="imageTypes">
  <xsd:restriction base="xsd:ENTITIES">
    <xsd:enumeration value="jpg"/>
    <xsd:enumeration value="gif"/>
    <xsd:enumeration value="png"/>
  </xsd:restriction>
</xsd:simpleType>
<!-- instance document -->
<gallery images="jpg gif png">Online_Brochure</gallery>
```

ENTITY

Constraining Facets

```
length

minLength

maxLength

pattern

enumeration

whiteSpace
```

Example

```
<!-- schema -->
<xsd:notation name="jpg" public="image/jpg"
    system="JPG_viewer.exe"/>
<xsd:complexType name="entityref">
  <xsd:sequence>
    <xsd:element name="picture">
      <xsd:complexType>
        <xsd:complexContent>
          <xsd:extension base="xsd:anyType">
            <xsd:attribute name="image"type="xsd:ENTITY"/>
          </xsd:extension>
        </xsd:complexContent>
      </xsd:complexType>
```

```
        </xsd:element>
      </xsd:sequence>
  </xsd:complexType>
  <!-- instance document -->
  <picture image="jpg">Brochure</picture>
```

ID

Constraining Facets

length

minLength

maxLength

pattern

enumeration

whiteSpace

Example

```
  <!-- schema -->
  <xsd:element name="bank">
      <xsd:complexType>
        <xsd:complexContent>
          <xsd:extension base="xsd:anyType">
            <xsd:attribute name="degree" type="xsd:ID"/>
          </xsd:extension>
        </xsd:complexContent>
      </xsd:complexType>
  </xsd:element>
  <!-- instance document -->
  <bank branch="412x">Northern</bank>
```

IDREF

Constraining Facets

length

minLength

maxLength

pattern

enumeration

whiteSpace

Example

```
<!-- schema -->
<xsd:element name="bank">
   <xsd:complexType>
     <xsd:complexContent>
       <xsd:extension base="xsd:anyType">
         <xsd:attribute name="branch" type="xsd:ID"/>
       </xsd:extension>
     </xsd:complexContent>
   </xsd:complexType>
</xsd:element>
<xsd:element name="city">
   <xsd:complexType>
     <xsd:complexContent>
       <xsd:extension base="xsd:anyType">
         <xsd:attribute name="branch_division" type="xsd:IDREF"/>
       </xsd:extension>
     </xsd:complexContent>
   </xsd:complexType>
</xsd:element>
<!-- instance document -->
<bank branch="412x">Northern</bank>
<city branch_division="412x">Chicago</city>
```

IDREFS

Constraining Facets

length

minLength

maxLength

enumeration

whiteSpace

Example

```
<!-- schema -->
<xsd:complexType name="bankref">
   <xsd:sequence>
     <xsd:element name="bank" minOccurs="0" maxOccurs="unbounded">
       <xsd:complexType>
         <xsd:complexContent>
           <xsd:extension base="xsd:anyType">
             <xsd:attribute name="branch" type="xsd:ID"/>
           </xsd:extension>
         </xsd:complexContent>
```

```
            </xsd:complexType>
          </xsd:element>
        </xsd:sequence>
      </xsd:complexType>
      <xsd:element name="city">
        <xsd:complexType>
          <xsd:complexContent>
            <xsd:extension base="xsd:anyType">
              <xsd:attribute name="branch_division" type="xsd:IDREFS"/>
            </xsd:extension>
          </xsd:complexContent>
        </xsd:complexType>
      </xsd:element>
      <!-- instance document -->
      <bank branch="412x">Northern</bank>
      <bank branch="513a">Central</bank>
      <bank branch="793c">Southern</bank>
      <city branch_division="412x 513a 793c">Chicago</city>
```

int

Constraining Facets

```
totalDigits

fractionDigits

pattern

whiteSpace

enumeration

maxInclusive

maxExclusive

minInclusive

minExclusive
```

Example

```
<!-- schema -->
<xsd:element name="ninedigits">
  <xsd:simpleType>
    <xsd:restriction base="xsd:int">
      <xsd:pattern value="\d{0,9}"/>
    </xsd:restriction>
  </xsd:simpleType>
</xsd:element>
<!-- instance document -->
<ninedigits>217748364</ninedigits>
```

integer

Constraining Facets

```
totalDigits

fractionDigits

pattern

whiteSpace

enumeration

maxInclusive

maxExclusive

minInclusive

minExclusive
```

Example

```
<!-- schema -->
<xsd:element name="myInteger" type="xsd:integer"/>
<!-- instance document -->
<myInteger>1</myInteger>
<myInteger>-35</myInteger>
<myInteger>+678432</myInteger>
<myInteger>5001182828293</myInteger>
```

language

Constraining Facets

```
length

minLength

maxLength

pattern

enumeration

whiteSpace
```

Example

```
<!-- schema -->
<xsd:element name="language_native">
   <xsd:simpleType>
      <xsd:restriction base="xsd:language">
```

```
        <xsd:enumeration value="de"/>
        <xsd:enumeration value="fr"/>
        <xsd:enumeration value="en-GB"/>
        <xsd:enumeration value="en-US"/>
      </xsd:restriction>
   </xsd:simpleType>
 </xsd:element>
 <!-- instance document -->
 <language_native>fr</language_native>
```

long

Constraining Facets

```
totalDigits

fractionDigits

pattern

whiteSpace

enumeration

maxInclusive

maxExclusive

minInclusive

minExclusive
```

Example

```
<!-- schema -->
<xsd:element name="bignumbers">
<xsd:simpleType>
   <xsd:restriction base="xsd:long">
     <xsd:enumeration value="2177483647"/>
     <xsd:enumeration value="-2177483647"/>
   </xsd:restriction>
</xsd:simpleType>
</xsd:element>
<!-- instance document -->
<bignumbers>2177483647</bignumbers>
```

Name

Constraining Facets

```
length

minLength
```

```
maxLength

pattern

enumeration

whiteSpace
```

Example

```
<!-- schema -->
<xsd:element name="group" type="xsd:Name"/>
<!-- instance document -->
<names xmlns="http://www.mycompany.org/schemas/e-commerce"
    xmlns:market="http://www.mycompany.org/schemas/market"/>
<market:group>Alpha</market:group>
```

NCName

Constraining Facets

```
length

minLength

maxLength

pattern

enumeration

whiteSpace
```

Example

```
<!-- schema -->
<xsd:element name="group" type="xsd:NCName"/>
<!-- instance document -->
<group>Alpha</group>
```

negativeInteger

Constraining Facets

```
totalDigits

fractionDigits

pattern

whiteSpace

enumeration
```

maxInclusive

maxExclusive

minInclusive

minExclusive

Example

```
<!-- schema -->
<xsd:simpleType name="neg_2">
   <xsd:restriction base="xsd:negativeInteger">
     <xsd:pattern value="-\d{2}"/>
   </xsd:restriction>
</xsd:simpleType>
<!-- instance document -->
<neg_2>-49</neg_2>
```

NMTOKEN

Constraining Facets

length

minLength

maxLength

pattern

enumeration

whiteSpace

Example

```
<!-- schema -->
<xsd:element name="title">
   <xsd:complexType>
     <xsd:complexContent>
       <xsd:extension base="xsd:anyType">
         <xsd:attribute name="degree" type="xsd:NMTOKEN"/>
       </xsd:extension>
     </xsd:complexContent>
   </xsd:complexType>
</xsd:element>
<!-- instance document -->
<title degree="MS">Mister</title>
```

NMTOKENS

Constraining Facets

length

minLength

maxLength

enumeration

whiteSpace

Example

```
<!-- schema -->
...
<xsd:attribute name="degree" type="xsd:NMTOKENS"/>
<!-- instance document -->
<title degree="BA MS">Mister</title>
```

nonNegativeInteger

Constraining Facets

totalDigits

fractionDigits

pattern

whiteSpace

enumeration

maxInclusive

maxExclusive

minInclusive

minExclusive

Example

```
<!-- schema -->
<xsd:element name="bank_balance" type="xsd:nonNegativeInteger"/>
<!-- instance document -->
<bank_balance>32</bank_balance>
```

nonPositiveInteger

Constraining Facets

totalDigits

fractionDigits

pattern

whiteSpace

enumeration

maxInclusive

maxExclusive

minInclusive

minExclusive

Example

```
<!-- schema -->
<xsd:simpleType name="BC">
   <xsd:restriction base="xsd:nonPositiveInteger">
     <xsd:minInclusive value="unbounded"/>
     <xsd:maxInclusive value="-2001"/>
   </xsd:restriction>
</xsd:simpleType>
<!-- instance document -->
<BC>-5365</BC>
```

normalizedString

Constraining Facets

length

minLength

maxLength

pattern

enumeration

whiteSpace

Example

```
<!-- schema -->
<xsd:element name="myString">
```

```
  <xsd:simpleType>
    <xsd:restriction base="xsd:normalizedString">
      <xsd:maxLength value="50"/>
    </xsd:restriction>
  </xsd:simpleType>
</xsd:element>
<!-- instance document -->
<myString>Here's one.</myString>
```

positiveInteger

Constraining Facets

```
totalDigits

fractionDigits

pattern

whiteSpace

enumeration

maxInclusive

maxExclusive

minInclusive

minExclusive
```

Example

```
<!-- schema -->
<xsd:complexType name="record_sets">
  <xsd:sequence>
    <xsd:element name="record" minOccurs="0"
      maxOccurs="unbounded">
      <xsd:simpleType>
        <xsd:restriction base="xsd:positiveInteger">
          <xsd:pattern value="555\d{3}"/>
        </xsd:restriction>
      </xsd:simpleType>
    </xsd:element>
  </xsd:sequence>
</xsd:complexType>
<!-- instance document -->
<record>555158</record>
<record>555687</record>
<record>555736</record>
```

short

Constraining Facets

totalDigits

fractionDigits

pattern

whiteSpace

enumeration

maxInclusive

maxExclusive

minInclusive

minExclusive

Example

```
<!-- schema -->
<xsd:complexType name="shortlist">
   <xsd:sequence>
     <xsd:element name="to_do" minOccurs="0"
       maxOccurs="unbounded">
       <xsd:complexType>
         <xsd:complexContent>
           <xsd:extension base="xsd:anyType">
             <xsd:attribute name="recur" type="xsd:short"/>
           </xsd:extension>
         </xsd:complexContent>
       </xsd:complexType>
     </xsd:element>
   </xsd:sequence>
</xsd:complexType>
<!-- instance document -->
<to_do recur="365">wake up</to_do>
<to_do recur="365">brush teeth</to_do>
<to_do recur="250">go to office</to_do>
```

token

Constraining Facets

length

minLength

```
maxLength

pattern

enumeration

whiteSpace
```

Example
```
<!-- schema -->
<xsd:element name="label" type="xsd:token"/>
<!-- instance document -->
<label>This is a token string</label>
```

unsignedByte

Constraining Facets
```
totalDigits

fractionDigits

pattern

whiteSpace

enumeration

maxInclusive

maxExclusive

minInclusive

minExclusive
```

Example
```
<!-- schema -->
<xsd:complexType name="RGB">
   <xsd:sequence>
     <xsd:element name="red" type="xsd:unsignedByte"/>
     <xsd:element name="green" type="xsd:unsignedByte"/>
     <xsd:element name="blue" type="xsd:unsignedByte"/>
   </xsd:sequence>
</xsd:complexType>
<!-- instance document -->
<red>33</red>
<green>255</green>
<blue>99</blue>
```

unsignedInt

Constraining Facets

```
totalDigits

fractionDigits

pattern

whiteSpace

enumeration

maxInclusive

maxExclusive

minInclusive

minExclusive
```

Example

```
<!-- schema -->
<xsd:simpleType name="grains_of_sand">
   <xsd:restriction base="xsd:unsignedInt">
     <xsd:maxInclusive value="4000000000"/>
   </xsd:restriction>
</xsd:simpleType>
<!-- instance document -->
<grains_of_sand>4000000000</grains_of_sand>
```

unsignedLong

Constraining Facets

```
totalDigits

fractionDigits

pattern

whiteSpace

enumeration

maxInclusive

maxExclusive

minInclusive

minExclusive
```

Example

```
<!-- schema -->
<xsd:simpleType name="distance_sun">
   <xsd:restriction base="xsd:unsignedLong">
      <xsd:pattern value="\d{8}"/>
   </xsd:restriction>
</xsd:simpleType>
<!-- instance document -->
<distance_sun>93000000</distance_sun>
```

unsignedShort

Constraining Facets

totalDigits

fractionDigits

pattern

whiteSpace

enumeration

maxInclusive

maxExclusive

minInclusive

minExclusive

Example

```
<!-- schema -->
<xsd:element name="shortstop">
   <xsd:simpleType>
      <xsd:restriction base="xsd:unsignedShort">
         <xsd:enumeration value="15515"/>
         <xsd:enumeration value="38860"/>
      </xsd:restriction>
   </xsd:simpleType>
</xsd:element>
<!-- instance document -->
<shortstop>38860</shortstop>
```

Glossary

A

annotations   An annotative mechanism that provides information about a schema component.

atomic datatypes   Datatypes that have a value that is considered indivisible and cannot be further broken down into other parts. Atomic datatypes can be primitive or derived. All primitive datatypes are atomic.

attribute   A name-value pair (where the value may be a single value or a list of values) that modifies or adds information to a specific element instance. In an SGML content model, attributes can be optional or required and may be assigned default values as needed.

attribute declaration   In XML Schema, a declaration that identifies which elements may have attributes, what attributes they may have, what values the attributes may hold, and what the default value is.

attribute definition   A specific type of declaration that defines an individual attribute's name, its associated value or values, a datatype, and an optional default value.

attribute group definitions   A set of attribute declarations that are defined as a group and are incorporated as a group in a complex type definition.

attribute list   A collection of one or more attributes associated with a specific document element.

attribute uses   A secondary schema component identified by the use attribute, which controls the occurrence of the element. It can have one of three values: required, prohibited, or optional.

attribute-list declarations   In DTDs, declarations that identify which elements may have attributes, what attributes they may have, what values the attributes may hold, and what the default value is.

B

B2B (business-to-business) transactions   E-commerce transactions that take place between businesses. Also known as inter-company e-commerce.

base document element   An element found in every SGML document (it's also called the root element, particularly when talking about XML documents).

binding   A protocol and a data format specification for a specific port type.

BizTalk Framework   A framework for implementing schemas and XML elements for messages between applications.

built-in datatype   A datatype that's already defined for you by the Datatypes specification.

C

canonical lexical representation   For any given datatype, the subset of literals that corresponds one to one to the values in the value space.

CDATA   Character data that is treated as raw input in an SGML or XML document without further interpretation or examination.

character reference   A reference to a character entity that is used in place of reserved symbols. For example, < is the character reference for the less than symbol (<).

character set   A named collection of character codes with associated renderings used to represent textual data in markup language documents.

comment   Data inserted into a markup language document or DTD solely for the purpose of explaining or elucidating its content (comments are not parsed and are generally ignored by document processors).

complex type   An element that allows for child elements and/or that can take attributes.

compositor   An element used within a `complex-Type` element to define content model behavior.

conditional element   An element whose existence depends on the existence or inclusion of another, related element within a data collection.

content   Document element data (normally text) that makes up the information contained within a document.

content model   In a document definition or a schema, a description of the structure and contents of an element type.

D

data collection   A set of multiple data elements that may represent a database, a document, or other collections of data elements.

data domain   The set of all possible values that a data element can assume.

data element   A specific item of data within some data collection.

data range   The set of all possible values that performing a function or an operation on some

data value may produce (similar to a data domain, but representing the result of some operation or another on a data domain).

database   A data collection that consists of one or more organized sets of element values, where such sets may be called records or tables (see *record* and *table* for more information about these element value sets).

database structure   The metadata that describes how a database is organized or what forms of organization or sequences of data elements it may take; information about element values or representations is part of the schema but not necessarily part of the database structure.

data-centric   Term used to describe a content model that's easier to process with computer programs because the data is better organized. Data-centric documents are those in which XML is used as a data format for data transport (e-commerce and B2B).

data-intensive   Term used to describe XML documents in which the content consists almost entirely of record- or table-structured data.

datatype   A specific form that the value or values associated with a data element may assume; alternatively, you may assume that an element value's datatype describes how to represent and interpret any associated value or values.

DCD (Document Content Description)   A schema that specifies the content and structure rules for XML documents.

derivation   A method that allows you to derive new types by restricting or extending the type definition. Extension is allowed only for complex types.

derived datatype   A datatype that is derived from a base type.

document   A data collection that consists of content (usually, but not always, textual data) along with metadata that in turn consists of content labels plus processing or rendering instructions. (Sometimes, but not always, this metadata is also in text form and is called markup; for XML documents, this is always the case.)

document definition   A type of metadata that defines valid content models and document elements and attributes (including rules governing element content and properties) for some specific document or class of documents.

document element   Any named document component with an associated content model, optional attribute definitions, and default value(s).

document instance   A specific document that belongs to a document type and that conforms to the content model for that document type.

document structure   The metadata that describes how a document's data elements may or must be organized or what forms of organization or sequences of data elements it may follow; information about element values or content is part of a document definition or schema but not necessarily part of the document structure. See also *content model*.

document-centric   A term that describes a content model that involves a liberal use of free-form text such as paragraphs and other block-level elements. This type of document is designed to store content fragments, such as paragraphs, chapters, and glossary entries, and may include document metadata, such as author names, revision dates, and document numbers.

DSD (Document Structure Description)   An XML Schema language developed by AT&T Lab Research and BRICS, University of Aarhus, Denmark. DSD is designed to provide stronger document descriptions than currently possible with DTDs or the current W3C XML Schema Recommendation and to further XML technologies such as Cascading Style Sheets (CSS) and XSL Transformations (XSLT).

DSDL (Document Schema Definition Language)   An XML Schema language designed to integrate descriptions of document structures, datatypes, and data relationships. It's based on extensions to RELAX NG.

DTD (Document Type Definition)   A special form of document definition that is expressed with SGML and that defines a content model and document elements (including rules governing element content and properties) for some specific document or class of documents.

E

element attribute   See *attribute*.

element content   For XML documents, refers to text associated with some specific, nonempty XML document element. In general, it refers to the data associated with any specific element and is also called an *element value*, which is more in keeping with database schema terminology.

element declaration   In a DTD, a special declaration in which an element is named and its associated datatype and/or content model information is defined.

element name   A string identifier associated with an element that identifies an element within the context of a particular data collection, be it a document (part of a content model), a database (an element in a table or a record), or some other kind of data collection (a named component of that other collection, whatever it may be).

element value   The actual data associated with a specific data element in a document, database, or some other data collection as distinguished from an element name (which identifies the element) or an element's properties or attributes (which qualify or identify an element and its associated content or value[s]).

entity declarations   Declarations that allow you to associate a name with some other fragment of content, which can be a chunk of regular text, a chunk of the document type declaration, or a reference to an external file containing either text or binary data.

entity   A type of markup that defines information—such as strings, pointers to external resources, and so on—that is parsed in at the beginning of document processing and then substituted for entity references that are encountered as a document is processed.

entity reference   DTD syntactical structure that references an entity. Entity references come in two flavors: a general entity reference (&*entity-name*;) and a parameter entity reference (%*entityname*;).

Examplotron   A language designed to use instance documents as a simple schema language.

external parsed general entity   An entity used to reference parseable XML data. Because external parsed general entities reference external files, they're useful for creating a common reference that can be shared among multiple documents.

external parsed parameter   An entity that used to reference external files that contain the replacement text.

external subset   Some element, attribute value, link, or other data resource that is defined outside the scope of the XML document.

external unparsed general entity   The only type of entity not parsed by the XML processor. It allows you to reference external files that don't contain XML data, such as graphics, sound, or other multimedia objects. Also known as an unparsed entity.

F

facets   The aspects that define a datatype.

function   A form of data analysis, extraction, abstraction, or transformation that performs various operations on the values in a data collection to produce some kind of desired result, be it a report, trending information, ad hoc query processing, or other kinds of output.

G

general entity   An entity that stores text for use within a document instance. General entities are referenced inside the XML document, not in the DTD.

H

HTML (Hypertext Markup Language) A mechanism to identify and mark up content to deliver online.

HTTP (Hypertext Transfer Protocol) A protocol for transferring information between browsers and Web servers.

I

ID A unique identifier used to distinguish each individual component within an SGML document or DTD.

identifier A unique name or attribute value that permits single element instances in a data collection to be unambiguously identified.

identifier value The unique value that pinpoints a single element instance in a data collection.

Infoset See *XML Information Set.*

instance An occurrence of a document type that conforms to your document description.

internal parsed general entity An entity that the XML processor parses as XML text. Also called internal general entity.

internal parsed parameter entity An entity used to declare entities existing solely in the DTD. Also known as an internal parameter entity.

internal subset Some element, attribute value, link, or other data resource that is completely defined within the scope of the current XML document. Internal subsets take precedence over external subsets.

K

key A special identifier—usually in a database—that identifies some specific instance of an element with special significance or meaning.

L

lexical space The set of valid literals, also known as lexical representations, for a specific datatype.

list datatypes A group of defined, finite-length sequences of atomic values. The atomic datatype included in the definition of a list datatype is known as the itemType of that specific list datatype. List datatypes are always derived.

M

markup minimization feature A feature of SGML that permits markup that identifies elements (also called tags) to be shortened or omitted. It also permits abbreviation of entity references.

MathML An XML language that defines both presentational and content markup for mathematical formulas and notations.

metadata Literally, data about other data. Metadata is what defines structure, organization, data elements and interpretation, and even sometimes functions or operations of elements in a data collection. In the context of this book, *metadata* effectively means the DTDs or XML Schema documents that govern XML documents and related content.

MIME (Multipurpose Internet Mail Extensions)   A standard developed to extend the capabilities of e-mail by allowing it to include types of data other than just plain text.

model group definitions   Definitions that reference a model group by assigning it a name.

model group   A collection of element declarations or references grouped using a *compositor*.

N

namespace   In XML, a special attribute used to uniquely identify a set of elements.

Namespaces in XML   A W3C recommendation that provides a means to qualify XML elements and attributes by associating them with a namespace.

notation   A way of defining content data when the built-in lexicon of SGML datatypes does not suffice to represent particular element or attribute values. Invoking a specific notation often permits the document processor to call another program to handle that specialized data; the other program then returns control to the processor when its work is done.

notation declarations   Declarations that identify specific types of external binary data. This information is passed to the processing application.

O

operation   A form of data analysis, extraction, abstraction, or transformation that performs various systematic functions on the values in a data collection to produce some kind of desired result—be it a report, trending information, ad hoc query processing, or some other kind of output.

optional element   Within a content model, elements that may or may not appear, depending on the specific content to be represented within a document, a database, or some other form of data collection.

P

parameter entity   An entity used solely within the DTD.

particles   An element declaration, a model group, or a wildcard combined with a value for minOccurs and/or maxOccurs to control occurrence.

PCDATA   Parsed character data that is subject to parsing and analysis (and can therefore include entity references) as a document is handled.

PICS (Platform for Internet Content Selection)   A method of associating metadata (PICS labels) with Internet content.

port   In WSDL, an element that is specified by associating a network address with a *binding*.

primitive datatype   A datatype not defined in terms of other datatypes. Primitive datatypes are the basis for all other datatypes.

private external entity   An entity identified by the keyword SYSTEM and intended for use by a single author or group of authors.

processing instruction   Instructions in an XML document that provide the processing applications with details about the XML document and help ensure that they process the XML document correctly.

public external entity   An entity identified by the keyword PUBLIC and intended for more general use.

public identifier   A special identifier that provides a location for a DTD or other external data on a system other than the one on which a document resides; public identifiers often point to public, standard DTDs and related resources and are generally accessible from anywhere on the Internet.

R

RDF (Resource Description Framework)   A system for describing and interchanging metadata about resources on the Web.

record structure   Within a specific type of database, a structure that defines the map for a single, coherent collection of data elements that together define a single database entry. Inherent in record structure are the results of applying value, existence, and other constraints to data elements and their associated values within that collection.

record   Within a specific type of database, a set of related data elements that together define a single, coherent database entry of some specific kind or another; the kind of database entry is subject to the database's schema and any applicable constraints.

regular expression   An expression that uses character sequences to describe patterns for string values. In terms of XML Schema, regular expressions are used to define datatype patterns for character data.

RELAX (REgular LAnguage description for XML)   A schema language developed at the Information

Technology Research and Standardization Centre (INSTAC) in Japan by Makoto Murata. RELAX uses XML document syntax to describe XML document structures and supports validation of these documents.

RELAX NG (REgular LAnguage for XML Next Generation)   A schema language based on RELAX and TREX.

required element   Within a content model, an element that must appear with a document, a database, or some other form of data collection to meet the structure and content requirements defined within that model.

Russian Doll design   An element declaration model in which the element declarations are nested within other element declarations; therefore, the structure of the element declaration mirrors the instance document structure.

S

Salami Slice design   An element declaration model in which each element declaration is defined globally and therefore referenced from within other complex types.

schema components   The building blocks that make up the abstract data model of the schema. Element and attribute declarations, complex types, simple types, and notations are all examples of schema components.

Schematron   A structural-based schema language based on patterns that contain rules that enforce logical constraints. In other words, it doesn't validate elements and attributes; instead, it validates patterns of relationship between items.

service   In WSDL, a collection of *ports*.

SGML (Standard Generalized Markup Language)
A markup language that separates information that describes the contents and structure of a document from information that describes how that document should appear when displayed, printed, or otherwise rendered for viewing.

simple type   An element that cannot contain child elements and that's based on built-in datatypes. By default, an attribute is also a simple type.

SMIL (Synchronized Multimedia Integration Language)   A markup language designed specifically for multimedia. It synchronizes multimedia files (audio, video, animation) to play in the order and time sequence you specify and to act as a single stream during download and playback.

SOAP (Simple Object Access Protocol)   A protocol that specifies a method that uses XML to perform remote procedure calls (RPCs) with HTTP as the underlying protocol.

substitution   A method that allows you to completely redefine content models. Substitution is only defined for complex types.

SVG (Scalable Vector Graphics)   An XML language used to describe two-dimensional graphics.

system identifier   A special identifier that provides a location for a DTD or other external data on the same local system where the document resides.

T

table structure   The way in which a set of related data elements is organized, wherein by convention, the columns define individual elements in database records and the rows define individual records of the same type.

table   Within a specific type of database, a set of related data elements that together define a single, coherent set of database information.

text-intensive   A term used to describe XML documents in which the content consists almost entirely of text.

TREX (Tree Regular Expressions for XML)   A schema language developed by James Clark. A TREX document is an XML document that specifies a pattern for other XML documents and supports validation of documents that match the pattern.

U

UDDI (Universal Description, Discovery and Integration Service)   A mechanism for dynamically finding Web services. A UDDI interface is used to connect to services provided by external partners. A UDDI registry provides a place for businesses to publish services as well a place for clients to obtain services. UDDI is built upon SOAP. It's cross-platform and cross-industry.

union datatypes Datatypes that are derived from atomic or list datatypes and include the value spaces and lexical spaces of all the datatypes used to derive the union datatype. The group of datatypes included in a union datatype is known as the memberTypes of that specific union datatype.

user-derived datatypes Datatypes that allow developers to build upon predefined datatypes (such as decimal, date, or string) to create their own datatype libraries.

V

validity The result of an XML document conforming to the constraints expressed by the associated XML Schema documents.

value domain The set of all possible values that a data element or attribute may assume.

value space The set of values for a specific datatype.

Venetian Blind design An element declaration model that is similar to the Salami Slice design; each item is defined globally as its own individual component.

W

Web service A set of functions grouped into a unit that can be published to a network for use by other programs.

well formed The condition of a document that meets all the well-formedness constraints defined by XML 1.0 (Second Edition).

wildcards A special type of particle, specified by using any, for validating an attribute or element dependent on the namespace name but independent of the local name.

WSDL (Web Services Description Language) A language that provides a method to describe the basic form of Web service requests with different network protocols and message formats. An XML format that is extensible to any network protocol or message format.

X

XDR (XML-Data Reduced) A schema language developed prior to the W3C XML Schema Recommendation. XDR has a very similar structure to XML Schema and does not support inheritance or other features of object-oriented design.

XForms An XML vocabulary for Web forms that separates the user interface from the data and logic. This type of Web form would allow users to complete it on a computer desktop, personal digital assistant (PDA), or mobile phone.

XLink (XML Linking Language) An XML application that provides complex linking capabilities.

XML Information Set An abstract data set that specifies the definitions of a well-formed XML document. Also called Infoset.

XML Schema The new validation tool for building XML document models. XML Schema also brings datatypes and complex content models to XML and allows developers to take advantage of namespaces.

XPath (XML Path Language)   A language that provides a method to address parts of an XML document as well as ways to manipulate strings, numbers, and Booleans. XPath is used heavily in conjunction with XSLT.

XSL-FO (Extensible Stylesheet Language Formatting Objects)   A style sheet language that provides formatting for XML documents.

XSLT (Extensible Stylesheet Language Transformations)   A style sheet language that allows developers to transform an XML vocabulary into HTML, text, or another XML vocabulary.

Resources

I f you didn't find what you were looking for in the book, you'll definitely find it on one of the resources listed in this appendix. Keep in mind, however, that the Web is a rapidly changing environment. Therefore, by the time you read this, some of these URLs may change or may not exist anymore. If you encounter a URL that doesn't work, go to the root of the URL and look for a search utility or a site map. It's possible that the information is still on the site but just not where it was before.

Organizations

The following are some organizations that you might find useful in your exploration of markup languages and XML Schema-related info:

World Wide Web Consortium (W3C)
www.w3.org

OASIS
www.oasis-open.org

Internet Engineering Task Force (IETF)
www.ietf.org

Dublin Core Metadata Initiative (DCMI)
http://purl.org/dc

International Organization for Standardization (ISO)
www.iso.org

Unicode
www.unicode.org

Mailing Lists

The following are some markup language mailing lists you may find helpful:

XML-DEV
http://lists.xml.org/archives/xml-dev

xml-l
http://listserv.heanet.ie/xml-l.html

xhtml-l
www.egroups.com/group/xhtml-l

Web Sites

Chances are you'll find some useful information on the following Web sites:

XML.com
www.xml.com

Robin Cover's SGML/XML page
www.oasis-open.org/cover

XML FAQ
www.ucc.ie/xml

Eclectic (xml-dev)
http://weblogs.userland.com/eclectic

Cafe con Leche
www.ibiblio.org/xml

WDVL XML
http://wdvl.Internet.com/Authoring/Languages/XML

ZVON.org
www.zvon.org

Repositories

The following repositories contain information that you will find very helpful in your schema journey:

XML.org
www.xml.org

BizTalk.org
www.biztalk.org

SCHEMA.NET
www.schema.net

Bibliography

The following are books that we recommend if you need more information on XML Schemas and related material:

- Cagle, Kurt, Jon Duckett, Oliver Griffin, et al. *Professional XML Schemas.* Chicago: Wrox Press, 2001. ISBN 1861005474.

- Cagle, Kurt. *XML Developer's Handbook.* Alameda, Calif.: Sybex, Inc., 2001. ISBN 0782127045.

- Goldfarb, Charles F. *The XML Handbook, 3/e.* Upper Saddle River, N.J.: Prentice Hall, 2001. ISBN 013055068X.

- Harold, Elliotte Rusty, and Scott Means. *XML in a Nutshell.* Cambridge, Mass.: O'Reilly and Associates, 2001. ISBN 0596000588.

- Harold, Elliotte Rusty. *XML Bible, 2nd Edition.* Indianapolis: Hungry Minds, 2001. ISBN 0764547607.

- Harold, Elliotte Rusty. *XML: Extensible Markup Language.* Indianapolis: Hungry Minds, 1998. ISBN 0764531999.

- Holzner, Steven. *Inside XML.* Indianapolis: New Riders Publishing, 2000. ISBN 0735710201.

- Kay, Michael. *XSLT Programmer's Reference.* Chicago: Wrox Press, 2000. ISBN 1861003129.

- Ray, Eric T. *Learning XML.* Cambridge, Mass.: O'Reilly and Associates, 2001. ISBN 0596000464.

- Tittel, Ed, Chelsea Valentine, Lucinda Dykes, and Mary Burmeister. *Mastering XHTML Premium Edition.* Alameda, Calif.: Sybex, Inc., 2001. ISBN 0782128181.

- White, Chuck, Liam Quin, and Linda Burman. *Mastering XML Premium Edition.* Alameda, Calif.: Sybex, Inc., 2001. ISBN 0782128475.

- Sybex, Inc. *XML Complete.* Alameda, Calif.: Sybex, Inc., 2001. ISBN 0782140335.

Tools

The following tools are available to help you create and view your XML Schema documents:

XSV (XML Schema Validator) online validator
www.w3.org/2001/03/webdata/xsv

XSV executable
ftp://ftp.cogsci.ed.ac.uk/pub/XSV/XSV12.EXE

IBM XML Schema Quality Checker
www.alphaworks.ibm.com/tech/xmlsqc

MSXML 3
http://download.microsoft.com/download/xml/Install/3.0/WIN98Me/EN-US/msxml3.exe

MSXML 4 (Technology Preview)
http://msdn.microsoft.com/library/default.asp?url=/library/en-us/dnmsxml/html/
dnmsxmlNewInJuly.asp

dtd2xs
http://puvogel.informatik.med.uni-giessen.de/dtd2xs/download

Sun XML Datatypes Library (trial version)
www.sun.com/software/xml/developers/xsdlib/download.html

XML Spy
www.xmlspy.com

Turbo XML
www.tibco.com/products/extensibility/solutions/turbo_xml.html

Tools for Schema Alternatives

The following are tools available for alternative schema languages:

DTD2RELAX
www.horobi.com/Projects/RELAX/Archive/DTD2RELAX.html

Style sheet to convert a RELAX grammar to a TREX schema
www.thaiopensource.com/trex/from-relax.xsl

DTDinst
www.thaiopensource.com/dtdinst

Files for Schematron
www.ascc.net/xml/schematron

Saxon XSLT processor
http://saxon.sourceforge.net

Book Web Site

The URL for this book's Web page is www.lanw.com/books/xmlschemas.

The Web site contains the following information:

- Easy-to-link URLs from the book
- Listings from each chapter

In addition, should we document any errata for this book, a link to that information will also be available through this page.

NOTE   You can also find the code listings and any errata by going to www.sybex.com and following the link to the page for this book.

Index

Note to the reader: Throughout this index **boldfaced** page numbers indicate primary discussions of a topic. *Italicized* page numbers indicate illustrations.

B

C

D

M

O

P

S

T

U

Z

TELL US WHAT YOU THINK!

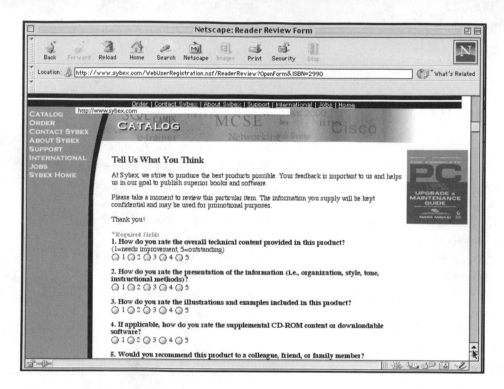

Your feedback is critical to our efforts to provide you with the best books and software on the market. Tell us what you think about the products you've purchased. It's simple:

1. Visit the Sybex website
2. Go to the product page
3. Click on **Submit a Review**
4. Fill out the questionnaire and comments
5. Click **Submit**

With your feedback, we can continue to publish the highest quality computer books and software products that today's busy IT professionals deserve.

www.sybex.com

SYBEX Inc. • 1151 Marina Village Parkway, Alameda, CA 94501 • 510-523-8233

The quotation on the bottom of the front cover is taken from the fourth chapter of Lao Tzu's Tao Te Ching, *the classic work of Taoist philosophy. These particular verses are from the translation by D. C. Lau (copyright 1963) and are part of a larger exploration of the nature of the Tao, sometimes translated as "the way."*

It is traditionally held that Lao Tzu lived in the fifth century B.C. *in China, but it is unclear whether he was actually a historical figure. The concepts embodied in the* Tao Te Ching *influenced religious thinking in the Far East, including Zen Buddhism in Japan. Many in the West, however, have wrongly understood the* Tao Te Ching *to be primarily a mystical work; in fact, much of the advice in the book is grounded in a practical moral philosophy governing personal conduct.*